Wealth Effects and Monetary Theory

RICHARD J. SWEENEY

Wealth Effects and Monetary Theory

Basil Blackwell

Library of Congress Cataloging in Publication Data

Sweeney, Richard J. (Richard James), 1944–
  Wealth effects and monetary theory / Richard J. Sweeney.
    p. cm.
  Bibliography: p.
  Includes index.
  ISBN 0-631-15846-4
  1. Wealth. 2. Monetary policy. 3. Macroeconomics. I. Title.
HB251.S94   1988
339.3—dc19   87-36077

British Library Cataloguing in Publication Data

Sweeney, Richard J.
  Wealth effects and monetary theory.
  1. Macroeconomics. Microeconomic aspects
  I. Title
  339

  ISBN 0-631-15846-4

Typeset in 10 on 12pt Times
by Colset Private Limited, Singapore
Printed in the United States

Contents

Preface

Why do various economists get such different answers about the size or even sign of macroeconomic wealth effects? One reason is that they commonly approach wealth effects by first defining wealth and then differentiating the wealth expression by, say, the price level to find the price-induced effect on wealth, or by the interest rate to find the interest-rate-induced effect on wealth. This is not, however, the approach the same economists take to wealth effects in their microeconomic work. There we are all committed to the substitution and income (or wealth) effects apparatus in Hicks's (1939) *Value and Capital*. When economists talk about microeconomic wealth effects, they mean wealth effects in the sense of Hicks. It makes sense, then, to analyze macroeconomic wealth effects with the same approach. Macro effects are, after all, an aggregate of individual effects.

Strangely enough, however, no one seems to have systematically analyzed the range of macroeconomic wealth effects with the Hicksian apparatus. That is the approach and one of the major contributions of this book. Of course, some economists have applied the standard micro analysis to particular questions or special cases in analyzing macro-economic wealth effects – Patinkin (1965), for example, is very careful to argue that his real balance effect really is a Hicksian wealth effect. Never-theless, a great deal of controversy could have been avoided if all questions on macroeconomic wealth effects had been dealt with in the same Hicksian mold.

Use of Hicks's approach to analyze macroeconomic wealth effects could have been made decades ago. Indeed, the elements were there in the 1946 revised edition of *Value and Capital*, but they were somewhat inaccessible, for three reasons. First, many of the interesting issues in macroeconomic wealth effects turn on multi-period analysis, and the large majority of readers did not devote much attention to the second half of *Value and Capital*, parts III and IV on dynamics, where Hicks took up multi-period questions. Second, much of the mathematics for the model with production and for the multi-period case is left for the reader to fill in, and this requires a significant amount of work. Third, Hicks's treatment of "outside" money in the revised edition is hidden away in the short and cryptic Additional Note B where he corrects the first edition's serious flaw of leaving out outside money.

If it was difficult for the reader to seize on Hicks' methods and hints to analyze macroeconomic wealth effects, why did Hicks himself not do it? Several years ago, I asked him that question. In particular, it seemed to me that Hicks's (1957) review of Patinkin's (1956) first edition would have been an ideal time to present an analysis that had much of Patinkin's as a special case, an analysis that would have short-circuited much of the controversy over wealth effects for the next 15 years. He replied along the lines that, since his work on *Value and Capital*, he had become convinced that the important issues in macroeconomics were in the Keynesian area of fixed-price macroeconomics, rather than in the debates over wealth effects set off by Patinkin's work. He allocated his time accordingly.

This seems a good time, however, to consider once again macroeconomic wealth effects. These issues were overlooked for more than a decade in the excitement and passions of the rational expectations revolution. That revolution is dying down, though its important lessons remain. Meanwhile, macroeconomics manifestly has a long way to go in explaining the economy, and more focus on wealth seems to be one promising path. Indeed, in empirical work, use of wealth variables has become very frequent. In this environment, then, perhaps a book that tries to clear up some of the issues in the wealth effects literature and put the range of questions in a common framework serves a good purpose.

This book is theoretical, but addresses issues both of theory and of empirical practice. It turns out that the variables commonly used in empirical work as measures of real wealth often do not move in the same way as our theoretical measures of changes in real wealth. This does not mean that past empirical work is "wrong." It does mean that, whatever the effects past work has been measuring, these have not been the effects of changes in wealth, at least not changes in wealth as understood in terms of the standard wealth and substitution effects. There is some hope that measures corresponding more closely to theoretical changes in wealth will produce better results.

Hicks and his great work *Value and Capital* deserve much credit for whatever contribution this book makes. It was a joyous moment when I saw that in principle the whole range of questions about macroeconomic wealth effects could be handled by the same simple, coherent approach we use in microeconomic analysis. This is, I think, one important meaning of the "integration of value and monetary theory" that has been for so long a desideratum in monetary economics.[1] And it was another joyous moment when I decided that the approach not only worked in principle but paid off in practice.

Axel Leijonhufvud was kind enough to read some of these chapters, and to give good advice and great encouragement. More important, he has been a friend and a source of inspiration since 1964.

Professors Hiroshi Imamura, Tatsuo Iwane and Kazumi Nakamura of Doshisha University, Kyoto, have undertaken the huge task of translating this book into Japanese. They have been of immense help for this English-language version in finding my mistakes and insisting on a clarity more in line with my tastes than my frequent practice. In particular, extensive conversations with and long letters from Professor Nakamura have been of great help in each chapter – he is a most valuable friend.

Comments over the years by colleagues and students have been of great help in stimulating extensions, corrections and revisions. I am very grateful.

Often this book refers to other works to criticize, or to claim that they fell into error or were not general enough. In these passages, I hope the tone is not ungracious; it is not meant to be. The books by Patinkin, Gurley and Shaw, and Pesek and Saving, and the articles by many authors, but particularly Harry G. Johnson, were tremendously stimulating and are the base for whatever incremental improvement this book offers. Let me note that this book began with the well-merited suspicion that I had earlier erred in my own treatment of wealth and wealth effects (Sweeney, 1974).

Pamela Martin of The Claremont Graduate School read the entire manuscript for style and consistency, and helped with both the page proofs and the index.

This book required many, many drafts. Perhaps a dozen typists worked on it over the years. Most of it was typed, however, by Theresa Hidalgo and Jackie Huntzinger, and Carol Bovett did the final corrections. They did a good and cheerful job, with a lot less complaining than my handwriting deserved.

I close this preface, and the part of my life that went into this book, with thoughts of my family: my parents, Johnny and Peggy; my brother Mike and sister Mary; my daughters, Robin and Erin; and of course my wife, Joan.

NOTE

1 Patinkin (1956, rev. edn 1965) subtitles his landmark book *An Integration of Monetary and Value Theory.*

Part I
INTRODUCTION

1
Introduction

1.1 The Purpose of this Book

Wealth and wealth effects have been curiously neglected for more than a decade, both in monetary theory and theoretical macroeconomics in general. The time seems right for a fresh look at these topics that received so much attention in the 1950s and 1960s.

After a brief flurry of interest in wealth effects in the early 1970s, the economics profession did little new research in the area. This was not so much, I think, because there was perfect satisfaction with the state of knowledge, but rather because the expected payoff seemed small from using the same old approaches to cover the same old questions.

Further, in the 1970s the excitement in macroeconomics mainly centered on the rational expectations revolution, with a great deal of emphasis on the proposition that anticipated monetary policy is ineffective. The models used in this discussion were quite stripped-down (Lucas, 1972; Sargent, 1973, 1976; Sargent and Wallace, 1975), and probably this was good scientific strategy. Most of these models neglected the wealth accounts altogether, and had no role for wealth effects. Now, however, the early phase of the rational expectations revolution is over and economists in this mold are turning to more detailed models, for example, of the investment process and capital structure. Perhaps it is also time once again to analyze the wealth accounts.

Ever since the 1960s the large econometric models, mostly Keynesian, have included wealth variables and the frequency of inclusion has generally increased over time. Many researchers view changes in wealth as an important transmission channel for economic effects and as having an important quantitative role, for example, on the size of policy multipliers. In some areas our theoretical understanding of how wealth should enter and what to expect empirically is limited, however, to what we knew 15–20 years ago. This is unsatisfactory because there are some large gaps in this knowledge, which this book tries to reveal and to fill. A particularly important gap addressed is how to develop measures of changes in wealth that correspond to the implications of theory. Unfortunately, commonly used measures have serious shortcomings.

The overall purpose of this book is to use the standard analytical apparatus of microeconomics to investigate systematically the range of macro wealth effects. In microeconomics, we analyze behavior in terms of substitution and income or wealth effects, following fairly closely the analysis Hicks developed in *Value and Capital* (1939; rev. edn., 1946). This apparatus can be used on a multi-period economy as well as on the more frequently encountered single-period, static economy. Unfortunately, this set of tools has never been systematically used to investigate the full range of macro wealth effects. Researchers have used it correctly to investigate particular effects in special cases, such as the real balance effect when the money supply is constant over time. The special nature of the results has seldom been stressed; in more general and quite plausible models a very wide range of results is possible, including a zero price-induced effect on wealth. Moreover, in many past discussions the reader does not receive a sense of how all effects on wealth have much in common and can be analyzed in the same framework.

This book has three particular purposes. One is to lay some of the theoretical groundwork for correctly measuring changes in wealth. The other two purposes are to present consistent, integrated discussions of, first, the change in wealth due to an increase in the overall price level, and, second, the change in wealth due to an increase in the general level of interest rates. These two changes in wealth are of substantial interest in their own right in the literature. The discussions of them also serve as detailed case studies of the general problem of measuring changes in wealth and the serious defects in the types of measures currently used.

From a theoretical point of view, standardly used wealth variables do not accurately reflect true changes in wealth; in fact, they are constructed in such a way that they cannot do so. An example is the change in wealth due to a rise in the general level of interest rates. This will lead to a decline in the value of firms' equity and hence a fall in measures of wealth that focus on non-human wealth. Under some circumstances, however, discussed in detail in chapter 8, the true effect on wealth is zero. In essence, what the conventional measures overlook is that, if households hold constant their intertemporal consumption, the present value of their future expenditures falls at the same time that the present value of equity income from firms falls. Properly measured, the two effects cancel under certain assumptions and the economy experiences no change in wealth. Under other assumptions, the effects do not exactly cancel, but conventional measures of wealth will still overstate the fall in wealth.

Wealth variables are important in many of the larger macroeconometric models. As shown below, changes in these measured wealth variables generally are not changes in wealth in the way we mean in micro-economics; they are not Hicksian changes in wealth. This does not mean that the conventional wealth measures should therefore be deleted from models, or that their use is somehow incorrect. It does mean that we cannot understand the meaning of changes in these measured wealth variables in terms of the usual apparatus of substitution and wealth effects with which economists are trained to explain phenomena. Also, it suggests that it might be worthwhile reworking econometric models using wealth variables that correspond to those used in theoretical work.

The basic complaint here is that conventional wealth variables are constructed so that they do not change in ways that theory specifies they must change if the theory is valid. As seen below, one implication is that theory must play a deeper role than before in designing measures of wealth. Another implication is that a theory cannot be tested very powerfully if use is made of wealth variables that are constructed incorrectly from the point of view of the theory. Theoretically correct measures of changes in wealth are those constructed to give the same wealth changes that theory implies as responses to the range of proximate causes of changes in wealth, for example, changes in the price level, interest rates, or technology. Hence, we have to study these theoretical issues to build correct measures of wealth changes.

Two other purposes of this book are to investigate in detail induced effects on wealth due to changes in the overall price level and due to changes in the general level of interest rates. The change in wealth induced by a change in the price level has been studied very extensively in the literature on the real balance effect, after Patinkin's (1956, 1965) usage. In this book the change is referred to more generally as the price-induced effect on wealth, after Pesek and Saving's (1967) usage. (Note that, in some discussions in the literature, the term "real balance effect" is used to refer to the effect on demand for output due to a price level change, or is equal to the price-induced effect on wealth multiplied by a marginal propensity to demand output out of wealth.) The conventional real balance effect of a rise in the price level, $-M^s/P^2$, arises when the government money supply M^s is constant over time; when the government money supply varies over time, the price-induced effect on wealth can be much different, even zero. Chapters 4–7 try to straighten out many of the controversies over the price-induced effect on wealth, and in a framework more general than previously used. In particular, chapters 6 and 7 take a new look at the conditions under which bank money enters the price-induced effect on wealth; binding interest rate regulations may well make bank money part of the effect.

Chapter 8 analyzes the interest-rate-induced effect on wealth. This effect has received substantially less attention than the price-induced effect on wealth, but plays a key role in correctly measuring changes in wealth. Both of these particular applications are of interest in their own right as they deal with topics that have received a great deal of attention in the literature. Both are illustrations of the overall approach to measuring changes in wealth. Both play an important role in the analysis in chapter 10 of how to measure changes in wealth correctly and how currently used types of measures are mismeasurements of true changes in wealth.

In the remainder of this introductory chapter, section 1.2 discusses why interest in the real balance effect tailed off in the early 1970s at the time of the rational expectations revolution. Why did the real balance effect, the effect on wealth that received the most theoretical attention, go from a hot topic to one that was so far on the back burner that few rational expectations models explicitly include it? Section 1.3 gives an introduction to some of the issues covered in the book and some of its characteristic results. Section 1.4 stresses that a goal of this book is integration – integration of micro and macro analysis, integration of the household, business, and government sectors, and integration of the analysis of bank and government monies. Section 1.5 concludes with a brief outline of the contents of the rest of the book.

1.2 The Real Balance Effect – The 1950s to the 1980s

In the mid-1950s, the real balance effect was a major issue in monetary economics; now it receives relatively little attention. Relatively few journal articles appear on the topic, and while Patinkin (1965) is still assigned in many graduate monetary courses, the book receives much less attention in such courses than a decade or two ago. Gurley and Shaw (1960) and Pesek and Saving (1967), two other books that enjoyed vogue with their discussions of wealth effects, are little read these days.

In the mid-1950s, a key issue was whether money mattered. The real balance effect showed that it did, and for many observers the real balance effect was thus a *raison d'être* for the field of monetary economics. The real balance effect was used to argue that the price level is determinate. Further, the real balance effect in the output market directly generated excess demand and supply for output, which in turn pushed the system toward a general equilibrium with full employment; money affected the excess demand for output without having first to affect the interest rate and then work through the interest elasticity of demand for output as in many Keynesian discussions.

The emphasis on the role of the real balance effect in adjustment showed up also in discussions of the transmission mechanism from monetary policy to prices, the interest rate, and real activity. In Friedman and Schwartz's (1963) paradigm, an increase in the stock of money relative to the price level increased consumption demand, reduced the interest rate, and hence increased investment demand. This led to increased output in the short run until the equilibrium level of real balances was restored, and to an increase in the price level in the longer run. Through the "liquidity effect," the initial increase in the money stock transitorily lowered the real rate of interest and led to adjustments in markets for all interest-sensitive goods, until the induced price level increases offset the injection of money and eliminated the liquidity effect.

Wealth Effects and the Rational Expectations Revolution

With the rational expectations revolution of the 1970s, interest in the real balance effect waned for a number of reasons. First, most economists had by then acknowledged that money mattered. The issue was by how much, when and under what circumstances. Second, for reasons of convenience many researchers omitted real balance effects from the output market in their rational expectations models. Often this vastly simplified the mathematics of the solution and reduced the difficulty of interpreting the solution (Lucas, 1975). This did not mean, however, that the real balance effect was absent from such models. Rather, it was confined to the bond market, as discussed in chapter 4.

Third, a key topic in many rational expectations discussions is the effects of unanticipated changes in the money supply. These unanticipated money supply changes work by unexpectedly shifting the aggregate demand curve. In turn, the position of the aggregate demand curve is sensitive to the money supply even if the real balance effect is absent from output markets, as is clear from intermediate textbook discussions. All that is required is a non-horizontal LM curve and some interest sensitivity of the demand for output (typically, investment demand in textbook discussions, but many empirical models show interest sensitivity of consumption). Hence, the central problem of many rational expectations discussions, the effect of unanticipated money supply changes, can be analyzed in the absence of the real balance effect from the market for output.

Fourth, rational expectations models often analyzed equilibrium in the face of anticipated monetary policy changes. Provided such monetary changes are neutral, it is a convenient shortcut to forgo explicit analysis of price-induced effects on wealth. These effects are "in" the models, but show up only in the bond markets, which are not explicitly analyzed (for example, Sargent, 1973). For example, a doubling of the money stock leads analytically to an increase in wealth, when evaluated at initial equilibrium prices, and in consequence to a doubling of the price level. The doubling of the price level creates an effect on wealth that is equal, but opposite, to the effect of the doubling of the money stock. At the new price level, the stock of real balances is the same as before. There is no change in real wealth between the two equilibria. Furthermore, consider an equilibrium time path where the money stock grows at a constant rate. In many rational expectations models (for example, Lucas, 1972; Sargent, 1973; Sargent and Wallace, 1975) such anticipated increases in the money stock are always accompanied by simultaneous changes in prices that keep real balances constant at their equilibrium level. Prices move instantly from one equilibrium level to another. Whether there is the potential for a change in real balances to affect excess demand for output, such a change never occurs in this experiment of anticipated monetary policy changes. Convenience then argued for leaving the real balance effect out of explicit modeling.

Even with anticipated monetary policy changes, some results characteristic of early rational expectations models require the absence of a price-induced effect on wealth in the output market. The monetary policy changes just discussed were neutral; for example, a sudden doubling of the money stock, or a 10 percent increase in the money stock as part of an ongoing process of 10 percent monetary growth, would leave real balances constant. Early rational expectations models, however, often gave the "policy irrelevance" result that an increase in the rate of growth of the money stock, from say 10 percent to 20 percent, would have no affect on such real variables as consumption, investment, employment and output. Policy irrelevance requires the strong assumption of "super neutrality," as Tobin (1973) pointed out at an early stage. Super neutrality assumes that changes in the rate of inflation or growth rate of money do not affect consumption through a real balance effect (as in Mundell, 1963) or affect investment through a portfolio effect (as in Tobin, 1965a). Thus, some characteristic rational expectations results argued, along with analytical tractability, for ignoring modeling the price-induced effect on wealth. This also illustrates the fact that inclusion of wealth effects can lead to important results that are overlooked in simpler models.

Wealth effects that enrich models on the demand side are also useful in analyzing such phenomena as "persistence" in real macroeconomics variables. A key distinction in the rational expectations literature is between anticipated versus unanticipated changes in monetary policy. In such models an unanticipated policy change affected the equilibrium in the current period. But in the earliest articles, for example Lucas (1972), the system was back on its previous intertemporal equilibrium path by the following period in the absence of further shocks. It was evident, however, that in the real world real variables showed much more persistence than this simple view allowed. Models soon allowed "persistence" by making aggregate supply depend on lagged values of real output (Lucas, 1973). This persistence on the supply side was argued to arise from inventory adjustments, firms' adjustment costs, the time needed to shift labor from one use to another, and so forth.

Current disturbances will also have long-lasting effects on household behavior in both the output and labor markets, though early rational expectations models often neglected these effects. A monetary disturbance that reduces output this period will cause a reduction in wealth, and thus in aggregate demand, for the next several periods, even if output were to return to its previous level next period. Current disturbances, then, have lagged effects on the demand as well as the supply side. One powerful channel of lagged demand-side effects is through wealth effects.

There is nothing intrinsic to rational expectations models that requires neglect of wealth effects; often these play a key role in "real business cycle" models (see Long and Plosser, 1983; King and Plosser, 1984). Indeed, as the demand side becomes more sophisticated in rational expectations models, it is inevitable that attention will focus on wealth effects. This book is a contribution in that direction.

1.3 Issues in Measuring Effects on Wealth

This book focuses on two effects on wealth. The first is the price-induced effect on wealth, as Pesek and Saving (1967) call it, so extensively analyzed by Patinkin and many others. If the current aggregate price level rises, what happens to peoples' wealth? The second effect is the much less frequently discussed interest-rate-induced effect on wealth. If the general level of interest rates rises, what is the effect on peoples' wealth?

In some ways, it is easier to see what is new in this book by looking first at the interest-rate-induced effect on wealth. This is obviously a multiperiod problem; there must be at least two periods to make the interest rate have any kind of useful interpretation. When the interest rate i rises, I am better off if I am a lender, and you are worse off if a borrower. Provided our planned borrowing and lending match over time, my gain in wealth must equal your loss. In fact, if the economy as a whole is planning on intertemporal market-clearing quantities, and if price expectations are the same across all actors, then the individual changes in wealth must cancel in the aggregate, giving a zero interest-rate-induced effect on wealth. The rise in i alters behavior through wealth effects, then, only through distribution effects. Note that the usual discussion finds the interest-rate-induced effect on wealth ambiguous at the level both of the individual and the economy. In this book, the effect on any individual can be ambiguous, but under the conditions outlined above is zero in the aggregate. Note further that empirical measures of wealth are likely to fall in this case where the true change in wealth is zero. For example, a general rise in discount rates will depress the value of the stock market and thus reduce measures of wealth that include equities.

Of course this brief intuitive discussion has many complications, which are discussed in chapter 8. Nevertheless, it conveniently raises a number of general points that are treated at length in later chapters. First, how does the price-induced effect on wealth differ in a multi-period model from the usual real balance effect, $d(M^s/P)/dP = -M^s/P^2$, discussed by Patinkin and many others? In particular, the government need not keep the stock of its fiat money constant over time, and this can cause substantial changes from the usual assumptions. The conventional result is merely a very special case. Other discussions have often been set in a multi-period framework, but simplifying assumptions have eliminated many of the interesting results that can arise. Chapters 4 and 5 focus on these issues.

Second, even if we think we know how to measure the price-induced effect on wealth, how do we measure the interest-rate-induced effect? It turns out that the answer is straightforward. We want effects on wealth that fit into the standard analysis of substitution and wealth (or income) effects, as developed by Hicks (1939; rev. edn 1946) and others. After all, economists have aimed for decades at an integration of value and monetary theory, and value theory is firmly Hicksian.

We are used to analyzing the effect of a rise in the price of X on an individual's demand for X as the substitution effect plus the wealth effect. In turn, the wealth effect is "MPC_W times the induced change in wealth," where MPC_W is the individual's marginal propensity to consume X out of a change in wealth. The induced change in wealth is often measured as an "equivalent variation." For example, suppose the individual initially consumes the amount X and has an endowment $\overline{X}$. A one-dollar rise in P_X, the price of X, induces a change in his/her wealth of $\overline{X} - X$, or $\overline{X} - X$ is the induced effect on wealth. This book measures effects on wealth throughout as equivalent variations. Assuming that there are no distribution effects, these induced changes in wealth can simply be added across households to find the aggregate change in wealth. Chapter 3 analyzes these issues.

In terms of the familiar Slutsky equation, the above analysis is

$$\frac{\mathrm{d}X}{\mathrm{d}P_X}$$ = substitution effect + wealth effect
= substitution effect + MPC$_W$(change in wealth)
= substitution effect + MPC$_W$($\overline{X} - X$).

In other words, the induced effect on wealth is the consumer's endowment $\overline{X}$ less his/her consumption X, with X evaluated at its initial level. While this is a familiar result from price theory, the question of how the change in wealth is found when there is production is less familiar.

Third, how are effects on wealth measured when there is production? In particular, firms vary both their output and factor use in response to price and interest rate changes. Think of any particular firm as being owned by a household. It turns out that the same "equivalent variation" measure, $\overline{X} - X$, can be used as in the case where $\overline{X}$ is a fixed endowment. Simply interpret $\overline{X}$ now as the initial equilibrium quantity produced. When P_X rises, $\overline{X}$ will likely change, and the owner of the firm is wealthier not only by $\overline{X} - X$ but also by the value of the change in production less the change in cost, or by the change in $\overline{X}$ multiplied by P_X minus marginal cost (MC). With a price-taking, profit-maximizing firm, the optimizing condition is $P_X - MC = 0$, so the second part of the effect on wealth is zero. This is covered at some length in chapter 3.

Fourth, in this framework, what is the price-induced effect on wealth through bank money? Pesek and Saving (1967) and Saving (1970) argue that the effect is negative, while Patinkin (1965, 1969, 1970, 1972) argues that it is zero. Strangely, none of the many discussions on this topic makes use of marginal conditions from optimizing behavior, as just used above. Suppose banks pay a competitive rate of interest r on their demand deposits, where r is less than the interest rate i on bonds as long as banks have to use real resources in their activities. Suppose further that banks are all optimizing price and interest-rate takers, and quantity-setters who view themselves as able to supply whatever quantity they like at the going prices and interest rates. Then the price-induced effect on wealth through bank money reduces to the question of whether banks' real resource demands are homogeneous of degree zero in nominal values – the same homogeneity needed for neutrality of the money supply. With this homogeneity, there is a zero price-induced effect on wealth through bank money. Of course infra-marginal banks will earn rents, and the whole price-taking banking sector can earn "monopoly" rents if there is restricted entry. Patinkin derives his zero price-induced effect on wealth through bank money by assuming zero bank profits in equilibrium, but this zero-profit condition is irrelevant. He fails to focus on the key issues of optimizing behavior and a competitively determined r. Chapters 6 and 7 give a detailed discussion of these analytical results and how they fit in with previous discussions.

Fifth, what happens if the government pays interest on its fiat money? If the government sets the interest rate $r*$ on its money by a marginal condition similar to that for banks, and if its resource use for money is homogeneous of degree zero in nominal values, then there is a zero price-induced effect on wealth through government money, just as with bank money. This is an intellectually satisfying result because, after all, it should not matter for this question whether the money is supplied by government or banks. Chapter 7 analyzes this issue and its relationship to the role of bank money in the price-induced effect on wealth.

Sixth, if there is no price-induced effect on wealth, because all monies pay a competitive rate of interest, what renders the price level determinate? Chapters 4 and 5 discuss a new effect, the initial-condition effect, that exists even when there is a zero price-induced effect on wealth and can render the price level determinate in this case. The initial-condition effect turns on the fact that the money stock is given at any instant, so an increase in the price level reduces the stock of real balances available right now for transactions and thus affects current excess demands in markets, as required for price level determinacy in discussions such as those of Patinkin (1956; rev. edn 1965) and Gurley and Shaw (1960).

Seventh, what are the implications of interest rate regulations for the price-induced effect on wealth? Governments typically pay no interest on their fiat monies. Even after the deregulation of the late 1970s and early 1980s, United States banks have some lingering restrictions. As was discussed in questions four and five above, if all money supplies are subject to optimizing conditions, if their resource use is homogeneous of degree zero in nominal values, and if the interest rates on the monies are set at competitive, market-clearing levels, then there is no price-induced effect on wealth. If the interest rates paid on monies are set below market-clearing levels, however, either by bank regulation or a government decision not to pay interest on its fiat money, then banks may become quantity-takers, with the marginal conditions not holding. It is the failure of these marginal conditions to hold that gives a non-zero price-induced effect on wealth, as shown in chapter 7. The real balance effect through government money exists in the conventional analysis because government typically does not pay interest on its fiat money. In a similar way, when the interest rate paid on bank money is set below the market-clearing level, this may well make banks quantity-takers, with bank money also contributing to the price-induced effect on wealth.

Eighth, in a multi-period framework, what is the role of older and younger generations in the interest-rate-induced effect on wealth? If the constant population consists of immortal individuals, then the interest-rate-induced effect is zero if the economy as a whole is planning on inter-temporal market-clearing quantities and if price expectations are the same across actors, as discussed above. Any individual's increase in wealth from a rise in the interest rate is offset by another's loss; assuming no distribution effects, the net effect on current aggregate demand is zero. An alternative model, however, has finite-lived generations with no bequests. In this case, the newer generations must literally buy the economy's physical capital and money stock from the older generation before that generation dies. If we think of the younger generation as saving to do this, it is clear that a rise in the general level of interest rates makes this purchase easier. Hence, the interest-rate-induced effect on wealth is positive for the younger generation. But the net effect for the two generations together must be zero, so the effect is negative for the older generation. Since the older generation is active in current markets, while some of the younger generation is yet unborn, the older generation's negative effect on wealth dominates in current markets. Thus, in current markets we observe a negative interest-rate-induced effect on wealth in this case of no bequests. This result is then an intergenerational distribution effect, since under the assumed conditions the net effect on wealth is zero for all generations combined. Chapter 8 analyzes a variety of cases in some detail.

Ninth, what is the interest-rate-induced effect on wealth when the current generation makes bequests based on maximizing its utility? The key here is that, with planned market-clearing quantities over time and the same expectations across actors, the net effect on wealth across generations must be zero. Hence, the current generation can offset any effect on itself and all other generations by altering bequests, and will in fact do so since it determines bequests through maximizing utility. In other words, chapter 8 shows that utility-maximizing bequests lead the current generation to offset any distribution effects due to a rise in the general level of interest rates.

Tenth, in this framework, are government bonds net wealth? Under certain conditions, government bonds are not net wealth if the bequest motive operates, much as Barro (1974) argued. This result requires, however, that the government plans both on ultimately paying the interest on its debt and on redeeming the principal by taxation or money creation. If the government instead plans simply to print new bonds to finance old ones, there does not exist an equilibrium, as shown in chapter 8.

1.4 A Goal of this Book: Integration

This book aims at integration. One goal is integrating monetary and value theory. The book uses precisely the same apparatus of Hicksian wealth and substitution effects to discuss issues in monetary economics as economists standardly use in discussions of micro problems. It uses exactly the same approach and assumptions to discuss both the interest-rate-induced and price-induced effects on wealth. It approaches both in a multi-period framework. The effects of business and government decisions are systematically reflected in household sector wealth.

Integration of the Business Sector

Integration of the household and business sectors clarifies a number of issues. A change in the price level or the general level of interest rates affects the household sector's wealth position for any given level of non-labor income from the business sector, but also affects this non-labor income. This book integrates these two effects and shows how to measure the net effect as an equivalent variation.

Patinkin (1965) argues that the real balance effect on households is $-MH/P^2$, where MH is nominal holdings by households of government fiat money, while the effect on businesses is $-MB/P^2$, where MB is nominal holdings by businesses of government fiat money. In his view, a rise in the price level reduces consumption demand through the household sector real balance effect and reduces investment demand through the business sector real balance effect. He assumes that the marginal propensities to consume and invest out of real balances are equal, so there are no distribution effects, and a rise in the price level reduces aggregate demand through the economy's real balance effect. He views the real balance effect for the economy as being equal to $-M^s/P^2$, where M^s ($=$ MH $+$ MB) is the total stock of government fiat money.

This argument is incorrect, as chapter 4 shows. It is true that the total real balance effect does depend on the sum of government money held by both sectors. A rise in the price level, however, reduces consumption demand but does not affect investment demand. The total effect on aggregate demand is from consumption and this effect depends on $-M^s/P^2$. Investment demand is modeled as independent of current real balances. MB/P does, however, affect business profits and thus household wealth, because ultimately businesses are owned by households. There is no issue of distribution effects between the household and business sectors. Indeed, there cannot be, because the household sector owns the business sector.

Integration of the Government Sector

Integrating the effects of government decisions on the household sector's wealth position clarifies a number of issues. In conventional analysis, the government money stock that enters the price-induced effect on wealth is the current stock M_0^s. However, this is so because of the implicit or explicit assumption that the money stock is constant through time. More generally, though, government plans on financing part of its future deficits by new money issues. If the current and expected future price levels rise, then the real value of given amounts of money creation declines. In turn, this means that the government sector must sooner or later raise taxes on the private sector of the economy – an effect on wealth. This effect will of course depend on what sequence of new money creation the government plans, and hence will not depend solely on the current money stock. Chapters 5, 7, and 8 discuss these issues in some detail.

It is sometimes suggested that the government suffers from money illusion. When the price level rises, there is a negative real balance effect on the private sector, which then cuts back on current planned spending. Since the government money stock is a liability of the government, in this view, the rise in price creates an equal but positive wealth effect for the government. Yet government does not increase its expenditure in a way that offsets the price-induced fall in private demand. The fall in aggregate demand might then be said to arise merely as a distribution effect. This view is incorrect, however. There are no distribution effects across sectors, only amongst individuals in the household sector. The net negative real balance effect in the output market arises, not because of money illusion on the government's part or a distribution effect across sectors, but because government does not pay a competitive rate of interest on its money, as argued in chapter 7.

Integrating Analysis of Government and Bank Monies

The issue of a competitive rate of interest on money integrates the analysis of bank and government money and the role of each in the price-induced effect on wealth, as discussed in chapter 7. If banks pay a competitively determined rate of interest r on their deposits, then r is determined by demand and supply equilibrium. Banks are quantity-setters, viewing themselves as able to choose any level of deposits they like at the going r. At this r, banks acquire or accept deposits up to the point where the marginal profit of another dollar of deposits is zero. If costs are homogeneous in nominal values, another way of putting the marginal condition is that banks set their real deposits where the marginal real profit from another unit of real bank money equals zero. From the marginal condition, a rise in the general price level has a zero effect on the flow of real bank profits. In turn, the real wealth accruing to the owners of banks from these flows is unchanged; thus the price-induced effect on wealth through bank money is zero in this case.

Imagine government also pays a competitive rate of interest r^* on its fiat money, and its real resource use in maintaining the money stock is homogeneous of degree zero in nominal values, so that the marginal real profit from one more real government dollar is zero. This is exactly parallel to the case of banks discussed in the preceding paragraph. A rise in the price level reduces the level of real government money but has no effect on the flow of real profits from the government's "money business" because of the government's marginal condition. Any change in real profits would be reflected in changes in government's real taxation of the private sector, but since real profits do not change, there is no effect on wealth from this direction.

This result depends on the government's marginal condition holding, which in turn depends on the government paying a competitive r^*. When r^* is not at a competitive level, a rise in price affects the real value of the government's "money business" and thus the taxes that government levies on the private sector of the economy. It is in this way that a non-zero price-induced effect arises through government money.

Thus, the analysis of bank and government money is integrated. If each pays a competitive rate of interest, neither contributes to a price-induced effect on wealth. When government does not pay competitive interest, there may well arise a non-zero price-induced effect on wealth. But, similarly, if banks do not pay a competitive rate of interest on their deposits and banks become quantity-takers, then bank money will also enter the price-induced effect on wealth.

1.5 Brief Outline of the Book

Chapter 2 surveys the price- and interest-rate-induced effects on wealth as discussed in the literature and shows how later chapters fit in with previous analyses. Chapter 3 gives a review of the Hicksian apparatus of wealth and substitution effects, with an emphasis on issues that arise in later chapters that explicitly deal with macro level wealth effects. Much of the material is familiar, but some is seldom discussed. An example is the role of production in wealth effects. Changes in expected prices are discussed in relation to rational expectations.

The next four chapters, chapters 4–7, deal with the price-induced effect on wealth. Chapter 4 discusses the case of a constant stock of fiat money, the case closest to conventional analysis. In chapter 5, the stock of government fiat money is allowed to vary over time and in response to price level changes. The usual real balance effect is a very special case in this more general analysis. Indeed, the price-induced effect on wealth may be zero here. A new effect, the initial-condition effect, acts to render the price level determinate in the absence of a non-zero price-induced effect on wealth.

Chapters 6 and 7 deal with bank money and questions about interest payments on bank and government monies. In chapter 6, price-taking banks pay a competitively determined interest rate r on their demand deposits. Each optimizes by picking a money stock where marginal profits equal zero. If banks' real resource use is homogeneous of degree zero in nominal values, it turns out that optimizing behavior by banks at a competitive rate r gives a zero price-induced effect on wealth through bank money. Similarly, chapter 7 shows that if the government pays an interest rate r^* on its money based on a marginal condition such as the banks' in chapter 6, and its resource use for this purpose is homogeneous of degree zero in nominal values, then the price-induced effect on wealth through government money is zero. If market-clearing competitive interest rates on money are not paid, however, then under reasonable conditions both money stocks enter the price-induced effect on wealth.

Chapter 8 discusses the interest-rate-induced effect on wealth. Under conditions discussed there, the effect is zero. A key issue is whether the current generation's utility maximization includes bequests for coming generations. With such bequests, the interest-rate-induced effect on wealth is zero. In the absence of such bequests, the effect on wealth in current markets is likely to be negative. This chapter also discusses the issue of whether government bonds are net wealth. In this world of perfect certainty and lump-sum taxation, government bonds are not net wealth if the government plans to repay its bonds with taxation or money creation and the current generations' utility maximization involves leaving bequests. But if the government plans simply to roll over its debt, paying interest by selling new bonds, no equilibrium exists.

Chapter 9 deals with further questions about whether government bonds are net wealth, using stochastic models. It considers the question of whether private individuals use a higher discount rate on their tax liabilities than on bonds. It deals with the case where some individuals are liquidity constrained as well as wealth constrained. It also discusses the case where marginal tax rates are used rather than lump-sum taxation. All these arguments are less than persuasive that, on balance, government bonds are part of the net wealth of the household sector. An argument that does have force is that some parents do not leave bequests, and other people simply have no children; in such cases, the bequest motive does not operate and, as argued in chapter 8, government bonds do show up as net wealth in current markets.

Chapter 10 asks how changes in wealth implied by theory correspond to changes likely to be observed in wealth variables measured in conventional ways. Often the correspondence is very poor indeed. The chapter spells out the reasons for the mismeasurement, the consequences of mismeasuring changes in wealth, and some ways to try to overcome mismeasurement.

2

A Survey of Analysis of Wealth Effects

2.1 Introduction

Views on wealth effects have varied greatly over the past four or five decades. This chapter gives a selective history of the analysis of wealth effects, and comments on various authors' discussions in light of the material developed later in this book. The discussion serves as a review of the past and an intuitive introduction to the rest of the book. It also tries to create a context in which to make some sense of the shifting views over time of the importance and role of wealth effects.

The importance of wealth effects in monetary theory is obscured by the fact that these effects play different roles in the models of different economists. While economists may discuss the same effects, they may use these effects in very different ways in their overall arguments. Thus, wealth effects may be very contentious in one context and either used or ignored at will in other contexts.

It is useful to distinguish five roles that wealth effects have played in the literature. First, authors such as Pigou (1943) used the price-induced effect on wealth to argue that an unemployment equilibrium could not persist, that the economy would by itself produce forces propelling it back to full-employment equilibrium. Similarly, the interest-rate-induced effect on wealth can be used as part of an argument that an unemployment equilibrium cannot persist, as Pesek and Saving (1967) illustrate when they assume that a fall in the interest rate induces a rise in wealth and thus an increase in aggregate demand.

Second, the price-induced effect on wealth can be used to argue that the price level is determinate, as Patinkin (1956, 1965) does. The argument, however, is often turned around. The reader's willingness to believe in the determinacy of the price level is sometimes used to argue that the price-induced effect must enter the output or bond market and is economically significant even if perhaps not easily detected econometrically.

Third, the price-induced effect on wealth has played a major role in arguments about the "transmission mechanism" from monetary policy to effects on real activity and prices in the economy. Patinkin (1956, 1965) argues that the price-induced effect on wealth exists, in fact in many cases has to exist for determinacy of the price level. Assuming current output is a superior good, current aggregate demand must respond to price level changes, that is, must respond to changes in current real balances. Thus, an increase in the money stock that raises real balances must also have a direct effect on demand for output. Monetary policy "works" in this view, and without having to go through the Keynesian sequence of first reducing the interest rate, then raising the quantity of investment demanded and finally affecting the level of consumption through the multiplier process as income begins to rise. This result was particularly important to monetary economists who were fighting the battle in the 1950s and 1960s over whether money mattered and whether it mattered only because of effects on the interest rate and the level of investment demand, a channel many Keynesians viewed as unreliable. Friedman and Schwartz (1963) emphasize how in the short run the "liquidity effect" of an increase in the money stock raises demand for many goods as well as pushing down interest rates, and increases demand for a wide range of interest-sensitive consumer goods.

Fourth, wealth effects are sometimes investigated to see whether they give monetary and fiscal policymakers a handle on the real economy. The protracted discussions about the neutrality of money are an example. Metzler (1951) and Gurley and Shaw (1960) argued that increases in the money supply through open market operations are not neutral and hence allow some government influence through this channel even after the price level has adjusted. Patinkin (1965) accepted this view to the extent that government bonds are viewed as net wealth. The issue of whether government bonds are net wealth, as raised by Barro (1974) for example, is the same as whether cuts in current taxes financed by government bond sales will stimulate current aggregate demand. If government bonds are not net wealth, then money would seem to be neutral and (lump-sum) tax policies ineffective. Only government expenditures have more than transitory real effects on equilibrium in such models.

Fifth, the wealth accounts may be viewed as a set of variables that may influence equilibrium quantitatively, but not qualitatively. Hence, these accounts, and wealth effects in general, may or may not be included in models depending on the aims and convenience of the model builder. In the rational expectations models of the 1970s, it was taken for granted that money was neutral, at least in the long run. It was also taken for granted that unanticipated monetary policy had real effects; all that was needed was for aggregate demand to depend on the level of real balances. In turn, aggregate demand can depend on real balances even if there is no price-induced effect on wealth in the output market; it is sufficient to have the Keynesian linkage of making the interest rate depend on real balances through the money demand function, and the level of aggregate demand depend on the interest rate through the investment function. Inclusion of the price-induced effect on wealth in the consumption function was a great analytical inconvenience (Lucas, 1975) without qualitatively changing results and so was quietly omitted. Some propositions developed in the rational expectations literature, pre-eminently that anticipated monetary policy has no real effects, depend on "super neutrality" and thus the absence of a price-induced effect on wealth that shows up in the output market. Others, such as Lucas's (1973) discussion of output-inflation trade-offs, can conveniently omit discussion of the price-induced effect on wealth without altering the key results. As argued in chapter 4, the price-induced effect on wealth is not absent from these models, but shows up in the bond market rather than the output market. Since the bond market is left implicit, the effect is not explicitly discussed.

Of course, at much the same time other economists with different goals viewed wealth variables as quite important. For example, estimates of consumption functions typically used wealth or permanent income variables, and this was sometimes done in estimates of money demand functions.

The view economists took on wealth effects depended strongly on which battle was being fought. In the 1950s and 1960s, the existence, size, and economic significance of the real balance effect in the consumption function was a key skirmish in the battle over whether money mattered, because this channel allowed monetary policy to work outside the interest-rate-investment mechanism. In this context, Pesek and Saving's (1967) argument that bank money entered the real balance effect was quite important, for it much enlarged the money stock on which the effect worked and thus made the effect more important.

Less than a decade later, however, the battle was quite different. Keynesians, or many of them, believed that money mattered and that money was neutral, at least in the long run. Modigliani (1977), for one, argued that the economy would return on its own to equilibrium, though this might take a decade. The major macroeconomic debates from 1973 on, say, seemed to have little to do with wealth effects, but instead were dominated by the typical rational expectations questions. Do people form expectations rationally? Do prices and wages adjust as rapidly as many rational expectations models assume? Does anticipated monetary policy matter?

Fashions change, in economics as elsewhere. Wealth effects are much less frequently discussed now, but not because all of the important questions about them have been asked, let alone answered. Take one example of such important questions. How do future money supplies enter the price-induced effect on wealth? Patinkin, Gurley and Shaw, and Pesek and Saving use the current money stock for evaluating this effect. Yet models by Brock (1975) and Fischer (1979a) show anticipated future money stocks affecting current behavior. Do these future money stocks work, at least in part, through wealth effects? Take another example. What happens to the price-induced effect on wealth if government pays a competitively determined rate of interest on its money? Take a final example. What is the sign of the interest-rate-induced effect on wealth? This has been discussed for more than 50 years, without resolution.

Although a host of unresolved questions was left, interest in wealth effects waned for at least two reasons. First, Patinkin (1965) set a paradigm in terms of which the debate was carried on. This paradigm was highly useful for focusing on some issues but was less useful for others. By the early 1970s, much of the scope of the paradigm was exhausted and the debates had become somewhat picayune. For example, the framework was geared to answer questions about the price-induced effect on wealth, not the interest-rate-induced effect. Further, the focus was on one money stock, the current one.

Second, the rational expectations revolution set the agenda for a decade of macroeconomic debates. Wealth effects were not central to these issues and indeed were not even needed explicitly in most of the models.

Now the steam seems to have gone from the rational expectations revolution. It no longer dominates debates as it once did, though the tool of rational expectations remains and the effects of the revolution persist. No one can be sure where the monetary and macroeconomic literature will turn. One guess is that we shall see more interest in the wealth accounts.

The remainder of this chapter gives a selective review of past analyses of wealth effects and comments on them in light of material developed later in this book. Section 2.2 discusses the price-induced effect on wealth and section 2.3 the interest-rate-induced effect.

2.2 The Price-Induced Effect on Wealth

In the first two decades after Keynes's *General Theory* (1936), many economists took as a key part of the Keynesian revolution the view that there could exist an unemployment equilibrium. The endogenous work-ings of the market were supposed to be unable to move the system to full employment. This view then supported the notion that active fiscal policy was needed to propel the system to full employment.

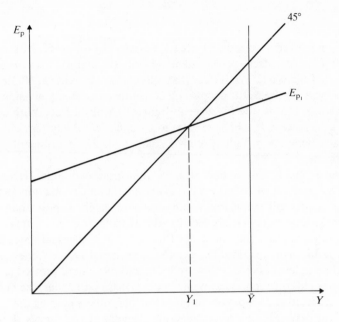

Figure 2.1 Income determination in the 45° line analysis

The "Keynesian cross" or "45° line" analysis was a simple model capturing the view of the possibility of unemployment equilibrium. Up to the full employment level $\overline{Y}$, equilibrium real output and income Y is demand determined along the 45° line in figure 2.1. If planned expenditure is given by the curve E_{p_1}, the equilibrium is at $Y_1 < \overline{Y}$. Fiscal policy can be used to shift up the E_p curve to run through the intersection of $\overline{Y}$ and the 45° line.

In finding E_p, a common formulation was the simple consumption function

$$C = a + b(Y - T), \qquad a > 0, \qquad 0 < b < 1, \tag{2.1}$$

where C is real consumption demanded, a and b are parametric, and T is real taxation and thus $Y - T$ is real disposable income.

Pigou's Analysis

Pigou (1943) objected to the notion of an unemployment equilibrium from which the economic system could not rescue itself. In effect, he modified (2.1) by including the term M/P, the real value of the stock of money, or

$$C = a + b(Y - T) + cM/P, \quad c > 0. \tag{2.2}$$

Pigou considered a stationary state where (net) investment is zero, so price adjustments can affect private demand only through C. From the consumption function (2.2) it is clear that falls in P will increase M/P. Because of this larger real wealth, people will consume more at any given level of real income, that is, the E_p curve in figure 2.1 will shift up. With a large enough decrease in P, and hence a large enough M/P, the system will automatically generate a high enough E_p curve to give a full-employment equilibrium.

Pigou explicitly did not urge reliance on price level declines. He argued that these might have to be very large, and might take a long time to move the system to full employment. Others were quick to point out other problems. Kalecki (1944) argued that the M in M/P should refer only to gold, not bank money. Even before Pigou, Irving Fisher had warned how a debt deflaton process could lead to idle resources. In Fisher's view, as the overall price level falls, debtors are more and more hard pressed to meet their nominal contractual payments, and when they go under, their capital goods are idled and employment falls. Further, others pointed out that to the extent that declining prices generate expectations of further declines, substitution effects will occur that, by themselves, make consumers want to defer purchases until prices fall in the future.

Nevertheless, Pigou's argument had an important, unambiguous implication. If rises in M/P brought about by declines in P could return the system to full employment, so could rises in M/P brought about by increases in M. Monetary policy could be used to stabilize the economy. Indeed, sufficiently vigorous monetary policy would necessarily have major effects on the economy.

Money in the IS–LM *Analysis*

Keynesians in the two decades after the *General Theory* (1936) tended to dismiss monetary policy. In many of their minds there was a real issue as to whether money mattered. To other Keynesians money clearly mattered, but the channels through which it worked were different from those of Pigou. Modigliani (1944) argued that unemployment could arise through too small a level of M/P. The argument, however, depended on M/P influencing the interest rate i, which then influenced investment I, and hence aggregate demand Y^d – and only then Y. The argument can be seen in the IS–LM diagram in figure 2.2. An increase in M/P shifts the LM curve down to LM_2. At Y_1, this reduces i to i_2 and raises I. Y^d goes up and through the multiplier process Y rises to Y_2 with the new equilibrium i_3.

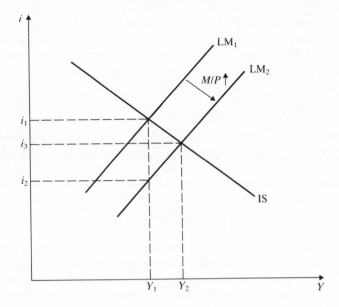

Figure 2.2 The interest rate as a transmission mechanism for monetary policy

Many early Keynesians were very skeptical that this process was important or reliable. The increase in M/P might not reduce i by much, the increase might take some (variable) time to reduce i, I might not respond much to the fall in i, and the response might take a long (variable) time. Further, the investment function itself was viewed as unstable and quite capable of shifting unpredictably and swamping the effects of the fall in i.

In Pigou's argument, of course, the increase in M/P shifted the IS curve to the right and hence Y would rise, however tenuous might be the links between M/P and i and between i and I. Keynesian use of the general equilibrium IS–LM apparatus thus allowed for money logically to play a role in determining equilibrium, but also allowed the analyst to minimize the role and stress the number and unreliability of the steps through which money's influence worked. Pigou's analysis was often ignored, minimized, or dismissed, along with the counter-revolutionary monetarists to whom the argument had much appeal.

Metzler's Analysis

Metzler (1951) investigated the effects of adding to the economy's money stock in two different ways, and thought he had found a mechanism whereby money affected the economy's equilibrium. Similarly to Pigou, Metzler assumed that the level of consumption and saving depended on real income and on real wealth W/P. Real wealth in turn equals real balances plus the capital stock in Metzler's analysis, or

$$\frac{W}{P} = \frac{M}{P} + K. \tag{2.3}$$

In Metzler's first experiment, the stock of money is increased by transfer payments from the government, which prints the extra money to finance these transfers; think of the transfers as a random drop of money from helicopters. Before there is any change in price, M/P is larger and from (2.3) so is real wealth W/P. If M is doubled and P is doubled, M/P and W/P are both at their same old levels. The result in this case of the increase in the money stock is a proportionate increase in the price level. Money is neutral in the sense that the increase in M does not affect the long-run real equilibrium but only induces a proportional increase in P.

The second way of increasing M is through open market operations. Since real balances and capital are the only assets in the model, Metzler has the government increase M, and hence M/P, and reduce K in private hands by an equal amount. Before any price level change, W/P in (2.3) is thus unchanged. The stock of real balances has increased, however, while the quantity of real balances demanded is unchanged. Thus, while the change in M causes no change in wealth, there is a portfolio effect that causes an excess supply of real balances. This excess supply of real balances in turn causes an increase in the price level. As P rises, M/P falls and hence so does W/P. As W/P falls, the level of desired saving out of $\overline{Y}$ rises. Since equilibrium requires equality between desired saving and investment, investment is induced to rise by a fall in the (real) interest rate. Clearly, this second form of money creation has real effects on the economy.

Another way of seeing these real effects is tentatively to suppose that the monetary expansion is neutral or simply results in a proportionate increase in the price level. This keeps M/P constant, but since K in private hands is down, W/P falls, and there must be a change in private sector behavior. In other words, money in this experiment cannot be neutral.

Metzler's analysis neglects to ask what happens to that part of K, dK, that the government has acquired. Presuming the government rents it back to private sector entrepreneurs, the total stock of capital available for production has not changed, and hence neither has $\overline{Y}$, the level of full employment or the equilibrium real wage rate. However, where the private sector used to earn revenues on dK, now the government sector does. Assuming that the government sector does not increase its spending, it must use the revenues on dK either to decrease taxes or increase transfer payments, or taxes net of transfer payments must fall by the revenue associated with dK.

Thus, on the one hand private income is reduced by the revenue from dK, but on the other hand the private sector finds its net taxes reduced by the same amount. Once the public catches on to this, their behavior should be unaltered by the shift of dK to the government. The open market increase in M should simply result in a proportional increase in P. The analysis of this case can be made substantially more complex, for example, in terms of expectations or changes in marginal tax rates, and these complexities can allow the method of monetary expansion to have some presumably minor real effects. However, it is clear that Metzler overlooked a key issue, the implied change in net taxation, and this oversight vitiates much of his argument that how the money stock is changed affects the real equilibrium.

Patinkin's 1956 Analysis

Patinkin's 1956 book was the culmination of a series of articles he had been writing since the late 1940s. He argued in 1956 that changes in P could move the system to a full-employment equilibrium. Further, the real balance effect was argued to be necessary for a determinate price level. He was clear that the real balance effect need not show up in the output market, but might arise in the bond market only. He considered implausible, however, the possibility that the real balance effect would be absent from the output market, since presumably consumption is a superior good.

Similarly to Pigou, Patinkin argued that a real balance effect that affected the output market would eventually return the system to equilibrium. This led to much discussion in the 1950s and 1960s of how large the real balance effect was, how long it took to operate, how far prices would have to fall, and whether the real balance effect could be detected in the output market. While Patinkin argued that the real balance effect must show up in some non-money market for the price level to be determinate, he showed that the effect need not logically show up in the output market, but might instead appear in the bond market (he does not analyze the possibility of the real balance showing up only in the money and labor markets). In the case where the real balance effect shows up in the bond but not output market, it first affects the interest rate and through the interest sensitivity of aggregate demand then affects the output market – the same sort of indirect channels allowed in conventional IS–LM analysis. When the real balance effect works in the output market, money directly affects aggregate demand without first affecting the interest rate and investment. Hence, in terms of the Keynesian–monetarist controversies of the 1950s and 1960s, it is easy to see why monetarists were interested in having the real balance effect show up in the output market and why Keynesians were so often hostile to the real balance effect, particularly in the output market.

Another major concern of Patinkin (1956) was the closely related issues of the neutrality of money and the determinacy of the price level. For neutrality, he imagined a once and for all doubling of the money supply. Assuming static expectations and neglecting distribution effects, a corresponding doubling of the price level leaves all relative prices unchanged, including intertemporal relative prices, and leaves wealth unchanged. Hence, the previous real equilibrium remains an equilibrium with only the nominal scale of the system changed – in this case, doubled. Money is neutral.

In the case of determinacy, Patinkin does not ask whether an equilibrium can be shown to exist or whether there is only one equilibrium, the existence and uniqueness questions of general equilibrium theory. Rather, assuming that an equilibrium exists, he asks whether an increase in the price level will cause a disequilibrium that makes the system tend back to the initial equilibrium. In other words, the issue is whether the increase in the price level causes non-zero excess demands to arise, with these non-zero excess demands then causing changes in the price level towards its initial value. Using Walras's law, Patinkin focuses on non-money excess demands. At the constant initial interest rate, assuming static expectations and neglecting redistributions of wealth caused by the price level increase, a rise in the price level causes no change in relative prices. Hence, in terms of the Hicksian analysis of wealth and substitution effects, there are no substitution effects on excess demands, and only wealth effects are left to make the excess demands non-zero. The only wealth effect is the real balance effect, and hence the real balance effect must exist and show up in *some* non-money market to make excess demands non-zero and render the price level determinate.

Patinkin (1956, pp. 204–8) includes a few pages introducing government bonds into his analysis. While he regards the net liquid assets of households and firms as "now equal to the total of their money and government-bond holdings" (p. 205), he does not write the sum as one argument but enters both separately. He argues that a doubling of the money supply, similar to Metzler's non-open market operation, or random distribution of money, is not neutral because the real value of government bonds falls. This non-neutrality could be removed by indexing. Even if bonds are indexed, however, an open market operation that increases the money stock will not simply lead to a proportionate increase in the price level because the stock of real government bonds is decreased by the operation, similar to Metzler's discussion.

Patinkin clearly misses the tax implications of bonds in his discussion. The interest and principal on government bonds must be paid by taxation in Patinkin's model and eventually decision-makers must catch on to the fact that (or act as if) government bonds are not net wealth, as discussed in chapter 8.

Gurley and Shaw's Analysis

Gurley and Shaw's (1960) book is an ambitious attempt to fit monetary theory into a discussion of the development of financial institutions in the course of overall economic development. They introduce the influential distinction between inside and outside money. They argue that money is not necessarily neutral. Further, they argue that there need not be a real balance effect, a price-induced effect on wealth, for the price level to be determinate.

In Gurley and Shaw's analysis, outside money is unbacked by other assets, while inside money is backed by other assets. For example, gold is outside money, and so is money distributed as transfer payments, as in Metzler's analysis. If all money is outside money, then the system is as Patinkin (1956) described. Money is neutral and the real balance effect is necessary for a determinate price level.

Suppose, however, that the only money is government fiat money that is introduced into the system by exchanging it for private sector bonds. Then, on the government's balance sheet the outstanding money is balanced by these bonds. Similarly, the total net assets of the private sector are unchanged, with this sector now having more money but owing the government an equal amount in the form of bonds. This is an example of inside money.

Suppose that money is initially all outside money and the government doubles the money supply through an open market operation by buying private sector bonds. This leaves initial private sector wealth unchanged, but creates an excess supply of real balances. As the price level rises to eliminate this excess supply, the private sector's real wealth falls because the real value of outside money falls. Hence, they argue, it cannot be that the price level simply changes proportionately with the money supply in this case, because such a change would result in a lower level of real wealth and necessarily some impact on the system's equilibrium. Money in this case is not neutral. Indeed, assuming the money stock is partly inside and partly outside money, the inside component insures that money is generally not neutral unless the two components are changed in a way that keeps their ratio constant.

It is clear that Gurley and Shaw's analysis falls into the same trap as Metzler's earlier work, of neglecting to ask what happens to the interest the government earns on its holdings of private sector debt. If these interest payments are returned to the private sector in the form of a reduction in net taxation, then to at least a first approximation the liability of making these payments is canceled by the reduction in net taxation. The private sector's balance sheet shows an increase in money on the asset side; on the liabilities side its debt to the government rises but the present value of its net tax liabilities falls by an equal amount. Looked at this way, the inside–outside money distinction and the differential analytical results following from it are simply mistaken.

While Gurley and Shaw's analysis is seriously flawed, they do introduce a useful new effect, the "portfolio effect," in considering the determinacy of the price level. Suppose that all money is inside money and the price level doubles. According to Gurley and Shaw, there is no real balance effect to cause non-zero excess demands and thus push the price level back to its initial value. While wealth has not changed in Gurley and Shaw's view, the total amount of real balances in existence has been halved. Thus, the composition of the unchanged real wealth in the household sector's portfolio has been altered. Since the quantity of real balances demanded is unchanged, but the supply has fallen, here is the non-zero excess demand needed to provide a determinate price level. Balancing this excess demand for real balances is an excess supply of real bonds, since the real value of the bond debt that the private sector owes the government has been cut in half. While Gurley and Shaw are incorrect in arguing that there is no real balance effect in this case, because they neglect government's use of its interest earnings, it is useful to look beyond wealth and substitution effects and consider other effects like portfolio effects. A portfolio effect is used, for example, in chapter 7 to argue for determinacy of the price level.

Johnson (1961)

In his 1961 survey article, Harry G. Johnson discusses Patinkin's (1956) result that the real balance effect is necessary for a determinate price level. Johnson points out that, when the initial price level doubles in Patinkin's experiment, the government could if it liked increase the money supply proportionately, so that the price level would not be determinate. Thus, the determinacy of the price level is in some ways a historical accident that depends on government not responding to price level changes by ratifying them with proportional increases in the money supply. In the decades since Johnson wrote, such inflationary ratification by policymakers appears much more likely. Even with such government behavior, however, this book shows that the price level is determinate by introducing a new effect, the initial-condition effect.

The Initial-Condition Effect

In the usual demonstration of the determinacy of the price level, M is assumed to be constant over time and this seems to be what returns P to its initial level. However, the constant M over time is not at all necessary for price level determinacy. To see this, consider the case Johnson (1961) proposes where the price level is supposed to be indeterminate if government were, say, to double M when P suddenly doubles. To sharpen the analysis, suppose that there is no bank money and that, whatever is the initial sequence of government money, each period's M is unit elastic with respect to the initial period's price level P_0. Thus, if P_0 doubles, then M_1, $M_2, M_3, \ldots$ also all double.

The key to understanding why the price level is still determinate is to examine the timing of money stock accumulation relative to its use. Similarly to Patinkin (1956, 1965), assume nominal balances are accumulated by the end of period t to be used for transactions in period $t+1$. Hence, given the price level P_{t+1}, the real balances used in period $t+1$ are predetermined by actions in period t.

When P_0 doubles and so does the sequence $M_1, M_2, M_3, \ldots$, there is a zero price-induced effect on wealth, as discussed in chapter 5. For M_1 to double, the government must inject extra money into the system over the course of period 0. But this extra money is not available at the start of the period for carrying out transactions. Instead, transactions will be made with the M_0 that is available from the previous period's decisions about accumulating money balances. The adequacy of the initial real balances, M_0/P_0, falls when P_0 doubles and M_0/P_0 is halved. It is almost surely true that this fall in M_0/P_0 will affect behavior in the current period and thus lead to excess demands in some current markets. This effect of the price level on excess demands is precisely the chain of reasoning Patinkin habitually uses to demonstrate determinacy of the price level.

Patinkin (1965)

In his 1965 revised edition, Patinkin took account of the analyses of both Gurley and Shaw and Johnson. He also took into account the analysis of Mundell (1963) as well as Christ's (1957) review of Patinkin (1956), which pointed out the implications of tax liabilities that both Metzler (1951) and Patinkin had overlooked.

Supposing that government and private sector bonds are perfect substitutes, the Gurley and Shaw analysis of inside money says that private sector wealth is reduced by the amount of its bonds that the government holds and increased by the amount it holds of government bonds. If the number of government bonds held by the public, net of government holdings of private sector bonds, is V and the price of bonds is P_b, then in Gurley and Shaw's analysis private sector real wealth is

$$\frac{W}{P} = \frac{M + P_b V}{P} + K \qquad (2.4)$$

Patinkin, however, writes

$$\frac{W}{P} = \frac{M + kP_b V}{P} + K$$

where $0 \leqslant k \leqslant 1$. In response to Christ's (1957) discussion, Patinkin (1965) allows the extent of capitalization of taxes to be an empirical matter of k's value. If taxpayers fully take into account the tax liabilities "associated" with government bonds, then $k = 0$. If these liabilities are not taken fully into account, however, k may be positive; and if the liabilities are ignored, k presumably equals unity. Thus, Patinkin views a "real financial effect" as arising from (2.4), an effect more general than the real balance effect. The real financial effect of an increase in the price level is

$$\frac{d(W/P)}{dP} = -\frac{M}{P^2} - \frac{kP_b V}{P^2}.$$

If $k = 0$, the real balance and the real financial effects are the same. If $k > 0$, then the real financial effect is even more powerful than the real balance effect, assuming $V > 0$. If there is a negative V, so government holds private sector bonds, and also $M = -P_b V$, this is simply Gurley and Shaw's case of pure inside money; it is a special case of Patinkin's general analysis. In the special case where all money is inside money and no account is taken of implied tax liabilities ($k = 1$), Patinkin finds no real financial effect, but argues that the price level is still determinate. This is because an increase in the price level from its equilibrium value reduces the stock of real balances but not the demand for them (since there are no wealth or substitution effects). This creates an excess demand for money (balanced by an excess supply of bonds) that moves the price level back to its initial value. Hence, Patinkin now recognizes real balance effects, real financial wealth effects (of which the real balance effect is a component) and portfolio effects as forces in the system's adjustment.

Patinkin's (1965) analysis goes into little detail regarding what the value of k should be on theoretical grounds. Suppose that people are ignorant of the relationship between their holdings of V and the increased taxes that someone must pay to finance the interest on these bonds compared with the case where $V = 0$. Still, over time people will become aware of the taxes actually being paid and will know they are poorer than they would otherwise be. If they eventually form accurate expectations, they will come to see that in the aggregate the present value of their tax liabilities has risen by $P_b V$. This of course does not require people to link in a causal way their extra tax liabilities to their extra holdings of government bonds. As a first approximation, $k = 0$, though Patinkin accepts $k \geqslant 0$. Chapters 8 and 9 go into the complexities of these issues in some detail.

Patinkin responds to Johnson's (1961) comment by noting that his analysis (1965) does assume an asymmetry between the government and private sectors in order to achieve determinacy of the price level. When P rises, the private sector feels poorer and cuts back on its expenditures because the real value of its asset money has fallen. The government sector, however, is assumed not to change its expenditures when the real value of its liability, money, falls. Thus, there is an asymmetry, but it seems reasonable and realistic to Patinkin.

Patinkin (1965) does not include bank money in the stock of money in the real balance effect. His view is that bank money is the asset of its holders and the liability of its issuers. A rise in P reduces the real value of the assets of the holders of bank money, but also reduces equally the real value of the liabilities of banks and hence increases equally the real wealth of bank owners. The net effect is zero.

In his discussion in 1965, Patinkin assumes banks pay a rate of interest r on their deposits that equals zero. Thus, in his 1965 view, it is solely the accounting requirement that bank assets and liabilities must be equal that implies that bank money is not part of the real balance effect. The level of r, and whether it is competitively determined or not, has no bearing on the issue in Patinkin's analysis.

Pesek and Saving's Analysis

A key point in Pesek and Saving's (1967) book is the argument that bank money is a part of net wealth and also a part of the real balance effect. They reject the argument, used from Kalecki (1944) through Patinkin (1965), that bank money is not part of net wealth just because bank liabilities equal assets.

Suppose that a bank is allowed to issue $100 of its money, subject only to the requirement that it keep on hand enough government money or reserves to be able to convert its money on demand into government money. Suppose the amount of reserves necessary is e times the amount of bank money issued, or for concreteness is $10 with $e = 0.1$. The bank then creates $100 of its money and uses it to buy $10 of government money and $90 of private sector bonds. Its balance sheet shows $100 of assets ($= $90 of bonds + $10 of reserves) and $100 of liabilities in the form of demand deposits. In Patinkin's (1965) analysis this $100 of bank money would not add to the real balance effect (or what Pesek and Saving call the price-induced effect on wealth), because the assets and liabilities of the bank are equal.

Pesek and Saving argue, however, that bank money does enter the effect. One way of seeing this is to argue that the non-bank public now has $100 more of bank money than before and $10 less of government money, or is $90 richer. The real value of this $90 is, for example, halved if the price level doubles, and the private sector of the economy is worse off while banks are unchanged in net terms. Alternatively, the amount of government money in private non-bank hands plus the amount of bank money enters the price-induced effect on wealth, and this total is higher by $90.

A third way of viewing this same issue, due to Patinkin (1969, 1972), is perhaps more illuminating. While the values of the bank's assets and liabilities are equal, the bank's stock (or ownership rights) has a positive value. The $90 worth of bonds held by the bank will provide a dividend stream to customers that has a net present value and market value of $90. Now, the non-bank sector gave up $10 of government money and $90 of bonds to buy $100 of bank money – this nets to zero so far. But the non-bank sector owns the bank sector which is worth $90, and thus the economy is richer by $90. When the price level doubles, the real value of this $90 is halved. The $90 must enter the price-induced effect on wealth.

Pesek and Saving argue vigorously that one point their analysis shows is that the quantity of bank money must be restricted. Otherwise, the issuers who are $90 ahead so far will issue more and more money. They will cease only when the real value of one more dollar has been driven down to the real cost of printing that dollar. Thus, they argue, restrictions on issuance of bank money are inherent if this fiat money is to have an equilibrium value in excess of its resource content.

Patinkin's (1969) Review of Pesek and Saving

Patinkin argues that Pesek and Saving's inclusion of bank money in the price-induced effect on wealth follows not from any innate property of money or a banking system but rather from monopoly restrictions that they include in their analysis. Recall that the inclusion of bank money in the price-induced effect on wealth arose in one view because the banks' dividend stream had a positive net present value. Suppose that there are many banks that compete with each other. Patinkin's view is that a competitive banking system implies that zero profits are made and hence the value of banks is zero; competition will dissipate the $90 present value. Further, when the price level doubles, say, bank profits remain zero, as does the value of the banking system. Thus, competition insures that bank money is not part of the price-induced effect on wealth. Even if banks operate as a cartel, Patinkin views free entry as reducing bank profits to zero and hence making the price-induced effect on wealth through banks also equal zero.

In 1965, Patinkin argues that assets-equals-liabilities is sufficient for bank money not to enter the price-induced effect on wealth, and he explicitly assumes that the rate r paid on deposits is equal to zero. In 1969, he abandons assets-equals-liabilities and uses competition-implies-zero-profits to keep bank money from being a part of the price-induced effect on wealth. He no longer assumes $r = 0$, but it seems that bank money is excluded whether $r = 0$ or not. He views competition, specifically free entry, as driving bank profits to zero whether r is set competitively or not.

Patinkin (1969, 1972) evaluates the price-induced effect on wealth at the initial nominal quantity of bank money, as does Saving (1970, 1971), though it is never clear why this is done. Government money is generally held constant in evaluation of the real balance effect under the assumption that it is in fact constant. Bank money is highly likely to vary endogenously in response to price level changes, and indeed it might seem more cogent to evaluate the real balance effect at a given level of real bank money balances.

In any case, it is curious that neither Patinkin (1969, 1971, 1972) nor Saving (1971, 1973) make use of banks' first-order conditions when evaluating the effect of a price level change on the real value of the banks' dividend stream. Suppose that the banks' real choices are independent of the nominal scale of the system, i.e. of the price level; this requires that bank resource use be homogeneous of degree zero in nominal values. (This homogeneity condition is also required for neutrality.) Then in any period each bank chooses its real deposits and real reserves to maximize its real value. Explicitly, at a profit maximum a marginal change in real deposits has a zero effect on the bank's real value, and the same with a change in real reserves. Now let the price level rise while the bank's nominal deposits and reserves are held constant. The increase in P reduces real deposits and real reserves. The change in the real value of the bank in reaction to this is also zero, however, because of the first-order conditions.

Profit-maximizing behavior by r-taking, quantity-setting banks is thus a key condition for the bank money to have no role in the price-induced effect on wealth. The reason that bank money does not enter the price-induced effect on wealth is not the zero-profit condition as argued by Patinkin but rather the competitive determination of r with wealth-maximizing banks subject to the homogeneity condition. Further, when bank money and reserves are allowed to vary in response to price level changes, the price-induced effect on wealth is still zero, as shown in chapter 6.

Note that the change in the real value of the future profit flows from the bank is zero[1] even if the real value of the bank is positive. For example, restrictions on entry into the banking industry may insure that while the average bank is a price-taker (including r) it also reaps some monopoly rents. Further, in an increasing-cost banking industry, some factors will earn rents, with the rents playing a role analogous to any monopoly rents. These issues are discussed in detail in chapters 6 and 7.

The preceding discussion assumed that the individual bank was initially at an optimum where it picked its real quantity of deposits, but government interest rate regulations can prevent banks from achieving their optimum. Suppose each bank is an r-taker and a quantity-setter, and in this sense a competitor, whether or not restrictions on entry give monopoly rents or specialized factors earn scarcity rents. The role of r is to adjust in order to equate the quantities of bank money demanded and supplied. If the equilibrium level is r_0 and r is set below r_0, then the average bank will find that its real deposits are less than desired. This means that its marginal condition for real bank money does not hold. The bank has become a quantity-taker rather than a quantity-setter. Further, since its real deposits are too small, an increase in real deposits raises the bank's real value.

Suppose, now, that P rises and this causes a decline in wealth through government money, leaving aside any effect through bank money. The reduction in wealth reduces the quantity of real bank balances demanded and hence the real value of banks. This reduction in the real value of banks follows from the fact that their marginal conditions for deposits do not hold and a rise in real deposits would increase the banks' real value. In other words, if banks do not pay a competitively determined rate of interest on their deposits, then bank money *is* a part of the price-induced effect on wealth. This is discussed at length in chapter 7.

Restrictions on banks' deposit rates will push them to compete on other margins. It is possible, though perhaps unlikely, that this competition will allow them to return to being quantity-setters. The key point is that as long as regulation leaves them as quantity-takers, bank money enters the price-induced effect on wealth.

The conclusion is this: if banks are price-taking quantity-setting optimizers, and if their real decisions are independent of the price level (the homogeneity condition), then bank money does not enter the price-induced effect on wealth. For this result, it is not at all necessary that the real value of banks be zero, as Patinkin assumes.

Johnson's (1969) View on Money Paying a Competitively Determined Interest Rate

In the course of a wide-ranging discussion, Johnson (1969) suggests that the distinction between inside and outside money is irrelevant, and that the important distinction is between monies that do or do not pay a competitive rate of interest. In his view, monies paying a competitive rate of interest are not part of the price-induced effect on wealth, and this is true of either bank or government money. Johnson's argument is short and sketchy and assumes that there are zero resource costs for the monetary services provided by either banks or government. Further, he seems to argue that real balances must be held constant in the face of price level increases; in this case it is not clear whether the government can use control of its money stock to control the price level or whether government money is fully endogenous.

As discussed above, bank money is not part of the price-induced effect on wealth if competitively determined interest is paid and if banks are optimizers subject to the homogeneity condition. Chapter 6 discusses this in detail. If competitive interest is not allowed on bank money, bank money enters the price-induced effect on wealth if the restriction makes banks quantity-takers. Thus, this book reaches conclusions somewhat similar to Johnson's (1969) for bank money, and in a far richer model.

The book also reaches the conclusion that government money does not enter the price-induced effect under certain conditions, including government paying a competitively determined rate of interest on its money. The case where government sets up a "money business" is discussed in chapter 7. All of the profits of the business go to reduce net taxation, and the real value of the "government money business" is equal to the real present value of the associated reduction in net taxation from this source. Government money's role in the price-induced effect on wealth is simply the change in the real present value of future cash flows from this "business" less future costs.

Suppose government chooses a given sequence of M in order to try to control the price level. Every period, however, let it also set the interest rate r^* that it pays on its money. Neglecting its monopoly power, it chooses r^* to set equal to zero the marginal revenue minus the marginal cost to its money business of a change in the real value of government money outstanding. In particular, the government sets M, the economy generates P, and the government then sets r^* in order to make the marginal condition hold. This role generates a competitive rate r^* in the sense of balancing marginal benefit with marginal cost.

If the current price level now rises, and all future price levels rise proportionately, this reduces M/P in every period and thus affects the real present value of the cash flows of the government's money business. Assuming government resource use is homogeneous of degree zero in nominal values, the change in each period is marginal revenue minus marginal cost for that period, and from the marginal condition is thus zero. In other words, if the government pays a competitive rate of interest on its deposits and its resource use is homogeneous of degree zero in nominal values, the price-induced effect on the real value of its money business is zero and hence so is the price-induced effect on wealth through government money. This is completely symmetric to the banking sector.

For clarity, suppose there is no banking sector. A rise in the price level reduces the real present value of revenue from the government's money business and also the real present value of the cost of its money business, and by equal amounts. Thus, there is no price-induced effect on wealth.

The real value of the money stock falls, however, while the demand for real balances stays the same, setting up an excess demand for money (equal to the excess supply of bonds) to return the system to its initial price level, the sort of portfolio effect that Gurley and Shaw (1960) and Patinkin (1965) use. In addition, there exist initial-condition effects that also help to render the price level determinate.

Thus, Johnson's (1969) intuition is basically correct. There is no price-induced effect on wealth through money that pays a competitive rate of interest, whether the money is from banks or government, provided that optimizing conditions hold and the homogeneity condition is met. It is important to note, however, that government retains full control over the stock of money and thus can set the money supply to control the price level. These issues are discussed in some detail in chapter 7.

The Rational Expectations Revolution

With Lucas (1972, 1973, 1975), Sargent (1973, 1976), Sargent and Wallace (1975) and others, the rational expectations revolution was under way and dominated macro and monetary discussions for more than a decade. Wealth effects played virtually no role in these models and were generally either ignored or assumed away. This made the theoretical models less sophisticated in their treatment of wealth accounts than the models of the 1950s and 1960s used by Patinkin, Gurley and Shaw, Pesek and Saving and others. The wealth accounts, however, were seen as not playing a crucial role in the debates over theory and hence could be neglected on grounds of convenience.

The empirical models produced by rational expectations exponents also typically neglected wealth variables except for including prominently some measure of the money stock; almost always there was no real balance effect in the output market. In contrast, since the early 1960s Keynesian econometric models have generally made increasingly sophisticated use of the wealth accounts in explaining behavior in many different markets. This difference may be explained in part by the monetarist preference for small versus large models. This preference was given additional support by the Lucas and Sargent (1979) critique of Keynesian econometric models. Further, the somewhat common monetarist preference for using permanent income rather than wealth variables may also have played a role.

Figure 2.3 gives the spirit of the simpler rational expectations monetary models. For various levels of price that are expected, the aggregate supply curve AS is vertical. If the price level P_1 is expected but the actual price

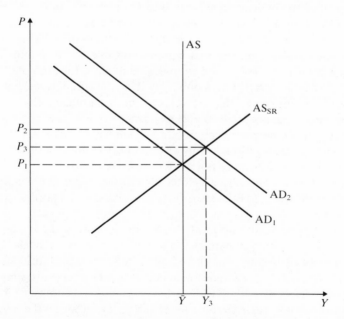

Figure 2.3 Aggregate demand, aggregate supply, and rational expectations

level is different from P_1, the economy moves along the short run AS_{SR}. The demand side of the economy is shown in the aggregate demand curve AD. AD is found from the usual IS–LM analysis by varying P and seeing how the Y at the IS–LM intersection varies. At a qualitative level, it is a matter of indifference in constructing AD whether there are price- or interest-rate-induced effects on wealth that show up in the IS curve, but such effects can make the mathematics more cumbersome. Hence such effects are ignored or assumed away. As shown in chapter 4, this does not mean that there are no wealth effects in such models, but rather that they are not explicitly analyzed and may be missing from the output market.

In equilibria where the price level is expected, the economy is at an AD–AS intersection. For example, an increase in M shifts the AD curve from AD_1 to AD_2 and, if this shift is expected, price rises from P_1 to P_2. Money is neutral and the economy moves itself to a full-employment equilibrium at $\overline{Y}$.

Up to this point, many Keynesians have no major objections to this as an analysis of long-run equilibrium. The AD curve is a Keynesian device. Many would agree that in the long run the economy will end up at the full-employment equilibrium $\overline{Y}$ and that the stock of money is neutral.

Many rational expectations models focus on changes in money as the source of changes in the AD curve. If the AD curve shifts to AD_2 because of an unexpected increase in M, P rises to P_3 rather than to P_2 and output goes from $\overline{Y}$ to Y_3. The unexpected increase in M causes a transitory increase in Y. In the simpler rational expectations models, monetary policy has no effect on the real equilibrium unless it is unanticipated (though this is not true in more complicated models, for example, Lucas (1975), Fischer (1979a)). The economy is always at equilibrium, but there can be deviations from long-run values if decision-makers find their *ex ante* optimal forecasts are incorrect *ex post*.

The typical Keynesian objections are well known. Most of them turn on arguments that expectations are not as rational as assumed in such models, or that prices and wages are not as flexible as assumed.

The important point is that neither the rational expectations modelers nor their critics have to raise issues about wealth effects in order to make their points.

Neglecting the wealth accounts leads, however, to some impoverishment of the transitory dynamics in rational expectations models. It was noticed at an early stage that there had to be some lagged influences on behavior to make these models produce results even broadly similar to reality. For example, when a disturbance puts the economy at Y_3, the simple models say that in the absence of further disturbances the economy should return to $\overline{Y}$ in the next period, but actual movements in Y show much greater persistence. Lucas's (1973) model and later models add lags to aggregate supply. Thus, after Y_3 the vertical AS curve is somewhere between Y_3 and $\overline{Y}$ and takes several (perhaps many) periods to shift back to $\overline{Y}$ even in the absence of further disturbances.

Another channel for lagged behavior, however, is through aggregate demand. With the economy at Y_3, the private sector will have accumulated more wealth than otherwise and will want to take several periods to work it off. Then, even with no further disturbances, the AD curve should be higher than AD_2 and only gradually work its way back to AD_2. Demand-side persistence has been somewhat neglected in theoretical rational expectations discussions (but see, for example, Long and Plosser, 1983).

2.3 The Interest-Rate-Induced Effect on Wealth

There are three pieces of conventional wisdom concerning the interest-rate-induced effect on wealth, or the effect on wealth of a rise in the current and all future one-period interest rates. The first says the effect is indeterminate; the second says it is zero; and the third says it is negative.

Famous economists can be lined up for each position. Hicks (1939, 1946) argues that the effect is indeterminate for any one individual, but is zero for society as a whole in the absence of distribution effects. Chapter 8 of this book derives this conclusion for certain cases. Keynes (1936), however, argued that a fall in the long-term rate of interest would cause a windfall capital gain that raised consumption demand. While Keynes's *General Theory* predates Hicks's analytical apparatus of wealth and substitution effects, later economists interpret Keynes's windfall effect as a statement about a wealth effect, namely that the interest-rate-induced effect on wealth is negative. This is the view, for example, of Pesek and Saving (1967) and Leijonhufvud (1968).

Chapter 8 shows that the debate turns mainly on whether the life of the economy is longer than the economic life of the representative individual currently alive. In a world with mortal individuals who will expire before the economy, the issue then turns on what bequests those who are currently alive and economically active make for their heirs.

Both Hicks (1939, 1946) and Matthews (1963) show that an increase in the long-term rate of interest has an ambiguous or indeterminate effect on an individual's wealth. The ambiguity arises from the timing of the individual's borrowing and lending. In a two-period world, suppose that I lend to you now in order for me to enjoy extra consumption next period (extra consumption beyond what I would have had without the lending). A rise in the interest rate i means the same lending will allow me to enjoy even higher second-period consumption, and clearly I am better off. For me, as a "net lender," the rise in the interest rate induces a positive effect on wealth. Since you are a "net borrower," clearly the effect on your wealth is negative. Hence, although the effect can be computed in principle for any individual, the effect is ambiguous in the absence of detailed knowledge about his or her borrowing or lending.

Hicks, however, assumes that the effect for each individual is calculated at equilibrium, and hence what I lend, you borrow. The effect on wealth for each individual turns on the net borrowing or lending position. Since you are borrowing what I lend, you are hurt as much as I am helped and the net change in wealth is zero. Assuming no distribution effects, the system's behavior shows a zero interest-rate-induced effect on wealth.

Pesek and Saving (1967) rather casually assume that the representative individual currently active in the economy is in effect a "net borrower" (p. 362) and hence is hurt by the rise in the interest rate. Leijonhufvud (1968) tries to deduce the circumstances under which Keynes would be correct about the interest-rate-induced effect on wealth being negative, and following Cassel (1903) assumes that the representative individual currently active in the economy is in effect a "net borrower." Chapter 8 shows that this assumption will reasonably give a negative interest-rate-induced effect on wealth. The question arises, though, of who are the "net lenders" corresponding to our desire to be a "net borrower." The answer is, our children and their children.

Chapter 8 investigates the case where those of us currently alive plan to leave no bequests. The capital stock and real balances of the economy, however, will go on after we are gone. In effect, we must sell these assets to the younger generation during that period when the two generations overlap. The younger generation must do some net saving and "net lending" during the overlap period in order to buy the economy's non-human capital from us. Of course a rise in i makes their lending more remunerative and as "net lenders" they are better off. As "net borrowers" we are worse off.

Those people who benefit by the rise in i are by definition not currently economically active, while those of us who lose are active. The current generation cuts back on its current consumption due to our loss in wealth. The coming generation does not balance this cutback because it is not currently active. In the aggregate, current consumption demand falls.

This apparent wealth effect is really a distribution effect across generations. Hicks assumes in effect that all individuals in the economy are as long-lived as the economy, and all those who will ever live are alive today. Hence, he can assume the wealth effects on behavior simply cancel. In a world with mortal individuals and no bequests, the intergenerational redistribution effects cannot net to zero in the current period, though their present value across all people who will ever live is zero.

Suppose, however, that the current generation leaves bequests to the future generation. The issue of whether the interest-rate-induced effect on wealth has effects on current consumption then turns on whether the bequests are determined by optimizing behavior on the part of the current generation, as discussed in chapter 8. For example, suppose that i falls, thus making the current generation better off and the future generation worse off. The sum of these effects on wealth must equal zero. This means that the current generation could return both generations to the same levels of utility as before by simply increasing its bequests to the younger generation. In fact, if positive bequests are optimally set by the current generation, it will simply offset such redistributions and there will be no wealth effect on current consumption, as shown in chapter 8.

Things are more complicated if there is a long succession of future generations. Leijonhufvud (1968) notes that Cassel lets "his representative transactor . . . take an interest in the consumption needs of his children. But he had to draw the line somewhere . . ." Leijonhufvud (1968, p. 252) then quotes Cassel:

> More cannot reasonably be asked for. It would simply be absurd to consider and try to provide for the needs of our grandchildren or for still more distant generations.

In another context, however, Barro (1974) puts forward an argument that the current generation must act "as if" concerned about all future generations. Suppose that the current generation's overall welfare depends only on its own direct utility and the overall welfare of its children. The next generation's overall welfare depends only on its own direct utility and the overall welfare of its children, and so on. Let a fall in i make the current generation's wealth rise and that of all other generations fall. Since the changes in wealth of all the generations sum to zero, the current generation could arrange bequests to leave all generations as well off as before. Each generation cares about the welfare of the succeeding generation, so simply allowing bequests to return the direct utility of a generation to the previous level will not return that generation's overall welfare to its previous level. In this way, there is a chain where the first generation is concerned indirectly about the third's welfare because the second generation is concerned. The upshot is that the current generation acts as if concerned about all future generations.

Concern is not enough, of course. It is the current generation acting on this interdependence through constrained utility maximization that leads it to change its bequests exactly to offset the interest-rate-induced wealth redistribution. Chapter 8 goes into some of the complexities of the argument.

Barro's (1974) Analysis of Government Bonds as Net Wealth

Barro put forward his discussion of how the current generation is linked to all future generations in the context of whether tax policy affects aggregate demand. Suppose that the government cuts taxes, financing this by an increase in its bond sales. Does this have an effect on the current generation's wealth and hence current demands for goods?

Suppose initially that all taxes are lump sum and the government ultimately pays all of the interest and principal on its debt through taxation. Neglecting any issues of uncertainty, it is clear that a cut in the first generation's taxes in this period, matched by an increase in the first generation's taxes in the next period of the same present value, has no effect on the first generation's wealth or behavior.

If the extra taxes, however, are levied on a later generation whose welfare does not enter the first generation's utility, it might appear that the first generation would be wealthier at the expense of later generations, and this is certainly so in the absence of bequests. But suppose the current generation does leave optimally determined bequests. From the previous argument, it is clear that the first generation and all intermediate generations will increase their bequests by the present value of the initial tax cut in order to compensate the future generation which suffers the tax increase.

Government Bonds as Net Wealth – Paying Interest on the Debt by Issuing New Debt

It is sometimes argued that, in a world that goes on forever, there is no need for the government ever to raise taxes to pay the interest and principal on its debt. It can simply issue more new debt for this purpose. Chapter 8 shows that in a finite-lived world, there cannot exist an equilibrium if government tries this sort of perpetual refinancing. Intuitively, this is clear from imagining the consequences if private individuals were to try the same thing, that is, to die owing creditors. No one would lend in this case. Similarly, if the government is planning to pay its debt in the final period by selling yet more debt that can never be redeemed, no one will buy this debt and the government will be unable to meet its obligations. In an argument by recursion, debt holders will not buy government debt in earlier periods. Chapter 8 also shows that even in an infinitely lived world no equilibrium can exist under such a perpetual refinancing scheme for government debt.

Tobin's (1980) Analysis of Government Bonds as Net Wealth

Chapter 9 deals with other issues in the controversy surrounding government bonds as net wealth. Many of these were raised in a persuasive way by Tobin (1980) to argue that tax cuts stimulate current consumption demand. First, taxes may be collected with positive marginal tax rates rather than as lump sums, and positive marginal rates are distorting. Second, people may be able to avoid paying taxes. Third, taxes may be uncertain. Fourth, the tax system may improve welfare by offering a type of diversification of risk. Fifth, a tax cut may spur consumption by those subject to a liquidity constraint as well as an intertemporal budget constraint. Chapter 9 finds these arguments fairly unconvincing on balance; essentially many of the arguments overlook general equilibrium effects that actually lead to a reversal of the predicted positive impact on demand.

NOTE

1 Suppose the current price level rises. Under the text's assumptions, banks hold their real activities constant. Since the real value of banks' money initially outstanding is halved, they must double the stock of bank money in the current period. Thus, profits rise in the current period through this expansion. This current period change is really a distribution effect, for while the owners of the banks benefit, the holders of bank money lose. Thus, the issue for wealth effects is what happens to future real profit flows from banks, and these are unchanged.

Part II
REVIEW

3
Wealth and Substitution Effects:
The Analysis of *Value and Capital*

This chapter reviews the Hicksian analytical apparatus of substitution and wealth effects from *Value and Capital*. The review is selective, and focuses on results that will be used in the analyses of macro wealth effects in later chapters. The economy analyzed is non-monetary; money is introduced and analyzed in chapters 4–7.

Section 3.1 examines an exchange economy, where there is no production and people trade exogenously given stocks of goods. It shows the well-known result that the effect of any parametric change on a consumer's demand for a particular good can be divided into substitution and wealth effects. Further, the effect on wealth of a change in price is shown to be the change in wealth that would be needed to allow consumption patterns to remain unchanged. In other words, the discussion of wealth effects focuses on Hicks's "equivalent variation." If there are no distribution effects, a change in price has an aggregate effect on wealth just in case the economy as a whole would require a change in wealth to maintain consumption patterns; an exactly analogous result holds for monetary economies, as discussed in chapters 4–7. Finally, section 3.1 illustrates how the Hicksian system analyzes the effects of a parametric change: such a change has an initial effect on excess demands, and then induced wealth and substitution effects occur to set all excess demands equal to zero again.

Section 3.2 generalizes the analysis by including production by firms, which are of course owned by the household sector. The major result is that the inclusion of the production sector does not significantly alter the analysis based on the exchange economy. In particular, the same equivalent variation is used to measure the effect on wealth. The firm's optimum conditions play a key role in this result, as they do in analysis of banks in chapter 6 and 7. Again, the analysis of firms' behavior generalizes to monetary economies.

Section 3.3 considers intertemporal choice and production. This allows investigation of the interest-rate-induced effect on wealth. If there are no distribution effects, and if (a) all markets are initially clearing intertemporally and (b) individuals all hold the same intertemporal price expectations (whether or not these are correct), then changes in long-term interest rates cause no aggregate effects on wealth. Section 3.4 discusses expectations of future prices in the Hicksian analysis, particularly the elasticity of expectations. The discussion also touches on rational expectations.

The key results of this chapter are as follows: (a) the change in wealth is measured by a specific change in the budget constraint; (b) ignoring distribution effects makes it possible to look simply at the economy's aggregate budget constraint in measuring the aggregate effect on wealth; (c) when production is allowed, economic analysis must assume that all firms tell stockholders the dividends they will receive at any given price vector that the economy tries;[1] (d) multi-period analysis uses the same analytical constructs and techniques as the single-period case.[2]

3.1 The Exchange Economy – Wealth Effects

For the past 30 years, the undergraduate exposition of demand theory has been the Hicksian analysis of the substitution and income effects. "Income effect" is Hicks's term and is ingrained usage in the single-period case for the exactly analogous wealth effect of the multi-period case. In what follows, the effect is labeled the wealth effect in both the single-period and the multi-period case.[3] The mathematical development of the analysis is also well known, as is the difference between Hicks's own mathematical and graphical development. His mathematical treatment in *Value and Capital's* appendices uses calculus to develop the wealth effect as the so-called "equivalent variation," while the text presents graphically the "compensating variation."[4] Since many of the results that follow turn on the mathematical development of the static (single-period) theory it is worthwhile to review it here.[5] Only the two-good, two-person case is considered here, but the results are perfectly general.

Assume person A has an endowment – goods he is given, the quantities of which he cannot affect at all. A's endowment is $\overline{X}_{1,a}$ and $\overline{X}_{2,a}$ of goods 1 and 2, the bars indicating endowments. The goods are bought and sold under conditions of perfect competition; the buying and selling prices are equal, and no buyer or seller can affect them. Then if P_1 and P_2 are the prices of goods 1 and 2 the value of A's endowment is $P_1\overline{X}_{1,a} + P_2\overline{X}_{2,a}$.

The value of A's consumption is $P_1 X_{1,a} + P_2 X_{2,a}$, where $X_{1,a}$ and $X_{2,a}$ are A's demands for goods 1 and 2 as opposed to the barred endowments.

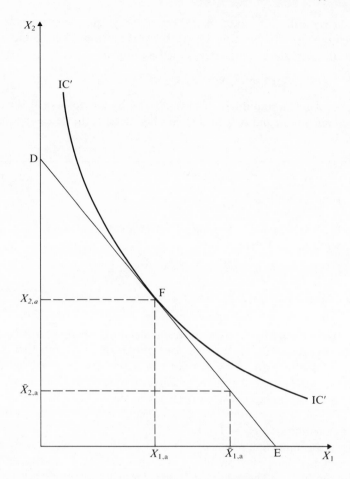

Figure 3.1 Consumer equilibrium

The value of demands cannot exceed the value of endowments (A can demand only what can be paid for), that is, the budget constraint is

$$P_1 X_{1,a} + P_2 X_{2,a} \leqslant P_1 \overline{X}_{1,a} + P_2 \overline{X}_{2,a}.$$

In figure 3.1, A can choose any bundle on or below the budget constraint DE. Given non-satiation, A chooses some point F on DE where an indifference curve IC′ is tangent. Tangency requires that the slope of the IC – the marginal rate of substitution (MRS) – equals the slope of the budget constraint, which is $dX_{2,a}/dX_{1,a} = -P_1/P_2$. Depending on tastes and on endowments – given the value of endowments – $X_{1,a}$ may be greater or less than $\overline{X}_{1,a}$.

Mathematically, A maximizes[6] the strictly quasi-concave, twice-differentiable utility function $U(X_1, X_2)$ subject to his/her budget constraint, or equivalently, maximizes the Lagrangian

$$L = U(X_1, X_2) - \lambda(P_1 X_1 + P_2 X_2 - P_1 \overline{X}_1 - P_2 \overline{X}_2), \qquad (3.1)$$

where λ (>0) is a multiplier. If both X_1 and X_2 are positive at the constrained maximum and A spends all his/her income, the necessary conditions are

$$\begin{aligned}
U_1 - \lambda P_1 &= 0 \\
U_2 - \lambda P_2 &= 0 \\
- P_1 X_1 - P_2 X_2 + P_1 \overline{X}_1 + P_2 \overline{X}_2 &= 0
\end{aligned} \qquad (3.2)$$

where U_j is the partial derivative of $U(\cdot)$ with respect to X_j ($j = 1,2$). Eliminating λ, (3.2) gives

$$- P_1 X_1 - P_2 X_2 + P_1 \overline{X}_1 + P_2 \overline{X}_2 = 0$$

$$- \frac{U_1}{U_2} = - \frac{P_1}{P_2},$$

or A must be on his/her budget constraint at a point where the MRS (equal to $- U_1/U_2$) equals the slope of the constraint ($- P_1/P_2$). Note that dividing the budget constraint by P_2 does not change its meaning, but does make it easy to see that, if P_1 and P_2 change in the same proportion, there is no change in the budget constraint. This is the standard result that only the relative price P_1/P_2 matters in a non-monetary economy. Thus, with no loss of generality, set $P_2 = 1$.

One of the important points of this chapter is how to measure the effect on wealth of a change in a parameter. For this, the "equivalent variation" is used, as illustrated below. In each case, the effect on wealth is found by differentiating

$$- P_1 X_1 - P_2 X_2 + P_1 \overline{X}_1 + P_2 \overline{X}_2,$$

the budget constraint that must equal zero when non-satiation is assumed.

To consider the effect on A of parametric changes, imagine that he/she receives funds not only from his/her endowment but from some source giving $Y\$$. In this case, A's budget constraint is

$$- P_1 X_1 - P_2 X_2 + P_1 \overline{X}_1 + P_2 \overline{X}_2 + Y\$ = 0,$$

and when $Y\$$ equals zero the necessary conditions are (3.2). Now consider the effects of parametric changes in terms of wealth and substitution effects.

If $Y\$$ increases by one unit, the changes induced are

$$
\begin{bmatrix}
U_{11} & U_{12} & -P_1 \\
U_{12} & U_{22} & -P_2 \\
-P_1 & -P_2 & 0
\end{bmatrix}
\begin{bmatrix}
\dfrac{dX_1}{dY\$} \\
\dfrac{dX_2}{dY\$} \\
\dfrac{d\lambda}{dY\$}
\end{bmatrix}
= -
\begin{bmatrix}
0 \\
0 \\
1
\end{bmatrix},
\tag{3.3}
$$

or

$$
[\mathbf{D}]
\begin{bmatrix}
dX_1 \\
dX_2 \\
d\lambda
\end{bmatrix}
= -
\begin{bmatrix}
0 \\
0 \\
1
\end{bmatrix},
$$

where the $U_{ij} = \partial^2 U / \partial X_i \partial X_j$. Then,

$$
\frac{dX_1}{dY\$} = - \frac{|\mathbf{D}_{31}|}{|\mathbf{D}|} \gtreqless 0
$$

where $|\mathbf{D}|$ is the determinant of $[\mathbf{D}]$ and $|\mathbf{D}_{31}|$ is the $(3,1)$ minor of $[\mathbf{D}]$, that is, the determinant obtained when the third row and first column are struck out. If A is initially at an interior constrained maximum, $[\mathbf{D}]$ must be negative definite.[7] For $[\mathbf{D}]$ to be negative definite, its nested principal minors of order greater than 2 must alternate in sign, with those of the third order being positive. In the present example with only two goods, this simply requires $|\mathbf{D}| > 0$. However, $|\mathbf{D}_{31}|$ $(= -U_{12}P_2 + P_1 U_{22})$ may take any sign. Hence, $dX_1/dY\$$ is ambiguous in sign. This merely restates the conventional result that a parallel outward shift in the budget constraint may induce either (a) an increase in the demand for both goods, or (b) a fall (or no change) in the demand for one and an increase in the demand for the other.

Now, suppose $Y\$ = 0$, and P_1 increases. From (3.2) this gives

$$
[\mathbf{D}]
\begin{bmatrix}
\dfrac{dX_1}{dP_1} \\
\dfrac{dX_2}{dP_1} \\
\dfrac{d\lambda}{dP_1}
\end{bmatrix}
= -
\begin{bmatrix}
-\lambda \\
0 \\
\overline{X}_1 - X_1
\end{bmatrix}
$$

and so

$$\frac{\mathrm{d}X_1}{\mathrm{d}^r} = \lambda \ \frac{|\mathbf{D}_{11}|}{|\mathbf{D}|} - (\overline{X}_1 - X_1) \ \frac{|\mathbf{D}_{31}|}{|\mathbf{D}|}$$

$$= \lambda \ \frac{|\mathbf{D}_{11}|}{|\mathbf{D}|} + (\overline{X}_1 - X_1) \ \frac{\mathrm{d}X_1}{\mathrm{d}Y\$}. \tag{3.4}$$

This says that the change $\mathrm{d}X_1/\mathrm{d}P_1$ in A's demand for X_1 equals the substitution effect plus the wealth effect. The substitution effect is $\lambda \, |\mathbf{D}_{11}|/|\mathbf{D}|$. Inspection of [D] in (3.3) shows that

$$|\mathbf{D}_{11}| < 0, \qquad |\mathbf{D}_{22}| < 0. \tag{3.5}$$

Hence the substitution effect must be negative since λ is positive ($\lambda = U_1/P_1$).

It is useful to decompose the wealth effect $(\overline{X}_1 - X_1)\,\mathrm{d}X_1/\mathrm{d}Y\$$ into two terms: the wealth effect is the change in the value $P_1(\overline{X}_1 - X_1)$ when P_1 rises, times the effect on A's demand for X_1 of a one-unit increase in wealth (i.e. $\mathrm{d}X_1/\mathrm{d}Y\$$). Note in particular that the change in wealth is the change in P_1 multiplied by $\overline{X}_1 - X_1$; however, the wealth effect is this change in wealth multiplied by $\mathrm{d}X_1/\mathrm{d}Y\$$. Thus, the wealth effect equals the change in wealth multiplied by the marginal propensity to consume good 1 out of a one-unit change in wealth.

The first term in (3.4) is a substitution effect, and the second is the wealth effect of the increases in P_1. Notice that the change in wealth is the partial derivative with respect to P_1 of the value of A's endowment of $\overline{X}_1$ less his/her demand for X_1 evaluated at the initial demand. In other words, the effect on wealth is found by differentiating the budget constraint with respect to the parameter changed, in this case P_1, while holding constant the endowments and initial levels of demand. Thus, the effect on wealth of an increase in P_1 is positive, zero or negative if A afterwards has funds left over when just consuming his/her old bundle, can just afford still to consume the old bundle, or cannot now afford to consume the bundle. This is the "equivalent variation" measure of the change in wealth. When distribution effects are ignored, the conditions for the sign of society's change in wealth are the same as for the individual: can society more than afford, just still afford, or not now afford its old choice pattern?

It is useful to note here that the effect on X_1 of an increase in $\overline{X}_1$ is $-P_1\,|\mathbf{D}_{31}|/|\mathbf{D}|$ and of an increase in $\overline{X}_2$ is $-P_2\,|\mathbf{D}_{31}|/|\mathbf{D}|$. These are pure wealth effects. Each is composed of (a) the net effect of the change on the value of endowment over consumption (for example, P_1 when $\overline{X}_1$ rises one unit), multiplied by (b) the effect on the consumption of X_1 of a one-unit increase in wealth $(-|\mathbf{D}_{31}|/|\mathbf{D}|)$.

Some Graphical Analyses

It is worthwhile to relate the above development to the usual graphical discussions. Changes in wealth are usually handled graphically by a "compensating variation." The mathematical development in the previous subsection, however, treats the change in wealth as an "equivalent variation." Because it is substantially easier to use the straightforward mathematics of an equivalent variation, this book uses that measure of changes in wealth throughout.

A \$1 increase in P_1 serves to illustrate the previous subsection's discussion. This increase in P_1 rotates the price line clockwise through the

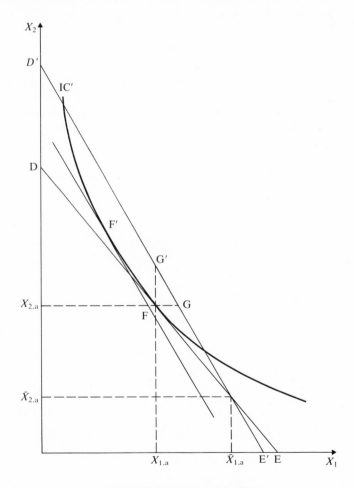

Figure 3.2 The wealth effect

endowment to D'E' in figure 3.2. In the text of *Value and Capital*,[8] Hicks uses the graphical technique of removing the wealth effect by taking away enough of the endowment of good 1 or good 2 (or some combination) to move the new price line leftward until it is tangent to IC' at F'.[9] (Notice that this requires taking away more of good 1 than FG.) Then, the reduction in X_1 between F and F' is the substitution effect against good 1 due to a rise in P_1, and the change in X_1 in moving from F' to the new point of tangency on D'E' is the wealth effect. That is, the wealth effect is removed by shifting the new price line until it is tangent to IC'.

The mathematics give FG as the increase in wealth in terms of good 1, and FG' as the increase in terms of good 2, for the initial consumption

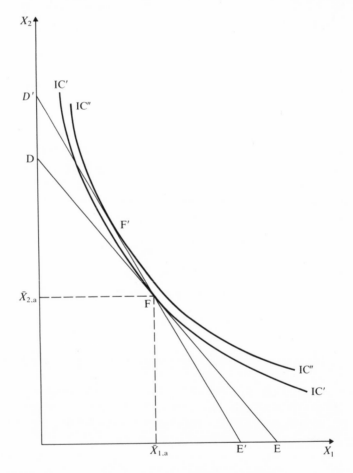

Figure 3.3 A zero effect on wealth

basket F can now be augmented by either FG or FG' (or by some combination along G'G). If $\overline{X}_1$ is reduced by FG, the wealth effect is removed. This shifts D'E' till it runs through the initial consumption basket F; the substitution effect is measured by the fall in X_1 found by running the steeper price line through F, and the wealth effect is the change in X_1 found by shifting this price line rightward to D'E'. This substitution effect is, of course, negative.

The first method of separating the wealth and substitution effects is the "compensating variation;" it compensates the consumer for any price change by allowing the same IC to be reached as before. The second method is the "equivalent variation," first derived mathematically by Slutsky, and also the result of Hicks's mathematical analysis in the appendix to *Value and Capital*.[10]

For more insight about the second method, consider the case where prices just make A want to consume his/her endowment point. In figure 3.3, DE is tangent to the IC through the endowment at the endowment point. Expression (3.4) says there is no wealth effect if P_1 increases, because $\overline{X}_1 = X_1$, and that X_1 necessarily falls, since the substitution effect is negative. When P_1 increases, DE rotates to D'E' and the point of tangency shows X_1 falling as (3.4) predicts. (Any tangency showing X_1 increasing necessarily involves an intersection of this IC with IC', a logical contradiction since non-intersecting ICs are always assumed.) Of course, the first method, the compensating variation, reaches this result, but can give no intuitive reason for it: there is a wealth effect in the compensating variation, since the higher IC" can be reached and the method cannot say why the substitution effect is necessarily dominant.

Türn now to an example of how wealth and substitution effects can be used to analyze the equilibrium adjustment of a system to a disturbance; the same method is used at the macro level.

Stability of Equilibrium

Hicks was fundamentally interested in fluctuations in prices and quantities, and his analysis led him to think these were intimately connected with the stability of equilibrium. By this he meant that, if the system starts with a non-equilibrium set of prices (no matter how it gets into this situation), will it return to equilibrium?[11] The easiest problem of this sort is the case of two goods. If the market for one is stable, the market for the other must also be stable, from Walras's law.

Hicks was interested in the slope of the excess demand curve for good 1 at equilibrium, because this determined the stability of equilibrium in his analysis.[12] Following Walras, he considered market equilibrium to be

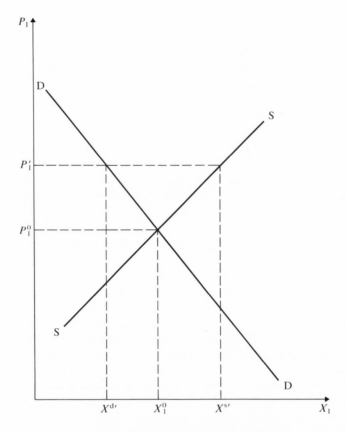

Figure 3.4 Stability of equilibrium

stable (when there are only two goods) if and only if an increase in price caused the quantity supplied to exceed the quantity demanded, as in figure 3.4. The excess of the quantity supplied over that demanded was seen as driving price down; similarly a price below P_1^0 would cause the quantity demanded to exceed that supplied and drive price up. If excess demand (ExD) is defined as the quantity demanded minus the quantity supplied, clearly the stability condition is that an increase in P_1 should reduce ExD. Thus, in Hicks's famous diagram, here figure 3.5, equilibria H and J are stable and equilibrium G is unstable.

Since Hicks was concerned with stability (in his and Walras's sense), he was concerned with how an equilibrium such as G might come about and how likely it was. With two individuals A and B, and no production, the economy's total supply of good 1 is the sum of the endowments of A and B, $\overline{X}_{1,a} + \overline{X}_{1,b} = \overline{X}_1$, and so excess demand for good 1 is

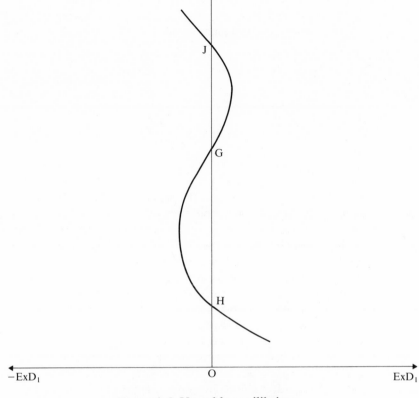

Figure 3.5 Unstable equilibrium

$$\text{ExD}_1 = (X_{1,a} + X_{1,b}) - (\overline{X}_{1,a} + \overline{X}_{1,b}).$$

The change in ExD_1 with an increase in P_1 is

$$\frac{d\text{ExD}_1}{dP_1} = \frac{dX_{1,a}}{dP_1} + \frac{dX_{1,b}}{dP_1}$$

if all endowments are held constant. In terms of wealth and substitution effects for A and B,

$$\frac{d\text{ExD}_1}{dP_1} = \left\{ \lambda^a \frac{|D_{11}^a|}{|D^a|} - (\overline{X}_{1,a} - X_{1,a}) \frac{|D_{31}^a|}{|D^a|} \right\}$$

$$+ \left\{ \lambda^b \frac{|D_{11}^b|}{|D^b|} - (\overline{X}_{1,b} - X_{1,b}) \frac{|D_{31}^b|}{|D^b|} \right\}. \tag{3.6}$$

Since both substitution effects are negative, the slope $d\mathrm{ExD}_1/dP_1$ could be positive only because of the sum of the wealth effects. Two things are noticeable. If the system of two persons is initially in equilibrium, the value of $\overline{X}_{1,a} - X_{1,a}$ equals $- (\overline{X}_{1,b} - X_{1,b})$: what one sells, the other buys. Next, if A and B are somewhat similar so that

$$\frac{|\mathbf{D}_{31}^a|}{|\mathbf{D}^a|} \doteq \frac{|\mathbf{D}_{31}^b|}{|\mathbf{D}^b|}$$

then

$$(\overline{X}_{1,a} - X_{1,a}) \frac{|\mathbf{D}_{31}^a|}{|\mathbf{D}^a|} + (\overline{X}_{1,b} - X_{1b}) \frac{|\mathbf{D}_{31}^b|}{|\mathbf{D}^b|}$$

is approximately zero, or the wealth effects cancel.

Thus, Hicks has the desired result of Walrasian stability if (a) the system is evaluated at equilibrium, and (b) people are similar enough that an increase in wealth affects each about the same.

As Hicks noted, if the system is at equilibrium and the effect on every person of an increase in his/her wealth is to increase demand for X_1 (X_1 is a superior good), then the wealth effects of the buyers and sellers must tend to offset each other. But if the wealth effect of the sellers is strong enough relative to that of the buyers, $d\mathrm{ExD}_1/dP_1$ may be positive – implying Walrasian instability. For example, suppose in equilibrium I sell you ten oranges and the price of oranges rises by \$1. Then I am richer by \$10 and you are poorer by \$10. I increase my demand for oranges by three units because of this increase in wealth, while your demand falls by approximately three since we have similar propensities to consume oranges out of changes in wealth. This gives a net change in demand of approximately zero due to wealth effects. However, if my demand were to rise by seven while yours fell by three, there would be a four-unit increase in demand due to wealth effects when price rises. If this aggregate wealth effect is stronger than the total of substitution effects, say a fall of two, then excess demand rises by two when price rises – implying Walrasian instability.

Distribution Effects

In monetary analysis, it is common to assume that arbitrary shifts in wealth from one actor to another have no effects on market demands (Patinkin, 1956, 1965; Gurley and Shaw, 1960). If such shifts do have market level effects, these effects are referred to as distribution effects. In the same way, if the individuals' wealth effects in the previous subsection do not cancel, these are distribution effects. Following the convention in monetary analysis, distribution effects are mainly ignored in this book (though intergenerational distribution effects are discussed in chapter 8). Thus, we assume the individual wealth effects cancel.

Individual wealth effects can cancel for two reasons. First, propensities to consume a particular good out of changes in wealth may be approximately equal across individuals, as emphasized above. Second, when the price of a good rises the wealth effect for an individual is this propensity times the value of his/her $\overline{X} - X$ for the good in question. Thus, if $\overline{X} - X$ is zero or close to zero, each individual's wealth effect is zero (or close to it) and so is the aggregate wealth effect. There is nothing inherent in a competitive economy that implies $\overline{X} \neq X$, and hence distribution effects need not exist even if marginal propensities differ.

To explore this second reason, note that at the initial equilibrium price vector there is an infinite number of redistributions of endowments that leave each person's consumption bundle the same and do not change the initial equilibrium price vector. At least one distribution also causes the wealth effects of an increase in P_1 to cancel. If the system is in equilibrium, A's and B's endowments can be altered without affecting either individual, or the equilibrium, as long as the value of each endowment is unchanged. The conditions are

$$P_1 d\overline{X}_{1,a} + P_2 d\overline{X}_{2,a} = 0 \tag{3.7}$$

$$P_1 d\overline{X}_{1,b} + P_2 d\overline{X}_{2,b} = 0. \tag{3.8}$$

(Satisfying (3.7) satisfies (3.8), since the totals $\overline{X}_1$ and $\overline{X}_2$ are given.) Is there some redistribution of endowments that preserves the value of both individuals' endowments but sets the sum of wealth effects equal to zero or sets

$$(\overline{X}_{1,a} - X_{1,a}) \frac{|\mathbf{D}_{31}^a|}{|\mathbf{D}^a|} + (\overline{X}_{1,b} - X_{1b}) \frac{|\mathbf{D}_{31}^b|}{|\mathbf{D}^b|} = 0?$$

Clearly, if $\overline{X}_{1,a} = X_{1,a}$, then $X_{1,b} = \overline{X}_{1,b}$, $X_{2,a} = \overline{X}_{2,a}$, and $X_{2,b} = \overline{X}_{2,b}$. From the above analysis, all individuals' wealth effects are then zero. Thus, if the wealth effects do not net to zero in the simple case considered above, it is only because of "bad luck" in the initial distribution of resources.

In such a simple case, there is no reason to assume A to have one endowment or another relative to demands, and thus it seems reasonable to ignore distribution effects, which is monetary theory's approach throughout. (Indeed, this is so even in cases where there are perfectly good reasons for not ascribing society's existing distribution of assets and liabilities to chance.[13]) Thus, in practice monetary theory recognizes a change in wealth only if it appears in the aggregate budget constraint; otherwise, it assumes that the same change (but with offsetting signs) in two individuals' budget constraints has exactly offsetting effects.[14]

Comparative Statics

One result of Hicks's concern with stability was comparative statics. Since only the relative price P_1/P_2 matters, assume $P_2 = 1$. In an exchange economy, P_1 will change as a result of (for example) an increase in $\overline{X}_{1,a}$, and the Hicksian apparatus can be used to analyze the direction of change. In the simple two-good, two-person economy, equilibrium requires $\text{ExD}_1 = 0$; Walras's law then implies $\text{ExD}_2 = 0$. An increase in $\overline{X}_{1,a}$ raises the supply $\overline{X}_1$ and causes $\partial \text{ExD}_1/\partial \overline{X}_{1,a} \gtreqless 0$, and usually makes $\text{ExD}_1 \neq 0$. In order to return to $\text{ExD}_1 = 0$, P_1 must adjust to set

$$\frac{\partial \text{ExD}_1}{\partial \overline{X}_{1,a}} + \frac{\partial \text{ExD}_1}{\partial P_1} \frac{dP_1}{d\overline{X}_{1,a}} = 0. \tag{3.9}$$

$\partial \text{ExD}_1/\partial \overline{X}_{1,a}$ is the impact effect on ExD_1 of an increase in $\overline{X}_{1,a}$; $\partial \text{ExD}_1/\partial P_1$ is the effect on ExD_1 of an increase in P_1, and $dP_1/d\overline{X}_{1,a}$ is the induced change in P_1. The net effect must be zero to keep the economy at equilibrium. Once $\partial \text{ExD}_1/\partial \overline{X}_{1,a}$ and $\partial \text{ExD}_1/\partial P_1$ are known, $dP_1/d\overline{X}_{1,a}$ can be found from (3.9). The Hicksian apparatus allows us to find $\partial \text{ExD}_1/\partial \overline{X}_{1,a}$ as a wealth effect, and to find $\partial \text{ExD}_1/\partial P_1$ as a sum of wealth and substitution effects.

First, find $\partial \text{ExD}_1/\partial \overline{X}_{1,a}$. The effect on the aggregate supply $\overline{X}_1$ ($= \overline{X}_{1,a} + \overline{X}_{1,b}$) of an increase in $\overline{X}_{1,a}$ is $+1$. The effect on A's demand for 1, $X_{1,a}$, is the wealth effect $-P_1 |\mathbf{D}_{31}^a|/|\mathbf{D}^a|$. (The effect on $X_{1,b}$ is zero so far.) The initial effect on $\text{ExD}_1 = X_{1,a} + X_{1,b} - (\overline{X}_{1,a} + \overline{X}_{1,b})$ is then

$$\frac{\partial \text{ExD}_1}{\partial \overline{X}_{1,a}} = -P_1 \frac{|\mathbf{D}_{31}^a|}{|\mathbf{D}^a|} - 1.$$ Next, the expression $\partial \text{ExD}_1/\partial P_1$ is given

in (3.6) and can be seen to be the sum of the two individuals' wealth plus substitution effects. Since the system is initially at equilibrium, $\overline{X}_{1,a} - X_{1,a} = -(\overline{X}_{1,b} - X_{1,b})$. Thus, rearranging (3.9) and using (3.6) gives the comparative static result

$$\frac{dP_1}{d\overline{X}_{1,a}} = -\frac{\partial \text{ExD}_1/\partial \overline{X}_{1,a}}{\partial \text{ExD}_1/\partial P_1}$$

$$= -\frac{-1 - P_1 |\mathbf{D}_{31}^a|/|\mathbf{D}^a|}{[\lambda^a |\mathbf{D}_{11}^a|/|\mathbf{D}^a| + \lambda^b |\mathbf{D}_{11}^b|/|\mathbf{D}^b| - (\overline{X}_{1,a} - X_{1,a})/ \atop (|\mathbf{D}_{31}^a|/|\mathbf{D}^a| - |\mathbf{D}_{31}^b|/|\mathbf{D}^b|)]}.$$

Suppose that the numerator $\partial \text{ExD}_1/\partial \overline{X}_{1,a}$ is negative; this means that the increase in $\overline{X}_{1,a}$ raises $X_{1,a}$ by less than this increase, and thus $X_{2,a}$ is a superior good. Then, supply increases more than demand, so the excess demand curve shifts to the left. Thus, if price is to fall, the denominator must be negative. In the denominator, the first two terms are own-price substitution effects for A and B and hence are necessarily negative. The third term is the sum of the changes in individuals' wealth due to an increase in P_1, weighted by their responses to a unit change in wealth. If these responses are equal, the wealth effects cancel and only the negative substitution effects remain, so P_1 falls. In this case, equilibrium is necessarily stable.

Notice that if

$$\frac{|\mathbf{D}_{31}^a|}{|\mathbf{D}^a|} = \frac{|\mathbf{D}_{31}^b|}{|\mathbf{D}^b|},$$

that is, if there are no distribution effects, the only wealth effect that enters the result is in the numerator, through $P_1 d\overline{X}_1 (= P_1)$, the increase in the value of society's wealth over the value of its initial consumption basket. This illustrates the point that, when distribution effects are ignored, the only wealth effect is through the change in the real value of society's wealth relative to its initial real expenditures. Notice further that in the absence of distribution effects a one-unit increase in anyone's endowment of good 1 has the same effect on price as the increase in $\overline{X}_{1,a}$.

This example illustrates an important distinction regarding price-induced effects. The change in P_1 is $dP_1/d\overline{X}_{1,a}$ and, of course, the change would be different if another parameter, say $\overline{X}_{2,a}$, were to change. Thus, how price changes depends on which parameter changes. Nevertheless, it makes perfectly good sense to ask the effect on excess demand of a rise in P_1 without inquiring what causes P_1 to rise. This effect is $\partial\text{ExD}_1/\partial P_1$ in (3.9), and is composed of wealth and substitution effects. $\partial\text{ExD}_1/\partial P_1$ is the same whether it is $\overline{X}_{1,a}$ or $\overline{X}_{2,a}$ that rises. The impact effect, in this case $\partial\text{ExD}_1/\partial\overline{X}_{1,a}$, is different in different cases and is what leads to different changes in the equilibrium value of P_1 for a given $\partial\text{ExD}_1/\partial P_1$. In monetary economics, it is sometimes thought that the price-induced effect on wealth should depend on which parameter is changed to cause the change in the price level. This is not so. The actual change in price depends on the parametric change, but for a given economy the price-induced effect on wealth is the same for every parametric change.

Changes in Wealth over Time

Consider how $X_{1,a}$ and $X_{2,a}$ change over time. Suppose the periods are short enough in all cases in this book so that a continuous-time approximation is reasonable. Further, suppose for convenience that U is independent of time or $\partial^j U/\partial t^j = 0$ for all j. Then, neglecting the subscript a, differentiation of the system

$$U_1 - \lambda P_1 = 0$$
$$U_2 - \lambda P_2 = 0 \qquad\qquad (3.2)$$
$$- P_1 X_1 - P_2 X_2 + P_1 \overline{X}_1 + P_2 \overline{X}_2 = 0$$

with respect to time gives

$$U_{11} \frac{dX_1}{dt} + U_{12} \frac{dX_2}{dt} - P_1 \frac{d\lambda}{dt} - \lambda \frac{dP_1}{dt} = 0$$

$$U_{21} \frac{dX_1}{dt} + U_{22} \frac{dX_2}{dt} - P_2 \frac{d\lambda}{dt} = 0$$

$$- \frac{dP_1}{dt} X_1 - P_1 \frac{dX_1}{dt} - P_2 \frac{dX_2}{dt} + \frac{dP_1}{dt} \overline{X}_1 + P_1 \frac{d\overline{X}_1}{dt} + P_2 \frac{d\overline{X}_2}{dt} = 0,$$

under the assumption that P_2 is constant over time in this non-monetary economy. In turn, this can be written as

$$\begin{bmatrix} U_{11} & U_{12} & -P_1 \\ U_{21} & U_{22} & -P_2 \\ -P_1 & -P_2 & 0 \end{bmatrix} \begin{bmatrix} \dfrac{dX_1}{dt} \\ \dfrac{dX_2}{dt} \\ \dfrac{d\lambda}{dt} \end{bmatrix} = - \begin{bmatrix} -\lambda \dfrac{dP_1}{dt} \\ 0 \\ \dfrac{dP_1}{dt} (\overline{X}_1 - X_1) + P_1 \dfrac{d\overline{X}_1}{dt} + P_2 \dfrac{d\overline{X}_2}{dt} \end{bmatrix}.$$

Solving for the effect on X_1 gives

$$\frac{dX_1}{dt} = \left\{ \lambda \frac{|\mathbf{D}_{11}|}{|\mathbf{D}|} \right\} \frac{dP_1}{dt} - \left\{ (\overline{X}_1 - X_1) \frac{|\mathbf{D}_{31}|}{|\mathbf{D}|} \right\} \frac{dP_1}{dt}$$
$$- \left\{ P_1 \frac{|\mathbf{D}_{31}|}{|\mathbf{D}|} \right\} \frac{d\overline{X}_1}{dt} + \left\{ P_2 \frac{|\mathbf{D}_{31}|}{|\mathbf{D}|} \right\} \frac{d\overline{X}_2}{dt}. \qquad (3.10)$$

The first term in braces is the static own-price substitution effect discussed at (3.4) above. The second term in braces is the static wealth effect of a unit change in P_1, as discussed above. The third and fourth terms in braces are the wealth effects of unit changes in $\overline{X}_1$ and $\overline{X}_2$. From (3.10), dX_1/dt can be written as a function of X_1, $\overline{X}_1$, P_1, P_2, dP_1/dt, $d\overline{X}_1/dt$ and $d\overline{X}_2/dt$. Since X_1 depends on $\overline{X}_1$, $\overline{X}_2$, and P_1 (suppressing the constant P_2), it follows that dX_1/dt is a function of $\overline{X}_1$, $\overline{X}_2$, P_1, $d\overline{X}_1/dt$, $d\overline{X}_2/dt$, and dP_1/dt, and so is dX_2/dt. However, the equation for dX_2/dt is not independent of that for dX_1/dt; once you know dX_1/dt, X_1, $\overline{X}_1$, P_1, P_2, dP_1/dt, $d\overline{X}_1/dt$, and

$d\overline{X}_2/dt$, then from the derivative of the budget constraint dX_2/dt is implied.

The results in (3.10) imply that intertemporal movements in X_1 and X_2 can be analyzed with the static framework so far developed. The static wealth and substitution effects are used with the changes over time in price variables and endowments. In particular, price-induced effects on wealth are measured by the endowment minus consumption times the change in price, for example $(\overline{X}_1 - X_1)dP_1/dt$. Changes in wealth through endowments are measured by the change in endowment times the price, for example $P_1 d\overline{X}_1/dt$.

Notice that there is an apparent asymmetry here. For changes in price, both $\overline{X}$ and X enter the effect on wealth. For other changes in wealth, only the change in $\overline{X}$ enters, not the change in X. Thus, while both $d\overline{X}_1/dt$ and dX_1/dt may be non-zero, only the change in endowment is part of an effect on wealth. One way of viewing this is that dX_1/dt is a change that is in part induced by changes in wealth.

Wealth effects due to intertemporal movements in prices will tend to net to zero for the economy as a whole. If a two-person economy is in equilibrium with $\overline{X}_{1,a} - X_{1,a} = -(\overline{X}_{1,b} - X_{1,b})$, then $(\overline{X}_{1,a} - X_{1,a})dP_1/dt + (\overline{X}_{1,b} - X_{1,b})dP_1/dt = 0$. Assuming that propensities to spend out of changes in wealth are similar, there is no aggregate price-induced wealth effect. However, powerful intertemporal changes in wealth can arise at the aggregate level from changes in endowments. The aggregate effect on wealth of an increase in $\overline{X}_1$ is $P_1 d\overline{X}_1/dt = P_1(d\overline{X}_{1,a}/dt + d\overline{X}_{1,b}/dt)$, and there is no reason to suppose this is necessarily zero over time. These points generalize to intertemporal production economics. In chapter 10 this discussion is used to analyze empirical measures of changes in wealth. Such time series contain substantial variation equivalent to changes in P_1; these changes have no aggregate effect on wealth in the absence of distribution effects. A major point of chapter 10 is that empirical measures of changes in wealth often do not correspond to the theoretical measures developed in this book, precisely because usual empirical measures contain movements in wealth equivalent to those generated by changes in P_1.

The change in wealth for individual A from period 0 to period 1 is

$$\Delta W_0 \equiv W_1 - W_0$$
$$= \Delta P_{1,0}(\overline{X}_{1,0} - X_{1,0}) + P_{1,0}\Delta\overline{X}_{1,0} + P_{2,0}\Delta\overline{X}_{2,0}$$

where the subscript on say $P_{1,0}$ is for the price of good 1 at time 0, and $\Delta P_{1,0} \equiv P_{1,1} - P_{1,0}$, $\Delta\overline{X}_{1,0} \equiv \overline{X}_{1,1} - \overline{X}_{1,0}$. No change in P_2 is assumed in this non-monetary economy. Interaction terms such as $\Delta P_{1,0}\Delta\overline{X}_{1,0}$ are neglected under the assumption that the length of the period is short enough for these terms to be small. Aggregating over individuals, it is clear that the sum of terms such as $\Delta P_{1,0}(\overline{X}_{1,0} - X_{1,0})$ is zero under the assumption of no distribution effects.

In conclusion for this section, the wealth effect on A's demand for good 1 of a change in any parameter α is equal to the product of the change in wealth due to the change in α multiplied by A's marginal propensity to consume good 1 as wealth rises. The change in wealth is found by differentiating A's budget constraint, evaluated at initial amounts of consumption. Assuming that each person's marginal propensity is approximately the same as every other's, there is an aggregate net wealth effect only if the real value of society's endowment has changed relative to the real value of its initial demand. The effect of a parametric change on society's wealth can be found by differentiating society's budget constraint in the same way as any individual's.

3.2 The Production Economy – The Role of Production in Wealth Effects

To deal adequately with the problems of monetary theory, section 3.1 must be extended to include production.[15] In particular, in section 3.1 the aggregate effect on wealth of a \$1 increase in P_1 is $\overline{X}_1 - X_1$. Is this proposed measure valid when firms can alter production and $\overline{X}_1$ is not fixed? The answer is yes, as is shown below for a simple case. In general, all the results of this book turn on aggregation of household responses, not on aggregation over goods or firms. The discussion is carried on in terms of the smallest number of goods and firms possible for convenience only.

Consider a single-period world with no borrowing or lending, in which the only goods are consumption and leisure, and the only factor is labor. Let A maximize the utility function

$$U^a = U^a(C_a^d, \overline{L}_a - N_a^s),$$

where C_a^d is demand for the consumption good, N_a^s is supply of labor, and $\overline{L}_a$ is the total number of units of time in the period, so $\overline{L}_a - N_a^s$ is A's leisure Le$_a$. A maximizes U^a subject to

$$P_c C_a^d - w N_a^s = 0$$

where P_c is the price of the consumption good, w is the wage rate, and A is assumed unsatiated (so all income is spent).[16]

Let B own the only two firms in the economy. Then, B maximizes

$$U^b = U^b(C_b^d, \overline{L}_b - N_b^s)$$

subject to

$$P_c C_b^d - wN_b^s - \text{Div}_1 - \text{Div}_2 = 0$$

where Div_j $(j = 1,2)$ are the dividends (non-labor incomes) B receives from firms 1 and 2, and B is assumed unsatiated. Clearly, B wants Div_j to be as large as possible, for the larger is Div_j the higher can be C_b^d (or Le_b, or both).

Suppose there is perfect competition, with the supply of entrepreneurial ability so large that B does not have to pay the firms' managers positive salaries. Each firm tries to maximize

$$\text{Div}_j = P_c Y_j^s - wN_j^d, \qquad (j = 1,2)$$

where Y_j^s is firm j's output of the consumption good, N_j^d its demand for labor, and $Y_j^s = f(N_j^d)$, $f' > 0$, $f'' < 0$, its production function. If firm j is at an interior maximum then

$$P_c \frac{dY_j^s}{dN_j^d} - w = 0, \qquad (j = 1,2) \tag{3.11}$$

where dY_j^s/dN_j^d is the marginal physical product of labor in firm j.

If there are no distribution effects, analysis of wealth effects can use the aggregate household sector budget constraint,

$$wN^s + \text{Div}_1 + \text{Div}_2 - P_c C^d = 0.$$

wN^s is wage income, or in this single-period model the value of human wealth. $\text{Div}_1 + \text{Div}_2$ is dividend income, or in this single-period model the value of the business sector. To be concrete, take the case where P_c rises. Analogously to section 3.1, the rise in P_c has a positive, zero, or negative impact on wealth depending on whether the household sector would require a positive, zero, or negative transfer in order to maintain its initial consumption with its initial amount of labor supplied. From the household sector budget constraint, the change in wealth is[17]

$$\frac{d\text{Div}_1}{dP_c} + \frac{d\text{Div}_2}{dP_c} - C^d \gtreqless 0, \tag{3.12}$$

with C^d evaluated at its initial value. As before, the change in wealth depends on whether the household sector can now more than afford, just afford, or no longer afford its initial basket C^d, Le ($= \overline{L} - N^s$). The only change from section 3.1 above is that now the household sector receives non-labor income from the business sector and this income may vary with P_c.

The change in Div_j with P_c is found by differentiating the expression for Div_j:

$$\frac{d\text{Div}_j}{dP_c} = Y_j^s + P_c \frac{dY_j^s}{dN_j^d} \frac{dN_j^d}{dP_c} - w \frac{dN_j^d}{dP_c}$$

$$= Y_j^s + \left(P_c \frac{dY_j^s}{dN_j^d} - w \right) \frac{dN_j^d}{dP_c} \qquad (j = 1,2).$$

But since the firm's marginal condition (3.11) holds,

$$P_c \frac{dY_j^s}{dN_j^d} - w = 0 = \left(P_c \frac{dY_j^s}{dN_j^d} - w \right) \frac{dN_j^d}{dP_c}$$

and thus

$$\frac{d\text{Div}_j}{dP_c} = Y_j^s \qquad (j = 1,2).$$

Thus,

$$\frac{d\text{Div}_1}{dP_c} + \frac{d\text{Div}_2}{dP_c} = Y^s, \qquad (3.13)$$

where Y^s is the sum of businesses' initial outputs of the consumer good at the initial levels of P_c and w. Notice there has been no aggregation of production functions.

From (3.13), rewrite the change in wealth (3.12) as

$$Y^s - C^d \gtreqless 0. \qquad (3.14)$$

The term $Y^s - C^d$ resembles $\overline{X}_1 - X_1$ in section 3.1 when P_1 rose. Both X_1 and C^d are evaluated at initial values. However, in section 3.1, $\overline{X}_1$ is constant because it is given. Y^s is not a constant but the same sort of result has now been shown to hold. Fundamentally, this result arises because the changes in Y^s and N^d induced by a change in P just balance each other in value terms from the firms' marginal conditions.

When P_c rises with w unchanged, the effect on wealth from (3.14) is $Y^s - C^d$. Thus, in equilibrium with $Y^s = C^d$, the effect on wealth is zero, and is positive or negative as $Y^s \gtreqless C^d$. When P_c rises relative to w, then Y^s and N^d rise, but dY^s/dP_c and dN^d/dP_c do not enter the wealth effect from the marginal condition (3.11). Thus, only the initial Y^s enters the effect on wealth when P_c rises. This is a very general result which is used extensively below. Note that it requires that every firm is optimizing, but not that the effect on wealth is evaluated at equilibrium (that is, Y^s need not equal C^d).

Similarly, a rise in w with P_c constant gives an effect on wealth of

$N^s - N^d \gtreqqless 0$, with a zero effect if the economy is at equilibrium with $N^s = N^d$.

In order to find the effect on wealth when P_c and w rise proportionately, substitute the expression

$$\text{Div}_j = P_c Y_j^s - w N_j^d \qquad (j = 1,2)$$

into the household sector budget constraint

$$wN^s + \text{Div}_1 + \text{Div}_2 - P_c C^d = 0$$

to find

$$wN^s + P_c Y_1^s - w N_1^d + P_c Y_2^s - w N_2^d - P_c C^d = 0$$

or that

$$\frac{w}{P_c} (N^s - N^d) + (Y^s - C^d)$$

must equal zero (assuming non-satiation), where $Y^s \equiv Y_1^s + Y_2^s$ and $N^d \equiv N_1^d + N_2^d$. When w and P_c rise proportionately, w/P_c does not change. Further, C^d and N^s are evaluated at their initial values as in section 3.1. Y^s and N^d are evaluated at their initial values since neither is altered by the rises in w and P_c that leave the relative price w/P_c unaffected.

Finally, suppose there is technological progress as shown by a shift parameter α, where $\partial Y^s / \partial \alpha \equiv Y_\alpha^s > 0$. The change in Div is $P_c Y_\alpha^s$ since

$$P_c \frac{\partial Y^s}{\partial N^d} \frac{dN^d}{d\alpha} - w \frac{dN^d}{d\alpha} = \left(P_c \frac{\partial Y^s}{\partial N^d} - w \right) \frac{dN^d}{d\alpha} = 0.$$

Hence, the effect on wealth of technological progress is $P_c Y_\alpha^s$, the value of the increase in Y^s due to a rise in α with Y^s evaluated at the initial levels of Y^s and N^d.

The relationship between wealth effects and Walras's law can be seen by considering the impact on wealth of price changes dP_c and dw:

$$dP_c(Y^s - C^d) + dw(N^s - N^d). \tag{3.15}$$

Neither (3.14) nor (3.15) assumes the system is at equilibrium. Both expressions assume that Div_j is a profit maximum for the existing vector of prices, disequilibrium or not. The relationship of this to Walras's law is twofold. Firstly, Walras's law also assumes that dividends are evaluated at actual prices, whether equilibrium or not, and that the household sector is continuously apprised of how dividends change as prices change. Thus, the assumptions used here are exactly those needed for Walras's law.

Secondly, Walras's law states that the sum of the values of excess demand is zero; hence, if $Y^s = C^d$, then $N^s = N^d$ and (3.15) is zero.

In general, in equilibrium the changes in wealth due to price changes tend to cancel and they do so completely in this model – but see chapter 4 where outside money is analyzed. An increase in P_c hurts consumers but helps firms and thus the owners of firms. In this section's example, A is hurt but B gains. In equilibrium with $C^d = Y^s$ and $N^d = N^s$, the gains and losses exactly cancel and the net change in wealth is zero.

3.3 Multi-Period Analysis – Interest-Rate-Induced Effects on Wealth

The interest-rate-induced effect on wealth refers to a multi-period analysis – a market rate of interest arises in connection with intertemporal transactions.[18] Extending the discussion of preceding sections reveals many of the analytical difficulties encountered in later, more interesting, and more complete models. The primary problems in this analysis are that different economic units may expect different future prices, and even if all agree on expected prices, the planned quantities demanded and supplied may be inconsistent.[19] This allows for future disequilibria, but also influences wealth effects.

As Hicks pointed out in *Value and Capital* (1939; rev. edn 1946), there are great formal similarities between single-period and multi-period analysis. Essentially, there is no analytical difference between current and future goods, and the discounted prices of future goods can be directly compared to prices of current goods when the individual considers trade-offs. Further, the consumer's choice problem can be phrased as optimizing subject to one intertemporal budget constraint that plays the same role as the single-period budget constraint used in previous sections. In particular, changes in wealth can be found as equivalent variations, using the intertemporal budget constraint in a way exactly analogous to the above.

The Household Sector

Suppose that there are three periods, periods 0, 1, and 2. Investigation of interest-rate-induced effects on wealth requires the introduction of bonds. Suppose that all bonds are for one period, paying the holder $1 in the period after purchase. The short-term interest rate between periods 0 and 1 is i_1, and between periods 1 and 2 is i_2. Then, if individual A holds B_t bonds at the start of period t (that is, A bought B_t bonds during period $t - 1$), these are redeemed in period t for B_t "dollars," continuing to call the unit of account dollars. Each such bond was bought in the previous period for a price $P_{b,t-1}$ equal to its present value, that is

$$P_{b,t-1} = \frac{1}{1 + i_t},$$

where i_t is the common interest rate at which everyone may borrow and lend in period $t - 1$. Thus, to receive B_t dollars in period t, A spent $P_{b,t-1}B_t$ dollars in period $t - 1$. Note that the present value in terms of period $t - 1$ of the B_t he/she receives minus his/her outgo is

$$\frac{B_t}{1 + i_t} - P_{b,t-1}B_t = \frac{B_t}{1 + i_t} - \frac{B_t}{1 + i_t} = 0.$$

In formulating the individual's optimizing problem, there are two equivalent approaches. The first has A maximize utility subject to a budget constraint for each period, while the second has him/her maximize utility subject only to a single intertemporal budget constraint. In either case, suppose that individual A's utility function is

$$U = U(C_{a,0}^d, C_{a,1}^d, C_{a,2}^d, \text{Le}_{a,0}, \text{Le}_{a,1}, \text{Le}_{a,2})$$

where $\text{Le}_{a,t}$ is A's leisure in period t. If the total amount of time available in each period is $\bar{L}$, then

$$\bar{L}_a = N_{a,t}^s + \text{Le}_{a,t}.$$

Substituting, A's utility is

$$U = U(C_{a,0}^d, C_{a,1}^d, C_{a,2}^d, \bar{L} - N_{a,0}^s, \bar{L} - N_{a,1}^s, \bar{L} - N_{a,2}^s).$$

Individual A's budget constraint for any period t, assuming non-satiation, is

$$P_t C_{a,t}^d + P_{b,t}B_{a,t+1} = w_t N_{a,t}^s + B_{a,t}.$$

Rearranging and discounting, the budget constraint for period t becomes

$$\frac{w_t N_{a,t}^s}{\Pi_{j=1}^t (1 + i_j)} + \frac{B_{a,t}}{\Pi_{j=1}^t (1 + i_j)} - \frac{P_t C_{a,t}^d}{\Pi_{j=1}^t (1 + i_j)} - \frac{P_{b,t}B_{a,t+1}}{\Pi_{j=1}^t (1 + i_j)} = 0.$$

Summing budget constraints for the three periods ($t = 0, 1, 2$) yields the single intertemporal budget constraint[20]

$$\sum_{t=0}^{2} \left\{ -\frac{P_t C_{a,t}^d}{\Pi_{j=1}^t (1 + i_j)} + \frac{w_t N_{a,t}^s}{\Pi_{j=1}^t (1 + i_j)} \right\} + B_{a,0} = 0;$$

this uses the fact that since

$$P_{b,t} = \frac{1}{1+i_{t+1}},$$

$$\frac{P_{b,t}B_{t+1}}{\Pi'_{j=1}(1+i_j)} - \frac{B_{t+1}}{\Pi^{t+1}_{j=1}(1+i_j)} = 0$$

and also the fact that A must plan to end with zero bonds, or $B_3 = 0$.[21] In other words, this budget constraint says that A's current bond holdings plus the present value of A's labor supplies is used to finance the present value of his/her consumption.

In the first approach, formulate A's choice problem as maximizing

$$U - \lambda_0(P_0C_0^d + P_{b,1}B_1 - w_0N_0^s - B_0)$$
$$- \lambda_1(P_1C_1^d + P_{b,2}B_2 - w_2N_1^s - B_1)$$
$$- \lambda_2(P_2C_2^d - w_2N_s^s - B_2),$$

where the λ_j are Lagrangian multipliers and the restriction $B_3 = 0$ is imposed. A's choice variables are $C_t^d(t = 0, 2)$, $N_t^s(t = 0, 2)$, $B_t(t = 1, 2)$ and λ_t $(t = 0, 2)$. His/her optimum conditions are

$$U_{C_0} - \lambda_0P_0 = 0$$
$$U_{C_1} - \lambda_1P_1 = 0$$
$$U_{C_2} - \lambda_2P_2 = 0$$
$$U_{N_0} - \lambda_0w_0 = 0$$
$$U_{N_1} - \lambda_1w_1 = 0$$
$$U_{N_2} - \lambda_2w_2 = 0$$
$$- \lambda_0P_{b,0} + \lambda_1 = 0$$
$$- \lambda_1P_{b,1} + \lambda_2 = 0$$
$$- P_0C_0^d - P_{b,0}B_1 + w_0N_0^s + B_0 = 0$$
$$- P_1C_1^d - P_{b,1}B_2 + w_1N_1^s + B_1 = 0$$
$$- P_2C_2^d \qquad\quad + w_2N_2 + B_2 = 0.$$

These conditions can usefully be altered and rearranged. First, in the bond conditions, note that $P_{b,0} = 1/(1 + i_1)$ and $P_{b,1} = 1(1 + i_2)$. Second, use these amended bond conditions to express

$$\lambda_1 = \lambda_0/(1 + i_1)$$
$$\lambda_2 = \lambda_0/(1 + i_1)(1 + i_2).$$

Third, substitute these last results into the consumption and labor marginal conditions. Fourth, discount the budget constraints for periods 1 and 2, and then add together all three (discounted) budget constraints, to find the intertemporal budget constraint. These changes give the revised marginal conditions as

$$U_{C_0} - \lambda_0 P_0 = 0$$

$$U_{C_1} - \lambda_0 P_1/(1 + i_1) = 0$$

$$U_{C_2} - \lambda_0 P_2/(1 + i_1)(1 + i_2) = 0$$

$$U_{N_0} - \lambda_0 w_0 = 0$$

$$U_{N_1} - \lambda_0 w_1/(1 + i_1) = 0$$

$$U_{N_2} - \lambda_0 w_2/(1 + i_1)(1 + i_2) = 0$$

$$- P_0 C_0^d - \frac{P_1 C_1^d}{1 + i_1} - \frac{P_2 C_2^d}{(1 + i_1)(1 + i_2)} + w_0 N_0^s - \frac{w_1 N_1^s}{1 + i_1}$$

$$- \frac{w_2 N_2^s}{(1 + i_1)(1 + i_2)} + B_0 = 0.$$

While these changes have reduced the number of conditions by four, they have also eliminated four choice variables (λ_1, λ_2, B_1, B_2).

The alternative formulation has A maximize U subject to the intertemporal constraint, or maximize

$$U - \lambda^* \left\{ P_0 C_0^d + \frac{P_1 C_1^d}{1 + i_1} + \frac{P_2 C_2^d}{(1 + i_1)(1 + i_2)} - w_0 N_0^s - \frac{w_1 N_1^s}{1 + i_1} \right.$$

$$\left. - \frac{w_2 N_2^s}{(1 + i_1)(1 + i_2)} - B_0 \right\}.$$

The optimum conditions are

$$U_{C_0} - \lambda^* P_0 = 0$$

$$U_{C_1} - \lambda^* P_1/(1 + i_1) = 0$$

$$U_{C_2} - \lambda^* P_2/(1 + i_1)(1 + i_2) = 0$$

$$U_{N_0} - \lambda^* w_0 = 0$$

$$U_{N_1} - \lambda^* w_1/(1 + i_1) = 0$$

$$U_{N_2} - \lambda^* w_2/(1 + i_1)(1 + i_2) = 0$$

$$- P_0 C_0^d - \frac{P_1 C_1^d}{1 + i_1} - \frac{P_2 C_2^d}{(1 + i_1)(1 + i_2)} + w_0 N_0^s - \frac{w_1 N_1^s}{1 + i_1}$$

$$- \frac{w_2 N_2^s}{(1 + i_1)(1 + i_2)} + B_0 = 0.$$

Once it is recognized that $\lambda_0 = \lambda^*$, it is evident that the two formulations are equivalent.

In the formulation with an intertemporal budget constraint, consider the effects of a rise in P_0. Since all other prices and interest rates are constant, the other goods can be treated as a composite good. The rise in P_0 thus causes a substitution effect against C_0^d and in favor of the composite good. There is also a wealth effect on A's demand for C_0^d, composed of a change in A's wealth times a marginal propensity to consume C_0^d out of wealth. As is the general case, the change in wealth is found as an equivalent variation, by differentiating A's (intertemporal) budget constraint. Thus, A's wealth changes by $-C_0^d$.

Complete the household sector by adding individual B. B's intertemporal budget constraint, by analogy to A's, is

$$\sum_{t=0}^{2} \left\{ - \frac{P_t C_{b,t}^d}{\Pi(1+i)} + \frac{w_j N_{b,t}^s}{\Pi(1+i)} + \frac{\text{Div}_t}{\Pi(1+i)} \right\} + B_{b,0} = 0,$$

where Div_t is now the total business sector dividend payments in period t. In what follows, treat the business sector as a single entity, but recall that, as before, no result depends on aggregation of production functions or products.

Recall the previous discussion which showed that lack of distribution effects implies that the household sector's budget constraint can be aggregated when considering aggregate household consumption and labor choices. In this example, then, the household sector's constraint is that

$$\sum_{j=0}^{2} \left\{ \frac{w_j N_j^s}{\Pi(1+i)} + \frac{\text{Div}_j}{\Pi(1+i)} - \frac{P_j C_j^d}{\Pi(1+i)} \right\} \tag{3.16}$$

must equal zero (assuming non-satiation). Expression (3.16) uses the fact that this is a closed economy and the assumption made below that business issues no bonds. Hence, the bonds which one individual holds were issued by another, so net household bond holdings are zero, and $B_{a,0} + B_{b,0} = 0$. Note that $B_{a,0} + B_{b,0} = 0$ is not an equilibrium relationship in the first period but an accounting identity.

The Business Sector

Suppose, for convenience, that business issues no bonds. Then, the only variables that business considers in any period t are N_t^d and its capital stock

K_{t}^{d}, with the consequent output from the production function $Y_{t}^{s} = f(N_{t}^{d}, K_{t}^{d})$. With the introduction of capital, dividends in period t become

$$\text{Div}_{t} = P_{t}Y_{t}^{s} - w_{t}N_{t}^{d} - P_{t}(K_{t+1}^{d} - K_{t}^{d})$$
$$= P_{t}Y_{t}^{s} - w_{t}N_{t}^{d} - P_{t}\Delta K_{t}^{d}$$
$$= P_{t}(Y_{t}^{s} - \Delta K_{t}^{d}) - w_{t}N_{t}^{d},$$

where $\Delta K_{t}^{d} \equiv K_{t+1}^{d} - K_{t}^{d}$. Capital is bought in period t to be available in period $t+1$ and affect output Y_{t+1}^{s}. For convenience, capital has the same price as other output. The present value of the business sector is

$$\sum_{t=0}^{2} \frac{1}{\Pi(1+i)} \{\widetilde{P}_{t}(Y_{t}^{s} - \Delta K_{t}^{d}) - \widetilde{w}_{t}N_{t}^{d}\},$$

with K_{0} fixed by last period's decisions and $K_{3} = 0$ so that the firm does not end with negative capital or wastefully holding positive-valued capital. Necessary conditions for business to be at a present value interior maximum are

$$P_{0}\frac{\partial Y_{0}^{s}}{\partial N_{0}^{d}} - w_{0} = 0$$

$$\frac{\widetilde{P}_{1}}{1+i_{1}}\frac{\partial Y_{1}^{s}}{\partial N_{1}^{d}} - \frac{\widetilde{w}_{1}}{1+i_{1}} = 0$$

$$\frac{\widetilde{P}_{2}}{(1+i_{1})(1+i_{2})}\frac{\partial Y_{2}^{s}}{\partial N_{2}^{d}} - \frac{\widetilde{w}_{2}}{(1+i_{1})(1+i_{2})} = 0$$

$$\frac{\widetilde{P}_{1}}{1+i_{1}}\frac{\partial Y_{1}^{s}}{\partial K_{1}^{d}} - P_{0} + \frac{\widetilde{P}_{1}}{1+i_{1}} = 0$$

$$\frac{\widetilde{P}_{2}}{(1+i_{1})(1+i_{2})}\frac{\partial Y_{2}^{s}}{\partial K_{2}^{d}} - \frac{\widetilde{P}_{1}}{1+i_{1}} + \frac{\widetilde{P}_{2}}{(1+i_{1})(1+i_{2})} = 0.$$

There is no marginal condition corresponding to K_{0} since K_{0} is predetermined. The tilde indicates values expected by business. These need not be the same as those expected by households.

The Interest-Rate-Induced Effect on Wealth

Consider the impact on wealth of an increase in i, in two separate cases.

A Rise In the Short-Term Rate of Interest First, let i_{1} rise with i_{2} held constant. The, the impact on the household sector's wealth, found by differentiating (3.16), is

$$-\frac{\mathrm{Div}_1}{(1+i_1)^2} - \frac{\mathrm{Div}_2}{(1+i_1)^2(1+i_2)} + \frac{\mathrm{dDiv}_0}{di_1} + \frac{\mathrm{dDiv}_1/di_1}{1+i_1} + \frac{\mathrm{dDiv}_2/di_1}{(1+i_1)(1+i_2)}$$

$$-\frac{w_1 N_1^s}{(1+i_1)^2} - \frac{w_2 N_2^s}{(1+i_1)^2(1+i_2)} + \frac{P_1 C_1^d}{(1+i_1)^2} + \frac{P_2 C_2^d}{(1+i_1)^2(1+i_2)}. \quad (3.17)$$

The first five terms are the induced changes in the present value of dividends, the next two are the changes in the present values of future labor income, and the last two terms are (minus) the changes in the present value of future consumption. The last four terms are evaluated at initial values of N_1^s, N_2^s, C_1^d, C_2^d, following sections 3.1 and 3.2. Now,

$$\frac{-\mathrm{Div}_1}{(1+i_1)^2} = -\frac{\tilde{P}_1(Y_1^s - \Delta K_1^d) - \tilde{w}_1 N_1^d}{(1+i_1)^2}$$

and

$$\frac{-\mathrm{Div}_2}{(1+i_1)^2(1+i_2)} = -\frac{\tilde{P}_2(Y_2^s - \Delta K_2^d) - \tilde{w}_2 N_2^d}{(1+i_1)^2(1+i_2)}.$$

The next three terms in (3.17) are

$$\frac{\mathrm{dDiv}_0}{di_1} + \frac{\mathrm{dDiv}_1/di_1}{1+i_1} + \frac{\mathrm{dDiv}_2/di_1}{(1+i_1)(1+i_2)}$$

$$= P_0 \frac{\mathrm{d}Y_0^s}{di_1} - w_0 \frac{\mathrm{d}N_0^d}{di_1} - \tilde{P}_1 \frac{\mathrm{d}K_1^d}{di_1}$$

$$+ \left(\tilde{P}_1 \frac{\mathrm{d}Y_1^s}{di_1} - \tilde{w}_1 \frac{\mathrm{d}N_1^d}{di_1} - \tilde{P}_1 \frac{\mathrm{d}K_2^d}{di_1} + \tilde{P}_1 \frac{\mathrm{d}K_1^d}{di_1} \right) \frac{1}{1+i_1}$$

$$+ \left(\tilde{P}_2 \frac{\mathrm{d}Y_2^s}{di_1} - \tilde{w}_2 \frac{\mathrm{d}N_2^d}{di_1} + \tilde{P}_2 \frac{\mathrm{d}K_2^d}{di_1} \right) \frac{1}{(1+i_1)(1+i_2)},$$

where

$$\frac{\mathrm{d}Y_0^s}{di_1} = \frac{\partial Y_0^s}{\partial N_0^d} \frac{\mathrm{d}N_0^d}{di_1}$$

$$\frac{\mathrm{d}Y_1^s}{di_1} = \frac{\partial Y_1^s}{\partial N_1^d} \frac{\mathrm{d}N_1^d}{di_1} + \frac{\partial Y_1^s}{\partial K_1^d} \frac{\mathrm{d}K_1^d}{di_1}$$

$$\frac{\mathrm{d}Y_2^s}{di_1} = \frac{\partial Y_2^s}{\partial N_2^d} \frac{\mathrm{d}N_2^d}{di_1} + \frac{\partial Y_2^s}{\partial K_2^d} \frac{\mathrm{d}K_2^d}{di_1}.$$

Thus, the three terms are

$$\left(P_0 \frac{\partial Y_0^s}{\partial N_0^d} - w_0\right) \frac{dN_0^d}{di_1} + \left(\widetilde{P}_1 \frac{\partial Y_1^s}{\partial N_1^d} - \widetilde{w}_1\right) \frac{dN_1^d}{di_1} \frac{1}{1+i_1}$$

$$+ \left(\widetilde{P}_2 \frac{\partial Y_2^s}{\partial N_2^d} - \widetilde{w}_2\right) \frac{dN_2^d}{di_1} \frac{1}{(1+i_1)(1+i_2)}$$

$$+ \left\{\left(\widetilde{P}_1 \frac{\partial Y_1^s}{\partial K_1^d} + \widetilde{P}_1\right) \Big/ (1+i_1) - P_0\right\} \frac{dK_1^d}{di_1}$$

$$+ \left\{\left(\widetilde{P}_2 \frac{\partial Y_2^s}{\partial K_2^d} + \widetilde{P}_2\right) \frac{1}{(1+i_1)(1+i_2)} - \frac{\widetilde{P}_1}{1+i_1}\right\} \frac{dK_2^d}{di_1} = 0$$

from the business-sector marginal conditions. That is, K_1^d and N_1^d surely change with a rise in i_1, but these three terms net to zero. Note that this is exactly analogous to single-period results in the preceding section.

Thus, the interest-rate-induced effect on wealth (3.17) simplifies to

$$-\frac{\widetilde{P}_1(Y_1^s - \Delta K_1^d) - \widetilde{w}_1 N_1^d}{(1+i_1)^2} - \frac{P_2(Y_2^s - \Delta K_2^d) - \widetilde{w}_2 N_2^s}{(1+i_1)^2(1+i_2)}$$

$$+\frac{P_1 C_1^d - w_1 N_1^s}{(1+i_1)^2} + \frac{P_2 C_2^d - w_2 N_2^s}{(1+i_1)^2(1+i_2)}. \tag{3.18}$$

Note that (3.18) is just the result of differentiating the household sector budget constraint (3.16) with respect to i_1 with quantities held at their initial values.

If (a) everyone expects the same prices, so $P_t = \widetilde{P}_t$, and if (b) all future quantities demanded equal those supplied, $C_t^d = Y_t^s - \Delta K_t^d$, $N_t^d = N_t^s$ for all $t > 0$, then (3.18) equals zero; that is, in this case the interest-rate-induced effect on wealth is zero. Common expectations and intertemporal market clearing of quantities are sufficient here to guarantee no interest-rate-induced effect on wealth.

While it is often necessary to assume the same price expectations and the equality of future quantities demanded and supplied to say anything meaningful about the wealth effect in multi-period analysis, this is not always true and (3.18) is such a case, as is now shown. If business expectations are substituted for dividends, the household sector budget constraint (3.16) becomes

$$P_0(Y_0^s - \Delta K_0^d) - w_0 N_0^d + \frac{\widetilde{P}_1(Y_1^s - \Delta K_1^d) - \widetilde{w}_1 N_1^d}{1+i_1}$$

$$+ \frac{\widetilde{P}_2(Y_2^s - \Delta K_2^d) - \widetilde{w}_2 N_2^s}{(1+i_1)(1+i_2)} + w_0 N_0^s + \frac{w_1 N_1^s}{1+i_1} + \frac{w_2 N_2^s}{(1+i_1)(1+i_2)}$$

$$- P_0 C_0^d - \frac{P_1 C_1^d}{1 + i_1} - \frac{P_2 C_2^d}{(1 + i_1)(1 + i_2)} = 0. \tag{3.19}$$

Now, if spot markets are in equilibrium, $C_0^d = Y_0^s - \Delta K_0^d$, $N_0^d = N_0^s$. If this is so, dividing the budget constraint (3.19) by $1 + i_1$ transforms its left-hand side to (3.18), and the wealth effect of a change in i_1 is zero if the system is in current equilibrium and whether or not all price expectations agree and all quantity expectations are consistent. That is, only current equilibrium is necessary in this case for a zero interest-rate-induced effect on wealth. The reader can demonstrate for himself or herself that a change in the initial (but not future) price level or in the rate of inflation expected for next period (but not future periods) can all be derived independently of the more stringent assumption of intertemporal equilibrium, as was done in the case of a change in the current (but not future) interest rate.

A Rise in the Long-Term Rate of Interest   However, there are some interest rate changes for which only the assumption of intertemporal market clearing and commonly held price expectations give determinate results. Because it is a frequent question in the literature, consider the change in wealth from an increase in i when all current and expected rates are equal and move together;[22] this is a shift in the entire yield curve and is often discussed as a change in the long-term rate of interest. Corresponding to (3.18), the change in wealth is

$$- \frac{\widetilde{P}_1(Y_1^s - \Delta K_1^d) - \widetilde{w}_1 N_1^d}{(1 + i)^2} - 2 \frac{\widetilde{P}_2(Y_2^s - \Delta K_2^d) - \widetilde{w}_2 N_2^d}{(1 + i)^3}$$
$$+ \frac{P_1 C_1^d - w_1 N_1^s}{(1 + i)^2} + 2 \frac{P_2 C_2^d - w_2 N_2^s}{(1 + i)^3} \gtreqless 0. \tag{3.20}$$

Clearly, if all expected prices are the same for businesses and consumers (e.g. $\widetilde{P}_1 = P_1$) and there is intertemporal market clearing (e.g. $C_1^d = Y_1^s - \Delta K_1^d$), then (3.20) equals zero and the interest-rate-induced effect on wealth is zero.

When the current interest rate rises, however, previous discussion showed that current-period market clearing was sufficient to give an interest-rate-induced effect of zero. But, in the case where all rates rise, simply assuming current equilibrium is not sufficient to determine the sign of (3.20). To see this, proceed as in the case of a rise in only the current interest rate and note that corresponding to (3.19) the household sector's budget constraint is

$$P_0^s(Y_0 - \Delta K_0^d) - w_0 N_0^d + \frac{\widetilde{P}_1(Y_1^s - \Delta K_1^d) - w_1 N_1^d}{1+i}$$

$$+ \frac{\widetilde{P}_2(Y_2^s - \Delta K_2^d) - w_2 N_2^d}{(1+i)^2} + w_0 N_0^s + \frac{w_1 N_1^s}{1+i} + \frac{w_2 N_2^s}{(1+i)^2}$$

$$- P_0 C_0^d - \frac{P_1 C_1^d}{1+i} - \frac{P_2 C_2^d}{(1+i)^2} = 0. \tag{3.21}$$

Assuming that current markets are in equilibrium and dividing by $1+i$, (3.21) becomes

$$\frac{\widetilde{P}_1(Y_1^s - \Delta K_1^d) - w_1 \widetilde{N}_1^d}{(1+i)^2} + \frac{\widetilde{P}_2(Y_2^s - \Delta K_2^d) - \widetilde{w}_2 N_2^d}{(1+i)^3}$$

$$- \frac{P_1 C_1^d - w_1 N_1^s}{(1+i)^2} - \frac{P_2 C_2^d - w_2 N_2^s}{(1+i)^3} = 0. \tag{3.22}$$

Notice that, given households' expectations (P_1, P_2, w_1, w_2) and plans $(C_1^d, C_2^d, N_1^s, N_2^s)$, there are an infinity of business expectations $(\widetilde{P}_1, \widetilde{P}_2, \widetilde{w}_1, \widetilde{w}_2)$ and plans $(Y_1^s - \Delta K_1^d, Y_2^s - \Delta K_2^d, N_1^d, N_2^d)$ that satisfy the budget constraint (3.22) – but even when (3.22) is satisfied, the impact on wealth (3.20) may take on any value whatsoever.

The interpretation of the two sets of results for an increase in the short-term versus long-term interest rate is straightforward. Equation (3.18) is really an intertemporal version of Walras's law, saying that the present value of the differences between the values of the goods society plans to demand and the values of the goods it plans to supply must equal zero. Clearly, multiplying this by $1/(1+i)$ does not affect it. Assuming that current markets clear implies that the present value of the values of future demands minus future supplies must equal zero – which is what (3.22) says.

An increase in i_1 by itself decreases the present value of the value of any future demand or supply by the same percentage. Hence, if the present values summed to zero, they must still do so. But if all interest rates increase, more distant values decrease in present value by a larger percent than do closer values – as shown by the weights in (3.20). Thus, it is only by chance that the patterns of values of future demands and supplies are such that the present values of both decrease by the same amount. The only way to guarantee this is to have common expectations and market-clearing quantities in all future periods, or $P_t = \widetilde{P}_t$, $w_t = \widetilde{w}_t$ and $C_t^d = Y_t^s, N_t^d = N_t^s$, for all $t > 0$.

Interpretation of Results for an Increase in the Long-term Rate of Interest

Consider an economy with two people, Smith and Jones. Smith plans to consume less than his/her income in the next several periods and thus accumulate savings. These savings will earn interest, and both the principal and the interest will be used in later periods to finance consumption beyond income. If all interest rates rise, Smith is wealthier, in the sense that the same saving will now finance more future consumption than before. However, if Smith had been borrowing now, to pay back later, the rise in rates would have reduced his/her wealth. The point is, the pattern of saving and dissaving must be known to judge whether interest rate changes have a positive or negative effect on an individual's wealth.[23]

However, suppose that all markets are initially in intertemporal equilibrium when i rises. In any period, the change in Smith's wealth is proportional to the difference between the quantities demanded and supplied. The same is true of Jones. But equilibrium requires that Jones's demand minus supply must equal the negative of Smith's demand minus supply. Thus, Smith's change in wealth equals the negative of Jones's change, and hence the net effect is zero. Note that it is easy to imagine a disequilibrium where both Smith and Jones want, say, to be lenders. In this case, a change in interest rates causes changes in wealth of the same sign for each of them. Common price expectations and market-clearing planned quantities are needed to make the sign of change in the wealth determinate, in which case it is zero.

The use in (3.18) of an intertemporal version of Walras's law carries the same interpretation as the use in section 3.2 of the single-period version: the household sector is kept continuously abreast of the dividends (here, the present value of the dividends) that it will receive from the business sector. If the current market is one that determines not only all current purchases and sales but also all future contracts, that is, it is a spot market plus a complete futures market,[24] clearly such a version of Walras's law must hold for standard analysis to proceed in the usual way. But in the present certainty model, even if there are not future markets, it does not seem any more implausible that households be kept up on a present value sum over three periods than over one period.[25]

3.4 Expectations in the Hicksian Analysis

Expectations have always been difficult to handle analytically. They have received increasing attention, however, in the past two decades, particularly with the advent of debate over expectations that are "rational" in the sense of Muth (1961). This section reviews the analysis of expectations and their role in wealth effects in *Value and Capital*. It also relates this analysis to more recent work.

In Hicks's analysis, an exogenous shock affects excess demands in various markets, and thus induces changes in prices to return the system to equilibrium. These changes in prices cause wealth and substitution effects that just offset the initial impacts on excess demands, returning all markets to equilibrium. To illustrate this, consider the single-period case, and in a non-monetary economy suppose that there are n goods with $n-1$ independent market-clearing equations:

$$\text{ExD}_j = 0 \qquad (j = 1, n-1).$$

Prices are normalized by setting the sum of the n prices equal to an arbitrary number $\bar{P}$, or

$$\sum_{j=1}^{n} P_j = \bar{P}. \tag{3.23}$$

Then, when the parameter α changes, for the excess demand for good j

$$\frac{\partial \text{ExD}_j}{\partial \alpha} + \sum_{h=1}^{n} \frac{\partial \text{ExD}_j}{\partial P_h} \frac{\mathrm{d}P_h}{\mathrm{d}\alpha} = 0 \qquad (j = 1, n-1) \tag{3.24}$$

where from (3.23)

$$\sum_{h=1}^{n} \frac{\mathrm{d}P_h}{\mathrm{d}\alpha} = 0. \tag{3.25}$$

The impact effects are the $\partial \text{ExD}_j / \partial \alpha$, and the aggregated wealth plus substitution effects are the $\partial \text{ExD}_j / \partial P_h$, just as in section 3.1. The n actual changes in prices in response to α are the $\mathrm{d}P_h / \mathrm{d}\alpha$, where the n $\mathrm{d}P_h / \mathrm{d}\alpha$ are found from solving the $n-1$ equations (3.24) along with (3.25), with all $\partial \text{ExD}_j / \partial \alpha$ and $\partial \text{ExD}_j / \partial P_h$ taken as parametric.

Suppose, however, that there are two periods, with the second period's expected price for good j denoted P_j^*. There are now n commodities in both periods, and bonds with the interest rate i in the first period. If all P_j, P_j^* double with i held constant, all current and future excess demands are unaffected. That is, all excess demands are homogeneous of degree zero in P_j, P_j^* (but not i). Continue to assume that prices are normalized according to (3.23), so that (3.25) continues to hold. There are then $2n+1$ price variables – n P_j, n P_j^* and i. Assume that all expectations are held in common across actors. An increase in α gives

$$\frac{\partial \mathrm{ExD}_j}{\partial \alpha} + \sum_{h=1}^{n} \frac{\partial \mathrm{ExD}_j}{\partial P_h} \frac{dP_h}{d\alpha} + \sum_{h=1}^{n} \frac{\partial \mathrm{ExD}_j}{\partial P_h^*} \frac{dP_h^*}{d\alpha}$$

$$+ \frac{\partial \mathrm{ExD}_j}{\partial i} \frac{di}{d\alpha} = 0 \qquad j = 1, n-1;$$

$$\frac{\partial \mathrm{ExDB}}{\partial \alpha} + \sum_{h=1}^{n} \frac{\partial \mathrm{ExDB}}{\partial P_h} \frac{dP_h}{d\alpha} + \sum_{h=1}^{n} \frac{\partial \mathrm{ExDB}}{\partial P_h^*} \frac{dP_h^*}{d\alpha}$$

$$+ \frac{\partial \mathrm{ExDB}}{\partial i} \frac{di}{d\alpha} = 0,$$

(3.26)

along with (3.25), where B refers to bonds. For any given n values of $dP_h^*/d\alpha$ the current n values of $dP_h/d\alpha$ and $di/d\alpha$ can be found from the $n+1$ equations (3.25) and (3.26). However, $dP_h/d\alpha$ will vary with the dP_h^*/α specified. The system in (3.25) and (3.26) is underdetermined, and the values of $dP_h^*/d\alpha$ must be specified in order to determine $dP_h/d\alpha$, $di/d\alpha$.

Hicks's solution was to work in terms of elasticities of P_h^* with respect to P_h. A common assumption was unitary elasticity, so that if $(dP_h/d\alpha)$ $(1/P_h) = 0.2$ then $(dP_h^*/d\alpha)(1/P_h^*) = 0.2$. Thus $\dfrac{dP_h^*}{d\alpha} = \dfrac{dP_h}{d\alpha} \dfrac{P_h^*}{P_h}$.
System (3.26) then becomes

$$\frac{\partial \mathrm{ExD}_j}{\partial \alpha} + \sum_{h=1}^{n} \left(\frac{\partial \mathrm{ExD}_j}{\partial P_h} + \frac{\partial \mathrm{ExD}_j}{\partial P_h^*} \frac{P_h^*}{P_h} \right) \frac{dP_h}{d\alpha}$$

$$+ \frac{\partial \mathrm{ExD}_j}{\partial i} \frac{di}{d\alpha} = 0 \qquad (j = 1, n-1),$$

$$\frac{\partial \mathrm{ExDB}}{\partial \alpha} + \sum_{h=1}^{n} \left(\frac{\partial \mathrm{ExD}_j}{\partial P_h} + \frac{\partial \mathrm{ExD}_j}{\partial P_h^*} \frac{P_h^*}{P_h} \right) \frac{dP_h}{d\alpha}$$

$$+ \frac{\partial \mathrm{ExDB}}{\partial i} \frac{di}{d\alpha} = 0,$$

with (3.25) still holding, giving $n+1$ equations in the n $dP_h/d\alpha$ and $di/d\alpha$. In particular, unit-elastic expectations were often specialized to satic expectations by assuming that $P_h^* = P_h$, so that $\partial P_h^*/\partial \alpha = \partial P_h/\partial \alpha$. Perfectly inelastic expectations meant that, when P_h changed, P_h^* was not affected, or $dP_h^*/d\alpha = 0$. Elastic expectations meant that P_h^* changed proportionately more than P_h. More generally, the influence of the elasticity of expectations could be expressed as

$$\frac{dP_h^*}{d\alpha} = \frac{dP_h}{d\alpha} \frac{P_h^*}{P_h} (1 + \gamma_h)$$

where

$$\gamma_h \gtreqless 0 \qquad (h = 1, n).$$

Expectations, then, are taken in *Value and Capital* to depend only on current prices. Further, the elasticity of expectations is taken as exogenous. Finally, note that (a) the effect on wealth of an increase in P_h also incorporates the effect on wealth of a change in P_h^*, and (b) this change in P_h^* depends on the exogenous elasticity.

Rational expectations do not base P_h^* on P_h but instead on the entire structure of the model. In the case of a two-period equilibrium model with no stochastic component, they would require that $dP_h^*/d\alpha$ be formed from (3.25) and (3.26) plus

$$\frac{\partial \text{ExD}_j^*}{\partial \alpha} + \sum_{h=1}^{n} \frac{\partial \text{ExD}_j^*}{\partial P_h} \frac{dP_h}{d\alpha} + \sum_{h=1}^{n} \frac{\partial \text{ExD}_j^*}{\partial P_h^*} \frac{dP_h^*}{d\alpha}$$

$$+ \frac{\partial \text{ExD}_j^*}{\partial i} \frac{di}{d\alpha} = 0 \qquad (j = 1, n) \tag{3.27}$$

where ExD_j^* is the excess demand for good j in the second period. Equations (3.25), (3.26) and (3.27) can be solved for the $2n + 1$ values $dP_h/d\alpha$, $dP_h^*/d\alpha$, $di/d\alpha$. Clearly, that is a more satisfying formulation than elasticity of expectations. This is particularly true when it is noticed that the ratio of $\partial P_h/\partial \alpha$ to $\partial P_h^*/\partial \alpha$ from (3.25), (3.26) and (3.27) will likely differ with different disturbances α; the elasticity parameters γ_h cannot reasonably be viewed as fixed.

The following chapters often discuss the case where unitary elasticity of expectations is assumed. Partly, this is because this assumption is so common in monetary literature, particularly up until say 1975. In some cases, particularly of neutral money supply shocks, this assumption gives precisely the rational expectations results. Further, the assumption can be used as a first approximation, because it often produces results not "far" off the mark.

For example, most of the discussion in the following chapters assumes a single produced good. Hence, the assumption of unitary expectations leads one astray only in the case where intertemporal relative prices are actually going to change. First, if the changes are not large, neglecting them should cause small problems. Second, and more importantly, these problems can be removed by separately considering the changes in wealth due to relative intertemporal price changes; separate consideration of different effects is useful in any case. Third, if the system is "close" to intertemporal market clearing and price expectations are held in common, the changes in wealth due to changes in intertemporal relative prices will often be zero; this can be seen intuitively from the discussion above of the effect on wealth of a change in the long-term rate of interest. Thus, while the use of rational expectations is intellectually more satisfying for analyzing movement of the overall system, the analytically more tractable assumption of unitary elasticity of expectations seems to cause no important difficulties in analyzing induced changes in wealth.

NOTES

1 When government is introduced, it must tell the household sector the present value of its tax liabilities – see chapter 5.

2 One of the main justifications Hicks offers for his development of static theory is that the static apparatus also applies for the problems of intertemporal economics. See Hicks (1946 chapter 1, especially pp. 5–6).

3 Hicks suggests in his intertemporal theory that some new name for the income effect might be useful – perhaps the "capital effect" (not to be confused with Mosak's (1944) general equilibrium "capital effect"). Patinkin (1965) recognizes by his second edition that there are not three effects (substitution, income, and real balance effects) in his analysis, but only two (substitution and wealth effects), in which the income and real balance effects can be distinguished as particular types of wealth effects.

4 Hicks later developed six measures of the wealth effect in his *Revision of Demand Theory*; Machlup's (1957) review of this book is excellent.

5 See Hicks (1946, parts I and II, especially the Mathematical Appendix).

6 Where it will cause no confusion, the subscripts referring to an individual are not written.

7 See Hicks (1946, Mathematical Appendix), Kuenne (1963), Samuelson (1965).

8 See Hicks (1946, chapter 2).

9 In fact, Hicks assumed A's endowment is all in terms of one good (or a composite good, made up of goods whose relative prices are unchanging), which he then uses as the numeraire and calls "money," noting that the only relationship between his money and money used in actual economies is that they are units of account. The wealth effect is then removed by changing this endowment.

10 See the English-language translation "On the Theory of the Budget of the Consumer" of Slutsky's 1915 article in *Readings in Price Theory*. Hicks and Allen (1934) were unaware of this pioneering effort when they developed their own analysis, though they were aware (as Mosak (1944) notes) of W.E. Johnson's "mathematical development of a demand theory essentially free from the assumption of the measurability of utility. . . ."

11 He was also interested in the strength of the forces making for equilibrium. His opinion that (what came to be called) the real balance effect was so weak that it could not explain why fluctuations were not even more severe than they were led him to be lumped with those who acknowledge the theoretical validity of the real balance effect but immediately deny its practical importance for macro fluctuations. Unfortunately, Hicks's views on this issue also led other economists to overlook the fact that money can be straightforwardly integrated into the Hicksian apparatus with great success.

12 Between the two editions of *Value and Capital*, Samuelson developed his notion of stability which came to be called "true dynamic stability." It is well known that Hicksian and dynamic stability imply each other for the case of two goods, and when there are more than two goods, Hicksian stability is neither necessary nor sufficient for true dynamic stability. See Metzler (1945), Hicks (1946, Additional Note C), Samuelson (1947), Kuenne (1963).

In the two-good case, Walras's law implies that the market for good 2 is in equilibrium just in case the market for good 1 is. Consequently, if the market for good 1 is stable, when it returns to equilibrium so must the market for good 2. Hence, the market for good 2 need not be considered separately in the stability analysis.

13 Leijonhufvud (1968) remarks on the inappropriateness of netting out assets and liabilities when the disaggregated positions have been assumed on the basis of individual utility maximization. It amounts to denying the significance of differences among individuals, while the existence of individuals' differing asset/debt positions strongly suggests that the differences are significant.

14 Hicks (1946) often proceeds on this assumption, though always with the warning that facts may prove it a poor one. Patinkin (1965) uses it systematically, as do Pesek and Saving (1967). It is a key assumption in a demonstration by Saving (1970), and Patinkin's (1971) objection to the demonstration does not mention it at all. Gurley and Shaw (1960) repeatedly reiterate that the assumed absence of distribution effects is one of the rules in neo-classical monetary theory to which they adhere (in order to show that certain propositions follow even on these rules).

15 Patinkin (1965) somewhat slights production after devoting over half his book to a treatment of an exchange economy. For present purposes, Pesek and Saving (1967) also give much too cursory a look to the firm side of the product and labor markets.

16 An alternative and equivalent assumption is that A maximizes $U^a(C_a^d, \text{Le}_a)$ subject to $P_c C_a^d - w(\overline{L} - \text{Le}_a) = 0$. Chapter 5 uses both formulations to discuss the initial-condition effect.

17 The parameter that changes can be a variable that is exogenous from the viewpoint of each economic unit but endogenous to the system – for example, the price level as in the real balance effect. It can be exogenous to the system also – for example, the state of technology.

18 The ease with which the analysis is extended from the single- to the multiperiod case illustrates Hicks's point that it is worthwhile developing his statics first, as he does in parts I and II of *Value and Capital*, for the same principles

apply in multi-period analysis.

19 Hicks noted these two sources of future disequilibrium, saying that the latter was the more potent. He also pointed out their influence on wealth effects. See Hicks (1946, pp. 133–5).

20 Mosak (1944) also adds the discounted budget constraints to form a single intertemporal constraint.

21 Patinkin (1965) refers to this restriction as an "imperfection" because B_3 cannot be negative (that is, A cannot die a net debtor). This is, in fact, a sign of market perfection, because anyone buying a bond from A without this restriction makes a mistake, since A cannot redeem the bond. B_3 cannot be positive because of the assumption of non-satiation (that is, A does not want to die with net assets that could have been used on consumption or to finance leisure).

22 See, for example, Metzler (1951), Bear (1961), Patinkin (1965), Pesek and Saving (1967), Leijonhufvud (1968), Bailey (1971), Sweeney (1974).

23 See Hicks (1946) and Leijonhufvud (1968) for similar analyses.

24 See Hicks (1946) and Hansen (1970).

25 The assumption that households are kept up to date on the present value of dividends they can expect, and the present value of taxes for which they are liable, is crucial for the following chapters.

Part III

THE PRICE-INDUCED EFFECT
ON WEALTH

4
The Price-Induced Effect on Wealth:
A Fixed Money Stock

This chapter uses the Hicksian apparatus of chapter 3 to analyze the price-induced effect on wealth. The discussion purposely considers a simple world, where the economy is closed, there is a single produced good that is both consumed and invested, there is no government sector, the nominal money stock is fixed, and there is no banking system. Chapters 5–7 then relax some of these assumptions regarding the government sector, the money stock and the banking sector. If there are no distribution effects, the effect on wealth of an increase in the price level is found by considering the change in wealth that society would require to maintain its consumption pattern, exactly the same sort of problem as was considered in chapter 3.

The model assumes that each individual accumulates money balances in one period to have on hand at the start of the next period to facilitate that period's transactions. This is also the structure of Patinkin's (1956, 1965) model. Thus, the individual's initial stock of money balances in the current period is predetermined by the preceding period's choices; however, the real value of the given stock of nominal money balances depends on the current period's price level, and can be different from what was planned as the price level is different from what was expected.

This chapter serves partly as an introduction because it discusses the case closest to the usual analysis of the price-induced effect on wealth; even so, there are some new insights. Further, the analytical approach is the same here as in the more complicated discussion in later chapters. Section 4.1 shows that an increase in the price level has the conventional effect on wealth $(-M^s/P^2)$ if the current wage rate increases proportionately with the current price level, and if no interest rate or expected rate of price or wage inflation changes. Constant expected rates of wage and price inflation, in the face of changes in the current level of prices and wages, are the same as unit-elastic price and wage expectations. Section 4.2 shows that unit-elastic expectations are necessary to get the usual price-induced effect on wealth; for example, perfectly inelastic expectations give a zero price-induced effect on wealth if current output and labor markets clear. Consequently, as argued in section 4.3, in the conventional discussion of the neutrality of money the role of unit-elastic expectations is not only to prevent substitution effects but also to ensure that the net change in wealth, due to proportionate changes in the current price level and money stock, must be zero.

Section 4.4 briefly introduces the "initial-condition effect" which later chapters discuss at length. Section 4.5 takes up two issues. First, Patinkin (1965) derives the conventional real balance effect by assuming there are no distribution effects across the business and household sectors. This is analytically faulty and is shown to be unnecessary because the only relevant distribution effects are within the household sector, not across sectors. Second, it is shown that the source of money – business, government, foreigners, as transfers, etc. – is irrelevant. Section 4.6 discusses the quantitative significance of the price-induced effect on wealth. A substantial amount of argument in the 1950s and 1960s focused on the fact that the effect is likely to be small. However, with the newer equilibrium models of the rational expectations revolution, the issue is the existence of the price-induced effect on wealth rather than its size. In the context of the determinacy of the price level, the issue always was the existence rather than the size of the price-induced effect on wealth.

4.1 Yap-Island Money

The Hicksian analysis of wealth effects developed in chapter 3 can be applied to the simplest possible multi-period monetary economy, referred to here as "the Yap-Island monetary economy." In fact, this chapter deals with what is closest to the standard case in conventional monetary analysis.

In the traditional native economy of the Pacific's Yap Island, giant rocks were a form of wealth and performed money roles. They served as a unit of account and store of value, and by means of settling accounts were a medium of exchange.[1] Fascinating anthropological questions aside, the main analytical quality of these rocks was their fixed quantity – unaugmentable by any human agency.[2] How they got there makes no difference – whether placed there by gods, by a government, by private individuals, by financial (or non-financial) firms – and whether or not anyone initially received something in exchange for them is also irrelevant.

Assume there are no distribution effects. Then, as argued in chapter 3, analysis of wealth effects can use the aggregate household sector budget constraint.

The Household Sector Budget Constraint

Assuming non-satiation, the budget constraint of the household sector in this economy for any period t says that

$$P_t C_t^d + \Delta MH_t + P_{b,t} B_{t+1} = w_t N_t^s + Div_t + B_t, \qquad (4.1)$$

where $\Delta MH_t \ (\equiv MH_{t+1} - MH_t)$ is the sector's desired accumulation of (claims to) those giant rocks. Rearranging and discounting, (4.1) becomes

$$\frac{w_t N_t^s}{\Pi(1+i)} + \frac{Div_t}{\Pi(1+i)} + \frac{B_t}{\Pi(1+i)} - \frac{P_t C_t^d}{\Pi(1+i)} - \frac{\Delta MH_t}{\Pi(1+i)} - \frac{P_{b,t} B_{t+1}}{\Pi(1+i)}$$
$$= 0. \qquad (4.2)$$

Assume that the economy will go on forever. Adding together budget constraints (4.2) for all t gives

$$\sum_{t=0}^{\infty} \frac{w_t N_t^s}{\Pi(1+i)} + \sum_{t=0}^{\infty} \frac{Div_t}{\Pi(1+i)} - \sum_{t=0}^{\infty} \frac{P_t C_t^d}{\Pi(1+i)}$$

$$- \sum_{t=1}^{\infty} \frac{i_t P_t (MH_t / P_t)}{\Pi(1+i)} + MH_0 \qquad (4.3)$$

must be greater than or equal to zero (equal to zero with non-satiation), where MH_t / P_t are real balances in period t. Expression (4.3) makes use of the fact that the term MH_t enters the budget constraint for period $t-1$ in $\Delta MH_{t-1} \equiv MH_t - MH_{t-1}$ and the constraint for t in $\Delta MH_t \equiv MH_{t+1} - MH_t$. When the present values of the budget constraints are added,

$$\frac{MH_t}{\Pi^{t-1}(1+i)} - \frac{MH_t}{\Pi^t(1+i)} = \frac{MH_t(1+i_t)}{\Pi^t(1+i)} - \frac{MH_t}{\Pi^t(1+i)}$$

$$= \frac{i_t MH_t}{\Pi^t(1+i)} \qquad (t \geqslant 1).$$

However, there is only one MH_0 term, so it enters (4.3) separately. Similarly, B_t enters the budget constraint for t and is discounted by $\Pi(1+i)$ where the product runs to t. But it also enters the constraint for period $t-1$ in $-P_{b,t-1} B_t$ and is discounted by $\Pi(1+i)$ where the product runs to $t-1$. However, since $P_{b,t-1} = 1/(1+i_t)$, the discounted values of B_t and $P_{b,t-1} B_t$ are equal and all B terms cancel save B_0. For convenience only, assume that the business sector issues no bonds. Then, in this closed economy with no government, the household sector's initial bond holdings must equal zero, or $B_0 = 0$.

The Opportunity Cost of Using Real Balances

The expression

$$\sum_{t=1}^{\infty} \frac{i_t P_t (MH_t / P_t)}{\Pi(1+i)}$$

is easily interpreted. If the household sector has MH_t / P_t real dollars on hand in period t, it foregoes the nominal interest income it could have earned on these real balances. The interest payment foregone is equal to the nominal stock of money holdings, $P_t(MH_t / P_t)$, multiplied by the interest rate i_t, or is $i_t P_t(MH_t / P_t)$. This is the opportunity cost of using the M_t / P_t real dollars. The present value of period t's opportunity cost is $i_t P_t(M_t / P_t)/\Pi(1+i)$. The present value of all such opportunity costs is found by summing such expressions to infinity.

However, the summation begins at time 1, not time 0, since nominal money holdings at the very start of period 0 are what they are; for each individual, money holdings are those decided on last period. Money holdings in the first period cannot now be invested (though they could previously have been) to earn interest this period – there is no current opportunity cost because bygones are bygones. Money holdings at the start of one period are accumulated during the preceding period, as in Patinkin's (1956, 1965) model.

Interpretation of the Household Sector Budget Constraint

In (4.3), the term

$$\sum_{t=1}^{\infty} \frac{i_t P_t (MH_t / P_t)}{\Pi(1+i)}$$

is the present value of the nominal (opportunity) cost of the services from real balances that the household sector plans on holding. The other outgo item is $\sum_{t=0}^{\infty} \dfrac{P_t C_t^d}{\Pi(1+i)}$, the present value of the nominal consumption stream. These two costs must be financed from three sources. First, the household sector's present financial wealth is simply its money holdings MH_0. Second, the term $\sum_{t=0}^{\infty} \dfrac{w_t N_t^s}{\Pi(1+i)}$ is the present value of the nominal value of the stream of labor services which the household sector plans to supply. And finally, $\sum_{t=0}^{\infty} \dfrac{\text{Div}_t}{\Pi(1+i)}$ is the nominal present value of the dividend stream that the business sector plans to pay to its owners, the household sector.

In every period t, a unit of consumption sacrificed now will lose the marginal utility of consumption MUC_t, but will allow accumulation of one extra unit of real balances. This will give $1/(1 + \Delta P/P)$ extra real balances to use in $t+1$ each with marginal utility MUm_{t+1}, and will also allow $1/(1 + \Delta P/P)$ extra units of consumption in period $t+1$, each with marginal utility MUC_{t+1}. The extra benefits in period $t+1$ are $\{1/(1 + \Delta P/P)\}(\text{MUm}_{t+1} + \text{MUC}_{t+1})$. If these future marginal utilities are discounted by the factor β, the marginal condition is $\text{MUC}_t = \{1/(1+\Delta P/P)\}\beta(\text{MUm}_{t+1} + \text{MUC}_{t+1})$.[3]

The Business Sector's Dividends

The Yap-Island business sector maximizes the present value of planned dividends. These planned dividends equal actual dividends only if the economy is on an equilibrium time path. Planned dividends in period t are

$$\text{Div}_t = \widetilde{P}_t Y_t^s - \widetilde{w}_t N_t^d - \widetilde{P}_t \Delta K_t^d - \Delta \text{MB}_t,$$

where Y_t^s is the total quantity supplied of the single real output, ΔK_t^d ($\equiv K_{t+1}^d - K_t^d$) is investment in period t in units of eternal non-wasting capital,[4] ΔMB_t is the business sector's flow demand in period t for accumulation of (claims to) those giant rocks and, as in chapter 3, the symbol tilde refers to businesses' expectations of prices and wages. Thus, the household and business sectors are not necessarily assumed to have the same expectations. The present value of period t's dividends is (expected to be)

$$\frac{\widetilde{P}_t Y_t^s}{\Pi(1+i)} - \frac{\widetilde{w}_t N_t^d}{\Pi(1+i)} - \frac{\widetilde{P}_t \Delta K_t^d}{\Pi(1+i)} - \frac{\Delta \text{MB}_t}{\Pi(1+i)} \quad .$$

The present value of the stream of dividends is the summation

$$\sum_{t=0}^{\infty} \left\{ \frac{\widetilde{P}_t Y_t^s}{\Pi(1+i)} - \frac{\widetilde{w}_t N_t^d}{\Pi(1+i)} - \frac{\widetilde{P}_t \Delta K_t^d}{\Pi(1+i)} - \frac{\Delta \text{MB}_t}{\Pi(1+i)} \right\}. \tag{4.4}$$

Recalling the discussion in connection with (4.3) above, (4.4) may be written

$$\sum_{t=0}^{\infty} \left\{ \frac{\widetilde{P}_t Y_t^s}{\Pi(1+i)} - \frac{\widetilde{w}_t N_t^d}{\Pi(1+i)} - \frac{\widetilde{P}_t \Delta K_t^d}{\Pi(1+i)} \right\}$$

$$- \sum_{t=1}^{\infty} \left\{ \frac{i_t \widetilde{P}_t (\mathrm{MB}_t / \widetilde{P}_t)}{\Pi(1+i)} \right\} + \mathrm{MB}_0. \tag{4.5}$$

The expression (4.5) gives the present value of nominal dividends as depending on two revenue or wealth terms and three costs terms. First,

$\sum_{t=0}^{\infty} \dfrac{\widetilde{P}_t Y_t^s}{\Pi(1+i)}$ is the present value of nominal revenue from the pro-

duction and sales stream Y_t^s. MB_0 is the business sector's initial stock of wealth in the form of giant rocks. From these two credit items, costs are

deducted to find dividends. $\sum_{t=0}^{\infty} \dfrac{\widetilde{w} N_t^d}{\Pi(1+i)}$ is the present value of nominal

labor costs, and $\sum_{t=0}^{\infty} \dfrac{\widetilde{P}_t \Delta K_t^d}{\Pi(1+i)}$ is the present value of costs of capital

accumulation. Finally, similar to the household sector's budget con-

straint, $\sum_{t=1}^{\infty} \dfrac{i_t \widetilde{P}_t (\mathrm{MB}_t / \widetilde{P}_t)}{\Pi(1+i)}$ is the nominal opportunity cost of busi-

nesses' planned holdings of real balances over time.

The Business Sector's Optimum Conditions

Assume that Y_t^s depends positively on the quantities of labor, capital and real balances used in period t, or

$$Y_t^s = Y(N_t^d, K_t^d, \mathrm{MB}_t / \widetilde{P}_t).$$

Necessary conditions for the business sector to have chosen positive quantities $(N_t^d, K_t^d, \mathrm{MB}_t)$ that maximize (4.5) are

$$\widetilde{P}_t \frac{\partial Y_t^s}{\partial N_t^d} - \widetilde{w}_t = 0 \qquad\qquad (t \geqslant 0)$$

$$\widetilde{P}_t \frac{\partial Y_t^s}{\partial K_t^d} - \widetilde{P}_{t-1} \left(i_t - \frac{\Delta \widetilde{P}_{t-1}}{\widetilde{P}_{t-1}} \right) = 0 \qquad (t \geqslant 1) \tag{4.6}$$

$$\frac{\partial Y_t^s}{\partial (\mathrm{MB}_t / \widetilde{P}_t)} - i_t = 0 \qquad\qquad (t \geqslant 1)$$

Note that MB_0 and K_0 are determined by the preceding period's decisions on cash and capital accumulation, so (4.6) holds for these variables during period 0 only if the "right" decision were made in the past. For the given, predetermined values of MB_0 and K_0, N_0^d will be adjusted to make the labor marginal conditions hold in period 0.

As an alternative to having real balances as a factor of production, business could be faced with real transaction costs that depend on Y_t^s and MB_t/P_t, and perhaps on N_t^d. Div$_t$ then has these transaction costs subtracted. Either formulation of how money enters will do. The point is this: if business makes the sacrifice of acquiring costly real balances, it is because their real balances are useful. A change in P_0 that alters MB_0/P_0 will then affect business behavior, generally with regard to both Y_0^s and N_0^d.

The Budget Constraint in Real Terms

For convenience, assume for the present that business holds no money, or $MB_t = 0$ for all t. Divide the household sector budget constraint (4.3) and the present value of dividends (4.5) by P_0, to put the analysis in current-period real terms. Then insert the expression for businesses' dividends (4.5) in (4.3) to find

$$\sum_{t=0}^{\infty} \left\{ \frac{w_t N_t^s}{P_0 \Pi(1+i)} + \frac{\widetilde{P}_t(Y_t^s - \Delta K_t^d)}{P_0 \Pi(1+i)} - \frac{\widetilde{w}_t N_t^d}{P_0 \Pi(1+i)} - \frac{P_t C_t^d}{P_0 \Pi(1+i)} \right\}$$

$$- \sum_{t=1}^{\infty} \left\{ \frac{i_t P_t (\mathrm{MH}_t/P_t)}{P_0 \Pi(1+i)} \right\} + \frac{\mathrm{MH}_0}{P_0}. \tag{4.7}$$

Next, define the rate of increase in prices expected between two periods as $\Delta P_t/P_t$. Thus, households expect period t's price level to be P_t and the next period's to be $P_t(1 + \Delta P_t/P_t)$ – and similarly for expected wages. Using this formulation (4.7) becomes

$$\sum_{t=0}^{\infty} \left\{ \frac{w_0}{P_0} \frac{\Pi(1 + \Delta w/w)}{\Pi(1+i)} N_t^s + \frac{\Pi(1 + \Delta \widetilde{P}/P)}{\Pi(1+i)} (Y_t^s - \Delta K_t^d) \right.$$

$$\left. - \frac{w_0}{P_0} \frac{\Pi(1 + \Delta \widetilde{w}/w)}{\Pi(1+i)} N_t^d - \frac{\Pi(1 + \Delta P/P)}{\Pi(1+i)} C_t^d \right\}$$

$$- \sum_{t=1}^{\infty} \left\{ \frac{\Pi(1 + \Delta P/P)}{\Pi(1+i)} \right\} i_t\, \mathrm{mh}_t + \frac{\mathrm{MH}_0}{P_0}, \tag{4.8}$$

where mh$_t$ are planned household real balances in period t in terms of that period's prices. Note that MH_0 has to equal the stock M^s in existence, so that MH_0 can be replaced by M^s in (4.8). This equality of M^s and MH_0 is not an economic result but simply an accounting necessity since, for the time being, MB is assumed to be zero.

The Price-Induced Effect on Wealth

A major question in monetary theory since the mid-1940s has been the effect on wealth of an increase in the current level of prices accompanied by a proportionate change in the wage rate structure. Much of the analysis has centered around the case discussed here, where there is an initial given stock of money. The change in wealth due to an increase in P_0 is just the derivative of (4.8) with respect to P_0, with all real choice variables including mh_t held at their initial values. Suppose that when P_0 rises, no expected rate of price or wage inflation or rate of interest changes, and w_0 varies proportionately with P_0. Then, the price-induced effect on wealth is the conventional

$$-\frac{\mathrm{MH}_0}{P_0^2} = -\frac{M^s}{P_0^2}. \tag{4.9}$$

Note that in differentiating (4.8), Y_t^s, N_t^d, and K_t^d (and hence ΔK_t^d) do not change because all relative prices are constant.

The result in (4.9) is independent of whether rates of inflation expected by two sectors are equal, and of whether present or future quantities demanded equal those supplied. In essence, relative prices have not changed, and the price-induced effect on wealth depends on the fact that initial real balances have fallen since nominal balances are fixed.

4.2 Conditions for the Conventional Real Balance Effect

The price-induced effect on wealth in (4.9) is the conventional result in monetary theory. It is useful to consider in a little more detail the conditions under which this result was just derived here.

1 "w_0 varies proportionately with P_0." However, suppose that all sectors expect the same rates of wage inflation, or $\Delta w_t/w = \Delta \widetilde{w}_t/w$ ($t \geqslant 1$). Further, suppose that planned demands and supplies of labor are equal, or $N_t^d = N_t^s$ ($t \geqslant 0$). Then inspection of (4.8) shows that w_0 need not vary at all, and certainly not proportionately, for the price-induced effect on wealth to equal $-M^s/P_0^2$. In other words, if the household and business sectors have the same price and wage expectations, and if markets are clearing in every period, then w_0 need not rise proportionately with P_0. If w_0 does not vary proportionately with P_0, then real wages fall when P_0 rises; there is a redistribution between workers and firm-owners but no aggregate effect on wealth.

If wage expectations are not equal, however, or quantities of labor demanded and supplied are unequal,

$$\sum_{t=0}^{\infty} \frac{w_0}{P_0} \frac{\Pi(1 + \Delta w/w)}{\Pi(1 + i)} N_t^s - \sum_{t=0}^{\infty} \frac{w_0}{P_0} \frac{\Pi(1 + \Delta \tilde{w}/w)}{\Pi(1 + i)} N_t^d$$

(4.10)

does not equal zero, and consequently changes when P_0 rises; the most plausible way to maintain the same real value of (4.10) when P_0 increases is for w_0 to rise proportionately.

2 "Expected price and wage inflation must not vary with P_0 (and w_0)." Expression (4.10) provides the explanation: if (4.10) is non-zero, only very specialized changes in $\Delta w/w$ and $\Delta \tilde{w}/w$ leave the real value of (4.10) unchanged.

However, if $\Delta w_t/w = \Delta \tilde{w}_t/w$ and $N_t^d = N_t^s$ for all $t \geq 1$, then (4.10) equals zero and equal changes in $\Delta w/w$ and $\Delta \tilde{w}/w$ leave (4.10) equal to zero. Clearly, the same sort of thing holds true for changes in $\Delta P_t/P$ and $\Delta \tilde{P}_t/P$ in

$$\sum_{t=0}^{\infty} \left\{ \frac{\Pi(1 + \Delta \tilde{P}/P)}{\Pi(1 + i)} (Y_t^s - \Delta K_t^d) - \frac{\Pi(1 + \Delta P/P)}{\Pi(1 + i)} C_t^d \right\}.$$

However, notice that such changes in $\Delta P_t/P$ do affect

$$\sum_{t=1}^{\infty} \frac{\Pi(1 + \Delta P/P)}{\Pi(1 + i)} i_t \, \mathrm{mh}_t$$

and hence (4.8), and thus do enter the price-induced effect on wealth. In fact, (4.9) becomes

$$-\frac{M^s}{P_0^2} - \sum_{t=1}^{\infty} \frac{d\Pi(1 + \Delta P/P)/dP_0}{\Pi(1 + i)} i_t \, \mathrm{mh}_t.$$

Notice that if $\Delta w_t/w = \Delta \tilde{w}_t/w$ ($t \geq 1$) and $N_t^d = N_t^s$ ($t \geq 0$), then from (4.10) increases in any $\Delta w_t/w$ ($\Delta \tilde{w}_t/w$ varying equally) or in w_0/P_0 cause no wealth effects, though there are of course substitution effects. In particular, in empirical research in this case, an increase in w_0/P_0 has no effect on wealth, and thus the researcher has no problem of trying to separate substitution and wealth effects. Since the relative prices of labor in various periods have not changed, and the relative prices of consumption of goods and money services have not changed, labor in various periods is a composite good and so is consumption and money services. Thus, the substitution effect is between these two composite goods.[5]

The assumption that all $\Delta P_t/P$ are unaffected by changes in P_0 is equivalent to assuming that all ratios P_t/P_0 are unaffected, since

$$\frac{P_t}{P_0} = \frac{P_0\Pi(1 + \Delta P_j/P)}{P_0} = \Pi(1 + \Delta P_j/P).$$

Assuming that P_t/P_0 is unaffected is just the assumption of unitary elasticity of expectations, or that the price expected in period t changes proportionately with price in period 0. A subcase of unit-elastic price expectations is static price expectations where not only are price expectations unit elastic but $P_t = P_0$ for all t. Clearly, expectations need not be static to find the usual real balance effect. As will be shown, neutrality of money requires unitary price expectations; however, most discussions (for example, Patinkin, 1965; Gurley and Shaw, 1960) assume static price expectations, though it is often unclear whether this is viewed as a necessary condition.

The upshot of the discussion is this. The assumptions of w_0/P_0 constant, all interest rates constant, and unit-elastic price and wage expectations are sufficient to give the usual price-induced effect on wealth in the case of Yap-Island money. However, the assumptions of a constant w_0/P_0 and constant $\Delta w/w$, $\Delta \tilde{w}/w$ are not necessary if the two sector's expectations agree and output and labor markets are clearing. However, if price expectations are not unit elastic, the price-induced effect on wealth is different from the conventional, as is now discussed.

Elasticity of Expectations, and the Size of the Price-Induced Effect on Wealth

Suppose that prices and wages have the same degree of elasticity. Unit-elastic price and wage expectations are necessary for neutrality as discussed in the next section; this is also the only degree of elasticity that will give the usual magnitude of the price-induced effect on wealth. Power (1959) and Mayer (1959) claim that "the real balance effect of a price decline expected to be permanent is necessarily greater than that of a temporary one." Patinkin denies this, though admitting that under certain circumstances the price-induced effect on wealth does depend on the elasticity of expectations.[6]

To evaluate this controversy, compare the real balance effect with unitary versus perfectly inelastic expectations. As seen in section 4.1, unit-elastic price and wage expectations imply that an increase in P_0 gives a real balance effect of $-M^s/P_0^2$. Perfectly inelastic price expectations imply that changes in P_0 leave P_t and $\tilde{P}_t$ entirely unaffected. Suppose that w_0 and hence $\tilde{w}_0$ change proportionately with P_0. Differentiating (4.7) with respect to P_0 yields

$$- \sum_{t=1}^{\infty} \left\{ \frac{w_t}{P_0^2} \frac{N_t^s}{\Pi(1+i)} + \frac{\widetilde{P}_t}{P_0^2} \frac{Y_t^s - \Delta K_t^d}{\Pi(1+i)} - \frac{\widetilde{w}_t}{P_0^2} \frac{N_t^d}{\Pi(1+i)} \right.$$

$$\left. - \frac{P_t}{P_0^2} \frac{C_t^d}{\Pi(1+i)} - \frac{P_t i_t \text{mh}_t}{P_0^2 \Pi(1+i)} \right\} - \frac{M^s}{P_0^2} \qquad (4.11)$$

Now, divide the budget constraint (4.7) by $-P_0$, and suppose that current markets are clearing so that $N_0^s = N_0^d$ and $Y_0^s = C_0^d + \Delta K_0^d$. Then (4.7) becomes (4.11). Since (4.7) equals zero, the price-induced effect on wealth with perfectly inelastic price (and wage) expectations is necessarily zero. The intuitive explanation for the difference in the two cases is this: with unit-elastic expectations, your initial real balances will buy less in the future (provide fewer real money services) because prices are expected to be higher, but with zero-elastic expectations expected prices are unchanged and so is the value in the future of your initial real balances.[7]

Intermediate degrees of elasticity of expectations will give intermediate changes in wealth. Thus, only unit-elastic expectations will give the conventional effect on wealth in the present model.

It might be noted that as long as $N_0^s = N_0^d$ a rise in P_0 with w_0 held constant gives a price-induced effect on wealth of zero.

4.3 The Neutrality of Yap-Island Money

Neutrality of money requires that a one-time increase in the money stock, accompanied by a proportionate increase in the price level (and wage rate), have no real effects. This requires no net change in wealth and no substitution effects.

Sections 4.1 and 4.2 stressed the case of the price-induced effect on wealth where P_0 and w_0 increase proportionately, price and wage expectations have unitary elasticity, and expected interest rates do not vary. While other assumptions can generate the wealth change in (4.9), these (and only these) assumptions permit the neutrality of money to be the obverse of the real balance effect, since other assumptions cause substitution effects.[8]

Recall that under the above assumptions a small increase in P_0 reduces wealth by $-(M^s/P_0^2) \, dP_0$ (if business holds no cash balances; see (4.10) and section 4.2). Now, if the price level increases by x percent (where x is small), then $dP_0 = xP_0$ and the effect on wealth is

$$- \frac{M^s}{P_0^2} \, dP_0 = - \frac{M^s}{P_0^2} x P_0 = - \frac{M^s}{P_0} x.$$

Suppose that, at the same time, both MH_0 and thus M^s were to increase by x percent by virtue of a once and for all increase in the number of rocks. This increases real wealth by $(M^s/P_0)\, x$. Thus, the effects on wealth of increasing M^s by x percent and P_0 by x percent cancel, $(M^s/P_0)\, x - (M^s/P_0)\, x = 0$, leaving unaffected the budget constraint (4.8) and hence wealth. Note that increasing MH_0 and M^s by x percent always increases wealth by $(M^s/P_0)\, x$; however, increasing P_0 by x percent necessarily changes wealth by $(M^s/P_0)\, x$ (so that two effects on wealth cancel) only if price expectations are unit elastic.

Neutrality of money implies that a doubling of the money supply induces only a doubling of all prices. In Hicksian theory, the effects of economic changes on excess demands are divided into wealth and substitution effects. If there are neither wealth nor substitution effects, there are no effects on demands, supplies, excess demands, or equilibrium, exactly as neutrality requires. As just shown, under appropriate assumptions of unitary elasticity of expectations, the wealth effect is zero when both P_0 and the money supply increase by x percent at the same time. Equilibrium is invariant, however, only if there are also no substitution effects. Substitution effects arise if and only if some relative price changes. If w_0 varies proportionately with P_0, the current real wage rate is unaffected. If price and wage expectations are all exactly unit elastic, no intertemporal relative price or wage changes will occur, as long as expected interest rates remain constant. What concerns the decision-maker is relative discounted prices; if all prices vary proportionately with P_0 (unit-elastic price and wage expectations) and if no expected interest rate changes, then all relative discounted prices are unaffected. Hence, there are no substitution effects and no wealth effects, and the real equilibrium is unaffected.

Many discussions treat unit-elastic price and wage expectations (usually only the special case of static expectations is considered) as necessary just in order to avoid substitution effects.[9] However, if the rise in price is to change wealth by $-(M^s/P)\, x$ and exactly offset the change in wealth due to the x percent increase in M^s, a sufficient condition is that all price and wage expectations are unit elastic, as discussed in section 4.2.

Note in particular that money is neutral here under the same conditions as used to derive the change in wealth in (4.9). This implies that money can be neutral whether or not (a) price expectations are consistent ($\Delta P_t/P$ and $\Delta w_t/w$ need not equal $\Delta \widetilde{P}_t/P$ and $\Delta \widetilde{w}_t/w$), or (b) quantity expectations are consistent (N_t^d need not equal N_t^s, $C_t^d + \Delta K_t^d$ need not equal Y_t^s), or (c) expected future prices equal current prices ($\Delta P_t/P$ and $\Delta \widetilde{P}_t/P$ need not equal zero), or (d) price and wage expectations are static (though they must be unit elastic).

Suppose that the system is in intertemporal equilibrium, with correctly anticipated prices and market-clearing quantities, and suppose that prices vary over time. A necessary condition for the neutrality of money is that this once and for all doubling of the money supply and current prices does not affect expected rates of inflation. Clearly, the neutrality of money has nothing whatsoever to do with a constant time path of prices. Just as clearly, ΔK_t need not equal zero. Neutrality is consistent with real growth and with varying absolute and relative prices over time. It is worthwhile to stress the independence of neutrality from the assumptions of stationarity, no production and no price changes over time (either expected or actual), for many economists either explicitly claim or give the impression that some or all of these unnecessary assumptions are required for neutrality.[10]

Determinacy of the Price Level

Determinacy is typically discussed (Patinkin, 1965) by supposing that the economy is initially at an equilibrium and asking whether an increase in P_0 would create non-zero excess demands that would then tend to drive price back to its initial value (whether price gets there being a question of stability). Usual discussions rely on the real balance effect as in (4.9) to argue that the rise in price reduces wealth and hence must affect demand for output or bonds (the supply of labor is typically assumed not to be affected), causing non-zero excess demands in these markets.

If there is a price-induced effect on wealth, this must affect some current market. If it affects only the current demand for real balances, then the demand and supply of real balances rise equally here and the excess demand for money remains equal to zero, as do all other excess demands. Hence, the rise in the price level sets up no non-zero excess demands in this case. This is why determinacy is typically viewed as requiring that the real balance effect enter some non-money market in models such as this.

Clearly the usual sort of determinacy argument can be made in the present model. However, some qualifications are appropriate. If price and wage expectations are not unit elastic, the rise in P_0 can cause substitution effects that conceivably just offset the real balance effect in the output and bond markets. Beyond this, there exist other effects that have been overlooked in discussions of determinacy. The following section provides an introduction to these effects, and later chapters discuss them extensively.

4.4 The Case Where Business Holds Money Balances – A Preliminary Look at the Initial-Condition Effect

The analysis up to this point has assumed for convenience that business holds no money balances. This section introduces business money holdings and alters the conventional price-induced effect on wealth by introducing an "initial-condition effect." Chapter 5 deals extensively with the initial-condition effect. In essence, both business and households accumulate cash balances during period $t-1$ in order to have real balances in period t for making transactions; an increase in the price level P_t reduces the adequacy of cash balances initially held, and hence affects behavior in t. This is reflected in the economy's price-induced effect on wealth when business holds cash balances, as discussed in this section; chapter 5 discusses in detail other aspects of the initial-condition effect.

The present value of dividends is given in (4.5) as

$$\sum_{t=0}^{\infty} \left\{ \frac{\widetilde{P}_t Y_t^s}{\Pi(1+i)} - \frac{\widetilde{w}_t N_t^d}{\Pi(1+i)} - \frac{\widetilde{P}_t \Delta K_t^d}{\Pi(1+i)} \right\} - \sum_{t=1}^{\infty} \left\{ \frac{i_t \widetilde{P}_t \text{MB}_t / \widetilde{P}_t}{\Pi(1+i)} \right\} + \text{MB}_0.$$

When the expression for dividends (4.5) is inserted into the household budget constraint (4.3) and divided by P_0, the budget constraint says that

$$\sum_{t=0}^{\infty} \left\{ \frac{w_t}{P_0} \frac{N_t^s}{\Pi(1+i)} + \frac{\widetilde{P}_t}{P_0} \frac{Y_t^s - \Delta K_t^d}{\Pi(1+i)} - \frac{\widetilde{w}_t}{P_0} \frac{N_t^d}{\Pi(1+i)} \right.$$

$$\left. - \frac{P_t}{P_0} \frac{C_t^d}{\Pi(1+i)} \right\} - \sum_{t=1}^{\infty} \left\{ \frac{i_t P_t \text{MH}_t / P_t}{P_0 \Pi(1+i)} + \frac{i_t \widetilde{P}_t \text{MB}_t / \widetilde{P}_t}{P_0 \Pi(1+i)} \right\}$$

$$+ \frac{\text{MH}_0 + \text{MB}_0}{P_0} \tag{4.12}$$

must be greater than or equal to zero. Expression (4.12) in turn can be written as

$$\sum_{t=0}^{\infty} \left\{ \frac{w_0}{P_0} \frac{\Pi(1 + \Delta w/w)}{\Pi(1+i)} N_t^s + \frac{\Pi(1 + \Delta \widetilde{P}/P)}{\Pi(1+i)} (Y_t^s - \Delta K_t^d) \right.$$

$$\left. - \frac{w_0}{P_0} \frac{\Pi(1 + \Delta \widetilde{w}/w)}{\Pi(1+i)} N_t^d - \frac{\Pi(1 + \Delta P/P)}{\Pi(1+i)} C_t^d \right\}$$

$$- \sum_{t=1}^{\infty} \left\{ \frac{\Pi(1 + \Delta P/P)}{\Pi(1+i)} i_t \, \text{mh}_t + \frac{\Pi(1 + \Delta \widetilde{P}/P)}{\Pi(1+i)} i_t \, \text{mb}_t \right\}$$

$$+ \frac{\text{MH}_0 + \text{MB}_0}{P_0}, \tag{4.13}$$

where mh_t and mb_t are respectively household and business planned real balances in period t in terms of that period's prices. Since all of the giant rocks must currently be held, $\text{MH}_0 + \text{MB}_0 \equiv M^s$ as an accounting requirement.

To investigate the price-induced effect on wealth, hold constant all interest rates and inflation rates, as well as w_0/P_0, and differentiate (4.13) with respect to P_0 to give

$$-\frac{M^s}{P_0^2} - \frac{\partial Y_0^s}{\partial (MB_0/P_0)} \frac{MB_0}{P_0^2}, \qquad (4.14)$$

which uses the fact that $MH_0 + MB_0 \equiv M^s$. Expression (4.14) makes use of the fact that, with no change in any intertemporal relative price, the business marginal conditions (4.6) imply no change in Y_t^s, N_t^d, K_t^d, mb_t for $t \geq 1$, and hence no change in the real present value of dividends for $t \geq 1$. Period 0, however, is different, because both K_0 and MB_0 are pre-determined by decisions taken before period 0. An increase in P_0 affects Div_0 in two ways. First, in order to hold mb_1 constant, business must reduce Div_0 to increase its money accumulation to offset the higher price level. Secondly, with a reduced MB_0/P_0, business alters its production. The first influence shows up as part of $-M^s/P_0^2$ in the price-induced effect on wealth (4.14) while the second influence is precisely the term $-\{\partial Y_0^s/\partial (MB_0/P_0)\} MB_0/P_0^2$ in (4.14). The latter term is omitted in (4.9) because of the assumption used there that businesses hold no cash balances.

It is worthwhile to explore how the second term in (4.14) arises. Assuming that the economy is at the start of period 0, the only period 0 variable which business can control now is N_0^d. A present value maximum requires

$$P_0 \frac{\partial Y_0^s}{\partial N_0^d} - w_0 = 0,$$

but not that the capital stock and real balance marginal conditions in (4.6) hold for $t = 0$, since these are determined by decisions prior to $t = 0$. When P_0 increases and w_0 rises proportionately, the change in $Y_0^s - (w_0/P_0) N_0^d - \Delta K_0^d$ is

$$\frac{\partial Y_0^s}{\partial (MB_0/P_0)} \frac{d(MB_0/P_0)}{dP_0} + \frac{\partial Y_0^s}{\partial N_0^d} \frac{dN_0^d}{dP_0} - \frac{w_0}{P_0} \frac{dN_0^d}{dP_0}$$

$$= -\frac{\partial Y_0^s}{\partial (MB_0/P_0)} \frac{MB_0}{P_0^2} + \left\{ \frac{\partial Y_0^s}{\partial N_0^d} - \frac{w_0}{P_0} \right\} \frac{dN_0^d}{dP_0}.$$

This reduces to $-\{\partial Y_0^s/\partial (MB_0/P_0)\} MB_0/P_0^2$ since

$$\frac{\partial Y_0^s}{\partial N_0^d} - \frac{w_0}{P_0} = 0$$

at the present value maximum. Earlier sections assumed that the business sector held no cash balances. Now, however, with $MB_0 > 0$, $d(MB_0/P_0)/$

$dP_0 < 0$ and $\partial Y_0^s / \partial (\mathrm{MB}_0/P_0) > 0$, $-\{\partial Y_0^s / \partial (\mathrm{MB}_0/P_0)\}\, \mathrm{MB}_0/P_0^2 < 0$.

Expression (4.14) differs from the usual result (for example, Patinkin, 1965) by including the term

$$-\frac{\partial Y_0^s}{\partial (\mathrm{MB}_0/P_0)}\,\frac{\mathrm{MB}_0}{P_0^2}. \tag{4.15}$$

(4.15) exists for two reasons. First, the business sector marginal conditions (4.6) assume that Y_t^s ($t \geqslant 0$) depends on MB_t/P_t; thus the derivative $\partial Y_0^s / \partial (\mathrm{MB}_0/P_0)$ is positive unless business has unintentionally become *ex post* satiated in period 0 real balances. Second, only this one derivative is included because MB_0/P_0 is the only quantity of business real balances mb_t that business cannot control in period 0. Thus, in period 0, the firm can still plan on satisfying the conditions for a present value maximum for $t \geqslant 1$ and all conditions are satisfied by the same values of N_t^d, K_t^d and MB_t/P_t as before no matter what P_0 is.

If P_0 is initially equal to the value business expected, then $\partial Y_0^s / \partial (\mathrm{MB}_0/P_0)$ equals i_0 from the business marginal conditions (4.6). Hence the value $-\{\partial Y_0^s / \partial (\mathrm{MB}_0/P_0)\}\, \mathrm{MB}_0/P_0^2$ in (4.15) equals $-i_0 \mathrm{MB}_0/P_0^2$. Thus, the expression (4.14) becomes

$$-\frac{M^s}{P_0^2} - \frac{\partial Y_0^s}{\partial (\mathrm{MB}_0/P_0)}\,\frac{\mathrm{MB}_0}{P_0^2} = -\frac{\mathrm{MH}_0}{P_0^2} - \frac{\mathrm{MB}_0}{P_0^2} - i_0\,\frac{\mathrm{MB}_0}{P_0^2}$$

$$= -\frac{\mathrm{MH}_0}{P_0^2} - (1 + i_0)\,\frac{\mathrm{MB}_0}{P_0^2}.$$

In other words, taking account of the wealth implications of the business sector's initial-condition effect will raise the contribution of MB_0 to the price-induced effect on wealth by a percentage equal to the interest rate i_0. Thus, if $i_0 = 0.05$ or is 5 percent, the price-induced effect on wealth through business money holdings is 5 percent larger than otherwise due to the business sector's initial-condition effect.

The importance of this initial-condition effect is not just that it modifies the conventional price-induced effect on wealth. Rather, it also provides a stabilizing effect on the economy even in the absence of any wealth effect. A brief sketch of the reasoning follows, to be taken up in much greater detail in chapters 5 and 6. Suppose that M^s, instead of being fixed, varies proportionally with P_0. That is, if P_0 doubles, then some time during period 0 (but not at its beginning) the economy will be granted a "gift from the gods" of additional money equal to the original M^s. Thus, there is no net effect on wealth, as it is conventionally considered. However, since initial money holdings are not doubled, the business sector cannot fully carry out its plans, Y_0 falls and through this channel wealth is reduced.

This reduction in wealth, as well as the fall in Y_0, sets up excess demands that, with appropriate stability conditions, will push the economy back to its initial equilibrium. (Households will also be unable to carry out their prior plans, as discussed in chapter 5.)

Finally, the business sector initial-condition effect plays two roles, as do all of the initial-condition effects introduced in later chapters. First, this initial-condition effect is a part of the price-induced effect on wealth. But, second, independent of this role, this initial-condition effect alters current real output. Thus, supposing that the price-induced effect on wealth were zero, this initial-condition effect would still affect the economy if price were to rise.

Why has previous literature overlooked this initial-condition effect? Very little attention has been paid to firms' optimizing conditions in discussions of the price-induced effect on wealth. Amazingly, this is true both of non-financial firms as well as of banks, as seen in chapters 6 and 7.

4.5 Distribution Effects: Creators of the Money Stock

The Assumption of No Distribution Effects Across the Household and Business Sectors

The change in wealth in (4.9) is the price-induced effect on wealth under the assumption that business holds no money balances. Alternatively, if $MB > 0$, the change in wealth is still that in (4.9) if $- \{\partial Y_0^s / \partial (MB_0/P_0)\}$ MB_0/P_0^2 is tentatively neglected. The induced change in household demand for output is the marginal propensity to consume out of wealth multiplied by $- M^s/P_0^2$. Investment is unaffected in the simple model used here with the production function in section 4.1 above, since all K_t^d are unaffected under the assumption of constant expected interest rates and unit-elastic expectations. Hence the change in household consumption demand is the total effect on private sector demand for output when P_0 rises (see chapter 5 for the total effect on private sector excess demand).

This result is important because it removes any need for postulating a lack of distribution effects between the business and household sectors as Patinkin (1965) and Gurley and Shaw (1960) do. Patinkin's (1965) book can most favorably be taken as referring to Yap-Island money. He assumes that consumption demand depends *inter alia* on household sector real balances, and investment demand depends on businesses' real balances. Total private demand for output is taken to depend on the sum of business and household real balances, on the assumption that any redistribution of balances between sectors causes equal and offsetting changes in the two demands. The real balance effect is then $-1/P_0^2$ multiplied by total private money holdings.

The conventional monetary analysis is really quite strange. It refers to distribution effects between sectors, whereas all distribution effects in the Hicksian analysis of chapter 3 were among consumers. More importantly, it seems to imply that the household sector does not own the business sector. However, the peculiar assumption of no redistribution effects across the household and business sectors is not necessary in the approach adopted here, where the Yap-Island price-induced effect on wealth is $-M^s/P_0^2$ however M^s is divided between the two sectors. Intuitively, if P_0 increases and the real value of dividends is taken as constant, the household sector would have to receive a wealth transfer of MH_0/P_0^2 to make up for the price-induced fall in its wealth. However, real dividends are not constant; a price rise means that business will have to reduce its current real dividends by MB_0/P_0^2 to rebuild its real balances for the next period. Thus, the household sector is poorer by $MH_0/P_0^2 + MB_0/P_0^2 \equiv M^s/P_0^2$.

Does It Matter Who Created Yap-Island Money?

Another question in the literature is whether it matters who creates money (see Pesek and Saving, 1967; Johnson, 1969). An advantage of the current discussion of "giant rocks used as money" is that it clearly does not matter how they first got there. As becomes clear by contrast to chapter 5 below, what really matters is the fact that the stock cannot and will not be augmented. There is no analytical difference between gods creating the rocks in some previous period and men bringing them from a distant land. And it does not matter if the men who brought them were foreigners, government officials (placed in this governmentless model just for this one purpose), or businessmen (whether engaged in financial or non-financial business). Further, since distribution effects are ignored, it does not matter whether these rocks were initially put in circulation by just giving them to the populace (a gift if from the gods, a transfer payment if from government or business), or were sold to the general public – bygones are bygones.[11] Thus, labeling the rocks as commodity money if created by gods, as outside money if created by government and given as transfer payments, or as inside money if government sold them for assets, or labeling them as bank money (or inside money) if created by private business, is to create distinctions of no analytical use here. Chapters 6 and 7 return to this issue.

4.6 Quantitative Importance of the Price-Induced Effect
on Wealth

This section discusses the size of the price-induced effect on wealth (neglecting initial-condition effects) and its quantitative importance in various markets in terms of explaining movements in the economy. In the Yap-Island economy discussed above, the price-induced effect on wealth has the same value as found in conventional discussions of the real balance effect, depending only on the current stock of outside money. In later chapters, the price-induced effect on wealth will depend on future stocks of government money and under certain conditions on bank money, including future bank money.

The 1950s and 1960s saw a great deal of discussion of the real balance effect, particularly as it showed up in the aggregate demand for output. Overall, the real balance effect was often dismissed, or its importance minimized, by pointing to its small magnitude and its relatively unimportant role in the output market. Further, it was sometimes argued that effects of expectations could easily overwhelm the real balance effect. In the rational expectations revolution of the 1970s, the price-induced effect on wealth was virtually ignored. Nevertheless, the effect is implicit in these rational expectations models and plays a major role in adjustment of output and price, though the effect of wealth changes in the output market is of minor importance. Even in such models, the issue of badly behaved expectations remains, and seems to be a problem quite independent of the size of the price-induced effect on wealth.

Size of the Real Balance Effect and its Importance in the Output Market

The size of the real balance effect arose as an issue even in the first articles on the effect by Pigou (1943). Pigou argued that if aggregate demand is less than full-employment real output, a fall in the price level will increase the real value of money balances and eventually close this gap. This argument was aimed at showing that in principle price level adjustments will lead to equilibrium (see chapter 2).

In such arguments, the money to which this effect applied was acknowledged to be the monetary base in a fiat money economy, or the stock of gold in the gold standard case. If the monetary base is, say, $150 billion, a halving of the price level is equivalent to an increase in the base of $150 billion. If the marginal propensity to consume out of this increase in wealth is one-third, aggregate demand rises by $50 billion. Suppose, however, that the gap between aggregate demand and full-employment output is 5 percent of the full-employment level of $3 trillion; thus, the gap is $150 billion. The price level would need to be halved twice to close the gap. This huge deflation, it was argued, would require a substantial amount of time to occur, and would lead to grave difficulties due to previously arranged contracts specified in money terms. Thus, for example, Pigou treated the real balance effect as a refutation of the early Keynesian argument that no equilibrium price level existed, rather than urging massive deflation to return to equilibrium.

Prices were often modeled as adjusting at a rate proportional to the excess demand for output (Patinkin, 1965). In turn, this made the speed of adjustment depend directly on the size of the real balance effect on aggregate demand. With a small real balance effect relative to the gap (as in the above example), the output market could take a long time to reach equilibrium.[12] The dynamics of market-clearing rational expectations models completely remove this as an issue, as discussed below.

Much attention was focused on the existence and size of a real balance effect in the output market, partly because this allowed money to have a direct role in the output market rather than just influencing the interest rate and thus the level of investment demand and in this way aggregate demand (as discussed in chapter 2). Nevertheless, it was explicitly recognized that determinacy of the price level really only required a real balance effect in some non-money market(s). For example, Patinkin (1965) discussed the case where there is no real balance effect in the output market but one in the bond market.

It is worthwhile pursuing the discussion of adjustment when the price-induced effect on wealth plays only a minor (or even no) role in the output market. The effect in the bond market still has a role in adjustment. Using the familiar IS–LM analysis, suppose that the economy is initially at an underemployment equilibrium at the IS–LM intersection at $Y_1 < \overline{Y}$ in figure 4.1. The BB curve shows Y, i combinations where the excess demand for bonds is zero; the BB curve has to run through the IS–LM intersection. (Figure 4.1 shows the BB curve with a negative slope on the reasonable assumption that an increase in Y raises the real excess demand for bonds; otherwise BB has a positive slope less than that of LM.) Since the sum of the values of the excess demands for output, money, and bonds must equal zero, analysis can use any two of the three curves. Typically, the BB curve is suppressed, but it is useful here to keep it in view. Assume that the money demand function is $\ell n(M^d/P) = b_0 + b_1 \ell n\, Y - b_2 \ell n\, i (b_1, b_2 > 0)$, as is used in very many Keynesian and rational expectations discussions. Note that this formulation assumes that there is no real balance effect in the demand for money. Now let the price level fall by 10

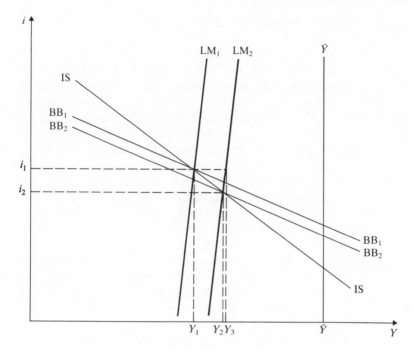

Figure 4.1 Price adjustment and the bond market

percent or the money stock rise by 10 percent. Assuming that $b_1 = 1$ or that the income elasticity of the demand for real balances is unity, this shifts the LM curve to the right by 10 percent at any i. If the LM curve is vertical ($b_2 = 0$), the new equilibrium Y must be 10 percent larger, at Y_3, no matter how the IS curve shifts due to the increase in real balances. That is, with a vertical LM curve equilibrium Y rises by 10 percent irrespective of the fraction of the increase in wealth that goes to an increase in the demand for output and no matter how large or small this increase in output demand is relative to initial real GNP. The adjustment mechanism that makes Y rise is the induced fall in the interest rate that moves the economy down along the IS curve.

Assume, however, that the LM curve is not vertical, and that there is no real balance effect in the output market so the IS curve does not shift. Then the new equilibrium is at Y_2. While $Y_2 < Y_3$, Y has risen substantially in the case drawn where there is, realistically, a relatively inelastic LM curve. It appears that the wealth effect has played no role in this adjustment in Y. The increase in real balances in the LM curve is a supply change and not an effect on wealth. By assumption, no effect on wealth enters the demand for output. The effect on wealth seems irrelevant to the adjustment process.

This, however, is a misimpression, as can be seen by carrying out the analysis with the IS and BB curves rather than the IS and LM curves. When M^s rises or P falls by 10 percent, real balances rise by 10 percent – an increase in wealth. However, by assumption this increase in wealth does not affect the demands for either output or money. Hence all of this increase in wealth must go to an increase in the demand for bonds. This shifts the BB curve down because i would have to fall at Y_1 to reduce the excess demand for bonds back to zero. In other words, the BB curve shifts down or to the left to BB_2, and the new IS–BB intersection is at Y_2.[13] Evidently, the increase in real balances plays a role as a wealth effect in the bond market in moving the economy to Y_2. Note that it does so, not by directly increasing the demand for output, but by raising the demand for bonds, bidding up the price of bonds and hence forcing the interest rate down, and by thus increasing the interest-sensitive demand for output and setting off a multiplier process in the output market. Thus, the price-induced effect on wealth works in a rather Keynesian way, as described in chapter 2, depending on interest rate linkages rather than on direct increases in demand for output.

If there is no wealth effect in the money demand function, a 10 percent rise in M^s or fall in P shifts the LM curve to the right by 10 percent, continuing to assume an income elasticity of demand for real balances of unity. If the LM curve is vertical, Y rises by 10 percent no matter how the increase in wealth affects output demand and shifts the IS curve. But with some elasticity of the LM curve, Y will rise more the greater the rightward shift in the IS curve. However, assuming that the monetary base is initially $150 billion, a 10 percent rise in M (or fall in P) is a $15 billion rise in wealth. Suppose that the marginal propensity to consume out of a current change in wealth is one-third, so output demand rises by $5 billion. In an economy with a $3 trillion GNP, aggregate demand increases by only 0.167 percent. If the multiplier is two (an estimate on the high end of the range), then the IS curve shifts to the right only by 0.333 percent. Clearly the real balance effect in the output market has to be of very secondary importance compared with the LM shift. In the conventional type of model analyzed here, the induced fall in the interest rate plays a very large role in the adjustment of output, with wealth effects having no additional effect if the LM curve is vertical. Even with an LM curve which is less than vertical but still relatively steep, real balance effects in the output market will have a much smaller comparative effect even if most of the real balance effect were to go to output rather than bonds.

Finally, suppose that the price-induced effect on wealth does enter the demand for money; say one-half of any wealth increase goes to raise the demand for real balances. Then the 10 percent increase in real balances is accompanied by a 5 percent increase in demand for them, and the LM curve shifts to the right by only 5 percent. The increase in *Y* is then smaller, being a maximum of 5 percent if LM is vertical. In terms of the BB curve, the more the increase in wealth goes to demand more money, the less to demand more bonds, and hence the smaller is the downward shift in the BB curve. Looked at either way, the power of the price-induced effect on wealth to move the system is reduced as more of the effect goes to the money market. In the limit, if all of the effect goes to the money market and none to either output or bonds, the rise in wealth does not affect any of the IS, LM, BB curves and hence does not affect the system; no fall in price or increase in the money supply can move the economy to $\overline{Y}$. This corresponds to the case where the price-induced effect on wealth does not affect either bond or output markets and hence the price level is indeterminate.

Destabilizing Expectations

In many of the pre-rational expectations discussions, it seemed plausible that expectations of inflation would depend on actual current and past inflation, as for example under adaptive expectations. Hence, if equilibrium required a fall in price, people would plausibly come to expect future deflation as they noticed actual deflation occurring. Thus, the fall in prices created two opposing effects. As prices fell, aggregate demand rose through the real balance effect in the output maket. But the falling price level caused people to expect higher deflation than otherwise, and this expectation likely led to a fall in aggregate demand.[14] Since a good deal of deflation might be required, people might come to expect so much deflation that the effect of such expectations dominated the real balance effect in the output market, leading to a fall rather than rise in aggregate demand. Hicks (1946) stressed this possibility in discussing how price expectations might be more than unit elastic, setting up explosive movements in the price level that would not lead to equilibrium but rather move the system farther away.

Rational Expectations Models

The size of the real balance effect and its role in the output market, and the issue of destabilizing price expectations, did not arise in the rational expectations models of the 1970s. Indeed, it was often explicitly assumed that there was no real balance effect in the output market (Sargent, 1973,

1976; Sargent and Wallace, 1975). These rational expectations models typically assumed that all markets adjust every period to equilibrium (Lucas, 1972, 1973; Sargent, 1973; Sargent and Wallace, 1975). In such models, the price level is at its market-clearing value in every period.

The only issue in these models concerning the price-induced effect on wealth is whether the price level is determinate, that is, whether a different price level would set up non-zero excess demands in at least some non-money markets (see section 4.3 above; chapter 5 discusses determinacy of the price level in some detail). A price-induced effect on wealth in the output market is not required for determinacy, as is well known (Patinkin, 1965), and little time was spent in these models in analyzing the real balance effect. In fact, these models often assume no real balance effect in the output market while adopting a money demand function that assures both determinacy of the price level and a real balance effect in the bond market. For example, take the conventional demand function for real balances, assumed above, $\ell n(M^d/P) = b_0 + b_1 \ell n\ Y - b_2 \ell n\ i$, where Y is real income and b_1, $b_2 > 0$. A given stock of money ensures that at given, equilibrium values of i, Y there is an equilibrium P; that is, changes in P cause $M^s/P \neq M^d/P$ and hence the price level is determinate. Of course, this means that the price-induced effect on wealth enters the current bond market as discussed above in connection with the BB curve, but the issue is not even raised in these models.

The speed of adjustment of the price level is not an issue in such models because they adopt a radically different approach to price dynamics from that of earlier discussions such as Patinkin's (1965), and typically assume market clearing in each period.

It is well known that rational expectations models can and very often will have at least some equilibrium time paths that are explosive, i.e. diverge from the initial steady-state equilibrium. While there is some work in the literature on conditions that would rule out divergent time paths (Brock, 1975; Obstfeld and Rogoff, 1983), the usual practice is simply to choose only convergent time paths and ignore the rest. Thus, rational expectations models cannot be said to have removed the problem of explosive time paths based on expectations. Note that the question in the earlier literature was whether from a disequilibrium position the system would converge to equilibrium. In market-clearing rational expectations models, the system is always in equilibrium, but the question is whether over time the system converges to a steady state.

In equilibrium models, and hence in those rational expectations models that assume equilibrium in every period, the size of the real balance effect might well not be much of an issue in analyzing many shocks, whether the effect is in the output market or other markets. Consider an economy where the exogenous shock is a decrease in the supply of energy. The change in all endogenous variables (prices, quantities, interest rates) between the two equilibria can be analyzed and measured quantitatively by the shock plus wealth and substitution effects, as in chapter 3, section 3.1. It could well be that the price-induced effect on wealth is not particularly influential in quantitative terms relative to other effects, and that in giving a rough description of the move from one equilibrium to another this effect could be omitted without causing substantial quantitative error. However, there still remains the role of the price-induced effect on wealth in rendering the (new) price level determinate (rather than playing a major role in the transition between equilibria) and this role might well involve only relatively small effects.

Does Equilibration Require Large Changes in the Price Level?

In considering the magnitude of the real balance effect, it is not very fruitful to think in terms of how far the price level would have to fall in order by itself to make aggregate demand equal full-employment real output, because there are other equilibrating effects. Consider a decline in current consumption demand matched by an increase in saving to finance increased future consumption, with the increased saving currently devoted to accumulating bonds. In the output market, the dominant equilibrating move will very likely be a rise in the level of investment. This will occur through better prospects for future sales inherent in the assumed change in consumption patterns, in combination with an induced fall in the interest rate. With a lower interest rate, the demand for real balances is larger if the demand for real balances displays any interest sensitivity, so the price level falls to generate a larger stock of real balances. It is likely that this induced increase in the stock of real balances has some positive wealth effect on aggregate demand, but the effect may be quite small compared with the others discussed.

Figure 4.2 illustrates the argument in the familiar IS–LM apparatus. Initial equilibrium is at the full-employment level of output $\overline{Y}$ at the IS–LM intersection with the interest rate i_1 and price level P_1. The decrease in consumption demand shifts IS_1 to IS_2. If this is all that happens, P_1 must fall to run the LM curve through the IS_2–$\overline{Y}$ intersection.[15] If the prospect of increased sales raises investment demand, as should happen if business foresees increased future consumption demand, IS falls only to IS_3 and the LM curve and P need not fall as far. Further, if aggregate demand depends on real balances, the rise in M^s/P due to the fall in P will shift IS_3 to IS_4, so the LM curve and P fall less than otherwise. It may be that the shift from IS_3 to IS_4 is much less important than any of the other IS shifts; and it may

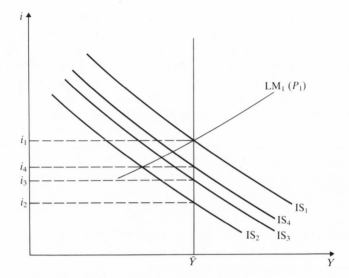

Figure 4.2 How far must the price level fall?

be that the price-induced shift from IS$_3$ to IS$_4$ is much less important quantitatively than the fall in i from i_1 to i_4. But this does not affect the determinacy of the price level. Indeed, the complete absence from the output market of the price-induced effect on wealth has the effect of eliminating the shift from IS$_3$ to IS$_4$, but has no qualitative effect on the analysis. This can be put more strongly. If the demand for real balances is interest inelastic, P does not change at all, there is no actual price-induced effect on wealth (though there might be if P were to change) and hence no shift from IS$_3$ to IS$_4$, and all of the burden of the adjustment is thrown on the interest rate.

The upshot is this. In the simple models discussed in this section, there must exist some sort of price-induced effect on wealth in order to render the price level determinate. However, this effect can be quite small in the output market. The effect will play a role in the adjustment of the system from one equilibrium to another when the system is disturbed, but for some disturbances the role may be trivial relative to other effects. Destabilizing expectations might lead to explosive movements away from equilibrium in older analyses. In rational expectations models, explosive movements are usually not a concern. This, however, is due more to defining them away rather than demonstrating analytically their unimportance.

NOTES

1 This is Einzig's (1949) view, but Herskovitz (1965) specifically and emphatically denies it. For analytical purposes, it does not matter that this description is hotly disputed. It has crept into textbooks as "fact" (see Haines, 1966).
2 In fact, the rocks apparently originally got to Yap by native boats from other islands. The supply seemed not to be much augmented over time, however.
3 See, for example, Brock (1975).
4 This assumption of a homogeneous output which can either be consumed or added to the stock of capital, and which when used as capital is eternal and non-wasting, is merely for convenience and to bring the analysis closer to the usual macro model. In fact, this chapter's results are perfectly valid in a model in which various types of capital depreciate at an exogenous rate or even where the firm partly controls the rate of depreciation through intensity of use and maintenance programs. Since this essay's results do not depend on aggregation over goods and factors, units of capital in different states of repair can be treated as different factors, and different rates of depreciation can be treated as yielding different output in a multiple-output process. See Haavelmo (1960) and Kuenne (1963). See also Keynes's (1936) discussion of user cost and Sweeney's (1974) treatment of depreciation as a factor of production.
5 For the fundamental development of the composite good theorem, see Hicks (1946, Mathematical Appendix). Hicks uses extensively the theorem that any set of goods whose relative prices do not vary can be treated as a single good.
6 See Patinkin (1965, pp. 140-4, especially 144n).
7 It is hard to find an explicit and correct statement of the dependence of the real balance effect on changes in expected future prices. Patinkin (1965) assumes expected equal future prices "for convenience." By the time he comes to discuss neutrality and the real balance effect (pp. 444ff) the assumption of static expectations is no longer explicit. Though Patinkin admits that the elasticity of expectations may affect the price-induced effect on wealth, he argues that the direction of change is ambiguous (p. 143).

   Saving (1970) discusses the real balance effect in a system where all price expectations are implicitly assumed to be static.
8 For example, if $\Delta w_t / w = \Delta \tilde{w}_t / w$ and $N_t^d = N_t^s$ ($t \geq 1$), equal increases in $\Delta w_t / w$ and $\Delta \tilde{w}_t / w$ create no additional impact on wealth if they occur with changes in P_0 but they do create substitution effects. For neutrality, an increase in M_0^s accompanied by a proportionate increase in P_0 and w_0 must have no wealth effect and no substitution effects.
9 For an example of such an erroneous treatment of the role of expectations, see Gurley and Shaw, and also Enthoven's (1960) mathematical appendix to their book.
10 For example, Enthoven (1960), Gurley and Shaw (1960), Patinkin (1965), Pesek and Saving (1967), Saving (1970).
11 If placed in circulation by businessmen in return for other assets, the shuffling

of these other assets among holders can only create redistribution effects among firm-owners which are ignored here. If placed in circulation by a government created only for one period for this purpose, any assets collected in exchange for the rocks must be redistributed as transfer payments (otherwise government is ongoing), and this reshuffling of other assets is ignored as a distribution effect among households.

12 Consider a simple illustration of this line of reasoning, based on Patinkin (1965). Let the time rate of change of price $\dot{P}$ depend on the positive constant α times the excess demand for output $\text{ExD}Q$, or $\dot{P} = \alpha \text{ExD}Q$ ($\ldots$, M^s/P, $\ldots$), where $\text{ExD}Q$ depends on real balances M^s/P. Linearizing the equation, local stability requires that the single root, $-\alpha\{\partial \text{ExD}Q/ \partial(M^s/P)\}$ M^s/P^2 (evaluated at equilibrium), be negative; this will be so if $\partial \text{ExD}Q/\partial(M^s/P) > 0$, as is so if an increase in real balances raises consumption demand. Further, the larger is $\partial \text{ExD}Q/\partial(M^s/P)$, the faster is the convergence to equilibrium (given α).

13 As mentioned above, the BB curve has a negative or positive slope as the real excess demand for bonds rises or falls with an increase in Y. In either case, an increase in real balances shifts down the BB curve. With a negative slope for BB, this downward shift is also a leftward shift, as the text describes. With a positive BB slope, the downward shift is a rightward shift. In either case, the equilibrium Y rises.

14 The price level in period 1 falls relative to current prices, or P_1/P_0 falls. However, P_2/P_1, P_3/P_2, etc. also fall. Consequently, there are many relative price changes and substitution effects, and no guarantee they all work against current demand. However, it seems very plausible that current demand will fall.

15 In a model with separate consumption and investment goods, it is clear that there may be a substantial period when resources are shifted from consumer to investment goods industries. A fall in i to i_2 would not keep full employment as judged by steady-state levels.

5

Government Fiat Money, the Price-Induced Effect on Wealth, and the Initial-Condition Effect

As noted in chapter 4, the distinctive feature of Yap-Island money is its fixed quantity. This is distinctly not the case with government fiat money in the real world. The analytical step after Yap-Island money is to consider a single type of money which is variable in quantity in response to government decisions and which can be used to finance government activity. In this chapter, the government sector purchases goods and services and makes transfer payments, financing these activities by taxation, bond sales, and money issue.

This chapter shows that the value of the price-induced effect on wealth found in chapter 4, the conventional value, is a very special case. In fact, the price-induced effect on wealth can even equal zero. Ever since Patinkin's (1956, 1965) analysis, a negative price-induced effect on wealth has been viewed as a necessary condition for a determinate equilibrium price level, at least in the case where there is a zero net supply of government bonds outstanding. However, this chapter introduces the "initial-condition effect," and shows how this effect can make the price level determinate even in the absence of a price-induced effect on wealth. The initial-condition effect says that an increase in the current period's price level reduces the real value of the money stock initially on hand and must affect private sector behavior. Hence, even if an arbitrary change in the initial price level sets up no corrective change through substitution or wealth effects, the initial-condition effect will generally cause non-zero current-period excess demands and, in terms of usual arguments for price level determinacy, cause the current period's price level to return to its initial equilibrium value.

Section 5.1 introduces the government sector, which finances its deficits by issuing money or selling bonds. The household sector's net taxes equal government spending less both money issue and the difference between the value of government's bond sales and its current interest payments and redemptions. When the government's budget constraint is substituted into the household sector's, initial holdings of government bonds cancel out, and government bonds do not enter the price-induced effect on wealth. The size of the price-induced effect on wealth depends crucially on the elasticity of future money stocks with respect to the current price level. At one extreme, the money stock is constant over time (Yap-Island money, as in chapter 4), and the price-induced effect on wealth has the conventional value $- M_0^s/P_0^2$. Alternatively, the future money stocks may be unit elastic relative to the current price level, yielding a price-induced effect on wealth of zero. Appendix 5B discusses some intermediate cases of the price-induced effect on wealth in models of money and growth.

The possibility of a price-induced effect on wealth with a zero value may be alarming, since current monetary theory has made a negative real balance effect the *sine qua non* for a determinate price level, at least in worlds where government bonds are not net wealth. Section 5.2 shows that the "initial-condition effect" can yield determinacy even in the absence of a negative price-induced effect on wealth. The initial-condition effect relies on the fact that a rise in the price level reduces the adequacy of initial nominal balances in carrying out planned real transactions in the current period; hence, some current plans will very likely change, creating non-zero excess demands and forcing the price level back to its initial value. While section 5.2 shows that a negative price-induced effect on wealth is not necessary to render the price level determinate, Appendix 5A shows that it is also not sufficient.

This essay adopts the common assumption that money balances for use this period must be accumulated in the previous period. An alternative and frequently used assumption is that assets are freely traded at the start of the period, on "market day" in Hicks's (1946) "weeks." Section 5.3 shows that the price level is still determinate in the case where this period's money balances are accumulated at the very start of this period.

The final three sections of this chapter discuss some debates in monetary theory. Section 5.4 discusses the common assertion that the real balance effect is simply a distribution effect and hence the price level is determinate only by an adventitious historical or institutional quirk. Section 5.5 discusses whether non-interest-bearing money is a part of government liabilities, or rather what interpretation should be put on this view. Section 5.6 analyzes the assumption used in this essay that the household sector is kept informed of the time path of its tax liabilities.

5.1 Government, Government Money, and the Price-Induced Effect on Wealth

This section examines the behavior of the government sector and shows how government decisions affect the household sector's budget constraint. When the initial price level rises, government may respond by issuing more money in the current or future periods. As a result, the price-induced effect on wealth takes on its conventional value only as a special case.

The Government Sector's Budget Constraint

The government's expected budget constraint for any period t is

$$\underset{\sim}{P_t} G_t - T_t = \Delta M_t^s + P_{b,t} V_{t+1}^s - V_t^s, \tag{5.1}$$

where $\underset{\sim}{P_t}$ is the price level government expects in period t, G_t is its planned purchases of real goods and services in that period,[1] T_t is its planned taxation net of nominal transfer payments but exclusive of interest payments, ΔM_t^s its new issue of fiat dollars, V_{t+1}^s its sales of bonds in t (the number of its bonds that will come due in period $t + 1$), and V_t^s the number of bonds it sold last period and must now redeem for \$1 each.

As in chapter 4, assume that the world goes on forever. Further, assume explicitly that government plans eventually to pay the interest and principal on its debt by taxation rather than simply rolling over the debt forever and paying any interest by issuing new debt. This assumption implies that government bonds are not net wealth and thus requires some justification; chapter 8 discusses this assumption in detail. Then, the government's budget constraint in present value terms is

$$\sum_{t=0}^{\infty} \frac{\underset{\sim}{P_t} G_t}{\Pi(1+i)} - \sum_{t=0}^{\infty} \frac{T_t}{\Pi(1+i)} = \sum_{t=0}^{\infty} \frac{\Delta M_t^s}{\Pi(1+i)} - V_0^s.$$

This says that the present value of government expenditures less net taxation is financed by the present value of money supply issuance less the value of initially outstanding government debt V_0^s that must be retired. Alternatively, the government budget constraint can be written as

$$\sum_{t=0}^{\infty} \frac{\underset{\sim}{P_t} G_t}{\Pi(1+i)} - \sum_{t=0}^{\infty} \frac{T_t}{\Pi(1+i)} = \sum_{t=1}^{\infty} \frac{i_t M_t^s}{\Pi(1+i)} - M_0^s - V_0^s, \tag{5.2}$$

which makes use of the discussion around (4.3). Notice that if $M_t^s = M_0^s$ for all $t \geqslant 0$, then $\sum_{t=1}^{\infty} \{i_t M_t^s / \Pi(1+i)\} = M_0^s$ and all the money supply terms in (5.2) drop out. This is just a reflection of the fact that money supply terms have to drop out if all $\Delta M_t^s = 0$, as must be so if $M_t^s = M_0^s$ for all $t \geq 0$.

The terms $\Sigma_{t=1}^{\infty} \{i_t M_t^s / \Pi(1+i)\} - M_0^s$ replace $\Sigma_{t=0}^{\infty} \{\Delta M_t^s / \Pi(1+i)\}$ in the government's budget constraint. The interpretation of $\Sigma_{t=0}^{\infty}$ $\{\Delta M_t^s / \Pi(1+i)\}$ as the present value of money issuance reducing the present value of taxation is clear. Alternatively, think of the government as renting to the public each period the use of money stock M_t^s at the rental rate i_t. The present value of the rent is $\Sigma_{t=1}^{\infty} \{i_t M_t^s / \Pi(1+i)\}$. From this must be subtracted the value of the money stock M_0^s already outstanding that the public owns.

Government is viewed as setting G_t for all periods and financing its expenditures with taxation and money issuance (since ultimately bonds are redeemed through the two channels). Thus, given G_t, a change in the price level must induce changes in T_t or M_t^s or both.

The Household Sector's Budget Constraint

With the introduction of the government sector, households must now pay taxes, so $\Sigma \{T_t / \Pi(1+i)\}$ enters the household sector's budget constraint. This constraint now says that

$$\sum_{t=0}^{\infty} \left\{ \frac{w_t N_t^s}{\Pi(1+i)} + \frac{\text{Div}_t}{\Pi(1+i)} - \frac{T_t}{\Pi(1+i)} - \frac{P_t C_t^d}{\Pi(1+i)} \right\}$$

$$- \sum_{t=1}^{\infty} \frac{i_t \text{MH}_t}{\Pi(1+i)} + \text{MH}_0 + V_0 \qquad (5.3)$$

must exceed or equal zero. Substituting in the values that government and business give for $\Sigma_{t=0}^{\infty} \{T_t / \Pi(1+i)\}$ and $\Sigma_{t=0}^{\infty} \{\text{Div}_t / \Pi(1+i)\}$ from (5.2) and (4.5), the household sector constraint (5.3) becomes

$$\sum_{t=0}^{\infty} \left\{ \frac{w_t N_t^s}{\Pi(1+i)} + \frac{\widetilde{P}_t(Y_t^s - \Delta K_t^d)}{\Pi(1+i)} - \frac{\widetilde{w}_t N_t^d}{\Pi(1+i)} - \frac{P_t C_t^d}{\Pi(1+i)} - \frac{\underaccent{\tilde}{P}_t G_t}{\Pi(1+i)} \right\}$$

$$- \sum_{t=1}^{\infty} \frac{i_t (\text{MH}_t + \text{MB}_t - M_t^s)}{\Pi(1+i)} \qquad (5.4)$$

which must exceed or equal zero. Expression (5.4) shows that all outstanding government bonds are held by the private sector and hence $V_0 - V_0^s = 0$; further, the sum of private sector current money holdings equals government money outstanding, or $\text{MH}_0 + \text{MB}_0 - M_0^s = 0$.

These cancellations are not economic implications but arise from this system's accounting identities. Note that this substitution of business and government budget constraints into the household sector's constraint is merely the multi-period analog of what is done to find Walras's law in the one-period case (see chapter 3, section 3.3).

Finally, divide (5.4) by P_0 to give the household sector budget constraint in real terms from the point of view of period 0, or

$$
\sum_{t=0}^{\infty} \left\{ \frac{w_0}{P_0} \frac{\Pi(1 + \Delta w/w)}{\Pi(1+i)} N_t^s - \frac{w_0}{P_0} \frac{\Pi(1 + \Delta \widetilde{w}/w)}{\Pi(1+i)} N_t^d \right.
$$

$$
+ \frac{\Pi(1 + \Delta \widetilde{P}/P)}{\Pi(1+i)} (Y_t^s - \Delta K_t^d) - \frac{\Pi(1 + \Delta P/P)}{\Pi(1+i)} C_t^d
$$

$$
\left. - \frac{\Pi(1 + \Delta P/P)}{\Pi(1+i)} G_t \right\} - \sum_{t=1}^{\infty} \frac{\Pi(1 + \Delta P/P)}{\Pi(1+i)} i_t \, \mathrm{mh}_t
$$

$$
- \sum_{t=1}^{\infty} \frac{\Pi(1 + \Delta \widetilde{P}/P)}{\Pi(1+i)} i_t \, \mathrm{mb}_t + \sum_{t=1}^{\infty} \frac{i_t M_t^s}{\Pi(1+i)P_0} \tag{5.5}
$$

must equal or exceed zero. In dividing (5.4) by P_0 to get (5.5),

$$
\sum_{t=1}^{\infty} \frac{i_t \mathrm{MH}_t}{\Pi(1+i)P_0} = \sum_{t=1}^{\infty} \frac{i_t P_t (\mathrm{MH}_t/P_t)}{\Pi(1+i)P_0}
$$

$$
= \sum_{t=1}^{\infty} \frac{i_t P_0 \Pi(1 + \Delta P/P) \, \mathrm{MH}_t/P_t}{\Pi(1+i)P_0}
$$

$$
= \sum_{t=1}^{\infty} \frac{\Pi(1 + \Delta P/P)}{\Pi(1+i)} i_t \, \mathrm{mh}_t,
$$

and similarly for MB and mb.

In comparing the household sector budget constraint (5.5) with the constraint (4.13) for the case of Yap-Island money, notice that M_0^s/P_0 enters for the Yap-Island case, while $\sum_{t=1}^{\infty} \{i_t M_t^s/\Pi(1+i)P_0\}$ enters in the present case. In general, M_0^s drops out when the government's constraint is substituted into the household sector's constraint, and only future money supplies (for $t \geq 1$) enter. This is because only future money supplies will affect household sector tax burdens. Of course the present general case must collapse to the Yap-Island case if the money stock is constant over time. If $M_t^s = M_0$ for all $t \geq 0$, then $\sum_{t=1}^{\infty} \{i_t M_t^s/\Pi(1+i)\} = M_0^s$ and the two cases are the same.

The Price-Induced Effect on Wealth

Differentiating (5.5) by P_0 gives the price-induced effect on wealth. Assuming that P_0 does not affect expected interest rates or expected rates of price or wage inflation (that is, assuming that price and wage expectations are unit elastic),[2] the effect reduces to

$$-\frac{\partial Y_0^s}{\partial (MB_0/P_0)}\frac{MB_0}{P_0^2}$$

plus the change in $\Sigma_{t=1}^{\infty}\ \{i_t M_t^s/\Pi(1+i)P_0\}$. To simplify exposition, suppose temporarily that business holds no cash balances, or $MB_t = 0$ $(t \geqslant 0)$; $MB_t > 0$ is considered in some detail in Appendix 5A. Under this condition, the price-induced effect on wealth is

$$\partial \left\{ \sum_{t=1}^{\infty} \frac{i_t M_t^s}{\Pi(1+i)P_0} \right\} \bigg/ \partial P_0.$$

Here are the many possibilities. At one extreme, if M_t^s is fixed and equal in all periods to the initial money stock M_0^s,

$$\sum_{t=1}^{\infty} \frac{i_t M_t^s}{\Pi(1+i)P_0} = \frac{M_0^s}{P_0},$$

and this part of the price-induced effect on wealth is

$$-\frac{M_0^s}{P_0^2}, \tag{5.6}$$

the conventional result. Put another way, the conventional result holds if the system is one with Yap-Island money, as in chapter 4.

But suppose that government decides that the number of dollars it has outstanding at the start of every period, from period 1 on, will vary proportionately with P_0; this is equivalent to deciding it will have given amounts of real balances in terms of period 0 prices outstanding in every future period, no matter what future prices are. That is, suppose the elasticity of every future (but not the initial) money supply with respect to the current price level is unity. Then, M_t^s/P_0 is constant $(t \geqslant 1)$,

$$\partial \left\{ \sum_{t=1}^{\infty} \frac{i_t M_t^s}{\Pi(1+i)P_0} \right\} \bigg/ \partial P_0 = 0 \tag{5.7}$$

and this part of the price-induced effect on wealth is zero.[3]

Further, note that suitable choice of the sequence M_t^s $(t \geqslant 1)$ can make the price-induced effect on wealth take on almost any particular negative value even if every future money supply is inelastic with respect to P_0.

The intuition behind these results depends on the fact that government decisions enter the household sector budget constraint through taxes, and taxes in turn depend on how the government varies (or plans to vary) M_t^s in response to increases in P_0, as can be seen from the government budget constraint (5.2). Think of the present value of government taxes as being net of M_0^s/P_0 and V_0^s/P_0 since these terms in (5.2) cancel with $(MH_0 + MB_0)/P_0$ and V_0/P_0 in the household sector constraint. Focus on the part of the present value of real taxation that depends on $\Sigma_{t=1}^{\infty}$ $\{i_t M_t^s/\Pi(1+i)\}$. When P_0 rises with fixed G_t, taxes must rise unless the government also increases the amount of money it prints. If, for example, P_0 doubles but $M_1^s, M_2^s, \ldots$ also doubles, then the real present value of taxation is constant, and there is no price-induced effect on wealth through taxation. (In cases where the effect $\{\partial Y_0^s/\partial(MB_0/P_0)\}\ MB_0^s/P_0^2$ arises, it does so through the business sector's dividends.) Clearly, the less elastic is M_t^s to P_0, the more the real present value of taxes must rise with P_0, since the less is G_t financed by real money issue.

An Example

Let $M_0 = M_1 = M_2 = \ldots$ to start with, and outstanding government bonds $V_0^s = 0$. Suppose $P_0 = 100$ initially and rises by 1 percent to 101. If $M_0 = 100$, this cuts the household sector's initial real balances by (approximately) 1 percent. In the Yap-Island case, this is all that happens; the price-induced effect is a fall of 1 percent of real balances. However, suppose the government responds by increasing the money stock by 1 percent. Then, M_0 is unchanged but $M_1^s, M_2^s, \ldots$ are all higher than M_0 by 1 percent. This increase in M_1^s, or $\Delta M_0^s \equiv M_1^s - M_0 = M_0 \times 0.01$, means that government can reduce taxes in the current period by an amount $M_0 \times 0.01$, or reduce taxes in real terms by an amount equal to 1 percent of real balances, M_0/P_0. On balance, then, the reduction in the household sector's real balances is matched by a cut in taxes, making the price-induced effect on wealth equal zero.

The Neutrality of Money

To understand (5.7) more clearly, consider an experiment of interest in its own right. Let (5.7) hold, in virtue of government varying all M_t^s proportionately with P_0, and ask whether money is neutral in this model. That is, starting from an initial equilibrium, if $MH_0 = M_0^s$ were twice as large, would all prices merely be twice as high, with the real equilibrium unchanged? As in chapter 4, this requires that there is no relative discounted price change and that the household sector budget constraint (5.5) continues to equal zero for the initial values of N_t^s, N_t^d, $Y_t^s - \Delta K_t^d$, C_t^d, G_t and mh_t ($t \geq 0$); recall that it is temporarily assumed that MB $= 0$. Considering the budget constraint (5.5), it is clear that doubling MH_0 and M_0^s has no effect on wealth, since MH_0 and M_0^s do not enter (5.5). If P_0 doubles and w_0 also doubles, while $\Delta \tilde{w}/w$, $\Delta w/w$, $\Delta \tilde{P}/P$, $\Delta P/P$, i_1 and all expected i_t ($t \geq 2$) are unchanged, then the change in (5.5) depends only on what happens to $\Sigma_{t=1}^{\infty} \{i_t M_t^s/P_0/\Pi(1+i)\}$. One way to get the net result that a doubling of MH_0, M_0^s, and P_0 gives a zero change in wealth is for all M_t^s ($t \geq 1$) to also double. This might occur because (a) $M_t^s = M_0^s$ (the Yap-Island money case), (b) when M_0^s doubles, government simply doubles the time path of M_t^s, that is, keeps all money stock growth rates constant, or (c) the money stock for all t is unit elastic relative to P_0.

Since w_0/P_0, all i_t ($t \geq 1$) and all $\Delta P_t/P_t$, $\Delta w_t/w_t$, $\Delta \tilde{P}_t/P_t$, $\Delta \tilde{w}_t/w_t$ and $\Delta \underset{\sim}{P}_t/P_t$, $\Delta \underset{\sim}{w}_t/w_t$ are unchanged, no relative price has changed, and hence there are no substitution effects. In the absence of substitution or wealth effects, there are no changes in any excess demand through these two channels. (Because the question plays such a large part in the next section, note that the household's initial real balances are unaffected.) In particular, if the system is initially in general equilibrium, temporary or intertemporal, it remains in general equilibrium.

5.2 The Determinacy of the Price Level – The Initial-Condition Effect

The preceding section showed that the system with government money is capable of displaying neutrality, in the sense that, if MB $= 0$ and if MH_0 is doubled when M_0^s doubles, then it is perfectly consistent that the only effect on the economy is a doubling of all current and future prices with no effect on the real equilibrium, provided price and wage expectations are unit elastic and all M_t^s ($t \geq 1$) take on double their initial values. In particular, two cases of neutrality in which the condition that all M_t^s double is automatically fulfilled are (a) the Yap-Island money case, $M_0^s = M_t^s$ ($t \geq 1$), and (b) when M_t^s ($t \geq 1$) varies proportionately with P_0. In case (b), (5.7) holds, and if business holds no cash balances an increase in P_0 has no impact on wealth.

Is the price level determinate in this second case? Current theory makes a negative impact on wealth of a rise in P_0 (the real balance effect)[4] the *sine qua non* of a determinate price level, at least when government bonds are not part of net wealth as in the present model. This section discusses the determinacy of the price level and shows that the so-called real balance effect is not necessary for determinacy (and Appendix 5A shows that in principle it is not sufficient). This section introduces instead the initial-condition effect, which supplements the price-induced effect on wealth in rendering the price level determinate.

Patinkin, the Real Balance Effect, and the Determinacy of the Price Level

The fundamental importance which current monetary theory assigns to the real balance effect begins with the problem Patinkin raises of whether the system's real excess demand functions for all non-money goods are homogeneous of degree zero in all current prices (save the price of bonds) – or, which is the same, dependent only on relative prices of commodities and labor services. If this homogeneity holds, then the absolute level of prices is indeterminate. For, suppose the system is in equilibrium with all non-money excess demands equal to zero. If all current prices double, no relative price has changed and thus (by homogeneity of degree zero) the excess demands for all non-money goods remain equal to zero. But from Walras's law the excess demand for money is thus equal to zero, and all markets are still in equilibrium when all prices have doubled. Thus the price level is indeterminate,[5] since any absolute price level is consistent with equilibrium. The doubling of the price level halves the stock of real balances, but the demand for real balances is also halved by implication of the zero-degree homogeneity. Think of this in the case of Yap-Island money. Then it is clear that the rise in the price level causes a conventional real balance effect; indeterminacy arises if the real balance effect shows up fully in the demand for money and not even partially in a non-monetary market. By contrast, the present problem is that the price-induced effect on wealth may be zero as in (5.7) and will thus show up in no market whether or not a non-zero effect would show up in some non-monetary market.

Patinkin's point is clearly valid, and implies that determinacy requires that the system of excess demand functions is not homogeneous of degree zero in all current (non-bond) prices.[6] Many economists would argue that a second restriction on the real excess demand functions is that lack of "money illusion" requires them to be homogeneous of degree zero in all non-bond prices *and* the quantity of (outside) money.[7] Thus, if this second requirement is met, a doubling of prices with no change in the quantity of money does not leave excess demands equal to zero; hence the system is out of equilibrium, and therefore the requirement that the system should not be homogeneous of degree zero in current non-bond prices is met and the price level is determinate.[8] Thus, establishing determinacy reduces to showing that excess demands depend on the real quantity of outside money in the system. The conventional method of demonstrating this is the "real balance effect" – a wealth effect. Typically, the first step is to establish the existence of a negative real balance effect, and then to argue that it must plausibly show up at least in part in some non-money market. The real balance effect is neither necessary nor sufficient, however, for the determinacy of the price level, or more generally a non-zero price-induced effect on wealth is neither necessary nor sufficient for the determinacy of the price level.[9] This section shows that the real balance effect is not necessary; sufficiency is discussed in Appendix 5A.

Given the usual approach in monetary theory, it is easy to fall into the error of thinking that if (5.7) holds and thus there is no effect on wealth when P_0 varies, then the price level is not determinate. The price level *is* determinate, though, and depends on the initial-condition effect, not the wealth effect; this part of contemporary monetary theory has overlooked the reasons for holding real balances.

Consider first the intuitive rational for a determinate price level. Let (5.7) hold and allow P_0 to double. Assuming unit-elastic price and wage rate expectations and neglecting

$$- \frac{\partial Y_0^s}{\partial (\mathrm{MB}_0/P_0)} \frac{\mathrm{MB}_0}{P_0^2}$$

(which may, of course, be zero – business may hold no cash balances), there are no wealth or substitution effects. But MH_0/P_0 has been halved, and this will affect current behavior. The mh_t in the budget constraint were not picked arbitrarily but because a particular level of real balances is desired. Suppose the arbitrary restriction is imposed that in period t the household sector can have real balances equal to only half the quantity it would otherwise desire. This imposes another constraint in addition to the wealth constraint and, at the initial set of prices, presumably manifests itself in many non-zero excess demands other than for money to hold in period t. In the same way, if M_0 is given, doubling P_0 constrains the household sector to have and use only half the real balances as before, and this presumably manifests itself in some current excess demand – rendering P_0 determinate on conventional monetary theory's own grounds. If (5.7) holds, there is no price-induced effect on wealth through government actions. P_0 increases and all future money supplies rise proportionately, but not the initial stock of money. In particular, during the course of time from 0 to 1, the government prints more money so M_1^s is higher than otherwise. Thus, there is no change in wealth with the rise in P_0, but M_0/P_0 and its adequacy are reduced.

The following three subsections analyze the initial-condition effect on the household sector. The first subsection analyzes the initial-condition effect by including the initial level of real balances in the utility function. The next subsection discusses hints of the initial-condition effect in the literature. The third analyzes the initial-condition effect through use of the budget constraint.

The Initial-Condition Effect – Real Balances in the Utility Function

Suppose that an increase in P_0 has no effect on wealth, because M_t^s ($t \geqslant 1$) increases proportionately with P_0. Further, suppose that w_0 changes proportionately with P_0, and no expected inflation or interest rates change, so that no relative prices have changed. Thus, there are no substitution or wealth effects.

The budget constraint, which has not shifted, is a hyperplane in the C_t^d, N_t^s ($t \geqslant 0$), mh_t ($t \geqslant 1$) space; note that mh_0 is not included since the household can no longer affect the predetermined MH_0. The first approach taken here is to assume that mh_0 enters the utility function. The issue of an initial-condition effect comes to whether the indifference surfaces in this hyperspace shift when this increase in P_0 reduces mh_0. If they do shift, then some demand(s) for C_t^d, N_t^s ($t \geqslant 0$), or mh_t ($t \geqslant 1$) change, and an excess demand becomes non-zero – just as in Patinkin's method for demonstrating a determinate price level. In particular, C_0^d or N_0^s is likely to change and thus cause non-zero excess demands in the current period.

An easy way to introduce the initial-condition effect for the household sector is to suppose that the usefulness of real balances during any period depends *inter ala* on transactions in that period. Suppose that every household's transactions involve time and trouble and that this can all be reduced to hours H spent in making transactions. Further, let[10]

$$H_t = H(C_t^d, \mathrm{mh}_t); \quad H_C \geqslant 0, \, H_{\mathrm{mh}} \leqslant 0 \quad (t \geqslant 0);$$

for large enough mh, $H_{\mathrm{mh}} = 0$ and $H_{C,\mathrm{mh}} = 0$. Then, leisure in period t (Le$_t$) is total time $\overline{L}$ minus H_t and the household's labor supply N_t^s, that is, Le$_t = \overline{L} - N_t^s - H_t$. Hence, the household's utility function has the argument

$$U = U(\ldots, \mathrm{Le}_0, \ldots)$$
$$= U[\ldots, \overline{L}_0 - N_0^s - H(C_0^d, \mathrm{mh}_0), \ldots], \quad U_{\mathrm{Le}} > 0.$$

Any household's initial nominal balances (MH_0) are given at time 0 by past actions. Its real balances (mh_0) are then determined solely by P_0 and vary inversely with P_0.[11] Changes in P_0 then affect mh_0, H_0, and Le_0 and hence the marginal utility of Le_0. They also affect the marginal utilities of C_t^d, Le_t, mh_t for all t unless U is separable in Le_0. These changes in marginal utilities are then likely to shift indifference surfaces.

As an example, the subjective trade-off between current consumption and labor is

$$\frac{U_{C_0} - U_{Le_0} H_{C_0}}{-U_{Le_0}} = \frac{\partial U}{\partial C_0^d} \bigg/ \frac{\partial U}{\partial N_0^s}, \tag{5.8}$$

which must equal $-P_0/w_0$ at a constrained interior maximum. If the increase in P_0 is not to change (5.8) and thus cause changes in some C_t^d, N_t^s ($t \geq 0$) and mh_t ($t \geq 1$) from their initial values, then

$$\frac{d(U_{C_0} - U_{Le_0} H_{C_0})/-U_{Le}}{dP_0} = \frac{d(U_{C_0} - U_{Le_0} H_{C_0})/-U_{Le_0}}{d\,mh_0} \left(-\frac{MH_0}{P_0^2} \right)$$

$$= [-U_{Le}\{U_{C,Le}(-H_{mh})$$

$$- U_{Le,Le}(-H_{mh})H_{C_0} - U_{Le}H_{C,mh}\}$$

$$- (U_C - U_{Le}H_C)\{-U_{Le,Le}(-H_{mh})\}]$$

$$(-U_{Le})^{-2} \left(-\frac{MH_0}{P_0^2} \right) \tag{5.9}$$

must equal zero when evaluated at the initial MH_0, C_t^d, N_t^s ($t \geq 0$) and mh_t ($t \geq 1$). In general, (5.9) is necessarily zero only if H_{mh} and $H_{C,mh}$ equal zero; this occurs only if the individual is accidentally satiated in real balances. In turn, such satiation occurs only if the initial P_0 is substantially lower than expected, for no one will forgo interest on the margin to hold redundant real balances. If (5.9) is non-zero, as is entirely probable, then (5.8) no longer equals the unchanged $-P_0/w_0$, the new higher level of P_0 is not consistent with previous decisions, and it is entirely probable that C_0^d, N_0^s, will be among the revised choices, implying current-period disequilibrium. In particular, if increases in leisure raise the marginal utility of consumption, then a fall in mh_0 will reduce current consumption unless consumers are satiated with initial real balances.

If by some chance (5.9) should equal zero in the neighborhood of the initial price level, it merely says that P_0 is not unique in the neighborhood. An increase in P_0 that reduces mh_0 virtually to zero must have some effect on current activity (and hence excess demands) if money is a necessary part of some transactions or, more generally, if the amount of leisure is not independent of real current balances over all values of mh_0.[12]

Thus, the household sector initial-condition effect plays a role in determining the price level exactly comparable to the price-induced effect on wealth. The absence of a price-induced effect on wealth does not necessarily make the price level indeterminate. Ignoring the household sector initial-condition effect is a logical error of the same order as ignoring a non-zero price-induced effect on wealth.

Hints of The Household Sector Initial-Condition Effect

The initial-condition effect presented here is entirely consistent with Patinkin's (1965) analysis, but is obscured and neglected there by concentration on the real balance effect. Patinkin's analysis explicitly makes each household's utility function depend *inter alia* on its initial real balances MH_0/P_0 but then mostly ignores this. Indeed, he treats the dependence of the utility function, and hence of excess demands, on initial real balances as tedious and analytically detrimental.

His position is as follows.[13] (a) Initial real balances are what they are – the ratio of the predetermined initial holdings of money to the current price level, just as assumed here. (b) The real value of initial money holdings enters the intertemporal budget constraint; here it does so only in the Yap-Island money case as discussed in section 5.1. (c) To generate a demand for money, real balances at all points in time enter the utility function;[14] it would not, then, be consistent to leave out initial real balances. (d) An increase in P_0 reduces wealth, shifting the budget constraint back toward the origin of the field of choice; if w_0 increases proportionately, all price expectations are unit elastic and all expected interest rates are constant, the new budget constraint is inside and parallel to the old constraint. (e) This change is due to the real balance effect. However, the workings of the real balance effect are obscured by (f) the shift in the indifference surfaces over the field of choice, the shift in indifference surfaces generated by the price-induced change in the utility function parameter MH_0/P_0, a *parameter* since no individual can affect P_0 and his/her initial money holdings were determined by past decisions to accumulate money.

Point (f) complicates the analysis to such an extent that Patinkin just ignores it, pointing out that if the utility function is separable the marginal rates of substitution between any two goods in the field of choice (and hence the indifference surfaces) are unaffected by changes in MH_0/P_0.[15]

While Patinkin neglects this reflection of the initial-condition effect, in at least two places he is on the verge of discovering the effect and its importance. In his discussion of the distinction between the marginal utility of real balances and Marshall's "marginal utility of money," he posits a one unit increase in (initial) nominal balances with no change in wealth as an illustration of the marginal utility of real balances.[16] But he does not take the further step of asking whether, if real wealth is held constant, a proportional increase in P_0 does not return the system to its old equilibrium (given the usual expectations assumptions). And he does not inquire whether the increase in MH_0 (with P_0 constant) will change excess demands even with wealth constant.

Earlier, in discussing money demand, he writes[17]

> It should be clear that the monetary demand now being discussed is that for next week. The foreknowledge that the payments of that week will be randomly timed is assumed to make the individual adjust his commitments of the current marketing period so as to provide for the money reserves he will then need. True, temporary insolvency of some of his buyers may (if they decide against an intraweek conversion of bonds into money) delay payment on their purchasing contracts with him. But since no one can obligate himself in excess of his budget restraint, our individual can be sure that such delays can at most be intraweek ones. Hence his money balances at the end of this week – or, equivalently, the beginning of next week – must be exactly at the level implied by his final current marketing decisions.
>
> Correspondingly, these decisions cannot affect the absolute level of the money balances with which the individual meets his liquidity needs of the current week, for these balances were in turn determined by the decisions of the preceding one. On the other hand, current decisions can very clearly affect the *relative* adequacy of these balances. This is nothing but the obverse side of the real-balance effect. In brief, at any given set of prices, the individual can always adjust his amounts of excess demand so as to enable his given initial money balances to provide any desired degree of security against insolvency during the ensuing week.

Of particular importance is the passage ". . . current decisions can very clearly affect the *relative* adequacy of these [initial] balances." Patinkin visualizes current demands adjusting in part to the initial real balances, and this relationship must be true whatever is the wealth constraint. If wealth is held constant and P_0 is raised and MH_0/P_0 decreases, continuity and consistency will generally require that (some) current demands adjust to the reduced adequacy of real balances. And this is not "nothing but the obverse side of the real balance effect." Similarly, the quote ". . . at any given set of prices, the individual can always adjust his amounts of excess demand so as to enable his given initial money balances to provide any desired degree of security against insolvency during the ensuing week" is true when P_0 rises and MH_0/P_0 falls even with an unchanged inter-temporal constraint.

The Initial-Condition Effect – The Budget Constraint

The preceding subsections approached the initial-condition effect through the utility function, as Patinkin (1965) approached the real balance effect in his chapters V and VI. However, an alternative, logically equivalent approach is through the wealth constraint. In this approach, a change in P_0 affects both the budget constraint and the implicit relative prices of goods. If the net effect of these two changes on individuals' choices is non-zero, then the change in P_0 affects excess demands and the price level is determinate in the absence of a non-zero price-induced effect on wealth.

Chapters 3 and 4 and the earlier parts of this chapter treated labor supply N_t^s ($t \geq 0$) as the choice variable, leaving leisure (Le) to be determined as a residual, the difference between total time ($\overline{L}$) and the sum of N_t^s and H_t. In this approach, the constraint that total time is devoted to leisure, work, and making transactions, $\overline{L} = \mathrm{Le}_t + N_t^s + H_t$, is imposed by substituting $\overline{L} - N_t^s - H_t$ for Le_t in the utility function, as above. Thus, utility is rewritten to depend on N_t^s and mh_t rather than on Le_t (for $t \geq 0$). An alternative is to treat Le_t and H_t as the choice variables and determine N_t^s as a residual. Then,

$$N_t^s = \overline{L} - \mathrm{Le}_t - H(C_t^d, \mathrm{mh}_t); \qquad H_C \geq 0, H_{\mathrm{mh}} \leq 0,$$

and, rewriting,

$$N_t^s = \phi(\mathrm{Le}_t, C_t^d, \mathrm{mh}_t); \phi_{\mathrm{Le}} = -1, \phi_C = -H_C \leq 0, \phi_{\mathrm{mh}} = -H_{\mathrm{mh}} \geq 0.$$

Thus, the budget constraint is

$$\sum_{t=0}^{\infty} \frac{w_0}{P_0} \frac{\Pi(1 + \Delta w/w)}{\Pi(1+i)} \phi(\cdot) + \sum_{t=0}^{\infty} \frac{\mathrm{Div}_t}{P_0\Pi(1+i)} - \sum_{t=0}^{\infty} \frac{T_t}{P_0\Pi(1+i)}$$

$$- \sum_{t=0}^{\infty} \frac{\Pi(1 + \Delta P/P)}{\Pi(1+i)} C_t^d - \sum_{t=1}^{\infty} \frac{\Pi(1 + \Delta P/P)}{\Pi(1+i)} i_t \mathrm{mh}_t$$

$$+ \frac{\mathrm{MH}_0}{P_0} + \frac{V_0}{P_0} .$$

In this approach, Le_t ($t \geq 0$) is left in the utility function, since the constraint $\overline{L} = \mathrm{Le}_t + N_t^s + H_t$ has been taken into account in the budget constraint.

A rise in P_0 reduces MH_0/P_0 and gives an initial-condition effect both through (a) the budget constraint and (b) altering relative prices. When P_0 rises, there is the effect on the budget constraint

$$\partial \left\{ \sum_{t=1}^{\infty} \frac{i_t M_t^s}{\Pi(1+i)P_0} \right\} \bigg/ \partial P_0,$$

as discussed above in section 5.1, plus the additional effect

$$\frac{w_0}{P_0} \frac{\partial\phi}{\partial mh_0} \left(-\frac{MH_0}{P_0^2} \right) = \frac{w_0}{P_0} (-H_{mh_0}) \left(-\frac{MH_0}{P_0^2} \right), \qquad (5.10)$$

which is negative as long as $-H_{mh_0} > 0$. Call (5.10) the initial-condition effect on wealth. If there is to be no initial-condition effect on wealth, then from (5.10) H_{mh_0} must equal zero. With $-H_{mh_0} > 0$, a rise in P_0 and fall in mh_0 reduces wealth and cuts C_0^d, on the assumption that C_0^d is a superior good.

For interpretation in later chapters, it is worthwhile expressing the initial-condition effect on wealth (5.10) in a somewhat different way. Consider consumer j's choice problem of the preceding period, where $t = -1$. He/she wants to maximize

$$U_j = U_j (C_{j,-1}^d, C_{j,0}^d, C_{j,1}^d, \ldots, \text{Le}_{j,-1}, \text{Le}_{j,0}, \text{Le}_{j,1}, \ldots)$$

subject to the intertemporal budget constraint

$$\sum_{t=-1}^{\infty} \frac{w_{-1}}{P_{-1}} \frac{\Pi(1 + \Delta w/w)}{\Pi(1+i)} \phi(\text{Le}_{j,t}, C_{j,t}^d, mh_{j,t}) + \sum_{t=-1}^{\infty} \frac{\text{Div}_{j,t}}{\Pi(1+i)}$$

$$- \sum_{t=-1}^{\infty} \frac{T_{j,t}}{\Pi(1+i)} - \sum_{t=-1}^{\infty} \frac{\Pi(1 + \Delta P/P)}{\Pi(1+i)} C_{j,t}^d$$

$$- \sum_{t=0}^{\infty} \frac{\Pi(1 + \Delta P/P)}{\Pi(1+i)} i_t \, mh_{j,t} + \frac{MH_{j,-1}}{P_{-1}} + \frac{V_{j,-1}}{P_{-1}}$$

where $\text{Div}_{j,t}$ and $T_{j,t}$ are j's dividend receipts and tax payments. Forming a Lagrangian, necessary conditions for an interior optimum are

$$\frac{\partial U}{\partial C_t} - \lambda \left\{ \frac{\Pi'(1 + \Delta P/P)}{\Pi'(1+i)} - \frac{w_{-1}}{P_{-1}} \frac{\Pi'(1 + \Delta w/w)}{\Pi'(1+i)} \frac{\partial \phi_t}{\partial C_t} \right\} = 0$$

$$t \geqslant -1$$

$$\frac{\partial U}{\partial \text{Le}_t} + \lambda \frac{w_{-1}}{P_{-1}} \frac{\Pi'(1 + \Delta w/w)}{\Pi'(1+i)} \frac{\partial \phi_t}{\partial \text{Le}_t} = 0 \qquad t \geqslant -1$$

$$\lambda \left\{ \frac{w_{-1}}{P_{-1}} \frac{\Pi'(1 + \Delta w/w)}{\Pi'(1+i)} \frac{\partial \phi_t}{\partial mh_{j,t}} - \frac{\Pi'(1 + \Delta P/P)}{\Pi'(1+i)} i_t \right\} = 0$$

$$t \geqslant 0,$$

where λ is a Lagrangian multiplier. Taking the mh marginal condition for $t = 0$,

$$\frac{w_{-1}}{P_{-1}} \frac{\Pi^0(1 + \Delta w/w)}{\Pi^0(1+i)} \frac{\partial\phi_0}{\partial mh_0} = \frac{\Pi^0(1 + \Delta P/P)}{\Pi^0(1+i)} i_0$$

and rearranging to

$$\frac{w_0}{P_0} \frac{\partial\phi_0}{\partial mh_0} = i_0,$$

rewrite the initial-condition effect on wealth as

$$\frac{w_0}{P_0} \frac{\partial\phi_0}{\partial mh_0} \left(-\frac{MH_0}{P_0^2}\right) = i_0 \left(-\frac{MH_0}{P_0^2}\right).$$

This assumes that the change is evaluated at the P_0 that people expected in period -1. A very similar derivation is used to measure the initial-condition effects on wealth through bank money and government money in chapters 6 and 7.

The other aspect of the initial-condition effect concerns changes in relative prices. In equilibrium, the subjective rate of trade-off between current leisure and consumption, $-U_C/U_{Le}$, is chosen so that

$$-\frac{U_C}{U_{Le}} = \frac{P_0 - w_0 \, \partial\phi/\partial C^d}{-w_0} = -\frac{P_0}{w_0}\left(1 + \frac{w_0}{P_0} H_C\right). \qquad (5.11)$$

If there is to be no initial-condition effect through a change in relative prices when a rise in P_0 reduces mh_0, then from (5.11) $H_{C,mh}$ must equal zero. With $H_{C,mh} < 0$, a rise in P_0 reduces mh_0 and induces the consumer to substitute against current consumption.[18] In the absence of satiation, the initial-condition effect works through relative prices and (under reasonable conditions) through the budget constraint to reduce current consumption.

5.3 An Alternative Assumption about Money Accumulation

Patinkin (1956, 1965) assumes that the money balances used in period t are accumulated in period $t - 1$. An alternative view is that money balances for use in period t are acquired at the very start of that period. This is like Hicks's (1939, 1946) "market day" at the start of his "week," where the week's flow contracts are made and the assets left over from the previous week are physically reshuffled. In particular, if person A starts the period with fewer real balances than desired, he/she can increase these by simply issuing a bond to acquire cash. In this case, there is not an initial-condition effect of precisely the sort described above. However, an increase in P_0 still creates non-zero excess demands.

More precision is needed regarding timing of government actions. As an example, take the case where all M_t^s ($t \geq 1$) vary proportionately with P_0, so that, assuming $MB_0 = 0$ and making the usual assumptions about expectations, there is no price-induced effect on wealth. The amount of money outstanding at the start of period 0, M_0^s, is given. If P_0 doubles, the government will double all M_t^s ($t \geq 1$). In particular, some time after the start of the initial period but before the period ends, the government will pump an extra amount of money into the system so that the money stock at the end of the period, M_1^s, will be doubled. This, however, will not allow the same volume of transactions to be carried out during period 0 as if the initial money stock were $2M_0^s$.

For concreteness, suppose that M_t^s would be constant in the absence of price level changes and would equal M. The doubling of P_0 means that M more dollars will be printed during period 0. In turn, net taxes will be reduced in period 0 by M. In principle, then, the household sector can use the cut in taxes on the private sector to increase its holdings of nominal balances just enough to keep its real balances constant. The problem is that these extra dollar balances are not available at the start of the period when they are needed. Initially, then, there will be an excess demand for money.

This excess demand must be balanced by an excess supply (or supplies) from Walras's law. The government is spending the same amount in real terms as before, and twice as much in nominal terms since P_0 has doubled, while it has cut taxes by the amount M. It can afford to do so because it is printing an extra amount of money M. These extra dollars can be thought of as printed and distributed over period 0 as real government expenditures occur. The household sector wants to double its money holdings at the start of the period, and to do this plans to issue bonds. It plans to redeem these bonds during the period with the tax cut (rise in transfer payments) and thus end the period with no extra debt. Hence, as of the start of period 0, the rise in P_0 creates an excess demand for money and an excess supply of bonds.

Thus, even with this alternative institutional arrangement regarding money accumulation, the price level is determinate.

5.4 Does Government Suffer from Money Illusion?

Is the real balance effect simply a distribution effect between the government and private sectors as Patinkin claims (1965, p. 288)? If so, does this not make monetary analysis simply an adventitious historical or institutional quirk (Johnson, 1962),[19] since in the absence of this distribution effect the price level would be indeterminate?

It is sometimes argued that the price level is determinate because "government, alone of all economic units, is unconcerned with the real value of its outstanding (non-interest-bearing) debt, and plans its demand for output accordingly" (Patinkin, 1965, p. 288).[20] Is government perhaps suffering from money illusion? And is this necessary to make the price level determinate?

Patinkin reaches this conclusion as follows. If the price level falls, the private sector is better off because the real value of its holding of government liabilities (money, in this case) is increased – and government is worse off to the same extent. If government does not change its demands for output in response to this but the private sector does, there is a net change in demand with no change in wealth – a distribution effect between the private and government sectors.[21] This distribution effect is necessary for a determinate price level.

This analysis is incorrect. It involves, first, the mistaken notion that there are distribution effects between sectors rather than only among households – just as if the consequences of government behavior (as business behavior) were not reflected in the household sector's budget constraint.

Second, as the above analysis of the initial-condition effect shows, a real balance effect is not necessary for a determinate price level. For example, if all future money supplies change proportionately with the current price level, there is a zero price-induced effect on wealth but the price level is determinate through the initial-condition effect.

Third, it is incorrect to say that the government does not respond to the fall in the price level. To the extent that M_t^s $(t \geqslant 1)$ is price elastic, or that there are any government bonds outstanding, the change in the price level affects the real present value of taxation for any given path of real government expenditure over time. This change in the time path of T_t shows up in the household sector budget constraint and is fully taken into account in the price-induced effect on wealth.

Further, consider the case of Yap-Island money, where the government initially issued the money but the stock is irrevocably fixed. It is possible to talk of this money as a government "liability." The word "liability," however, usually implies obligations and responsibilities. But the only government action really implied by the existence of this money is that the government will not change this stock. When P rises, there is no reason to believe that G_t should rise; this would require a rise in (the real net present value of) taxation. Economists who view the price-induced effect on wealth as a distribution effect really seem to be arguing that when P varies a rational government should change proportionately the quantity of Yap-Island money. It is not at all clear, however, why this should be so if government views itself as having fiduciary responsibility to aim for some degree of price level stability.

5.5 Is Money a Part of Government's Liabilities?

The discussion in section 5.4 touched on the issue of whether government fiat money should be viewed as a liability of the government. This section discusses this partly semantic issue by analyzing the government's inter-temporal budget constraint

$$\sum_{t=0}^{\infty} \frac{\Pi(1 + \Delta\underaccent{\tilde}{P}/P)}{\Pi(1+i)} G_t - \sum_{t=0}^{\infty} \frac{T_t}{\Pi(1+i)P_0} = \sum_{t=1}^{\infty} \frac{i_t M_t^s}{P_0\Pi(1+i)}$$

$$- \frac{M_0^s}{P_0} - \frac{V_0}{P_0}. \quad (5.12)$$

The discussion is also relevant to the "burden of the debt" and other questions in government debt management.

The economic interpretation of

$$\sum_{t=1}^{\infty} \frac{i_t M_t^s}{P_0\Pi(1+i)}$$

is that the government rents the use of its fiat dollars to the public at a per unit charge equal to $1 times the market rate of interest. However, the real present value of government's total income from such rentals is

$$\sum_{t=1}^{\infty} \frac{i_t M_t^s}{P_0\Pi(1+i)}$$

only if the number of fiat dollars outstanding at the start of period 0 is zero, for any dollars outstanding are owned by the public and the government is paid no rent on them. The real present value of the rent lost by having M_0^s outstanding at time 0 is M_0^s/P_0 and thus the total real rent earned is

$$\sum_{t=1}^{\infty} \frac{i_t M_t^s}{P_0\Pi(1+i)} - \frac{M_0^s}{P_0}.$$

The real present value of the net rent thus earned is subtracted from the sum of the real value of bonds outstanding (V_0/P_0) and the real present value of government expenditures,

$$\sum_{t=0}^{\infty} \frac{\Pi(1 + \Delta \tilde{P}/P)}{\Pi(1+i)} G_t,$$

to find the present value of real taxation net of (non-interest) transfer payments.

The question of whether the term M_0^s/P_0 represents real liabilities of the government is in part merely semantic, for no matter what terminological agreement might be reached, (5.12) still holds. But an interpretation of M_0^s/P_0 as a real liability is straightforward and meaningful. If the government wished to earn the real rent on future money supplies of

$$\sum_{t=1}^{\infty} \frac{i_t M_t^s}{P_0 \Pi(1+i)},$$

it must first redeem its liability M_0^s/P_0. Alternatively, the government earns the real rent

$$\sum_{t=1}^{\infty} \frac{i_t M_t^s}{P_0 \Pi(1+i)},$$

but the net real present value of its earnings is less by the amount of its real liabilities M_0^s/P_0. Again, as long as the real present value of the net income from money issue is recognized to be

$$\sum_{t=1}^{\infty} \frac{i_t M_t^s}{P_0 \Pi(1+i)} - \frac{M_0^s}{P_0}, \tag{5.13}$$

it really does not matter whether M_0^s/P_0 is referred to as a debt, or not.

Notice that this position is consistent with two conflicting current views in monetary theory.[22] The first view holds M_0^s/P_0 to be real government liabilities because money is a financial asset and any financial asset is *ipso facto* a liability of the issuer. If someone wants thus to designate M_0^s/P_0, there is no problem as long as such terminology is not taken to conflict with (5.12).

The second view holds that the government need never redeem M_0^s – there is no "redemption clause" or any other implied responsibility except to exchange one dollar bill for another – and *ipso facto* money is not a liability.[23] This view, too, is fine as long as it is recognized that the real present value of the income earned by having money supplies outstanding at various points in time is reduced by precisely M_0^s/P_0 as (5.13) says.[24]

5.6 The Household Sector Knows its Tax Liabilities

As noted previously, the influence of a non-constant M_t^s stream on the price-induced effect on wealth requires that the household sector be kept informed of the value of the net tax liabilities to which it is subject. This is completely parallel to the requirement that the business sector must keep the household sector informed of the value of the expected dividend stream if the analysis is to proceed as above. In single-period analysis, the government and business sectors must keep the household sector so informed if Walras's law is to hold for every vector of prices. Thus, the present requirement just generalizes this to a multi-period analysis, and as chapter 3, section 3.3, argues, is necessary if Walras's law is to hold for every price vector in a hypothetical economy in which all current and future contracts are made on a single initial market day.

The assumption about tax information is required for the mere possibility of general equilibrium. Suppose that the system is in (temporary) general equilibrium but all sectors have the same price, wage, and interest expectations, and planned quantities demanded and supplied are equal for all time periods, so that the system is in fact in intertemporal equilibrium. Let some parameter change. Then the adjustments of excess demand in reaction to this can be analyzed in terms of wealth and substitution effects (and now, the initial-condition effects). If the new temporary equilibrium requires a change in P_0, then either the government informs the household sector of its changed tax liabilities, as assumed here, or it does not. If it does not, then the household sector is unaware of an actual change in its wealth, and the new temporary equilibrium is established on the basis of ignoring this change in wealth. The future that the private sector contemplates must necessarily not come true, for in the future this neglected effect on wealth will manifest itself when net taxes are found to be different from expected.

If government informs the household sector of its changed tax liabilities, then the temporary equilibrium reflects this change in wealth and the future which the private sector expects may come about – at least expectations are not upset by unexpected government taxes. This is, in fact, just a way of saying that, in an economy with complete futures markets, the real present value of net tax liabilities must be known for equilibrium. Conversely, in an economy with no futures markets, intertemporal equilibrium is impossible (not just unlikely) if such liabilities are falsified (i.e. if changes in them due to changes in P_0 are not reported). Of course, even if such changes are reported, the temporary equilibrium may not be part of an equilibrium intertemporal time path, but correct reporting of such changes is a necessary condition for intertemporal equilibrium.

APPENDIX 5A A NON-ZERO PRICE-INDUCED EFFECT
ON WEALTH IS NOT SUFFICIENT TO RENDER
THE PRICE LEVEL DETERMINATE

Section 5.2 argued that a non-zero price-induced effect on wealth was not necessary for a determinate price level. This Appendix shows that a non-zero effect on wealth is also not sufficient for a determinate price level. The key to the argument is the fact that P_0 affects mb_0, and mb_0 affects both Y_0^s and N_0^d; the usual discussion neglects the latter channels.

Much of chapter 5's analysis assumed for convenience that business holds no money balances. Now, however, suppose that business does hold cash balances. Then, on the supply side of the market for output, doubling of P_0 cuts business's real balances MB_0/P_0 in half. Since K_0 and MB_0 are determined by accumulation decisions before time 0, business cannot satisfy all three of its marginal conditions in (4.6) for $t=0$. However, business can control N_0^d, and maximizing the present value of the dividend stream requires setting

$$\frac{\partial Y_0^s}{\partial N_0^d} - \frac{w_0}{P_0} = 0.$$

Presumably the quantity of business's real balances affects the marginal productivity of the other two factors; in particular, it is likely that all three are complements,[25] implying that an increase in MB_0/P_0 raises the marginal physical product of labor, $\partial Y_0^s/\partial N_0^d$. In any case, an increase in MB_0/P_0 yields

$$\frac{\partial^2 Y_0^s}{\partial N_0^d \, \partial(MB_0/P_0)} \gtreqless 0$$

as the two factors are complements, independent, or substitutes. Thus, from the labor marginal condition, when P_0 rises (w_0 rising proportionately to hold w_0/P_0 constant),

$$\frac{dN_0^d}{dP_0} = - \frac{\{\partial^2 Y_0^s/\partial N_0^d \, \partial(MB_0/P_0)\} \, (- MB_0/P_0^2)}{\partial^2 Y_0^s/\partial N_0^{d2}} \gtreqless 0$$

as the factors are complements, independent, or substitutes. (From diminishing marginal productivity, $\partial^2 Y_0^s/\partial N_0^{d2} < 0$.) Therefore,

$$\frac{dY_0^s}{dP_0} = \frac{\partial Y_0^s}{\partial(MB_0/P_0)} \left(- \frac{MB_0}{P_0^2} \right) + \frac{\partial Y_0^s}{\partial N_0^d} \frac{dN_0^d}{dP_0} \gtreqless \frac{\partial Y_0^s}{\partial(MB_0/P_0)}$$
$$\left(- \frac{MB_0}{P_0^2} \right)$$

as the factors are substitutes, independent, or complements.

Assume the case of a constant money stock over time, and let P_0 rise. Then, from differentiating (5.5) by P_0, when $M_t^s = M_0$ the change in wealth W is

$$\frac{dW}{dP_0} = - \left\{ \frac{\partial Y_0^s}{\partial (MB_0/P_0)} \frac{MB_0}{P_0^2} + \frac{M_0}{P_0^2} \right\}.$$

Let the effect of an increase in wealth on current consumption and household demand for real balances (MH_1/P_0) be $C_W, M_W > 0$; both goods are superior. The effect on labor supply is $N_W \gtreqless 0$; whether leisure is inferior or superior is assumed unknown. When P_0 rises, the change in excess demand for output is

$$C_W \frac{dW}{dP_0} - \frac{dY_0^s}{dP_0} = C_W \left\{ - \frac{\partial Y_0^s}{\partial (MB_0/P_0)} \frac{MB_0}{P_0^2} - \frac{M_0}{P_0^2} \right\}$$

$$- \left\{ - \frac{\partial Y_0^s}{\partial (MB_0/P_0)} \frac{MB_0}{P_0^2} + \frac{\partial Y_0^s}{\partial N_0^d} \frac{dN_0^d}{dP_0} \right\},$$

$$(5A.1)$$

because investment demand is unaffected from the model in chapter 4 and government expenditure is assumed constant. Since mb_1 is unaffected, given unit-elastic price and wage expectations and constant interest rate expectations,[26] the change in demand for real balances comes only through the household sector $(M_W dW/dP)$. This gives the change in the excess demand for real balances

$$M_W \frac{dW}{dP_0} + \frac{M_0^s}{P_0^2} = M_W \left\{ - \frac{\partial Y_0^s}{\partial (MB_0/P_0)} \frac{MB_0}{P_0^2} - \frac{M_0^s}{P_0^2} \right\} + \frac{M_0^s}{P_0^2}.$$

$$(5A.2)$$

The change in the excess demand for labor services due to a rise in P_0 is

$$\frac{dN_0^d}{dP_0} - N_W \frac{dW}{dP_0} = \frac{dN_0^d}{dP_0} - N_W \left\{ - \frac{\partial Y_0^s}{\partial (MB_0/P_0)} \frac{MB_0}{P_0^2} - \frac{M_0^s}{P_0^2} \right\}.$$

$$(5A.3)$$

It is perfectly possible that the changes in all three excess demands are zero.

As an example, if $C_W, M_W > 0$, $N_W > 0$ (leisure is an inferior good), $\partial^2 Y_0^s/\partial N_0^d \, \partial (MB_0/P_0) > 0$ (the factors are complements) so that $dN_0^d/dP_0 < 0$, then since necessarily $dY_0^s/dP_0 < 0$, (5A.1)–(5A.3) may well equal zero. That is, restrictions on the signs of C_W, M_W, $\partial Y_0^s/\partial (MB_0/P_0)$ and $\partial Y_0^s/\partial N_0^d$ are not sufficient to ensure that at least one of the changes in current excess demands is non-zero. In this case, a doubling of P_0 has no impact on the current market excess demands, and hence the wealth effect of a change in P_0 is not sufficient to make the price level determinate.

In the literature, the effect of business cash holdings on current production is assumed away,[27,28] and thus

$$\frac{\partial Y_0^s}{\partial (\text{MB}_0/P_0)} = 0, \qquad \frac{dN_0^d}{dP_0} = 0.$$

Therefore, $C_w \dfrac{dW}{dP_0} - \dfrac{dY_0^s}{dP_0} = C_w \left(-\dfrac{M_0^s}{P_0^2} \right) < 0$

is the change in excess demand for output when P_0 doubles. The change in the excess demand for real balances becomes

$$-M_W \frac{M_0^s}{P_0^2} + \frac{M_0^s}{P_0^2} > 0,$$

since M_W is taken to be positive but less than unity (other goods as a whole are superior). Finally, N_W is usually taken as zero, so there is no change in the excess demand for labor. The non-zero excess demands for output and real balances are taken as proving that the system is not homogeneous of degree zero in the price level alone, or the price level is determinate.

Note that the experiment just considered, starting from equilibrium and asking the consequences of a change in the price level, is precisely the sort which Patinkin (1965) insists that economists must perform if they are not to be suspected of engaging in the invalid dichotomy – they must raise price from its equilibrium level and, in a model with only government money where government bonds are not net wealth, show how this creates wealth effects, causes non-zero current excess demands, and propels price back to its initial level.

In the general case where there are both initial-condition effects and non-zero wealth effects, these may interact to offset each other and have all current excess demands equal to zero as P_0 varies over a range. This implies a range of price levels consistent with equilibrium. Thus, existence of the initial-condition effect is not sufficient to guarantee that there will not be a range in which P_0 is indeterminate. Rather, the initial-condition effect (a) opens another channel of economic causation beyond the standard wealth and substitution effects, and (b) shows that the existence of a price-induced effect on wealth is not at all necessary for the price level to be determinate.

APPENDIX 5B THE PRICE-INDUCED EFFECT ON
WEALTH IN MODELS OF MONEY AND GROWTH

The discussion of this chapter has an immediate application in the theory of money and growth. Suppose that a growth model with government fiat money is in steady-state equilibrium and real income is growing at the percentage rate n. Assume that the economy's demand for real balances is homogeneous of degree one in real income. If there is to be a zero rate of price inflation, the money supply must also grow at n. Breaking into the growth process at time 0, $M_t^s = (1+n)^t M_0^s$. Thus,

$$\sum_{t=1}^{\infty} \frac{i_t M_t^s}{\Pi(1+i)P_0} = \sum_{t=1}^{\infty} \frac{i(1+n)^t M_0^s}{(1+i)^t P_0} = \frac{M_0^s}{P_0} \frac{i}{i-n},$$

assuming that i is constant over time.

For convenience, assume that $MB_0 = 0$. When P_0 varies, consider two major possibilities. If all M_t^s ($t \geq 1$) change proportionately, that is, all M_t^s ($t \geq 1$) are unit elastic with respect to P_0, the change in wealth is zero as in (5.7). But a case closer to the usual analysis assumes that the sequence of M_t^s is invariant with respect to P_0. Here, the effect on wealth is

$$-\frac{M_0^s}{P_0^2} \frac{i}{i-n},$$

and

$$-\frac{M_0^s}{P_0^2} \frac{i}{i-n} \gtreqless -\frac{M_0^s}{P_0^2}$$

as $n \lesseqgtr 0$ (assuming $i > n$). This result says that if the economic system is in a non-inflationary steady state, the impact on wealth of an increase in P_0 is the same as the Yap-Island money real balance effect if and only if the real rate of growth is zero ($n = 0$). This has been noticed in no monetary growth model.[29] Monetary analysis in no way requires a stationary state; however, in a zero-inflation world the usual real balance effect holds only for such a state. With positive growth ($n > 0$), a rise in the price level causes a larger decline in real wealth than in a stationary state.

More generally, suppose that the economy is on a steady-state path with a real growth rate of n, and the money supply grows at the percentage rate u. Then, the rate of inflation is approximately[30] $u - n$ (so if $u = n$, the rate of inflation is zero). Then

$$\sum_{t=1}^{\infty} \frac{iM_t^s}{(1+i)^t P_0} = \frac{M_0^s}{P_0} \sum_{t=1}^{\infty} \frac{i(1+u)^t}{(1+i)^t} = \frac{M_0^s}{P_0} \frac{i}{i-u}. \tag{5B.1}$$

Suppose that the real rate of interest i' is approximately invariant with changes in inflation.[31] Then $i = i' + $ inflation $= i' + u - n$ and thus

$$\frac{M_0^s}{P_0} \frac{i}{i-u} = \frac{M_0^s}{P_0} \frac{(i'+u-n)}{i'-n}. \tag{5B.2}$$

Then, the effect on wealth of an increase in P_0 is

$$-\frac{M_0^s}{P_0^2} \frac{(i'+u-n)}{i'-n} = -\frac{M_0^s}{P_0^2} \left(1 + \frac{u}{i'-n}\right). \tag{5B.3}$$

If the price-induced effect on wealth is to equal the conventional result $-M_0^s/P_0^2$, the rate of monetary expansion u must equal zero - the Yap-Island case; in particular, the conventional result holds in monetary growth models just in case the steady-state rate of deflation equals the growth rate n.

From (5B.3), holding constant M_0^s/P_0, the absolute value of the price-induced effect on wealth increases with a rise in either the rate of monetary expansion u or steady-state inflation $u - n$. Further, the effect of changes in i' or n on the size of the price-induced effect on wealth depends on the growth rate of the money stock, u. With $u > 0$, a rise in i' or fall in n reduces $u/(i' - n)$ and thus reduces the absolute value of the price-induced effect on wealth. With $u = 0$, changes in i' or n have no impact on the price-induced effect on wealth. M_0^s/P_0 will of course vary with changes in u, i' or n, but their effects will not be offset if the common assumption that the demand for real balances is relatively inelastic is imposed.

NOTES

1 Government purchases of goods and services raise many welfare issues that are typically beyond the scope of essays in monetary theory, and thus such issues are ignored here. Pesek and Saving (1967) also choose not to discuss the welfare issues, and explicitly assume no government spending. Gurley and Shaw (1960) avoid the issue by assuming that any government spending is devoted to households' ends, and merely displaces private spending; this is a position Bailey (1971) analyzes. Note that this opposes the usual Keynesian stand that government spending does not just displace private spending. See also Hansen's (1970) comments.

2 As chapter 4 showed, the value of the price-induced effect on wealth is sensitive to the assumption of the degree of elasticity of price expectations.

3 This is the usual result in the argument that if government does not suffer from "money illusion" there is no "real balance" effect. The conclusion of this argument is that the price level is then indeterminate. But this essay shows below that the price level is determinate. For a further discussion of this

"money illusion" argument, see Johnson (1962), Patinkin (1965), Pesek and Saving (1967) and chapter 7 later.

4 Patinkin chooses to call his result the "real balance effect." As section 5.1 emphasized, the relationship between the price-induced effect on wealth and the initial quantity of real balances is (in general) variable, and indirect in the sense of depending on future taxes and hence future government money stocks. However, his result is just this essay's result for the Yap-Island money case with unit-elastic price and wage expectations.

5 This is Patinkin's (1965) succinct argument. Note that price expectations can be elastic to any degree at all, and if the non-money excess demand functions are homogeneous of degree zero in current prices, the current price level is indeterminate.

6 Any subset of the excess demand functions could be homogeneous of degree zero, but not the system as a whole. Thus, the excess demand for output might show no real balance effect; in this case, Patinkin argues that the real balance effect must show up in the bond market.

7 See Patinkin (1965). Note again that this homogeneity renders the price level determinate whatever the degree of elasticity of price expectations. See chapter 6 for the problems raised by including bank money in the system. The issue of outside versus inside money is discussed in chapters 6 and 7.

8 The price level is determinate in the sense that not all price levels yield a general equilibrium. The conventional demonstration does not show that the equilibrium is unique, nor that the number of equilibria is finite.

9 See note 4 for why the nomenclature "real balance effect" is unfortunate.

10 See Saving (1970) for more complex use of this approach to derive the properties of an individual's demand for money.

The transactions cost approach used by Saving and also here seems the natural neo-classical approach – constrained maximization of a utility function. And it seems the easiest way to extend Hicksian analysis the necessary distance. However, $H_t(\cdot)$ is not unalterably given but is the result of the interaction of the members of society. Once this interaction is explored, the economics can rapidly become very complex.

11 Where it makes no difference to understanding, the same variable is used for the typical household and the household sector, for example, MH_0.

12 For completeness, consider intertemporal trade-offs, in addition to the current period trade-off discussed in connection with (5.8) and (5.9).

The subjective rate of trade-off between current consumption and consumption in period t is

$$\frac{U_{C_0} - U_{Le_0} H_{C_0}}{U_{C_t} - U_{Le_t} H_{C_t}}$$

which in equilibrium must equal $\dfrac{\Pi(1+i)}{\Pi(1 + \Delta P/P)}$ where the Π product runs to t. Suppose for convenience that the utility of current consumption and leisure is independent of period t's consumption and leisure. Then, if the increase in P_0 is not to force a change in some household sector choice, the change in the ratio of marginal utilities,

$$\frac{d\{(U_{C_0} - U_{Le_0}H_{C_0})/(U_{C_t} - U_{Le_t}H_{C_t})\}}{dP_0}$$

$$= \frac{d\{(U_{C_0} - U_{Le_0}H_{C_0})/(U_{C_t} - U_{Le_t}H_{C_t})\}}{d\,mh_0} \left(-\frac{MH_0}{P_0^2}\right)$$

$$= \frac{U_{C_0,Le_0}(-H_{mh}) - U_{Le_0,Le_0}(-H_{mh})H_{C_0} - U_{Le_0}H_{C,mh}}{U_{C_t} - U_{Le_t}H_{C_t}} \left(-\frac{MH_0}{P_0^2}\right),$$

must equal zero. Again, for this necessarily to be zero, and thus the subjective rate of transformation to remain equal to the intertemporal discounted price ratio, H_{mh} and $H_{C,mh}$ for period 0 must equal zero; otherwise $U_{C_0,Le_0} > 0$ ensures that C_0^d will fall.

13 See Patinkin (1965, p. 107, especially footnote 36; and pp. 457–60, especially 460n).

14 This is so in Patinkin's chapters V and VI, but not in chapter VII.

15 In the transaction's costs formulation used in this essay, the marginal utilities of labor and real balances cannot be independent, since these variables enter through their effects on leisure,

$$Le = \bar{L} - N - H(C^d, mh).$$

16 See Patinkin (1965, pp. 114–15).

17 See Patinkin (1965, p. 83).

18 For completeness, consider some intertemporal effects. The total price of current consumption (including transactions costs) relative to either consumption or leisure in t is

$$\frac{P_0 - (\partial\phi_0/\partial C_0^d)w_0}{P_t - (\partial\phi_t/\partial C_t^d)w_t}\,\Pi(1+i) = \frac{P_0}{P_t}\,\frac{1 - (\partial\phi_0/\partial C_0^d)(w_0/P_0)}{1 - (\partial\phi_t/\partial C_t^d)(w_t/P_t)}\,\Pi(1+i)$$

or

$$\frac{P_0 - (\partial\phi_0/\partial C_0^d)w_0}{w_t}\,\Pi(1+i) = \frac{P_0}{w_t}\left(1 - \frac{\partial\phi_0}{\partial C_0^d}\frac{w_0}{P_0}\right)\Pi(1+i),$$

respectively. An increase in P_0 (and w_0 proportionately) raises P_t and w_t proportionately, under the assumption of unit-elastic price and wage expectations, and hence P_0/P_t and P_0/w_t are unaffected by an increase in P_0. But the increase in P_0 reduces mh_0 by $(MH_0/P_0^2)\,dP_0$. Assuming that an increase in mh_0 reduces the time involved in the marginal purchase of consumption goods, or $\partial^2 H_0/\partial C_0^d\partial mh_0 < 0$, then the increase in P_0 reduces mh_0 and increases $\partial\phi_0/\partial C_0^d$, thus raising the price of current consumption relative to either future consumption or future leisure. This creates a substitution effect against current consumption. In any case, there is a substitution effect just in case $\partial^2\phi_0/\partial C_0^d\partial mh_0 \neq 0$.

146   *The Price-Induced Effect on Wealth*

The total price of current leisure relative to either consumption or leisure in period t is

$$\frac{w_0}{P_t - (\partial\phi_t/\partial C_t^d)w_t}\,\Pi(1+i) \qquad \text{or} \qquad \frac{w_0}{w_t}\,\Pi(1+i),$$

respectively. With unit-elastic price and wage expectations, proportional increases in P_0 and w_0 leave w_0/P_t and w_0/w_t constant. $\partial\phi_t/\partial C_t^d$ is unaffected by the fall in mh_0. Hence, none of these relative prices change and there will be substitution against current consumption. As noted above, the price-induced decrease in mh_0 creates a negative wealth effect. Thus, it seems very likely that the price-induced decreases in mh_0 will create substitution and wealth effects against current consumption, and hence reduce current consumption demand through the household initial-condition effect. Without some assumption about whether leisure is normal or not, the net effect on the current demand for leisure is ambiguous, as is the net effect on labor supply.

The initial-condition effect on the demands for future consumption and money services is quite ambiguous. It comprises a negative change in wealth, which is likely to decrease all demands, plus increases in the price of current consumption and leisure relative to all other goods and services. These substitution effects may each be positive or negative.

19 See Johnson (1962), Pesek and Saving (1967), Saving (1970).
20 See Patinkin (1965), Hansen (1970).
21 Compare this distribution effect with that between the household and business sectors, and the discussion of this in chapter 4 and this section. See references in note 19.
22 See Pesek and Saving (1967) for their view and also for the views that they believe others hold. Note that their interpretations of others' views are controversial.
23 See Pesek and Saving (1967) for exhaustive exposition of this view.
24 Strictly speaking, the assumption that government fiat money bears only a "repurchase clause" and not a "redemption clause" – a promise to retire the money stock (or some part) at some point in time – is an assumption about the world, rather than a logical property of government money. Consider a proposed monetary union where national currencies are to be retired in exchange for the new union currency. A part of the agreement may well be that one country must reduce its money supply by a certain amount. This is certainly a sort of redemption clause, and its plausibility is evident in the reflection that any country entering a monetary union must be powerfully tempted to secure for its citizens as many units of new currency as possible.

Alternatively, consider a country on a gold standard that temporarily refuses to redeem government fiat money for gold during a crisis such as war. To the extent that the government plans to return to convertibility, it must plan to reduce the stock of its money in the future (cf. Friedman and Schwartz, 1985). This will be reflected in the expected course of M_t^s and hence in the price-induced effect on wealth.

25 It seems desirable that the economy be capable of steady-state balanced growth. In the absence of continuing and regular shifts in the production function, this requires that the production function be homogeneous of degree one (display constant returns to scale).

26 mb_1 is unaffected because none of the marginal conditions for $t = 1$ change, given the expectations assumption. Investment demand is unaffected for the same reason. In the literature, changes in demand for output and real balances are made to depend on $-M_0^s/P_0^2$ through the strained device of assuming no distribution effects between the household and business sectors. On this dubious view of distribution effects, see Patinkin (1965) and the discussion in chapter 4.

27 For example, see Enthoven's Appendix to Gurley and Shaw (1960), Patinkin (1965), Pesek and Saving (1967).

28 In models where business holds cash balances but the price level does not affect current output and labor demand, business real balances are allowed to affect investment demand, thus giving a motive for the previous decision to accumulate cash balances for this period. The total of consumption plus investment demand is then taken to depend on the private sector's total real balances, by assuming no distribution effects between sectors (see chapter 4). What is not noticed is that the rationale for a wealth-maximizing firm to hold real balances is that their quantity affects wealth. Therefore, a change in P_0 that affects their quantity also affects wealth and thus the effect on wealth is larger than M_0^s/P_0^2 (see the authors cited in the preceding note). Note especially that Patinkin (1965) grants that the demand and supply of labor "should" depend on the business and household sectors' real balances respectively, but that ignoring this is a reasonable simplification and makes no difference to neutrality; this seems to be a lack of perception that business real balances cause a wealth effect beyond their contributions to M_0^s/P_0.

29 For discussions which either assert or imply that the price-induced effect on wealth in steady-state growth is independent of the rate of growth, see Tobin (1955, 1965), Enthoven (1960), Patinkin (1965, 1969), Stein (1966), Sidrauski (1966, 1967), Villanueva (1970).

30 If Y^s grows at the continuously compounded percentage rate n and M^s at the continuously compounded percentage rate u, and if breaking into the steady-state time path at $t = 0$ finds the values Y_0^s, M_0^s, P_0 of output, the money supply and the price level, then a constant steady-state ratio of real values requires that

$$\frac{M_t^s/P_t}{Y_t^s} = \frac{M_0^s e^{ut}/P_0 e^{(u-n)t}}{Y_0^s e^{nt}} = \frac{M_0^s}{P_0 Y_0^s}.$$

However, if time periods are discrete $\dfrac{Y_{t+1}^s - Y_t^s}{Y_t^s} = n$ and

$$\frac{M_{t+1}^s - M_t^s}{M_t^s} = u,$$

then a constant steady-state ratio of real balances to output requires

$$\frac{M_t^s/P_t}{Y_t^s} = \frac{M_0^s(1+u)^t/P_0\{(1+u)/(1+n)\}^t}{Y_0^s(1+n)^t}$$

and

$$\frac{P_{t+1} - P_t}{P_t} = \frac{1+u}{1+n} - 1 = \frac{1}{1+n}(1+u-1-n) = \frac{u-n}{1+n}.$$

31 This assumption, and attending arguments designed to support it, are popular in the quantity theory tradition. See Irving Fisher (1911). Note the widespread argument that easy money can only temporarily lower nominal rates, for such a monetary policy causes increased inflation, which in turn causes nominal interest rates to rise to return real rates to their previous levels. Many rational expectations models do not allow for even a transitory fall in i' as monetary expansion rises, if decision-makers understand that money supply growth has risen.

6
Bank Money and Wealth Effects: Banks Pay a Competitive Rate of Interest

Chapter 5 analyzed the price-induced effect on wealth in an economy with government fiat money. A major controversy in monetary theory, however, is the extent to which and under what conditions bank money enters the effect. This chapter and the next discuss these issues in detail. This chapter discusses the role in wealth effects of fiat bank money, when the money is produced by competitive banks in an economic system with the same government sector as in chapter 5. The key characteristic of these banks is that they pay a competitively determined rate of interest on their deposits. They are price-takers and quantity-setters. Payment of a competitively determined rate of interest on deposits plays an important role in guaranteeing that the price-induced effect on wealth through bank money is zero. Indeed, if banks pay a competitively determined rate of interest on their money, if banks are wealth-maximizers, and if banks' real decisions are homogeneous of degree zero in nominal values as is required for neutrality, then the price-induced effect on wealth through bank money is zero. Chapter 7 extends this chapter's results by showing that if the government pays a competitive rate of interest on its money and if the government's costs of maintaining its money stock are homogeneous of degree zero as required for neutrality, then there is no price-induced effect on wealth through government money. Chapter 7 also shows that, if the government sector pays an interest rate below the competitive level on its money, then a price-induced effect on wealth through its money will exist. Similarly, if government restrictions on interest on bank money turn banks from quantity-setters into quantity-takers, bank money enters the price-induced effect on wealth. Thus, the price-induced effects on wealth through the two types of money are symmetric.

The banking sector described in section 6.1 is competitive in the sense that each bank is a price-taker and quantity-setter, though regulation might limit entry and thus allow monopoly rents to be made. Banks provide services to their customers and pay the competitively determined interest rate r to their customers. As with government fiat money, transactors accumulate bank money in one period to be used in the next. Section 6.1 finds the optimum conditions for a wealth-maximizing bank. As with previous discussions of bank money's role in the price-induced effect on wealth, this model ignores banks' service charges on customers' transactions. These service charges are considered in Appendix 6B and discussed at some length in chapter 7.

Section 6.2 discusses the price-induced effect on wealth. This is the same as in chapter 5, except for the inclusion of two changes in wealth arising through bank money. The first, referred to as the price-induced effect on wealth through bank money, is the discounted value of the price-induced effects on banks' dividends in future periods. Under plausible conditions, this effect is zero. The second effect focuses on the change in current profits. This second part of the effect is an initial-condition effect and on net is positive, as shown in section 6.3.

Section 6.4 introduces a new effect, the velocity effect of bank money. If people increase the velocity with which they turn over bank money, this raises banks' costs and reduces the wealth of bank shareholders. This effect has the same status as wealth, substitution and initial-condition effects in analysis of the transition from one equilibrium to another.

Section 6.5 briefly shows the conditions under which money is neutral. Suppose that banks are wealth-maximizers and their real decisions are homogeneous of degree zero in all nominal values. Then, doubling current prices and wages and the initial holdings of the household, business, and banking sectors of government and bank money will give the same real equilibrium if expected prices and wages are unit elastic. However, if bank money is not doubled when government money is doubled, the real equilibrium is affected because there are initial-condition effects. Over time, these effects disappear and bank money doubles endogenously, so even in this experiment government money is neutral in the long but not short run.

Chapter 5 showed that determinacy of the price level did not depend on the existence of a price-induced effect on wealth, since the initial-condition effect through government money would have impacts on excess demands. Section 6.6 adds bank money initial-condition effects on the household, business, and banking sectors to the initial-condition effects through government money on the household and business sectors. These effects, along with the velocity effect, show that absence of a price-induced effect on wealth does not imply indeterminacy of the price level.

Section 6.7 and 6.8 discuss a number of issues concerning the contribution of bank money to the price-induced effect on wealth. In particular, section 6.8 argues that restrictions on entry into the banking sector may allow the industry to make monopoly rents, but this has no effect on analysis of the price-induced effect on wealth. Further, neutrality requires that banks' demands for factors be homogeneous of degree zero in bank money and reserves, and reserve requirements can be designed to ensure that this homogeneity does or does not hold.

Section 6.9 shows that, in the absence of reserve regulations, this homogeneity is very likely to hold, ensuring neutrality.

Section 6.10 argues that there is no necessary relationship between the contribution of banks to society's welfare and the price-induced effect on wealth through bank money.

The "old view" and "new view" monetary theories are briefly discussed in section 6.11.

Finally, Appendix 6A discusses the Wicksellian cumulative process and shows that it can come about only if banks supply money in such a way as to remove any initial-condition effect through bank money. Appendix 6B reformulates the model of the banking sector to include banks' service charges on transactions made with bank money.

6.1 A Wealth-Maximizing, Price-Taking, Quantity-Setting Banking Sector

Banks issue deposits of bank dollars, which they promise to exchange on demand for government fiat dollars; following Pesek and Saving (1967), call this the "instant repurchase" requirement. It does not much matter for analytical purposes if banks' deposits are numbers on checks, in bank books and on balance sheets, or are bank-dollar bills (though the practical advance from bank currency to demand deposits was a major economy). Banks are assumed to be perfect competitors in the sense of being price-takers and quantity-setters, but there may be barriers to entry imposed by government limitations on the number of banks, thus yielding monopoly rents to the industry. Banks promise to pay the competitively determined interest rate r, on each of these bank dollars held at the end of period $t-1$ or at the (very) start of period t. Banks may use the funds they receive in exchange for new issues of bank dollars to buy bonds, to acquire government dollars, or to pay hired help; assume for convenience that the banking sector uses no real capital equipment.[1] Reserves of government dollars are useful in making good the instant repurchase guarantee, and labor is used to perform the services the bank offers, such as cashing checks, converting bank notes, clearing checks, bookkeeping, etc.[2]

Since banks are perfect competitors, any particular bank is a quantity-setter and can attract as many dollars of deposits as it likes in period $t - 1$ at the going rate r_t, to be paid at the very start of period t on each bank dollar then outstanding. It can use these deposits to buy bonds that pay interest, at the rate i_t, at the start of t. Let the number of units of labor necessary to perform a particular bank's services in period t depend on the quantity of its deposits, its reserves, the general level of prices, and the number of transactions using its money in that period. The determination of the quantities of deposits and reserves by the wealth-maximizing behavior of banks is discussed shortly.

This is clearly an abstract and stylized banking system. It corresponds in many ways to those analyzed by Gurley and Shaw (1960), Patinkin (1965, 1969, 1972), Pesek and Saving (1967) and others in the tradition of monetary general equilibrium models. Its primary shortcoming is its neglect of uncertainty, but the implications of uncertainty are neglected throughout this book save in chapter 9. For a survey of more detailed banking models, see Santomero (1984). Note that many of the conclusions developed below are robust to extension of the basic model used here.

The Bank's Dividend Stream

The dividends that the banking sector pays to households in period t are div_t (the lower-case d indicating bank dividends, a capital D indicating non-financial-sector dividends), with

$$\text{div}_t = \Delta \overline{M}_t + \overline{B}_t + \overline{V}_t - r_t \overline{M}_t - \tilde{w}_t \overline{N}_t^d - P_{b,t}(\overline{B}_{t+1}^d + \overline{V}_{t+1}^d) - \Delta \text{MF}_t,$$
(6.1)

where $\Delta \overline{M}_t$ is the flow supply of bank money and $\overline{M}_t$ is the quantity of bank money outstanding at the start of period t ($\Delta \overline{M}_t \equiv \overline{M}_{t+1} - \overline{M}_t$), the bars on the M, B, V, and N variables refer to the banking sector, and ΔMF_t is the financial sector's flow demand for government money in period t. Thus, dividends by the bank sector in period t are equal to the increase in bank money issuance, $\Delta \overline{M}_t$, plus the interest and principal from private and public sector bonds held, $\overline{B}_t + \overline{V}_t$, less interest payments on outstanding bank money, $r_t \overline{M}_t$, less banks' wage payments, $\tilde{w}_t \overline{N}_t^d$, less the value of banks' purchases of private and government sector bonds, $P_{b,t}(\overline{B}_{t+1}^d + \overline{V}_{t+1}^d)$, less banks' accumulation of government money, ΔMF_t. As with the non-financial business sector, this analysis does not pre-suppose any aggregation of production functions.[3]

Expression (6.1) assumes that banks retain no earnings and acquire any injections of equity funds by issuing new stock. Since this is a Miller–Modigliani (1961) world, dividend policy is irrelevant and (6.1) is adopted essentially as a notational convenience in what follows. If bank-owners put up no initial funds or contribute no financial "capital," then the frequent bank balance sheet "accounting identity" holds that

$$\overline{M}_t = P_{b,t-1}(B_t + V_t) + \mathrm{MF}_t$$

and thus

$$\overline{M}_{t+1} = P_{b,t}(B_{t+1} + V_{t+1}) + \mathrm{MF}_{t+1}.$$

In this case, (6.1) reduces to

$$\mathrm{div}_t = (1 - P_{b,t-1})(B_t + V_t) - r_t\overline{M}_t - \widetilde{w}_t\overline{N}_t^d,$$

or dividends in period t equal the interest earned on bonds held by banks less interest paid on bank money less the banks' wage bill. In equilibrium, div can easily be positive. First, there may be restrictions on entry so that, even though all banks are price-taking quantity-setters, the industry makes monopoly rents. Second, there may be some non-explicit differential rent-earning factors contributed by bank-owners, with the rents on these factors impounded in div. If the differential factors are not owned by bank-owners, the analysis is exactly the same in principle as in this chapter, as discussed in chapter 7.

As noted in the introduction, this model neglects service charges that banks levy on transactions using bank money, as is usual in models discussing bank money's role in the price-induced effect on wealth (Saving, 1977, p. 293, n. 10). Appendix 6B adds these considerations to the model, and chapter 7 discusses them in some detail.

The model assumes that bank money that is useful for transactions in period t must be on hand at the start of t, or acquired by the end of $t-1$. Interest is earned on these bank dollars at the rate r_t, set in period $t-1$ and paid in t. This parallels the treatment of government money in chapter 5.

Discounting (6.1) and summing yields

$$\sum_{t=0}^{\infty}\frac{\mathrm{div}_t}{\Pi(1+i)} = \sum_{t=1}^{\infty}\frac{(i_t - r_t)\overline{M}_t}{\Pi(1+i)} - \sum_{t=0}^{\infty}\frac{\widetilde{w}_t\overline{N}_t^d}{\Pi(1+i)} - \sum_{t=1}^{\infty}\frac{i_t\,\mathrm{MF}_t}{\Pi(1+i)}$$

$$+ (\mathrm{MF}_0 - \overline{M}_0 - r_0\overline{M}_0) + (\overline{B}_0 + \overline{V}_0), \qquad (6.2)$$

where in handling $\Delta\overline{M}$ and $\Delta\mathrm{MF}$ use is again made of the discussion around (4.3). Equation (6.2) says that the present value of the financial sector's dividends equals the present value of the net interest $(i-r)$ earnings induced by its deposits $\overline{M}$, less the present value of the wage bill and the cost of reserve holdings $(i_t\,\mathrm{MF}_t)$ necessary to sustain these deposits, plus the difference between the initial value of assets $(\mathrm{MF}_0 + \overline{B}_0 + \overline{V}_0)$ less the initial value of liabilities $\overline{M}_0$ and the interest that banks are currently committed to pay on the initial liabilities ($r_0 \overline{M}_0$).

As discussed above, if bank-owners contribute no financial capital, then

$$\overline{M}_t = P_{b,t-1}(\overline{B}_t + \overline{V}_t) + \mathrm{MF}_t.$$

In this case, (6.2) can be rewritten as

$$\sum_{t=0}^{\infty} \frac{\mathrm{div}_t}{\Pi(1+i)} = \sum_{t=1}^{\infty} \frac{(i_t - r_t)\overline{M}_t}{\Pi(1+i)} - \sum_{t=1}^{\infty} \frac{\widetilde{w}_t \overline{N}_t^d}{\Pi(1+i)} - \sum_{t=1}^{\infty} \frac{i_t \mathrm{MF}_t}{\Pi(1+i)}$$
$$+ (1 - P_{b,t-1})(\overline{B}_0 + \overline{V}_0) - r_0 \overline{M}_0 - \overline{M}_0 - w_0 \overline{N}_0,$$

where the summation on the wage bill now runs from $t = 1$ rather than from $t = 0$ as in (6.2).

Note that using the term "liabilities" to refer to $\overline{M}_0$ is perfectly analogous to the same description of government money (M_0^s) in the government's budget constraint (5.20). As chapter 5 points out, the matter is one of terminology; what is analytically important is that, given the values of the other variables in (6.2), a unit increase in $\overline{M}_0$ reduces the present value of the financial sector's dividend stream by \$1. Whether bank money is a debt in some "deeper" meaning (see section 6.3) is irrelevant for this point.

The Bank's Demand for Labor

Suppose that the banking system is unregulated, except for the requirement that bank money must trade at par with government money.[4] Each bank determines its supply of money, use of labor, and level of reserves to maximize its shareholders' wealth. Let the minimum quantity of labor in period t that suffices to service a given quantity of deposits $\overline{M}_t$ depend positively on $\overline{M}_t$, negatively on the bank's reserves of government money (MF_t) and the price level $\widetilde{P}_t$, and positively on the number τ_t of its customers' real transactions that use bank money in that period. The larger are reserves, the smaller the difficulty in meeting the repurchase guarantee; the larger the number of real transactions, the more bookkeeping and other services required. Thus,[5]

$$\overline{N}_t^d = \theta(\mathrm{MF}_t, \overline{M}_t, \widetilde{P}_t, \tau_t); \quad \theta_{\mathrm{MF}} < 0, \theta_{\overline{M}} > 0, \theta_P < 0, \theta_\tau > 0.$$

Further, let the bank have some expectation v_t of the average number of real transactions that will be carried out in period t per unit of real bank money balances. (The concept v_t is discussed below in detail.) Then, banks expect

$$\tau_t = v_t \, \frac{\overline{M}_t}{\widetilde{P}_t}$$

and thus

$$\overline{N}_t^d = \theta \left(\mathrm{MF}_t, \overline{M}_t, \widetilde{P}_t, v_t \, \frac{\overline{M}_t}{P_t} \right).$$

Finally, assume that θ is homogeneous of degree zero in the nominal values of $\overline{M}$, MF and $\widetilde{P}$, or

$$\overline{N}_t^d = \theta \left(\frac{\mathrm{MF}_t}{\widetilde{P}_t}, \frac{\overline{M}_t}{\widetilde{P}_t}, 1, \frac{v_t \overline{M}_t}{\widetilde{P}_t} \right) = \theta(m_t^F, \overline{m}_t, 1, v_t \, \overline{m}_t),$$

where m_t^F and $\overline{m}_t$ are the real values of the bank's reserves and money stock in period t. The homogeneity assumption is discussed extensively in section 6.9. As is intuitively clear, this homogeneity is required for neutrality (see Saving (1973) and the discussion in section 6.5).

The Bank's Optimum Conditions

Substituting the bank's labor demand function into (6.2), necessary conditions for an interior maximum, through choice of deposits $\overline{M}$ and bank reserves MF, are

$$(i_t - r_t) - \frac{\widetilde{w}_t}{\widetilde{P}_t} \, \theta_{\overline{M}} - \frac{\widetilde{w}_t}{\widetilde{P}_t} \, v_t \theta_\tau = 0 \qquad (6.3a)$$

$$(t = 1, \ldots, \infty)$$

$$-i_t - \frac{\widetilde{w}_t}{\widetilde{P}_t} \, \theta_{\mathrm{MF}} = 0. \qquad (6.3b)$$

The first condition balances the net interest return to having one more bank dollar outstanding $(i_t - r_t)$ against the extra costs of supporting that dollar, both directly, $(\widetilde{w}_t / \widetilde{P}_t)\theta_{\overline{M}}$, and through the dollar's indirect effect of leading to a larger number of real transactions, $(-\widetilde{w}_t / \widetilde{P}_t) v_t \, \theta_\tau$. The second condition balances the cost of holding an extra dollar in reserves, $-i_t$, versus the savings in labor costs of servicing deposits, $(-\widetilde{w}_t / \widetilde{P}_t)\theta_{\mathrm{MF}} > 0$. The index running from $t = 1$ in (6.3) reflects the fact that $\overline{M}_0$ and MF_0 have been predetermined from the viewpoint of period 0 by decisions in past periods, and $\overline{N}_0^d$ thus depends only on τ_0, over which banks now have no control since $\overline{M}_0$, P_0, and v_0 are parametric to them.

To find the real present value of the bank sector's dividend stream, divide (6.2) by P_0,[6] giving

$$\sum_{t=0}^{\infty} \frac{\text{div}_t}{P_0 \Pi(1+i)} = \sum_{t=1}^{\infty} \frac{\Pi(1+\Delta \widetilde{P}/P)(i_t - r_t)\overline{m}_t}{\Pi(1+i)}$$

$$- \sum_{t=1}^{\infty} \frac{\Pi(1+\Delta \widetilde{P}/P)i_t m_t^{\text{F}}}{\Pi(1+i)}$$

$$- \sum_{t=0}^{\infty} \frac{\Pi(1+\Delta \widetilde{w}/w)\overline{N}_t^{\text{d}} w_0/P_0}{\Pi(1+i)} + \frac{\text{MF}_0}{P_0} + \frac{\overline{B}_0}{P_0}$$

$$+ \frac{\overline{V}_0}{P_0} - \frac{\overline{M}_0}{P_0} - r_0 \frac{\overline{M}_0}{P_0}. \tag{6.4}$$

In (6.4), $\overline{m}_t$ and m_t^{F} are the financial sector's real supplies of bank money and real demands for reserves in period t (in terms of $\widetilde{P}_t$) and for example

$$\frac{\overline{M}_t}{P_0} = \frac{\widetilde{P}_t}{P_0} \overline{m}_t = \Pi\left(1 + \frac{\Delta \widetilde{P}}{P}\right)\overline{m}_t.$$

With the bank sector now characterized, the next step is to find the price-induced effect on wealth.

6.2 The Price-Induced Effect on Wealth – Bank Money

Consider the price-induced effect on wealth when there exists a banking system such as the one just described. The household sector budget constraint must be amended to include the banking sector's dividend payments. Further, both households and non-financial businesses hold bank money.

The Household Sector's Budget Constraint

The household sector's budget constraint, in real terms relative to period 0's price level P_0, now requires that

$$\sum_{t=0}^{\infty} \frac{w_0}{P_0} \frac{\Pi(1+\Delta w/w)}{\Pi(1+i)} N_t^{\text{s}} + \sum_{t=0}^{\infty} \frac{\text{Div}_t}{P_0 \Pi(1+i)} + \sum_{t=0}^{\infty} \frac{\text{div}_t}{P_0 \Pi(1+i)}$$

$$- \sum_{t=0}^{\infty} \frac{\Pi(1+\Delta P/P)}{\Pi(1+i)} C_t^{\text{d}} - \sum_{t=1}^{\infty} \frac{\Pi(1+\Delta P/P)}{\Pi(1+i)} i_t \, \text{mh}_t$$

$$- \sum_{t=1}^{\infty} \frac{\Pi(1+\Delta P/P)}{\Pi(1+i)} (i_t - r_t)\overline{\text{mh}}_t - \sum_{t=0}^{\infty} \frac{T_t}{P_0 \Pi(1+i)} + \frac{\text{MH}_0}{P_0}$$

$$+ r_0 \frac{\overline{\text{MH}}_0}{P_0} + \frac{V_0^h}{P_0} + \frac{\overline{\text{MH}}_0}{P_0} - \frac{B_0^h}{P_0} \tag{6.5}$$

be greater than or equal to zero; assuming non-satiation (6.5) must equal zero. Consider the new terms in (6.5). The term

$$- \sum_{t=1}^{\infty} \frac{\Pi(1 + \Delta P/P)}{\Pi(1 + i)} (i_t - r_t)\overline{\text{mh}}_t$$

shows the net cost per period of each bank dollar held at the start of period t as $i_t - r_t$. V_0^h is the household sector's initial holdings of government bonds and B_0^h its initial outstanding debt – for convenience, the non-financial business sector still issues no bonds but the household sector's bonds are now held by the banking sector and thus need not be zero in the aggregate. Government and household sectors' bonds are still assumed to be perfect substitutes.

The Non-Financial Business Sector

The real present value of the non-financial business sector's dividend stream is now

$$\sum_{t=0}^{\infty} \frac{\text{Div}_t}{P_0 \Pi(1 + i)} = \sum_{t=0}^{\infty} \frac{\Pi(1 + \Delta \widetilde{P}/P)}{\Pi(1 + i)} (Y_t^s - \Delta K_t^d)$$

$$- \sum_{t=0}^{\infty} \frac{w_0}{P_0} \frac{\Pi(1 + \Delta \widetilde{w}/w)}{\Pi(1 + i)} N_t^d$$

$$- \sum_{t=1}^{\infty} \frac{\Pi(1 + \Delta \widetilde{P}/P)}{\Pi(1 + i)} \{i_t \, \text{mb}_t + (i_t - r_t)\overline{\text{mb}}_t\} + \frac{\text{MB}_0}{P_0}$$

$$+ \frac{\overline{\text{MB}}_0}{P_0} + r_0 \frac{\overline{\text{MB}}_0}{P_0}, \tag{6.6}$$

where $\overline{\text{MB}}_0$ is businesses' initial holdings of bank money and $\overline{\text{mb}}_t$ is non-financial businesses' demands for real bank money balances (in terms of $\widetilde{P}_t$) in period t.

Suppose that business output in period t depends on N_t^d, K_t^d, and also on that period's real government money balances in terms of $\widetilde{P}_t$ ($\text{MB}_t/\widetilde{P}_t = \text{mb}_t$), as well as real bank money balances ($\overline{\text{MB}}_t/\widetilde{P}_t = \overline{\text{mb}}_t$), or $Y_t^s = f(N_t^d, K_t^d, \text{mb}_t, \overline{\text{mb}}_t)$. Then, in addition to (4.6), a marginal condition for the non-financial business sector to be at an interior maximum is, from (6.6),

$$Y_{\overline{\text{mb}}_t}^s - (i_t - r_t) = 0 \qquad (t \geq 1).$$

(Recall that none of the results depend on being able to aggregate production functions.) As chapter 5 discussed, the only reason a wealth-maximizing business ever incurs the cost of holding money balances, either government or bank money, is because such balances influence output (given N_t^d and K_t^d). Note that a positive value of r implies that the cost of using a bank dollar is less than the cost of using a non-interest-bearing government dollar. Hence, if firms are to hold both sorts of money, there must be some transactions that are more efficiently made with government money than with bank money.

Substitution for Dividends and Taxes

Let the government's budget constraint remain (5.2) – for simplicity, the government holds no bank money. Then, substituting the government's intertemporal budget contraint (5.2), the expression for the real present value of the banking sector's dividend stream (6.4), and the real present value of the non-financial business sector's dividends (6.6) into the household budget constraint (6.5) yields the household sector constraint that

$$\sum_{t=0}^{\infty} \frac{w_0}{P_0} \frac{\Pi(1+\Delta w/w)}{\Pi(1+i)} N_t^s - \sum_{t=1}^{\infty} \frac{w_0}{P_0} \frac{\Pi(1+\Delta \widetilde{w}/w)}{\Pi(1+i)} (N_t^d + \overline{N}_t^d)$$

$$+ \sum_{t=0}^{\infty} \frac{\Pi(1+\Delta \widetilde{P}/P)}{\Pi(1+i)} (Y_t^s - \Delta K_t^d) - \sum_{t=0}^{\infty} \frac{\Pi(1+\Delta P/P)}{\Pi(1+i)} C_t^d$$

$$- \sum_{t=0}^{\infty} \frac{\Pi(1+\Delta P/P)}{\Pi(1+i)} G_t$$

$$- \sum_{t=1}^{\infty} \frac{\Pi(1+\Delta P/P)}{\Pi(1+i)} \{i_t \, \mathrm{mh}_t + (i_t - r_t)\overline{\mathrm{mh}}_t\}$$

$$- \sum_{t=1}^{\infty} \frac{\Pi(1+\Delta \widetilde{P}/P)}{\Pi(1+i)} \{i_t \, \mathrm{mb}_t + (i_t - r_t)\overline{\mathrm{mb}}_t\}$$

$$+ \sum_{t=1}^{\infty} \frac{\Pi(1+\Delta \widetilde{P}/P)}{\Pi(1+i)} \{(i_t - r_t)\overline{m}_t - i_t \, m_t^F\} + \sum_{t=1}^{\infty} \frac{i_t M_t^s}{P_0 \Pi(1+i)}$$

$$(6.7)$$

must exceed or equal zero. Note that (6.7) uses the fact that

$$\frac{\mathrm{MH}_0}{P_0} + \frac{\overline{\mathrm{MH}}_0}{P_0} + \frac{V_0^h}{P_0} - \frac{B_0^h}{P_0} + \frac{\mathrm{MB}_0}{P_0} + \frac{\overline{\mathrm{MB}}_0}{P_0} + \frac{\mathrm{MF}_0}{P_0} - \frac{\overline{M}_0}{P_0} + \frac{\overline{B}_0}{P_0}$$

$$+ \frac{\overline{V}_0}{P_0} - \frac{V_0}{P_0} - \frac{M_0^s}{P_0} + \frac{r_0\overline{MH}_0}{P_0} + \frac{r_0\overline{MB}_0}{P_0} - \frac{r_0\overline{M}_0}{P_0} = 0,$$

which follows from the system's accounting identities

$$\text{MH}_0 + \text{MB}_0 + \text{MF}_0 = M_0^s,$$

$$V_0^h + \overline{V}_0 = V_0,$$

$$B_0^h = \overline{B}_0,$$

$$\overline{\text{MH}}_0 + \overline{\text{MB}}_0 = \overline{M}_0.$$

The Price-Induced Effect on Wealth

Differentiating (6.7) with respect to P_0, while holding constant w_0/P_0 as well as all intertemporal relative prices and interest rates, yields the price-induced effect on wealth:

$$- \left\{ \frac{\partial Y_0^s}{\partial(\text{MB}_0/P_0)} \frac{\text{MB}_0}{P_0^2} + \frac{\partial Y_0^s}{\partial(\overline{\text{MB}}_0/P_0)} \frac{\overline{\text{MB}}_0}{P_0^2} \right\} + \left\{ \sum_{t=1}^{\infty} \frac{i_t \, dm_t/dP_0}{\Pi(1+i)} \right\}$$

$$+ \left\{ \sum_{t=1}^{\infty} \Pi(1+\Delta\widetilde{P}/P) \frac{(i_t - r_t) \, d\overline{m}_t/dP_0 - i_t \, dm_t^F/dP_0}{\Pi(1+i)} \right.$$

$$- \sum_{t=0}^{\infty} \frac{w_0}{P_0} \frac{\Pi(1+\Delta\widetilde{w}/w)}{\Pi(1+i)} \frac{d\overline{N}_t^d}{dP_0} \right\}. \tag{6.8}$$

The first term in braces is the initial-condition effect on current business output, as discussed in chapters 4 and 5; however, now the increase in P_0 reduces Y_0^s because both government and bank real balances fall. The second term in braces depends on the response of future government money stocks, and was analyzed at length in chapter 5. Clearly, the only differences between the price-induced effect on wealth here and in chapter 5 turn on the third term in braces in (6.8). This term is more conveniently expressed as the sum of

$$\sum_{t=1}^{\infty} \Pi(1+\Delta\widetilde{P}/P) \frac{(i_t - r_t) \, d\overline{m}_t/dP_0 - i_t \, dm_t^F/dP_0}{\Pi(1+i)}$$

$$- \sum_{t=1}^{\infty} \frac{w_0}{P_0} \frac{\Pi(1+\Delta\widetilde{w}/w)}{\Pi(1+i)} \frac{d\overline{N}_t^d}{dP_0} \tag{6.9}$$

and

$$- \frac{w_0}{P_0} \frac{d\bar{N}_0^d}{dP_0}. \tag{6.10}$$

Expression (6.9) refers to effects on wealth through banks' behavior in the next period and beyond. Call (6.9) the price-induced effect on wealth through bank money. Expression (6.10) turns out to be an initial-condition effect.[7] These two impacts are discussed in turn.

Analysis of Bank Money in the Price-Induced Effect on Wealth

Assuming homogeneity of degree zero of banks' labor demand, as was done around (6.3), it is clear that $\bar{m}_t$, $\bar{m}_t^F$ and $\bar{N}_t^d$ ($t \geqslant 1$) are independent of the initial price level P_0, and hence (6.9) equals zero. It is useful, nevertheless, to spell out this result in more detail.

Expression (6.9) is very likely to equal zero. In fact, (6.9) is zero for any set of parameters if and only if the bank's labor demand function $\theta(\cdot)$ is homogeneous of degree zero in the nominal values M_t, MF_t and $\tilde{P}_t$. The reasons why $\theta(\cdot)$ is extremely likely to have this homogeneity property are discussed in section 6.9. Assuming homogeneity, the necessary conditions for a wealth-maximizing bank are shown in (6.3). Clearly, a rise in P_0, accompanied by a proportionate change in w_0, leaves these conditions unaffected for given real levels $\bar{m}_t$, m_t^F. Thus, the rise in P_0 has no effect on real bank behavior. Examination of (6.9) shows that if $\bar{m}_t$, m_t^F and hence $\bar{N}_t^d$ are unchanged, then (6.9) equals zero, and the price-induced effect through future bank money is zero.

This result depends on three assumptions. First, banks are price-takers and quantity-setters, paying a competitively determined r. Chapter 7 investigates the consequences of relaxing this assumption. Second, the banking firm is a wealth-maximizer, which gives the marginal conditions to determine bank behavior, so banks do not just arbitrarily or randomly change behavior as P_0 changes. Third, bank resource use is homogeneous of degree zero in nominal values. Thus, an increase in P_0 brings proportionate increases in $\bar{M}$ and MF from the marginal conditions.

Patinkin (1965, 1969, 1971, 1972), Pesek and Saving (1967), and Saving (1970, 1971), however, do not allow the stock of bank money to change with P_0. This suggests asking what happens in (6.9) if $\bar{M}_t$, M_t^F are held constant when P_0 rises. As long as the marginal conditions (6.3) hold, (6.9) remains equal to zero. That is, as long as banks are price-taking, quantity-setting wealth-maximizers, and given the homogeneity condition, the price-induced effect on wealth through bank money is zero even in the case where $\bar{M}_t$, M_t^F are held fixed. To see this, note that the effect of a rise in P_0 on period t's contribution to (6.9) is through the change in $\tilde{P}_t$, $d\tilde{P}_t/dP_0$.

The real present value of bank dividends can be written from (6.4) as

$$\sum_{t=0}^{\infty} \frac{\text{div}_t}{P_0 \Pi(1+i)} = \sum_{t=1}^{\infty} \frac{(i_t - r_t)(\overline{M}_t/\widetilde{P}_t)}{\Pi(1+i)} \frac{\widetilde{P}_t}{P_0}$$

$$- \sum_{t=1}^{\infty} \frac{(\widetilde{w}_t/\widetilde{P}_t)\overline{N}_t^{\text{d}}}{\Pi(1+i)} \frac{\widetilde{P}_t}{P_0} - \sum_{t=1}^{\infty} \frac{i_t(\text{MF}_t/\widetilde{P}_t)}{\Pi(1+i)} \frac{\widetilde{P}_t}{P_0}$$

$$+ \frac{(\text{MF}_0 - \overline{M}_0 - r_0\overline{M}_0) + (\overline{B}_0 + \overline{V}_0)}{P_0}.$$

Differentiating real bank dividends in period t with respect to $\widetilde{P}_t$, holding constant $\widetilde{w}_t/\widetilde{P}_t$, gives

$$\left\{ -(i_t - r_t) \frac{\overline{M}_t}{\widetilde{P}_t^2} + \frac{\widetilde{w}_t}{\widetilde{P}_t} \theta_{\overline{M}} \frac{\overline{M}_t}{\widetilde{P}_t^2} + \frac{\widetilde{w}_t}{\widetilde{P}_t} v_t \theta_r \frac{\overline{M}_t}{\widetilde{P}_t^2} + i_t \frac{M_t^{\text{F}}}{\widetilde{P}_t^2} \right.$$

$$\left. + \frac{\widetilde{w}_t}{\widetilde{P}_t} \theta_{\text{MF}} \frac{M_t^{\text{F}}}{\widetilde{P}_t^2} \right\} \frac{\widetilde{P}_t}{P_0 \Pi(1+i)}$$

$$= \left\{ -\frac{\overline{M}_t}{\widetilde{P}_t^2} \left[(i_t - r_t) - \frac{\widetilde{w}_t}{\widetilde{P}_t} \theta_{\overline{M}} - \frac{\widetilde{w}_t}{\widetilde{P}_t} v_t \theta_r \right] \right.$$

$$\left. - \frac{M_t^{\text{F}}}{\widetilde{P}_t^2} \left[-i_t - \frac{\widetilde{w}_t}{\widetilde{P}_t} \theta_{\text{MF}} \right] \right\} \frac{\widetilde{P}_t}{P_0 \Pi(1+i)}. \tag{6.11}$$

Since both the terms in square brackets in (6.11) equal zero from the marginal conditions under homogeneity (6.3), it is clear that the change in $\widetilde{P}_t$ for all $t \geq 1$ has no effect on real bank dividends or real wealth even when $\overline{M}_t$, MF_t are held constant.

The intuition for the result is this: for a profit-maximizing bank, if the homogeneity condition holds, its marginal condition implies that an increase in the real stock of its money outstanding or in its real holdings of government money causes a marginal change in profits of zero, and this is true even if the change is caused by variations in the price level.

Thus, whether future bank money and reserves change proportionately with prices, as banks plan, or whether the price-induced effect on wealth is evaluated at initial quantities, as Patinkin, Saving and others do, the price-induced effect on wealth through bank money is zero. With this zero effect, and neglecting all other price-induced effects on wealth, it might seem that the increase in P_0 creates no current disequilibrium between demand and supply of bank money, but this is not so. While total wealth is unchanged, the proportion of bank money held in wealth has fallen. However, the real amount of debt owed to banks has also fallen. Consequently, the private non-bank sectors can just afford to restore their levels of real bank balances, and the banks' homogeneity property means that banks are just willing to meet this demand.

Examination of (6.9), both when $\overline{M}_t$, MF_t are allowed to change to keep $\overline{m}_t$, m_t^F constant and when $\overline{M}_t$, MF_t are held constant, shows that the price-induced effect on future bank money is zero when the homogeneity condition holds. Further, in the case where banks are free to vary $\overline{M}_t$, MF_t, a rise in P_0 induces no change in $\overline{m}_t$, m_t^F and thus both $\overline{M}_t$ and MF_t rise proportionately with P_t. Hence, it follows that the price-induced changes in M_t and MF_t, dM_t/dP_t and dMF_t/dP_t, have no effect on wealth. This is discussed in chapter 7, section 7.3.

Expression (6.9) equals zero under homogeneity because banks are price-takers and quantity-setters in the sense that each can set its money stock at whatever level it pleases at the prevailing interest rate on bank money. If banks were somehow limited to smaller money stocks than desired, the marginal condition for bank money would not hold and there would be a price-induced effect on wealth through bank money, as shown in chapter 7. While banks must be price-takers and quantity-setters for (6.9) to equal zero, there is no presumption that (6.9) is evaluated at general equilibrium. Thus, whether or not the system is in equilibrium, the price-induced effect on wealth through bank money is zero.

Thus, in the analysis of the overall price-induced effect on wealth, there remains (6.10), an initial-condition effect.

6.3 The Banking Sector Initial-Condition Effect

The above result for (6.9) means that the part of the price-induced effect on wealth that works through banking activity after period 0 is zero. However, analysis below of (6.10) shows that the part of the price-induced effect on wealth that works through banking activity in period 0 is non-zero. The effect is very much like the business sector's initial-condition effect but now, since $\overline{M}_0$ is not an asset but a liability of the banking sector, the effect is positive. As with the business sector's initial-condition effect, the increase in P_0 not only has an effect on the wealth of the household sector, it also changes the banking sector's market behavior and thus affects current excess demands in two ways.

Recall that $\overline{M}_0$ and MF_0 are the quantities of bank money outstanding and banks' reserves at the start of period 0, determined by the past decisions and thus predetermined from the point of view of period 0. The quantity of labor necessary for banks to do their part in transactions involving bank money, an obligation they undertook by issuing the money, depends on the number of transactions for which the given $\overline{M}_0$ is used. In fact, given $\overline{M}_0$ and MF_0,

$$\frac{\partial \overline{N}^{\mathrm{d}}}{\partial P_0} = -\theta_{\overline{M}} \frac{\overline{M}_0}{P_0^2} - \theta_{\mathrm{MF}} \frac{\mathrm{MF}}{P_0^2} - \theta_\tau v_0 \frac{\overline{M}_0}{P_0^2} \tag{6.12}$$

With a constant w_0/P_0, (6.10) is thus

$$-\frac{w_0}{P_0} \frac{\mathrm{d}N_0^{\mathrm{d}}}{\mathrm{d}P_0} = \frac{w_0}{P_0} \left(\theta_{\overline{M}} \frac{\overline{M}_0}{P_0^2} + \theta_{\mathrm{MF}} \frac{\mathrm{MF}}{P_0^2} + \theta_\tau v_0 \frac{\overline{M}_0}{P_0^2} \right). \tag{6.13}$$

Suppose that in the previous period the banking sector expected the initial value of P_0 and set $\overline{M}_0$ and MF_0 accordingly. Then, from the marginal condition for $\overline{M}_0$ in (6.3)

$$(i_0 - r_0) \frac{\overline{M}_0}{P_0^2} = \frac{w_0}{P_0} \theta_{\overline{M}} \frac{\overline{M}_0}{P_0^2} + \frac{w_0}{P_0} \theta_\tau v_0 \frac{\overline{M}_0}{P_0^2}$$

and for MF_0

$$-i_0 \frac{\mathrm{MF}_0}{P_0^2} = \frac{w_0}{P_0} \theta_{\mathrm{MF}} \frac{\mathrm{MF}_0}{P_0^2}.$$

Thus, (6.10) or (6.13) is

$$(i_0 - r_0) \frac{\overline{M}_0}{P_0^2} - i_0 \frac{\mathrm{MF}_0}{P_0^2} > 0$$

if the bank is making positive profits, since this would require $(i_0 - r_0)M_0 - i_0\mathrm{MF} > 0$. (Even if the initial P_0 is different from what was expected, so the marginal conditions do not initially hold, it is hard to imagine that (6.10) would not be positive.)

The economic interpretation is that the net income from every bank dollar outstanding is fixed, but banks' costs go down because τ_0 falls when the rise in P_0 reduces $\overline{M}_0/P_0$ (with v_0 fixed).

Thus, analysis of (6.10) shows that the contribution of bank money to the price-induced effect on wealth is the positive initial-condition effect in (6.13). Note that among those analyses arguing that bank money plays a part in the price-induced effect on wealth, the usual contention is that the contribution is negative (for example, Pesek and Saving, 1967). Chapter 7 gives a detailed analysis of previous discussions of the banking sector's role in the price-induced effect on wealth; see also the discussion in chapter 2.

While the banking sector's initial-condition effect enters positively in the price-induced effect on wealth, the non-financial business sector's initial-condition effect through bank money enters negatively in (6.8), following the analysis in chapters 4 and 5. Similarly, if the household sector is thought of as choosing leisure, then an increase in P_0 reduces MH_0/P_0, increases household time spent on transactions, and reduces labor supply, and thus causes a household sector initial-condition effect that enters negatively into the price-induced effect on wealth, following the analysis in chapter 5. For the latter two sectors, assuming that the initial P_0 equals the value expected, an increase in real bank money has a marginal benefit equal to the opportunity cost $i_0 - r_0$. Hence a rise in the price level P_0 has the initial-condition effect through bank money of $-(i_0 - r_0)\overline{MB}_0/P_0^2$ and $-(i_0 - r_0)\overline{MH}/P_0^2$ for the business and household sectors.[8] Combining these with the banking sector's effect $(i_0 - r_0)\overline{M}/P_0^2 - i_0 MF/P_0^2$ gives $-(i_0 - r_0)\overline{MB}_0/P_0^2 - (i_0 - r_0)\overline{MH}_0/P_0^2 + (i_0 - r_0)\overline{M}/P_0^2 - i_0 MF/P_0^2 = -i_0 MF/P_0^2 < 0$, since $\overline{MB}_0 + \overline{MH}_0 \equiv \overline{M}_0$.

Call $-(i_0 - r_0)\overline{M}_0/P_0^2$ the initial-condition effect on the banking sector through bank money, and call $-i_0 MF_0/P_0^2$ the initial-condition effect on the banking sector through government money. Hence, the net effect on wealth of all the initial-condition effects through bank money is zero. This still leaves $-i_0 MF_0/P_0^2$, the initial-condition effect on the banking sector through government money. In words, the net initial-condition effect through bank money that enters the price-induced effect on wealth is simply the initial-condition effect on the banking sector through government money. (This result is important in the next chapter when the government pays a competitive rate of interest on its money.) Note that while the effects on wealth of the initial-condition effects tend to cancel, the direct effects of a reduction in $\overline{mb}_0$ on Y_0^s remain, as well as the induced effects on N_0^d and $\overline{N}_0^d$.

The Bank's Current Assets and Liabilities

Inspection of (6.4) shows that (6.10) is not the only effect on the real present value of banks' dividends through the current period. That is, the change in the real value of equity in banks is not simply (6.10). Instead, a rise in P_0 also gives

$$-\left(\frac{\overline{MF}_0}{P_0^2} + \frac{\overline{B}_0}{P_0^2} + \frac{\overline{V}_0}{P_0^2} - \frac{\overline{M}_0}{P_0^2} - r_0 \frac{\overline{M}_0}{P_0^2}\right).$$

$\overline{MF}_0 + \overline{B}_0 + \overline{V}_0$ can be called the banks' assets and $\overline{M}_0 + r_0 \overline{M}_0$ its liabilities (where $r_0 \overline{M}_0$ is an accrued payment obligation added to the more usual bank liability $\overline{M}_0$). Clearly the rise in P_0 affects the real value of assets less liabilities. There is no necessity for assets less liabilities to equal zero, since net worth is not included. However, these same terms show up in the household sector's budget constraint (6.5) and the government sector budget constraint, but with the opposite sign. Hence, when the expressions for the real present value of bank dividends and the government's budget constraint are substituted into the household sector budget constraint, these asset and liability terms cancel exactly. Thus, the net effect of a rise in P_0 on wealth through the banks' current operations is just the initial condition effect (6.10) even if banks' net worth is positive. This is important because many discussions (e.g. Patinkin, 1965, 1972) assume that assets equal liabilities.

Alternatively, suppose that banks' owners put up no financial capital so that the usual "accounting identity"

$$\overline{M}_t = P_{b,t-1}(\overline{B}_t + \overline{V}_t) + \mathrm{MF}_t$$

holds. Then, the expression

$$-\left(\frac{\mathrm{MF}_0}{P_0^2} + \frac{\overline{B}_0}{P_0^2} + \frac{\overline{V}_0}{P_0^2} - \frac{\overline{M}_0}{P_0^2} - r_0\,\frac{\overline{M}_0}{P_0^2}\right)$$

becomes

$$-\{(1-P_{b,-1})(\overline{B}_0 + \overline{V}_0) - r_0\overline{M}_0\}/P_0^2.$$

The second expression turns on the net interest banks earn on their assets, $(1 - P_{b,-1})(\overline{B}_0 + \overline{V}_0)$, less the interest they owe, $r_0\,\overline{M}_0$. This net interest need not equal zero if bank owners put up capital, supply a rent-earning resource, or if entry restrictions allow monopoly rents to be earned. (Banks' income this period is

$$(1-P_{b,-1})(\overline{B}_0 + \overline{V}_0) - r_0\,\overline{M}_0 - w_0\,N_0,$$

but $w_0\,N_0$ is included in the initial-condition effect.)

6.4 The Velocity Effect

The analysis of (6.9) and (6.10) treated $v_t\,(t \geqslant 0)$ as constant. However, in the move from one equilibrium to another, there will very likely be changes in v_t. The result of variations in v_t is a separate effect, the "velocity effect," just as there are separate wealth, substitution and three initial-condition effects (for the household, banking, and non-financial business sectors). In the simplest Hicksian theory, the sum of the wealth and substitution effects suffices to explain variations in behavior (see chapter 3). In this more complex model the sum of wealth, substitution, (the three) initial-condition and velocity effects suffices to explain variations in the system's behavior.

An increase in velocity reduces household sector wealth. To see this, suppose that all expected v_t ($t \geqslant 1$) are positively related to the actual current value v_0. Then, by disturbing the household sector's budget constraint (6.7), an increase in the current transactions velocity of bank money v_0 yields

$$- \sum_{t=0}^{\infty} \frac{w_0 \Pi (1 + \Delta \tilde{w}/w)}{P_0 \Pi (1 + i)} \, \theta_\tau \, \frac{dv_t}{dv_0} \, \overline{m}_t < 0,$$

where $dv_0/dv_0 = 1$, $dv_t/dv_0 > 0$. The economic interpretation is that the more rapid is the velocity of bank money, the more transactions services the bank must provide (given $\overline{m}_t$), and thus the more labor it must hire, thereby making the bank less profitable and reducing the real value of its dividends.

A rise in the velocity of bank money increases the financial sector's current labor demand. The change is

$$\frac{d\overline{N}_0^d}{dv_0} = \theta_\tau \, \overline{m}_0 > 0,$$

since $\overline{m}_0$ and m_0^F are predetermined from this period's point of view. Hence, an increase in bank money velocity disturbs the initial market equilibrium and requires changes in the price variables to re-establish equilibrium.

At the level of the economic system, velocity is not an exogenous variable of course, but is determined by people's reacting to parametric changes. Just exactly how various parametric changes (for example, a technological breakthrough, or a change in consumers' tastes) affect velocity, and through the velocity effect cause further repercussions in the economy, is very difficult to say, since it involves the entire social web of transactions, payments, trade credit accommodation, etc.[9] Will an autonomous decrease in consumption demand which causes a fall in the price level lead to an increase or decrease in v_0? Without further specification of the model, the answer is ambiguous.

Nevertheless, the velocity effect has an important role in two questions of interest here – neutrality and the determinacy of the price level.

6.5 The Neutrality of Money

Consider the neutrality of money. Suppose that by some sort of magic P_0, MH_0, MB_0, MF_0, $\overline{MH}_0$, and $\overline{MB}_0$ are all double their initial equilibrium values, and hence $M_0^s (= MH_0 + MB_0 + MF_0)$ and $\overline{M}_0 (= \overline{MH}_0 + \overline{MB}_0)$

are also doubled.[10] Assume that the wealth-maximizing banks' real decisions are independent of nominal values, or the bank homogeneity condition holds. If w_0 changes proportionately with P_0, if all interest rates are held constant, and if all expected prices and wages are unit elastic, then all (intertemporal and intratemporal) relative discounted prices are unchanged, and there are no substitution effects. All bank and non-financial business sector marginal conditions continue to hold at the same real quantities as before; the banks' homogeneity condition is clearly crucial here. Since MH_0/P_0 and $\overline{MH}_0/P_0$ are unchanged, there is no household sector initial-condition effect. Further, MB_0/P_0, $\overline{MB}_0/P_0$ and MF_0/P_0, $\overline{M}_0/P_0$ are constant, so there are no business or banking sector initial-condition effects, and thus there are no effects on household wealth through business or banking sector initial-condition effects. Further, if all M_t^s ($t \geqslant 1$) are unit elastic with respect to P_0 or all M_t^s double with M_0^s, there is no price-induced effect on household wealth through government money. The only remaining effect, and the only possible means of an effect on household sector wealth, is through the velocity effect, but in the absence of any of these other effects, there is no reason for velocity to alter when price rises. The velocity effect cannot by itself prevent neutrality.

Clearly, if only government money is doubled the real equilibrium must be affected because holding bank money constant sets up initial-condition effects when current prices double. However, assuming uniqueness and stability of equilibrium, over time banks can and will endogenously increase the stock of bank money to return long-run stocks of real bank money and reserves to their previous levels. In the short run, then, increases in government money by itself are not neutral, but they are in the long run.

Obviously the bank homogeneity condition is necessary for neutrality. In other words, if money is neutral, then a competitive, wealth-maximizing banking sector gives a zero price-induced effect on wealth through bank money.

6.6 The Determinacy of the Price Level, the Initial-Condition Effects with Bank Money, and the Velocity Effect

Consider the determinacy of the price level. As seen above, under certain conditions there is no price-induced effect on wealth through bank money. Suppose that all government money stocks M_t^s ($t \geqslant 1$) vary proportionately with P_0, and thus the price-induced effect on wealth through government money is zero. In the absence of effects on wealth through the two kinds of money, conventional theory relies on the "portfolio effect" to make the price level determinate (see Gurley and Shaw (1960), Patinkin (1965), and chapter 2 above). According to this effect, while wealth does not change with a rise in P_0, there is a decline in the amount of one or both kinds of real money balances that are available to hold at the end of the period. However, under present assumptions, both monies are unit elastic with respect to P_0, so the portfolio effect is absent. For conventional theory, then, P_0 seems to be indeterminate. But, as in chapter 5, there are initial-condition effects on the household, business, and banking sectors to ensure determinacy. Further, there is now the velocity effect.

Consider the household sector's initial-condition effect. As before, if P_0 doubles, the real value of its initial government money holdings is cut in half and these holdings are insufficient to make the transactions which were planned to be executed with government money. That is, executing this volume of transactions now requires a larger sacrifice of time than had been planned. In addition, the real value of the household sector's initial holdings of bank money is cut in half; households' real holdings of bank money are now insufficient to execute the transactions which the sector had planned to carry out with bank money. As in chapter 5, the household sector initial-condition effect can be viewed as leaving the budget constraint unchanged but shifting the indifference surfaces, if real balances enter the utility function, or as reducing wealth and rotating the budget constraint if leisure is viewed as the household choice variable in a context of transactions costs.[11] Through changes in both the initial real value of government money and bank money, consumer demands are very likely to change.

Further, the rise in P_0 is likely to affect consumer wealth through the effect on the non-financial business sector

$$- \frac{\partial Y_0}{\partial (MB_0/P_0)} \frac{MB_0}{P_0^2} - \frac{\partial Y_0^s}{\partial (\overline{MB}_0/P_0)} \frac{\overline{MB}_0}{P_0^2}$$

and the banking sector

$$(i_0 - r_0) \frac{\overline{M}_0}{P_0^2} - i_0 \frac{MF}{P_0^2}$$

in equations (6.8) and (6.13). Beyond these effects on wealth, the non-financial business and the banking sectors will alter Y_0^s, N_0^d and $\overline{N}_0^d$ when both types of real balances fall with a rise in P_0. In addition, the velocity of bank money is likely to change in response to these real changes. Thus, the current non-zero excess demands that are conventionally taken as showing the determinacy of the price level in this sort of experiment are likely to occur (see chapter 5).

As in chapter 5, the three initial-condition effects, plus the velocity effect, do not guarantee that doubling P_0 will produce disequilibrium.[12] Rather, they show that, even in the absence of substitution effects and a price-induced effect on wealth, there are still forces tending to ensure that the price level is determinate in the sense that doubling prices leads to disequilibrium.

6.7 The Role of Banks and Bank Money in the Price-Induced Effect on Wealth

The preceding discussion provides the basis for answering some questions in earlier literature. (A critical review of Patinkin's (1969) critique of Pesek and Saving's (1967) book is given in chapter 7 to clarify other important doctrinal issues.)

The Price-Induced Effect on Wealth – Initial Bank Deposits as a Liability

The early postwar literature held that the bank money in existence at a point in time was not part of net wealth,[13] and therefore a rise in P_0 had no effect on wealth through its impact on the real value of bank money, because for any bank money "asset" there was a matching and offsetting "liability." Pesek and Saving (1967) explicitly challenged this position on the basis that bank money is not a debt but rather an obligation to provide certain services. This is clearly a superior analytical formulation – indeed, it is the view which this essay has adopted above. Nevertheless, there is some truth in the older position. In the context of the above model, an increase in P_0 reduces the real value of the household sector's initial holdings of real bank money and thus reduces wealth. The increase in P_0 also reduces the present value of the real dividend stream that the non-financial business sector plans to pay the household sector, since business must now accumulate more bank money to rebuild its real holdings of bank money. The sum of these two reductions in household sector wealth is exactly the same amount that the real present value of the banking sector's dividend stream is increased due to outstanding issues of bank money; given the real amounts of bank money $\overline{m}_t$ that banks plan to have outstanding, a reduction in $\overline{m}_0$ due to a rise in P_0 increases banks' dividends. The three effects must net to zero, since $\overline{M}_0 = \overline{MH}_0 + MB_0$; none of these three terms is found in (6.7), since they cancel. Pesek and Savings's position that money is not just a debt is correct, but in the present model the net effect of the initial quantity of bank money on the price-induced effect on wealth is necessarily zero, just as earlier theorists maintained.[14] This of course is not the end of the matter of the role of banks in the price-induced effect on wealth; the remaining issues, as discussed above, are the price-induced effect on wealth through future bank money and the banking sector's initial-condition effect. A contribution of Pesek and Saving (1967) was that they jolted the profession to think in terms of banks' future net income rather than just banks assets versus liabilities (Patinkin, 1969, 1972). Chapter 7 argues that the literature is still quite unclear on the issue of how an increase in P_0 affects the real net present value of net bank income.

The Price-Induced Effect on Wealth: The Initial-Condition Effect, and Future Quantities of Bank Money

From (6.10) and (6.13), an increase in P_0 has an effect on wealth through banks' activities in period 0; this is the influence on wealth of the banking sector's initial-condition effect. But rather than this effect being negative or zero when P_0 rises, as have been the alternatives disputed, the effect is positive, as explained in detail in section 6.3. It is clear that there was no inkling in the earlier literature, and there is none in the most recent literature, of the banking sector's initial-condition effect and its role in the price-induced effect on wealth.

Previous discussions seem to have paid only slight attention to how future supplies of bank money enter the price-induced effect on wealth. However, as the preceding sections demonstrated in connection with (6.8)–(6.10), if the function $\theta(\cdot)$ is homogeneous of degree zero in $\overline{M}_t$, MF_t and $\widetilde{P}_t$ for all $t \geq 1$, and the wealth-maximizing banking sector pays a competitive rate of interest on its money, then activities of the banking sector in period 0 and beyond do not contribute at all to the price-induced effect on wealth[15] (see the discussion around (6.9)). It is possible to argue that earlier workers really did have something like the proper homogeneity of $\theta(\cdot)$ in mind – neutrality, after all, requires it, and neutrality was not seriously challenged (Saving, 1973).

Section 6.9 argues that $\theta(\cdot)$ is quite likely to be homogeneous of degree zero. But, supposing that it is not, an increase in P_0 accompanied by a proportionate rise in w_0 does lead to an effect on wealth through the banking sector's activities in future periods, but not necessarily a negative effect. To facilitate the argument, assume that $\theta(\cdot)$ is homogeneous of some degree λ in $\overline{M}_t$, MF_t and $\widetilde{P}_t$,[16] where $\lambda \gtreqless 0$. Thus $\overline{N}_t^{\mathrm{d}} = P_t^{\lambda}$ $\theta(\overline{m}_t, m_t^{\mathrm{F}}, 1, v_t\overline{M}_t/\widetilde{P}_t)$. This says that the effect on $\overline{N}_t^{\mathrm{d}}$ of a change in price that holds $\overline{m}_t$ and m_t^{F} constant but increases the nominal scale of operations is positive, zero or negative as $\lambda \gtreqless 0$. The financial sector's real wage bill in period t, as a function of $\bar{m}_t$ and m_t^F, is

$$\frac{w_0}{P_0} \frac{\Pi(1 + \Delta \tilde{w}/w)}{\Pi(1 + i)} \tilde{P}_t^\lambda \theta(\bar{m}_t, m_t^F, 1, v_t \bar{m}_t)$$

$$= \frac{w_0}{P_0} \frac{\Pi(1 + \Delta \tilde{w}/w)}{(1 + i)} \{P_0 \Pi(1 + \Delta \tilde{P}/P)\}^\lambda \theta(\cdot)$$

The effect on wealth of an increase in P_0 through future banking activity is (6.9) and, assuming unit-elastic price and wage rate expectations, equals

$$- \sum_{t=1}^{\infty} \frac{w_0 \Pi(1 + \Delta \tilde{w}/w)}{P_0 \Pi(1 + i)} \Pi\left(1 + \frac{\Delta \tilde{P}}{P}\right) \lambda \tilde{P}_t^{\lambda - 1} \theta(\cdot) \gtreqless 0 \quad \text{as} \quad \lambda \lesseqgtr 0.$$

$$(6.14)$$

This can be seen by noting that in any period t the change in (6.9) is

$$\left\{ \frac{\Pi(1 + \Delta \tilde{P}/P)}{\Pi(1 + i)} (i_t - r_t) - \frac{w_0}{P_0} \frac{\Pi(1 + \Delta \tilde{w}/w)}{\Pi(1 + i)} \frac{\partial \bar{N}_t^d}{\partial \bar{m}_t} \right\} \frac{d\bar{m}_t^d}{dP_0}$$

$$+ \left\{ -\frac{\Pi(1 + \Delta \tilde{P}/P)}{\Pi(1 + i)} i_t - \frac{w_0}{P_0} \frac{\Pi(1 + \Delta \tilde{w}/w)}{\Pi(1 + i)} \frac{\partial \bar{N}_t^d}{\partial \bar{m}_t} \right\} \frac{dm_t^F}{dP_0}$$

$$- \frac{w_0}{P_0} \frac{\Pi(1 + \Delta w/w)}{\Pi(1 + i)} \frac{\partial \bar{N}_t^d}{\partial P_0}.$$

From marginal conditions, the two expressions in braces are zero. The term $\partial \bar{N}_t^d / \partial P_0$ is $\partial \{\tilde{P}_t^\lambda \theta(\cdot)\}/\partial P_0 = \partial[\{P_0 \Pi(1 + \Delta \tilde{P}/P)\}^\lambda \theta(\cdot)]/\partial P_0 = \Pi(1 + \Delta \tilde{P}/P)\lambda \tilde{P}_t^\lambda \theta(\cdot)$. Expression (6.14) implies, then, that a negative price-induced effect on wealth through future banking activity would require $\lambda > 0$ in this case. However, if λ is not equal to zero – though a strong case for $\lambda = 0$ is made below – it seems just as likely that λ is less than zero as greater than zero.

6.8 Bank Profits, Restrictions on Entry, and Reserve Requirements

The above analysis of banking is distant from many real world complications, including government regulations. This section considers the effects of two pervasive regulations – entry to the industry and required reserves. Restrictions on entry have no effect on the price-induced effect on wealth. Patinkin (1969, 1972), however, makes free entry and consequent zero bank profits the key to his view that there is a zero price-induced effect on wealth (see the discussion of Patinkin's analysis in chapter 7).

Restricted Entry

Consider restricting entry. As long as none of the individual banks in existence can affect i or r, the analysis proceeds exactly as in sections 6.1 and 6.2, which never postulated free entry. Price-taking, quantity-setting behavior requires large numbers of firms, not necessarily free entry. Restrictions on entry make it very likely that revenues exceed cost, the difference being monopoly rents for the industry. Note that the level of the surplus does not alter the analysis of the price-induced effect on wealth through banks, as given in the discussion of (6.9) and (6.10). If the function $\theta(\cdot)$ is homogeneous of degree zero, a doubling of P_0 does not affect the contribution of future periods' bank money to wealth, (6.9) – though there still remains the bank sector initial-condition effect (6.10). But equation (6.9) still holds whether perfect competition and free entry make bank dividends zero or, alternatively, perfect competition and restricted entry make dividends positive. Whether bank dividends benefit from government restriction is irrelevant to proper competitive analysis of the effect of P_0 on wealth.

Reserve Requirements

Suppose that government regulation requires banks to hold government money equal to 20 percent of the stock of bank money, in addition to the reserves that banks themselves decide to hold for convertibility purposes. Then, if $\theta(\cdot)$ is homogeneous of degree zero, banks' decisions are still unaffected by the price level and (6.9) still equals zero. The reserve requirement means that $\theta(\cdot)$ is replaced by the new function $\bar{\theta}(\cdot)$, where $\bar{\theta} = \theta(\overline{M}_t, \text{MF}_t - 0.2\overline{M}_t, \widetilde{P}_t, r_t)$, to reflect the fact that an amount of reserves equal to $0.2\overline{M}_t$ is simply unavailable to aid in convertibility.[17] Clearly, in this case $\bar{\theta}(\cdot)$ is homogeneous of degree zero in $\overline{M}_t$, MF_t and $\widetilde{P}_t$ if and only if $\theta(\cdot)$ is.

Conversely, if $\theta(\cdot)$ is homogeneous of degree zero, the reserve requirement can be made non-proportional, thus ensuring that $\bar{\theta}(\cdot)$ is not homogeneous of degree zero. For example, if required reserves in period t are $a + b\overline{M}_t$, the required reserves show increasing, constant, or decreasing costs as $a \lesseqgtr 0$. Since price changes do have an impact on the real present value of future bank dividends unless $\bar{\theta}(\cdot)$ is homogeneous of degree zero (see section 6.7 above), government policy can ensure such effects by choosing a reserve policy to make $\bar{\theta}(\cdot)$ non-homogeneous of degree zero (and such a policy can be chosen whether or not $\theta(\cdot)$ is homogeneous of degree zero).[18]

Further, if $\theta(\cdot)$ is not homogeneous of degree zero, government can choose a set of reserve requirements to make $\bar{\theta}(\cdot)$ homogeneous of degree zero for a wide variety of $\theta(\cdot)$.

Consequently, when government regulates the banking industry's required reserves, the size and sign of the industry's contribution to the price-induced change in wealth is very much a matter of government choice.

Chapter 7 discusses another example of government regulation, restrictions on interest rates paid on demand deposits.

6.9 The Homogeneity Assumption

The issue of the homogeneity of degree zero of θ in nominal values is important for neutrality as well as for a zero price-induced effect on wealth through bank money. As noted above, none of this chapter's conclusions depends on aggregation over firms, or presupposes an aggregate industry $\theta(\cdot)$ function, though some arguments are stated in aggregate terms for convenience.

Start with the question of neutrality. Suppose that P_0 doubles, and $\bar{M}_t$ and MF_t $(t \geq 0)$ double with it. $\bar{m}_t$, m_t^{F} $(t \geq 0)$ are unaffected and so are real, physical bank transactions

$$\tau_t = v_t \frac{2\bar{M}_0}{2P_0\Pi(1 + \Delta P/P)} = v_t \frac{\bar{M}_t}{P_0\Pi(1 + \Delta P/P)}.$$

It is difficult to see how such a comparative statics experiment can make any real difference, and in particular how it could alter $\bar{N}_t^{\mathrm{d}}$. Conditions sufficient for the necessary zero-degree homogeneity are either (a) bank money and government money are bookkeeping entries, or (b) the two monies are (say) paper money but both institutions require (ensure) that all denominations of their money exchange at face value, and already provide sufficiently varied denominations so that the gap between one denomination and the next lower or higher is not "too large."

Under (a) with all money as bookkeeping entries, it should not matter to depositors, banks, and government whether or not the bookkeeping entries shuffled about are twice as large. It is often said that individuals adjust psychically to one level of prices, and a doubling causes psychic pain and readjustment. Probably this is quite right, but it is of no relevance to a comparative statics experiment. Second, it is said that a change in the rate of inflation means more time, trouble, and expense in calculating intertemporal relative prices. Again, this is true, but irrelevant to the experiment – no rate of inflation has changed. On the contrary, the rates are constant and the base price level changes.

As for (b) with paper money, suppose that both bank and government money come in (almost) continuous denominations. If a $5 bill (whether bank or government) is to sell for precisely one-half the price of a $10 bill, then the issuing institution must make $10 bills available on demand for two $5 bills.[19] Suppose that in the initial equilibrium everyone uses $10 bills, but no $5 or $20 bills. If prices double and if everyone must make transactions now with two $10 bills where previously they used one $10 bill, then there is a real difference, for money has become less convenient. For example, a radical inflation in a country on a copper standard can impose heavy burdens, as can a radical deflation in a country on the gold standard. However, if there exist $20 bills, freely exchangeable for two $10 bills, individuals will not have to undergo any added inconveniences, and hence there should be no effect.

This last experiment is similar to the traditional neutrality experiment where P_0, M_0^s and $\overline{M}_0$ all double and there is a simultaneous currency reform that replaces every two bills of a given denomination with one bill of a denomination twice as large. The point is, though, that such a "currency reform" automatically occurs if the monetary system has a sufficient range of denominations and freely buys and sells all denominations to maintain fixed exchange rates among them at the ratios of their face values. Aside from the initial conversion costs from one set of denominations to another twice as large, costs ignored in a comparative statics experiment, neither banks nor government should be affected.

Thus, in the absence of regulations such as those discussed in section 6.8, it seems very reasonable that $\theta(\cdot)$ is homogeneous of degree zero in nominal values, the assumption on which so many of this chapter's results depend.

6.10 Banks, Welfare, Wealth, and the Price-Induced Effect on Wealth through Banks

The world enjoys improved welfare through the existence of a banking system, rather than being restricted solely to government fiat money. However, this is an entirely separate issue from the price-induced effect on wealth through banks.

Conceptually, one could attempt to measure the improvement in welfare owing to the existence of the banking system first by prohibiting bank money and measuring national income before and after the regulation, or secondly by asking the community how much it would pay (in real terms) in order not to have this regulation imposed or to have it removed. In general, the two answers would differ, but they would provide some measure of the increase in welfare created by the existence of a private banking system. And they might be said to measure the increase in the community's "wealth" due to the existence of the bank system, and this wealth is higher the greater the efficiency of the bank sector.

All the results of this chapter are perfectly consistent with a wide range of values of these two measures. The price-induced effect on wealth is (6.8), whatever the efficiency of the banking system.

A third way of measuring the addition to wealth caused by the existence of the banking system is to value each bank dollar at its opportunity cost $i-r$. As Johnson (1969) points out, this method creates a "paradox" when $i = r$, for it seems to say the system has no influence on wealth; more generally, the less efficient the system is per bank dollar, so the wider must be the gap $i-r$, and the more highly does the method value each bank dollar (see also Friedman and Schwartz, 1969). Again, the value assumed by this measure has no necessary relationship to the correct method of evaluating the price-induced effect on wealth, as in (6.8).

Yet a fourth way – consumer surplus – is to compute the area under the demand curve for real balances, as Johnson (1969) does. This has the advantage over the third method that there is no paradox when $i = r$ and this fourth method yields answers more or less like the first two methods. Again, the value found by this measure has no necessary relationship to the price-induced effect on wealth. But the ease with which the two concepts can be confused is demonstrated by Johnson's (1969, p. 35) use of the term "wealth effect" to refer both to the price-induced effect on wealth and to the "wealth effect . . . from the existence of the bank."

A fifth attempt is to measure society's net assets,[20] the approach of much of monetary theory, which Pesek and Saving (1967) attribute to the "new view" and Patinkin (1969) to the "old view." By assuming that each bank's liabilities and assets exactly cancel – or defining assets and liabilities so that this is true – the banking system is said to cause no net addition to society's assets.

The first, second, and fourth measures are just attempts to quantify the fact that the economic system is better off with the banking system than if banks were prohibited; the third and fifth methods seem to deny this. In fact, these conflicting measures are merely examples of the ancient paradox of the difference between value in use and value in exchange. Pesek and Saving (1967), Johnson (1969) and Saving (1970) correctly deny that banks add nothing to welfare. But these economists go further and insist that the measures they choose in trying to quantify this contribution also have some role in the price-induced effect on wealth. However, the measure of welfare chosen does not affect the measurement of the Hicksian price-induced effect on wealth through banks.

6.11 The "Old View" and "New View" Monetary Theories, and Many Financial Assets

The conflict between the "old view" and "new view" schools of monetary theory raises other questions about the connection between the banking system and wealth. The debate has continued unresolved for three decades, and since some of the issues turn on elements not considered here (for example, uncertainty), this essay cannot resolve it. The essay can show, though, how the debate looks in a Hicksian neo-classical, certainty framework. Patinkin (1969, p. 1159) gives a summary of the "new view" as emphasizing

> . . . the necessity for banks to persuade individuals to demand their product (viz., bank money) as contrasted with other forms of money; the necessity for banks to compete for reserves; the costs of production of the banking industry; and, generally, the necessity for analyzing the behavior of the banking industry in terms of the profit-maximizing objective used for any other industry . . .

The "old view" is dominant in textbooks, and is perhaps most clearly symbolized by the description of the multiple expansion of the money supply due to an increase in reserves.

Banks as Firms

In this essay's framework, the "new view" is clearly better on several issues. Consider the "old view" belief that banks create money out of thin air (Tobin, 1963). As long as bank money is counted as a component of the money supply, then it is clearly true that the money supply is larger because bank money exists (as long as banks hold less than 100 percent reserves). In addition, society is better off through the existence of the banking system, and hence society is "wealthier." Both facts are consistent with the "new view." In this essay banks produce an output – bank money plus a repurchase guarantee – subject to a production function, and sell the output at a competitive price, just as they hire inputs (labor and reserves). As Gurley and Shaw (1960 and 1956) pointed out long ago, the economy is (presumably) better off because of the existence of a competitive automobile industry. The output of this industry is part of the supply of vehicles, and unless the auto industry uses more vehicles as inputs than it produces, the stock of vehicles is larger because of the industry – exactly analogously to the banking industry.

Multiple Expansion of the Money Supply

The usual exposition of the money supply process creates a bias toward the view that banks create money out of air. Suppose that a bank has $100 in unwanted reserves; this implies that the bank, and hence the economy, has not reached equilibrium. The bank can safely (that is, without fear of falling below its desired level of reserves) buy $100 worth of bonds with newly created bank money. Suppose there is no currency drain from the banking system; that is, if the non-bank sector receives this $100 in bank money, it does not want to hold part of it in cash and thereby reduce the stock of unwanted reserves. Hence, the banking system must ultimately end up holding the $100 in reserves. As the banking sector's demand deposit issues increase, its demand for reserves rises, continuing so until the $100 is absorbed in desired reserves. The money supply has increased, as have bank's earning assets and present values – all compared with the initial disequilibrium position.

An alternative description is that the bank uses the $100 (rather than newly created bank money) to buy bonds. By assumption the bond sellers do not desire government money (no currency drain) but want bank money; as in the other description, the system is not yet in equilibrium. Hence, the bond sellers deposit the $100 of government money at banks. The $100 in cash is "unwanted" by banks, or rather cash was not the optimum asset. At the competitively determined rates i and r, the banking system adjusted its quantity of bank money supplied and labor demanded. Now the household sector demands $100 more of bank money, in place of the $100 of government money it receives for its bond; hence i and r must vary to induce banks to raise $\overline{M}$ by $100. These changes in i and r change MF, presumably increasing it; so with the household deposit of $100 of government money, actual reserves are now too high by only (say) $90. The process is repeated until all $100 is absorbed in reserves.

The second example proceeds in terms of balance sheets (as did the first). But it is much more economically appealing. It shows how i and r must adjust to induce an increase in $\overline{M}$ supplied and an increase in the reserves demanded, and shows the equilibrium conditions: i and r must take on values where $\overline{M}^d = \overline{M}$ and MF has absorbed the extra $100 of government money. Note that the banking system increases the quantity of output it supplies in response to changes in price incentives, and increases its factor (reserve) demand in the same way. The money supply, banks' earning assets and present values have all increased relative to the disequilibrium position. But rather than describing the banks as engaged in creating money and dumping it on the household sector until reserves become just barely adequate and put a stop to the process, the second description shows banks as cajoled by changing prices into expanding $\overline{M}$ and MF until equilibrium is attained.

Banks Versus Other Financial Intermediaries

Another "old view" position is that bank money is different from the products of other financial firms, and different in a sense beyond the trivial (see Gurley and Shaw, 1956) that demand deposits are not savings deposits and also are not insurance policies. This "old view" position does not seem correct within the static framework used here. This chapter assumed that bank money was used to make transactions directly, just as was government money; of course for both to coexist with different opportunity costs, the two must not be perfect substitutes, or equally useful in all transactions. Suppose, though, that the variable $\overline{M}_t$ is now redefined as savings deposits which cannot be used directly to effect transactions, but must be first turned into government money at the (savings) bank. For example, the government might forbid the use of bank deposits as a medium of exchange, making all bank deposits savings rather than demand deposits. Such a change would be likely to have a large effect on the economy's welfare, but it would not affect the form of the household sector's budget constraint, or the nature of the price-induced effect on wealth and the initial-condition effects. That is, the two financial institutions – commercial banks and savings banks – have precisely the same analytical impact for present purposes.

It is easy to extend the analysis and include both commercial and savings banks. Within the static, certainty framework of this essay, risk and uncertainty cannot explain the demand for time deposits any more than they explained the demand for bank money. Rather, both demands are made to depend on transactions costs. If time deposits are to be analytically distinct from bonds, it must be true that holding wealth in the form of time deposits allows some transactions to be made more cheaply than if wealth is in bonds. This chapter's analysis applies with $\overline{M}_t$ interpreted as time deposits rather than as demand deposits. The main change in the surrounding story is that now transactions consummated with time deposits first require a stop at the bank to convert these deposits to government money.

Government money is superior to time deposits in making transactions, since any transaction with time deposits first requires conversion to cash.

But households maintain these deposits because they earn interest on them, and this interest compensates them for the costs of making conversion. The costs of making the conversion are lower when going from time deposits to cash than from bonds to cash if indeed conversion from bonds to cash is feasible within the period[21] (the transactor may have to resort to purely credit arrangements when his/her wealth is all in bonds). Thus, a given set of transactions requires smaller costs both the larger are cash holdings and the larger are time deposits. The smaller conversion costs in going from time deposits to cash rather than from bonds to cash also explain why the rate of interest on time deposits is smaller than on bonds.

Suppose that the number of assets expands to include bonds, cash, and demand and time deposits. Holding both cash and demand deposits is rationalized as before by the differential abilities of the two in effecting various exchanges. If time deposits are used for a transaction, they must first be converted to either cash or demand deposits, whichever is more convenient. The rationale just given for holding time deposits when cash exists applies *mutatis mutandis* for holding them when demand deposits also exist. A higher rate of interest on time deposits than on demand deposits compensates the holder for having to convert time deposits before consummating a transaction; but the lower costs of converting time deposits than bonds[22] make the bond rate of interest higher than the time deposit rate.

Note that the same sort of reasoning that allows demand and time deposits to coexist on the basis of transactions costs also allows the existence of a range of financial institutions, offering different assets, different interest rates, and different costs of conversion (time and trouble, penalties, and so forth). Each household has different sorts of transactions. Different households have different transactions patterns. Different entrepreneurs have more or less skill at different types of financial transactions and at managing different types of financial transactions, and at managing different types of financial institutions. Different factor mixes are more likely to be suitable for one sort of financial institution than for others. Thus, from both the demand and supply side, it seems plausible that there exists a range of assets with different interest rates and different costs, and that these rates and costs on different assets will shift relative to one another when demand and supply change. At going rates, some households find one asset dominant, others will find a different asset dominant; some households find a mix preferable. Sufficiently large changes in the interest rates and costs of one asset relative to others will change the preferred selection. In the same way, financial institutions offer a more or less large array of assets.

A static certainty theory that bases asset demand on transactions costs no doubt misses a good deal that depends on risk and uncertainty. Within these limitations, however, the "new view" seems clearly superior to the "old view."

APPENDIX 6A THE WICKSELLIAN CUMULATIVE PROCESS

The present chapter has implications for the Wicksellian cumulative process in a pure credit economy. Hicks (1946) interpreted Wicksell as discussing an economy with no government money, only bank money. Hicks argued that, given all interest rates, if all current and expected prices rise proportionately, no individual has any substitution effect. But further, any effect on wealth is just a distribution effect, and if distribution effects are ignored there is no wealth effect.

So far, this chapter's analysis agrees perfectly with Hicks. If all expected rates of inflation and interest are constant, as assumed, there are no changes in relative prices. Further, the effect on wealth depends on the sign of (6.8) and, if $M_t^s = 0$, there is no price-induced effect on wealth through government money in (6.8). Note that the non-existence of government money implies no reserves, and hence $\overline{N}_t^d = \theta(\overline{M}_t, \widetilde{P}_t, \tau_t)$. Hicks fairly clearly assumes the zero-degree homogeneity property, or $\theta(\overline{M}_t, \widetilde{P}_t, \tau_t) = \theta(M_t/\widetilde{P}_t, 1, \tau_t)$.

Hicks goes on to argue that P_0 can thus take any value; the price level is indeterminate. But in terms of this essay this conclusion is clearly wrong, for it ignores the three initial-condition effects through bank money. Though there is no effect on wealth through government or through future bank activities, an arbitrary increase in P_0 (a) reduces the real value of the household sector's initial holdings of bank money below the optimum level for executing planned transactions, (b) reduces the real value of the (non-financial) business sector's bank money holdings, hence reducing planned activities and household wealth, and (c) given v_0, reduces τ_0, hence reducing $\overline{N}_0^d$ and increasing household wealth.[23] The Wicksellian cumulative process, at least as pictured by Hicks, cannot come about on this essay's assumptions.

But Hicks had a different assumption. He pictured bank money as in instantaneous supply at the very beginning of the period. When P_0 rises, there are no wealth and substitution effects: the household and (non-financial) business sectors immediately (and exactly) replenish their real balances by issuing bonds (transactions which hold wealth constant), and the banking sector immediately issues new money to bring its real balances outstanding (and hence bank transactions) back to their old level. There are no initial-condition effects.

Note, however, that in a model with both bank and government money the absence of a bank money initial-condition effect still leaves a government money initial-condition effect to help render the price level determinate, even if the price-induced effect on wealth through government money is zero. As long as the government makes its transfer payments and bond sales and collects its taxes over the course of the period, the number of government dollars in existence at the start of the period is fixed – the mechanism of the initial-condition effect.

Thus, for convenience, suppose that the system has been in stationary equilibrium for several periods, and the government announces at the very start of a period that by the end of the same period the supply of government money will have doubled (say through transfer payments). If the current period's price level doubles, there is no wealth effect through government money, and, under Hicks's assumptions about the timing of acquisition of bank money, no initial-condition effect through bank money. Firms and households, however, do not yet have the increased stock of government dollars – they will not have all of them until the end of the period – and hence alter their real plans.

As an alternative experiment, suppose that future government money supplies are unit elastic with respect to the current price level. Then, if P_0 doubles, there is no effect on wealth through government money (say that the induced extra government money is disbursed as transfer payments). Given Hicks's assumption on the timing of acquisition of bank money, there is no initial-condition effect through bank money. However, each sector's initial real holdings of government money are halved, and as long as some sector is not satiated in government balances this causes an initial-condition effect through government money; real behavior is affected, and the doubled price level is not likely to be an equilibrium. The fact that the increase in government money, generated by the increase in P_0, is distributed over the period, and not in the initial instant, works to render the price level determinate.

It is sometimes asserted that "rationality" implies that the government must double the money supply when prices double[24] – see Hansen, 1970. It is then concluded that the price level is indeterminate in this case. However, the conclusion of indeterminacy follows from this prescription of rationality only if government money doubles with price in the initial moment of the period and bank money is acquired as assumed by Hicks. Thus, even accepting the dubious premise of what constitutes rationality, initial-condition effects work to render the price level determinate.

APPENDIX 6B   BANK SERVICE CHARGES ON CUSTOMER TRANSACTIONS

Models used to analyze bank money in the price-induced effect on wealth have not included bank service charges on customer transactions, as Saving (1977, p. 293, n. 10) has noted. Other economists, for example, Mitchell (1979), Saving (1979) and Merris (1985), suppose that banks charge fees for customers' transactions. To include this issue in the model developed above, suppose that banks charge a competitively determined nominal fee of s for each real transaction their customers carry out. This alters bank dividends in (6.1) to

$$\text{div}_t = \Delta \overline{M}_t + \overline{B}_t + \overline{V}_t + s_t \, \tau_t - r_t \, \overline{M}_t - w_t \, \overline{N}_t^{\text{d}} - P_{\text{b},t}(\overline{B}_{t+1}^{\text{d}} + \overline{V}_{t+1}^{\text{d}}) - \Delta \text{MF}_t. \tag{6.1'}$$

Continuing to assume that $\overline{N}_t^{\text{d}}$ is homogeneous of degree zero in nominal values, the banks' marginal conditions are now

$$(i_t - r_t) \, \frac{s_t \, v_t}{\widetilde{P}_t} - \frac{\widetilde{w}_t}{\widetilde{P}_t} \, (\theta_{\overline{M}} + \theta_\tau v_t) = 0 \tag{6.3a'}$$

$$- i_t - \frac{\widetilde{w}_t}{\widetilde{P}_t} \, \theta_{\text{MF}} = 0. \tag{6.3b'}$$

Compared with the earlier marginal conditions (6.3a) and (6.3b), the new (6.3a') includes the term $s_t v_t / \widetilde{P}_t$, while (6.3b) and (6.3b') are identical. Under the assumption that $\overline{N}_t^{\text{d}}$ is homogeneous of degree zero in nominal values, it is clear that proportionate changes in $\widetilde{w}_t$, $\widetilde{P}_t$, s_t have no effects on banks' decisions, or on $\overline{m}_t$, m_t^{F}, $\overline{N}_t^{\text{d}}$. From this result, it follows directly that the price-induced effect on wealth through future bank money, the analog of (6.9), must still be zero.

Note that the individual bank does not choose the real transactions τ_t of its customers. Rather, the bank chooses $\overline{M}_t$ and from $\tau_t = v_t \, \overline{M}_t$ its customers choose τ_t. Saving's (1979) assumption that the individual competitive bank sets not only $\overline{M}_t$ but also τ_t neglects the relationship $\tau_t = v_t \, \overline{M}_t / \widetilde{P}_t$, where the individual bank has no control over v_t. In general equilibrium, v_t varies endogenously of course and in particular is likely to be lower the higher is s_t. s_t is competitively determined, however, and is not under the control of the individual bank.

The present value of the banking sector changes by the inclusion in (6.2) of the term

$$\sum_{t=0}^{\infty} \frac{s_0}{P_0} \, \frac{\Pi(1 + \Delta s^{\text{e}}/s)}{\Pi(1 + i)} \, \tau_t^{\text{e}},$$

where $\Delta s^e/s$ and τ^e_t are banks' expected inflation in s and expected real transactions with bank money. Both business and households must now pay the service charge s_t on their transactions τ^B_t, τ^{HH}_t. The present value of these costs is

$$\sum_{t=0}^{\infty} \frac{s_0}{P_0} \frac{\Pi(1+\Delta\tilde{s}/s)}{(1+i)} \tilde{\tau}^B_t \text{ and } \sum_{t=0}^{\infty} \frac{s_0}{P_0} \frac{\Pi(1+\Delta s/s)}{\Pi(1+i)} \tau^{HH}_t.$$

Assuming that $\Delta s^e = \Delta\tilde{s} = \Delta s$ and $\tau^e_t = \tilde{\tau}^B_t + \tilde{\tau}^{HH}_t$, the revenue that the banks earn from s and the costs the other sectors pay for s net to zero, and these terms drop out of the household sector budget constraint (6.7) after substitutions are made for bank and non-financial business dividends. It is clear, then, that the analysis of the price-induced effect on wealth in a world with bank money is as given in chapter 6, even when the model is generalized to include service charges due to customers' transactions that use bank money. In particular, the price-induced effect on wealth through bank money, expression (6.9), and the banking sector's initial-condition effect, expression (6.10), are unchanged.

Looking ahead to chapter 7's discussion, it is worthwhile giving a further discussion of the case with service charges. From the banks' viewpoint paying interest on bank money and levying service charges are perfect substitutes at any given v. Define a net interest rate on bank money

$$r'_t = r_t - s_t v_t/\tilde{P}_t.$$

Examination of bank marginal conditions shows that only r' affects choice of $\overline{M}_t$, M^F_t, $\overline{N}^d_t$.

On the demand side, both r and s matter, not just r'. A high r and low s (holding r' constant) make holding bank money more attractive but using it for transactions less attractive. Even if s and r move in offsetting ways to keep r' constant, the rise in s affects banks' marginal conditions and hence overall general equilibrium. Thus, even though r and s are perfect substitutes on the supply side, the fact that they are not on the demand side argues for determinate equilibrium values of both r and s, not just r'.

NOTES

1 This assumption genuinely is merely for convenience. For the most part, allowing banks to buy capital goods merely makes the notation more cumbersome.

2 As cursory examination of the real world confirms, there are many possible mixes of services, with different deposit institutions offering different service mixes, charging for them in various ways, and offering different interest rates

to depositors. These differences are ignored here.

3 The use of $\tilde{w}_t$ in (6.1) assumes that the banking sector has the same expectations as the non-financial business sector. Since no use is made here of the possible differences, the notational convenience of assuming them the same is used.

4 The banking system may be required (by prohibitive penalties) to keep bank money at par with government money – Pesek and Saving's (1967) instant repurchase provision. Alternatively, even in the absence of such regulation, each bank may find it in its own interest to impose on itself the requirement that par be maintained. There are, after all, significant costs to users in varying exchange rates amongst monies used in the same area, and the premium that users are willing to pay to avoid this variability may be sufficient to eliminate it. See Klein (1974).

5 Assume, solely for convenience, that the function $\theta(\cdot)$ does not change over time. A detailed discussion of the properties of $\theta(\cdot)$ is given below.

6 For the assumption in (6.4) that banks expect the same inflation $\Delta \tilde{P}/P$ as non-financial business, see note 3 above.

7 Expression (6.10) plays essentially the same role for banks as the first term in braces in (6.8) does for non-financial firms. In both cases, the rise in P_0 necessarily changes initial real balances and hence affects behavior. It is useful to recall from chapter 3 that the fall in non-financial firms' real balances affects their labor use, but this effect drops out of (6.8) because of their optimum conditions; the net effect of an induced change in N_0^d is $\partial Y_0^s / \partial N_0^d - w_0/P_0 = 0$.

8 The result for non-financial firms follows from their marginal condition for bank money in section 6.2, $Y_{mb_t}^s - (i_t - r_t) = 0$. The derivation for the household sector exactly parallels the discussion in chapter 5, section 5.2, which shows that the initial-condition effect on wealth through government money is $i_0(-\text{MH}_0/P_0^2)$.

9 The inability readily to handle such questions is one of the chief liabilities in applying the standard, perfect competition value theory to monetary questions. This inability also makes radical shifts in perspective, for example to a game-theoretical approach, more appealing.

10 Note that V_1, V_1^s, $\bar{V}_1$, B_1^h and $\bar{B}_1$ do not appear in (6.7) and hence need not be doubled. Private sector bonds can be ignored under the assumption of no distribution effects. See chapters 5, 8 and 9 for discussions of when and why government bonds can be ignored.

11 There is no very good way of grafting into this essentially static, certain and riskless model the speculative, precautionary and portfolio holdings of money that are so dependent on uncertainty and risk. Hicks (1946) viewed the certainty equivalent approach as not very useful, though Mosak (1944) pushed it to the point of rudimentary portfolio theory within a Hicksian framework.

12 The household sector initial-condition effect may combine with the two business sector initial-condition effects, with the velocity effect, and with price-induced effects on wealth to leave all current excess demands equal to zero, though demands and supplies have changed (in offsetting ways) – see

chapter 5, Appendix 5A. Note that the changes in demands and supplies in such a case will virtually ensure a non-zero velocity effect.

13 See Kalecki's (1944) insistence on this in a comment on Pigou's (1943) article that provides the start of the Pigou effect debate – still continuing.

14 See Pesek and Saving (1967) for their views on earlier theorists' positions, but note that this exegesis is itself controversial – see Patinkin (1969).

15 However, see below for a discussion of how the existence of the banking system plays a role in society's welfare even though none in the price-induced effect on wealth.

16 This assumption of homogeneity of degree λ is merely for expository convenience.

17 Current United States required reserves are in fact prohibited from use to meet the convertibility requirement.

18 Various non-proportional reserve requirements are frequently found in the real world. Central banks have many devices beyond (and less crude than) non-proportionality for ensuring that, if $\theta(\cdot)$ has the proper zero-degree homogeneity, $\bar{\theta}(\cdot)$ does not.

19 A "coin shortage" means that the government is not supplying the desired ratio of coins to currency. Businesses are influenced in their choice of a bank by how available it makes the scarce coins; householders patronize businesses in part because of policy on change. Presumably a long or severe enough shortage leads to pecuniary (as well as imputed) discrepancies from par.

20 Pesek and Saving (1967) are justly and particularly critical of this approach and its influence. However, they seem to think (incorrectly) that the first two measures have some role in the analysis of the price-induced effect on wealth through banks. See also Saving (1970).

Pesek and Saving identify this fifth approach with the "new view" in monetary theory, and stress that their work is a revalidation of the "old view." Patinkin (1969), however, finds their work very "new view" in character, and believes this fifth approach is "old view," going back to Kalecki's (1944) note on Pigou's (1943) classic paper.

21 Patinkin (1965) allows this conversion, though it is costly.

22 Once the liquid assets cash, demand and time deposits are exhausted, the transactor may find it more expensive to use bonds than to make pure credit arrangements, which are more costly than using time deposits, or credit arrangements would have been resorted to before the exhaustion of liquid assets.

23 There would almost surely also be a change in velocity, and the resulting velocity effect would then disturb equilibrium.

Since there is no government money in this model, the changes in wealth due to the initial-condition effects through bank money are likely to cancel, along the lines discussed in section 6.3. However, as emphasized repeatedly, initial-condition effects play two roles. They alter household sector wealth and they directly affect demands in markets. For example, even if the change in wealth nets to zero, the non-financial business sector reduces Y_0^s and N_0^d (assuming that mb_0 and N_0^d are complements).

24 This is similar to Gurley and Shaw's (1960) device for removing any distribution effects: if the real value of a sector's financial assets or liabilities is affected by a price change, suppose that these financial variables change in proportion to price.

7

Interest-Bearing Money and the Price-Induced Effect on Wealth

The common thread of this chapter is how interest-bearing money enters the price-induced effect on wealth. This chapter discusses three main issues. First, US government regulations long kept the rates which banks could pay on deposits below market-clearing levels, and even with deregulation some vestiges still prevail. Section 7.1 shows that this regulation may change banks from price-taking quantity-setters into quantity-takers. If this happens, then bank money plays a role in the price-induced effect on wealth.

Second, governments choose not to pay interest on their fiat monies. If, however, they were to pay the analog of a competitively determined rate, where marginal benefit equals marginal cost, the price-induced effect on wealth through government money would be zero, as discussed in section 7.2. This makes the analysis of government money symmetric with that of bank money in chapter 6.

Third, Patinkin (1969, 1972) argues that any money, government or bank, enters the price-induced effect on wealth just to the extent that "there is a difference between the value of the stock of money and the present value of the costs of maintaining that stock constant" (1972, p. 190). Further, Patinkin concludes that payment of interest is not necessary for a particular money to fail to be included in the price-induced effect on wealth. Section 7.3 discusses Patinkin's analysis and disagrees with it.

One issue not covered in chapter 6 is the effect of interest rate regulations on the price-induced effect on wealth through bank money. The United States currently imposes a number of restrictions on bank behavior. Chapter 6 showed that restrictions on entry can create monopoly rents but will not affect the analysis of the price-induced effect on wealth provided that there is a large enough number of banks to create competitive, price-taking, quantity-setting behavior. Further, it showed that reserve requirements need not intrinsically affect the analysis, but can easily be designed to violate the homogeneity requirement. This chapter analyzes restrictions on the interest rate that banks are allowed to pay on demand deposits. While such restrictions have been relaxed, beginning in the mid-1970s, there are still some significant vestiges today. This chapter shows that these restrictions can easily cause a negative price-induced effect on wealth through bank money. This arises because the restriction implies that the average bank is not able to issue as large an amount of its real balances as it desires, in the sense that the marginal benefit to the bank of one more of its dollars outstanding would outweigh its marginal cost. Since (at least some of) the interest rates banks pay are below market-clearing levels, the actual level of bank money real balances is the level demanded, which is less than banks want to supply when the interest rate restrictions are effective. An increase in the price level that has a negative effect on wealth through government money will thus reduce the demand for real bank dollars, and hence reduce wealth even more by reducing real bank profits. This does not occur when price-taking, quantity-setting banks pay a competitively determined interest rate, because each chooses a level of deposits where marginal benefit equals marginal cost; a marginal reduction in demand for bank money has no influence on bank profits, since the last dollar issued adds a zero increment to profits.

Restrictions on the interest rate that banks can pay on their money will surely lead to other types of competition. As long as this competition leaves banks quantity-takers, bank money enters the price-induced effect on wealth. The non-interest-rate competition, however, may leave banks as price-taking quantity-setters, with bank money excluded from the effect. Section 7.1 discusses these issues.

A number of economists (Friedman, 1969; Johnson, 1969) have suggested that the government pay a competitive rate of interest on its fiat money. Johnson argues that competitive-interest-bearing money has the role which conventional analysis assigns to inside money, and, though he is not specific on this issue, it appears that he believes the price-induced effect on wealth through government money to equal zero in this case. It seems he believes this is so, however, under the assumption that the stock of real balances is held constant (Johnson, 1969, p. 33, figure 1), which corresponds in this analysis to future government money stocks M_t^s ($t \geqslant 1$) being unit elastic with respect to the current price level P_0; section 7.2 shows this unit elasticity is not at all necessary. Two criteria for government interest payments seem reasonable to explore: interest is paid (a) to set "marginal benefit equal to marginal cost" or (b) to give "zero profits" for the government's money supply operations. This chapter investigates these issues under the assumption, similar to that for banks, that real resource use for government money is homogeneous of degree zero. Section 7.2 shows that under criterion (a) the price-induced effect on wealth through future government money is zero, and this is so whatever the elasticity of M_t^s to P_0. Under criterion (b), the effect is positive or zero as government's marginal cost of its monetary operations is rising or constant.

Chapter 5 discussed government money that paid no interest, and found a negative price-induced effect on wealth in cases where the government varies future money supplies less than proportionately to changes in the current price level. Chapter 6 discussed a banking industry that pays a competitively determined rate of interest on the money it issues. That chapter argued that the price-induced effect on wealth through bank money was zero. In the conventional analysis, government money is viewed as "outside" money and bank money as "inside" money, so the results of chapters 5 and 6 seem to fit the usual view that outside money is part of the price-induced effect on wealth while inside money is not. However, Johnson (1969, p. 35) argues that the relevant distinction is not between outside and inside money but between non-interest-bearing and competitive-interest-bearing money, whether government or bank money. The discussion below supports Johnson's view.

The key issue for bank money, however, is whether restrictions on bank interest lead to forms of competition where banks remain price-taking quantity-setters. In this case, bank money does not enter the price-induced effect on wealth. If restrictions on bank interest turn banks into quantity-takers, then their money does enter the effect. The analysis is thus more complicated than Johnson's dichotomy.

Patinkin (1972, chapter 9, p. 190), however, argues that "what really matters from the viewpoint of the real balance effect is not whether the issuer of the money is the government or the private banking sector, but whether there are costs involved in maintaining constant the stock of money. More specifically, money is wealth from the viewpoint of the real-balance effect only to the extent there is a difference between the value of the stock of money and the present value of the costs of maintaining that stock constant." In Patinkin's view, bank money is part of the price-induced effect on wealth only if the banking industry makes positive profits. Further, while Johnson makes interest payments the key to his analysis, interest costs are not necessarily included in the costs Patinkin is discussing, since he argues (p. 189) that entry into the banking industry will make the present value of costs equal the value of the money issued even if banks pay no interest on deposits.

Chapter 6 showed that when price-taking, quantity-setting banks pay a competitively determined rate of interest, the key issues for the price-induced effect on wealth are, first, whether bank resource use is homogeneous of degree zero in nominal values, and, second, whether the bank is at a wealth maximum. Patinkin, however, does not discuss this homogeneity condition and ignores the bank's marginal conditions. Instead, his analysis focuses on the entirely different issue of whether or not banks make zero profits, in the belief that zero profits imply a zero price-induced effect on wealth through bank money. In turn, he argues that paying a competitively determined interest rate will ensure zero bank profits (though such interest payments are not necessary for zero profits in his view). Chapter 6 showed that if the banking industry is competitive but the number of banks is limited through restrictions on entry, then the average bank will earn "monopoly" rents but there will be a zero price-induced effect on wealth through bank money provided the homogeneity condition is met and the wealth-maximizing banks act as price-takers and quantity-setters, paying a competitively determined rate of interest.

Section 7.3 discusses Patinkin's analysis of the price-induced effect on wealth through bank money, and the role of competitively determined interest payments in price-induced effects on wealth through both bank and government money.

7.1 Interest Rate Regulation on Otherwise Competitive Banks

A potentially powerful channel of monetary influence on the economy arises through the regulation of the interest rates that banks are allowed to pay on their deposits. Different types of money require adjustment of the relative price of their services in order for the system to reach equilibrium. If adjustment is not allowed, the system does not show the equilibrium properties of chapter 6, but rather gives new, disequilibrium results.

Bank Money and Equilibrium in Competitive Markets

During the United States Civil War the Federal government issued greenbacks, fiat currency not convertible into gold. Greenbacks were legal tender but not required to be accepted at par with gold by private parties in an exchange. These non-interest-bearing bills were accepted in the quantity issued only by allowing variations in the gold price of greenbacks. ($10 bills currently exchange at par for ten $1 bills because the two are convertible on demand; hence currency-holders' preferences, not the government, determine the quantities of the two types of bills.) The relative price of gold and greenbacks fluctuated to make them perfect substitutes at the margin, just the way r varied in chapter 6 to equilibrate the system where both monies exchanged at par.

In the early twentieth century, banks paid interest on checking accounts, that is, on bank money. In the depths of the Great Depression, the Federal government forbade interest on demand deposits, since such interest payments seemed to many to have contributed to creating the Depression. Since the mid-1970s, interest rate regulations have been much relaxed, though they still influence banks' behavior.

Imposing such a restriction on chapter 6's model creates a disequilibrium system, for r can no longer adjust to equate demand and supply of bank money. For the moment, neglect the variety and effects of the non-price competition such a ruling encourages (as well as the role of the service charge s discussed in Appendix 6B), and concentrate on the influence of statutory regulation of r on the financial sector's role in the price-induced effect on wealth. Suppose both that such regulation is enforced and that the maximum allowable r is below what banks would pay in equilibrium. Then, whenever a parametric change induces an increase in the real demand for bank money, this in turn creates a positive effect on wealth because banks are able to issue more profit-making dollars. Consequently, if a fall in the price level causes an increase in wealth through government money and thus expands the demand for bank money, then the further expansion of the bank money component of the money supply is part of the price-induced effect on wealth. This result occurs because effective regulation means that banks cannot issue their dollars up to the point where the revenues they earn by issuing one more dollar equal the marginal cost of supporting that extra dollar. Hence, an increase in demand for bank dollars adds to the rent earned by banks (whether this rent is initially positive or zero). Note that the same sort of analysis holds for any industry that is regulated in the price it can pay or charge; there is nothing unique about money in this respect.

Bank Behavior Under Interest Rate Regulations

The restriction on r constrains banks only if the quantity demanded is less than banks would freely supply at the maximum allowable r. Suppose that when this is so, each bank has deposits which are largely proportional to what it would have in equilibrium. Each bank would like to have larger deposits. Instead of being a quantity-setter and having all the deposits it wants at competitively determined values of i and r, each faces a given quantity demanded of real balances. Instead of choosing values of deposits and reserves (and thus labor) to maximize profits (as in chapter 6), each chooses reserves to minimize costs for the given level of demand for deposits.

Thus, recall that the banking sector's demand for labor $\overline{N}_t^d$ is

$$\overline{N}_t^d = \theta(M_t^F, \overline{M}_t, \widetilde{P}_t, \tau_t) = \theta(M_t^F, \overline{M}_t, \widetilde{P}_t, v_t\overline{M}_tP_t). \tag{7.1}$$

Assume that $\theta(\cdot)$ is homogeneous of degree zero in nominal values, so that

$$\overline{N}_t^{\text{d}} = \theta(\overline{m}_t, m_t^{\text{F}}, 1, v_t \overline{m}_t). \qquad (7.2)$$

Then, if the r regulation is non-existent or is non-binding, the necessary conditions for a present value maximum when $\overline{m}$ and m^{F} can be freely chosen are, from the analysis of chapter 6,

$$(i_t - r_t) - \frac{\widetilde{w}_t}{\widetilde{P}_t} \theta_{\overline{M}} - \frac{\widetilde{w}_t}{\widetilde{P}_t} \theta_r v_t = 0 \qquad (7.3)$$

$$t \geqslant 1$$

$$- i_t - \frac{\widetilde{w}_t}{\widetilde{P}_t} \theta_{\text{MF}} = 0. \qquad (7.4)$$

It is useful to view (7.3) as the marginal condition for $\overline{m}$, and (7.4) for m^{F}, though in optimization by a competitive bank the two quantities are simultaneously chosen. When the r regulation exists and is lower than the equilibrium r and thus binding, $\overline{m}_t$ is determined by market demand and banks cannot supply all the money they wish. All banks can do is adjust reserves to minimize costs, or the constrained present value maximum requires only the second condition, equation (7.4), subject to the given $\overline{m}_t$. To say that the constraint on r is binding is to say that $\overline{m}_t$ is not as large as it would be at a present value maximum where both (7.3) and (7.4) hold. Instead, with r regulated, (7.4) holds but (7.3) is replaced with

$$(i_t - r_t) - \frac{\widetilde{w}_t}{\widetilde{P}_t} \theta_{\overline{M}} - \frac{\widetilde{w}_t}{\widetilde{P}_t} \theta_r v_t > 0. \qquad (7.5)$$

The pressure to raise r comes from the fact that doing so and attracting more deposits seems profitable from (7.5).

Figure 7.1 shows a representative bank's marginal cost (MC) of supplying real balances $\overline{m}$ (with m^{F} and $\overline{N}$ optimally adjusted), as well as net income $i - r$ from an extra unit of $\overline{m}$. The bank would like to supply $\overline{m}_1$, but customers demand only $\overline{m}_2$. At $\overline{m}_2$, (7.5) holds. In order to attract more deposits, the bank would be willing to raise the r it pays, and thus lower $i - r$ since i is given to the individual banks, but this is forbidden by the interest rate regulation.[1]

The discussion in chapter 6 of the real present value of the banking sector's dividend stream made no mention of the effect of an increase in the real demand for bank money. The simple reason is that with perfect competition and with freely varying and thus equilibrating prices and interest rates, the banks were price-takers and quantity-setters and were thus unconcerned with the quantity demanded. Each could have any quantity of deposits it liked at the going (competitively determined) i and r.

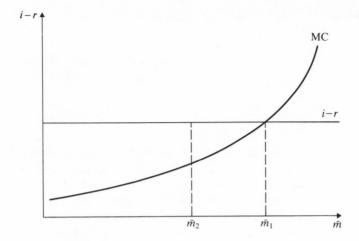

Figure 7.1 Bank's choice of its real balances

When the regulation of r constrains the system's pricing, banks cannot issue as many demand deposits as they would like. Their profits rise with an increase in the quantity they can issue. Period t's real dividends (in terms of that period's prices) are

$$\bar{m}_t^d (i_t - r_t) - i_t m_t^F - \frac{\widetilde{w}_t}{\widetilde{P}_t} \theta(\cdot), \qquad t \geqslant 0, \tag{7.6}$$

where the terms $\bar{m}_t^d$ specifically indicate that the real deposits outstanding are constrained not to exceed the quantity demanded, or rather to equal the quantity demanded since this quantity is less than what banks desire to supply. From (7.6), an increase in $\bar{m}_t^d$ raises period t's real dividends by

$$(i_t - r_t) - \frac{\widetilde{w}_t}{\widetilde{P}_t} \theta_{\overline{M}} - \frac{\widetilde{w}_t}{\widetilde{P}_t} \theta_\tau v_t + \left\{ - i_t - \frac{\widetilde{w}_t}{\widetilde{P}_t} \theta_{MF} \right\} \frac{dm_t^F}{d\bar{m}_t^d}$$

$$= (i_t - r_t) - \frac{\widetilde{w}_t}{\widetilde{P}_t} \theta_{\overline{M}} - \frac{\widetilde{w}_t}{\widetilde{P}_t} \theta_\tau v_t > 0. \tag{7.7}$$

The terms in braces equal zero from the first-order condition (7.4) since the industry always chooses m_t^F to minimize costs. Equation (7.7) is positive since the r constraint is assumed to be binding and thus (7.5) holds.

Suppose that the household sector decides in period 0 to accumulate more real bank money to be used in period 1, or $\bar{m}_1^d$ rises, and that demand also rises for real bank money in future periods. Using the result (7.7) in the household sector budget constraint (6.7), the effect on wealth of a change in $\overline{m}_1^d$ is

$$\sum_{t=1}^{\infty} \left[\frac{\Pi(1 + \Delta\widetilde{P}/P)}{\Pi(1 + i)} (i_t - r_t) - \frac{w_0}{P_0} \frac{\Pi(1 + \Delta\widetilde{w}/w)}{\Pi(1 + i)} \{\theta_{\overline{M}}(\cdot) + \theta_\tau v_t\} \right]$$

$$\times \frac{d\overline{m}_t^d}{d\overline{m}_1^d} > 0 \tag{7.8}$$

if $d\overline{m}_t^d/d\overline{m}_1^d > 0$, where $d\overline{m}_t^d/d\overline{m}_1^d$ is the change in the quantity $\overline{m}_t^d$ that banks expect in period t due to the increase in demand they currently experience. Thus the impact on wealth is unambiguously positive, though the magnitude depends on whether banks expect the constraint to be binding in the future, and if they do so expect for period t, on the elasticity of period t's expected demand with respect to current demand.

The Effect on Wealth of Expansionary Monetary Policy

As an application of these results, consider a government decision in period 0 to make all M_t^s ($t \geq 1$) x percent larger than previously planned (where x is small). This increase in M_t^s ($t \geq 1$) has *per se* a positive impact on wealth, as seen from the household sector budget constraint (6.7). From the government sector's budget constraint, this increase in all money supplies manifests itself as an increase in (the present value of) transfer payments or a decrease in net tax liabilities. Thus, the impact on wealth of this monetary policy first makes itself felt by the decrease in taxation it implies – the monetary expansion begins life by looking like fiscal policy.

Before any other change occurs, the increase in all M_t means that real wealth rises by

$$dW^* = \sum_{t=1}^{\infty} \frac{i_t M_t^s x}{\Pi(1 + i)P_0}. \tag{7.9}$$

Assuming that the demand for real bank money is positively related to wealth, and using η to denote the partial derivative of this demand with respect to wealth, then the change in the quantity of real bank money demanded is

$$d\overline{m}_1^d = \eta dW, \tag{7.10}$$

where dW is the total change in wealth due both to dW^* and the increase in demand for bank money. Using (7.8) and (7.10), the increase in wealth due to the increase in demand for bank money is

$$\left\{ \sum_{t=1}^{\infty} \left[\frac{\Pi(1+\Delta \tilde{P}/P)}{\Pi(1+i)} (i_t - r_t) \right. \right.$$

$$\left. \left. - \frac{w_0}{P_0} \frac{\Pi(1+\Delta \tilde{w}/w)}{\Pi(1+i)} \{\theta_{\bar{M}}(\cdot) + \theta_\tau v_t\} \right] \frac{d\bar{m}_t}{d\bar{m}_1^d} \right\} d\bar{m}_1^d = \{\cdot\} \eta dW.$$

$$(7.11)$$

The total change in wealth (before any repercussions on prices) is the sum of the change through government policy plus the change due to the increase in $\bar{m}_1^d$, or is

$$dW = dW^* + \{\cdot\} \eta dW = \sum_{t=1}^{\infty} \frac{i_t M_t^s x}{\Pi(1+i)P_0} + \{\cdot\} \eta dW, \qquad (7.12)$$

$$dW = \frac{\displaystyle\sum_{t=1}^{\infty} i_t M_t x / P_0 \Pi(1+i)}{1 - \{\cdot\}\eta} > \sum_{t=1}^{\infty} \frac{i_t M_t^s x}{P_0 \Pi(1+i)}. \qquad (7.13)$$

Clearly, the banking sector magnifies the increase in wealth.

Note that $\{\cdot\}\eta$ must be less than unity for the impact on wealth to be positive. This is just the analog of the condition in simple income–expenditure theory that the sum of the marginal propensities to consume and invest must be less than unity.

The Price-Induced Effect on Wealth under Interest Rate Regulation

Consider the price-induced effect on wealth when all government money supplies are fixed at the initial level M_0^s – the Yap-Island case. Through government money, the effect is the conventional real balance effect result $-M_0^s/P_0^2$. Analogously to (7.13), the total change in wealth, including banking sector reactions to changes in $\bar{m}_t^d$, is

$$\frac{dW}{dP_0} = \frac{-M_0^s/P_0^2}{1 - \{\cdot\}\eta} < -\frac{M_0^s}{P_0^2} < 0. \qquad (7.14)$$

In words, the price-induced effect on wealth through government money is negative in this case. This decline in wealth reduces the demand for bank money in current and future periods (that is, reduces $\bar{m}_t^d$, $t \geqslant 1$) and hence reduces banks' real profits. This decline in bank profitability further reduces wealth and hence $\bar{m}_t^d$, in a multiplier process. Thus, the ultimate fall in wealth is larger than the initial fall, or, as in (7.14), $dW/dP_0 < -M_0^s/P_0^2$.

Of course the analysis is much more general than the Yap-Island case chosen for illustration. If the price-induced effect on wealth through government money is dW_{GM}/dP_0, then the total price-induced effect on wealth is

$$\frac{dW}{dP_0} = \frac{dW_{GM}/dP_0}{1 - \{\cdot\}\eta}. \tag{7.15}$$

Measurement of the Price-Induced Effect on Wealth

The price-induced effect on wealth through government money is

$$\partial\left\{\sum_{t=1}^{\infty} \frac{i_t M_t^s}{P_0 \Pi(1+i)}\right\} \bigg/ \partial P_0 = \partial\left\{\sum_{t=1}^{\infty} \frac{i_t m_t^s \Pi(1+\Delta P/P)}{\Pi(1+i)}\right\} \bigg/ \partial P_0,$$

which allows for the possibility that M_t^s varies with P_0 (see chapter 5). The price-induced effect through bank money is

$$\partial\left(\sum_{t=1}^{\infty}\left[\left\{(i_t - r_t)\overline{m}_t^d \Pi\left(1 + \frac{\Delta\widetilde{P}}{P}\right) - i_t m_t^F \Pi\left(1 + \frac{\Delta\widetilde{P}}{P}\right)\right.\right.$$

$$\left.\left. - \frac{w_0}{P_0}\; \overline{N}_t^d \Pi\left(1 + \frac{\Delta\widetilde{w}}{w}\right)\right\}\{\Pi(1+i)\}^{-1}\right]\right) \bigg/ \partial P_0$$

$$= \sum_{t=1}^{\infty}\left\{\frac{(i_t - r_t)\,\Pi(1+\Delta\widetilde{P}/P) - MC_t}{\Pi(1+i)}\; \frac{d\overline{m}_t^d}{dP_0}\right\},$$

where again MC_t is the real marginal cost in t of an increase in $\overline{m}_t$, with m_t^F optimally adjusted. For simplicity, assume no price or wage inflation, that i and r are constant, that v is constant, that $d\overline{m}_t^d/dP_0$ is the same for all t ($t \geqslant 1$), and that the change in M^s with a rise in P_0 is the same for all periods. Thus, $\Pi(1+\Delta\widetilde{P}/P) = \Pi(1+\Delta\widetilde{w}/w) = 1$ and MC is constant over time. Under these assumptions, the price-induced effect on wealth through government money is dm^s/dP_0, and through bank money is $(d\overline{m}/dP_0)(i-r-MC)/i$. Hence, the total price-induced effect is

$$\frac{dm^s}{dP_0} + \frac{d\overline{m}}{dP_0}\; \frac{(i-r) - MC}{i}.$$

Thus, in this simple example, the price-induced effect on wealth is a weighted sum of the change in the two forms of real balances, where the weight on government money is unity. The weight on bank money varies between zero, when regulation allows the bank marginal condition

$i - r - MC = 0$ to hold, and unity when no bank interest r is allowed and marginal cost is insignificant ($MC \doteq 0$).

This suggests that attempts to measure the price-induced effect on wealth with fixed weights of unity assigned to both monies are mis-specified. The weight on bank money is greater than zero when regulation is significant, and the weight varies as regulations change.

This discussion also suggests the magnitude of the price-induced effect on wealth through bank money under regulation. From (7.15), bank money affects the overall price-induced effect on wealth through the term $\{\cdot\}\,\eta$ in the denominator. From (7.11), $\{\cdot\}$ depends on $d\bar{m}_t^d/d\bar{m}_1^d$; assume this thus equals unity for all t. From the discussion of the above few paragraphs, $\{\cdot\}$ then equals unity in the extreme case where $r = MC = 0$, and will thus generally be less than unity. The marginal propensity to hold bank money from increases in wealth, η, may be, say, 0.05. Hence, $\{\cdot\}\,\eta$ may be approximately 0.05 as a maximum, with $1 - \{\cdot\}\,\eta$ perhaps 0.95 as a minimum. Thus, from (7.15), the overall price-induced effect on wealth is perhaps 5 percent larger than otherwise due to interest rate regulations.

Competition on Other Margins

When regulation of r is effective, banks will naturally turn to other avenues beyond price (r) competition to attract the extra deposits they desire. It may be that all such avenues of competition are effectively ruled out by regulation (banks may view such competition as "wasteful" and urge regulation to eliminate it). In this case, the above analysis goes through unaltered. But competition is like crabgrass – tough to eliminate, with victories mostly temporary. If non-r competition allows banks to settle back into being price-taking quantity-setters, the analysis reverts to one similar to that of chapter 6 and bank money does not enter the price-induced effect on wealth. If, however, banks are quantity-takers under the new r-induced competition, then this section's analysis holds and bank money does enter the effect. Examples of each type of competition follow.

Service Charges on Transactions with Bank Money Appendix 6B modified the model developed earlier in that chapter by introducing the service charge s_t on each real transaction τ_t. This added the term

$$\left[\sum_{t=0}^{\infty} \frac{s_0}{P_0} \frac{\Pi(1 + \Delta s^e/s)}{\Pi(1 + i)} \tau_t^e \right]$$ to the expression (6.4) for the real present

value of bank dividends, where $\Delta s^e/s$ and τ^e are the rate of service charge inflation and the number of real transactions expected by the bank.

Assuming that the τ_t banks are planning on is the same for all t as the sum planned on by households and non-financial businesses, and that all sectors expect the same service charge inflation rates $\Delta s^e/s$, the planned real service charges paid and received net to zero and hence these expressions drop out of the household sector budget constraint after substituting for bank and non-financial business dividends, as Appendix 6B points out.

The bank's optimum conditions, continuing to assume zero-degree homogeneity, become

$$(i_t - r_t) + s_t \, v_t/\widetilde{P}_t - \frac{\widetilde{w}_t}{\widetilde{P}_t} \, \theta_{\overline{M}} - \frac{\widetilde{w}_t}{\widetilde{P}_t} \, \theta_\tau v_t = 0 \qquad (7.3')$$

$$- i_t - \frac{\widetilde{w}_t}{\widetilde{P}_t} \, \theta_{\mathrm{MF}} = 0. \qquad (7.4')$$

(7.3') differs from (7.3) above by including $s_t \, v_t/\widetilde{P}_t$, while (7.4) and (7.4') are the same. Clearly, a proportionate change in all w, P, s has no effect on $\overline{m}$, MF, $\overline{N}^d$.

As Appendix 6B points out, r and s are perfect substitutes on the supply side. Thus, in (7.3'), $r_t - s_t \, v_t/P_t$ can be replaced with

$$r_t' = r_t - s_t \, v_t/P_t$$

to give

$$(i_t - r_t') - \frac{\widetilde{w}_t}{\widetilde{P}_t} \, \theta_{\overline{M}} - \frac{\widetilde{w}_t}{\widetilde{P}_t} \, \theta_\tau v_t = 0. \qquad (7.3'')$$

When r is restricted below its competitive level, banks' competition can reduce s to offset exactly this restriction and leave r' unchanged. If r and s are perfect substitutes on the demand side, restricting r will then have no effect.

r and s are highly unlikely to be perfect substitutes on the demand side, as Appendix 6B points out. A regulated decrease in r is likely to lead to a decrease in general equilibrium in the quantity of real bank balances held, even as an accompanying reduction in s would be likely to lead to a rise in v. Thus, even if r' stays constant due to offsetting changes in r and s, the rise in v will affect banks' supply of their real balances, as can be seen from condition (7.3''').

For present purposes, the issue is whether the economy settles down to a new equilibrium – with a lower, restricted r and a presumably lower s – where each bank is a price-taking quantity-setter. Such an equilibrium would not be the same as the equilibrium with an unrestricted r, and under appropriate assumptions removing the r restriction would cause the economy to revert from the restricted-r equilibrium to the unrestricted-r equilibrium. In principle, however, there is no reason why a restricted-r equilibrium cannot arise; this is somewhat similar to the case where regulation forces banks to hold a level of reserves beyond that desired without regulation.

It is quite possible that r is restricted to such a low level that s would have to be negative to give a restricted-r equilibrium. In this case, regulators might require $s \geqslant 0$ and this effectively rules out a restricted-r equilibrium.

Further, adjustments in s are likely to be viewed as more or less satisfactory substitutes for a higher r by those bank money holders who have higher or lower than average transactions velocities. Someone holding large balances but planning low turnover is unlikely to be pleased by falls in r and s – the decrease in r hurts a lot and the decrease in s helps only a little. Hence, there may well spring up some partially segmented markets, leading to imperfect, quantity-taking competition.

Imperfect Competition　If r is restricted and competition on the service charge margin is either infeasible or leaves some customers willing to consider switching banks, competition may arise on other margins. Banks may, for example, offer free toasters in each period (TO_t) to influence their deposits. Each bank will "give away" toasters until the marginal benefit equals marginal cost. Each toaster attracts $d\bar{m}/dTO$ deposits for a marginal benefit of $(i-r) \, d\bar{m}/dTO$, but costs the price of the toaster (P) plus the marginal cost of servicing the extra deposits (MC), or the marginal condition is

$$(i-r) \, \frac{d\bar{m}}{dTO} - MC \, \frac{d\bar{m}}{dTO} - P = 0,$$

$$(i - r - MC) \, \frac{d\bar{m}}{dTO} = P.$$

Since $P > 0$, both $i - r - MC > 0$ and $d\bar{m}/dTO > 0$.

$i - r - MC$ remains the marginal profit due to an autonomous increase in depositors' demand for bank money, as above. Just as before, such an increase in demand raises the wealth of the banks' owners. Wealth rises even if competition on the toaster margin, and other margins, has set the representative bank's profit equal to zero. The issue of whether initial profits equal zero is irrelevant.

Wealth-maximizing banks set marginal benefit equal to marginal cost.

The issue is whether or not the optimum is found subject to regulation. If regulation bites, the bank cannot fully optimize on one of the margins. Hence, a shift that reduces the bite on this margin will increase wealth, while the same shift would have no effect on wealth if the bank were a quantity-setter and already optimizing on that margin.

7.2 Interest-Bearing Government Money

Much of monetary theory assumes that government fiat money is non-interest-bearing. Government could, of course, pay interest on its fiat money, a possibility that has been raised on efficiency grounds, for example by Friedman (1969) and Johnson (1969). This section examines the price-induced effect on wealth through government money in such a case. If government pays a rate analogous to what competition would determine, so marginal benefit equals marginal cost, then the price-induced effect on wealth through government money is zero.

Discussions in previous chapters of the terms

$$\sum_{t=1}^{\infty} \frac{i_t M_t^s}{P_0 \Pi(1+i)} - \frac{M_0}{P_0}$$

in the government budget constraint interpreted

$$\sum_{t=1}^{\infty} \frac{i_t M_t^s}{P_0 \Pi(1+i)}$$

as the real present value (in terms of P_0) of the income the government earns by renting the stock M_t^s in period t to the public at the rate i_t per period. This present value is reduced by the amount of real government money outstanding, M_0/P_0, which is owned by the private sector and hence not rented from the government. The larger is

$$\sum_{t=1}^{\infty} \frac{i_t M_t^s}{P_0 \Pi(1+i)} - \frac{M_0}{P_0},$$

the smaller is the present value of real government taxation, given government's planned real expenditures. Since the term M_0/P_0 enters the household sector constraint, the net is

$$\sum_{t=1}^{\infty} \frac{i_t M_t^s}{P_0 \Pi(1+i)}$$

and it is the change in this term with respect to P_0 that is the price-induced effect on wealth through government money.

Introducing government interest payments, at the rate r_t^*, is usefully accompanied by considering the labor services (N_t^d) that the government uses to maintain (collect, replace, supply in demanded denominations, protect from counterfeiting, etc.) its stock of fiat money. Labor is assumed to be the only factor used for this end, for the same reasons of convenience as in the discussion of bank money. The part of the government budget constraint dealing with its monetary activities is now

$$\sum_{t=1}^{\infty} \frac{(i_t - r_t^*)M_t^s}{P_0\Pi(1+i)} - \sum_{t=0}^{\infty} \frac{w_0\Pi(1+\Delta w/w)}{P_0\Pi(1+i)} N_t^d - \frac{M_0}{P_0} - r_0^* \frac{M_0^s}{P_0}.$$

The government's "money business" now makes less profit than before, since r^* is paid and explicit attention is focused on the resource cost of N^d.

The household sector budget constraint for period t is

$$w_t N_t^s + \text{Div}_t + \text{div}_t - P_{b,t} V_{t+1}^h + V_t^h - T_t - P_t C_t^d - \Delta MH_t$$
$$- \Delta \overline{MH}_t - P_{b,t} B_{t+1}^d + B_t^h + r_t \overline{MH}_t + r_t^* MH_t = 0. \qquad (7.16)$$

Discounting (7.16), summing over all t ($t \geq 0$), and dividing by P_0 yields the constraint that

$$\sum_{t=0}^{\infty} \frac{\Pi(1+\Delta w/w)}{\Pi(1+i)} \frac{w_0}{P_0} N_t^s + \sum_{t=0}^{\infty} \frac{\text{Div}_t}{P_0\Pi(1+i)} + \sum_{t=0}^{\infty} \frac{\text{div}_t}{P_0\Pi(1+i)}$$

$$- \sum_{t=0}^{\infty} \frac{\Pi(1+\Delta P/P)}{\Pi(1+i)} C_t^d - \sum_{t=1}^{\infty} \frac{\Pi(1+\Delta P/P)}{\Pi(1+i)} (i_t - r_t^*) \, mh_t$$

$$- \sum_{t=1}^{\infty} \frac{\Pi(1+\Delta P/P)}{\Pi(1+i)} (i_t - r_t) \, \overline{mh}_t - \sum_{t=0}^{\infty} \frac{T_t}{P_0\Pi(1+i)}$$

$$+ \frac{MH_0}{P_0} + \frac{\overline{MH}_0}{P_0} + r_0^* \frac{MH_0}{P_0} + r_0 \frac{\overline{MH}_0}{P_0} + \frac{V_0^h}{P_0} - \frac{B_0}{P_0} \qquad (7.17)$$

must equal or exceed zero (assuming non-satiation, must equal zero).

The Government's Budget Constraint

The expressions for Div_j and div_j are only slightly altered from previous chapters to take account of r^*, and the main difference is in T_t, net government taxation in period t. Government's budget constraint for period t is

$$T_t = P_t G_t - (\Delta M_t + P_{b,t} V^s_{t+1} - V^s_t - r^*_t M^s_t - w_t \underset{\sim}{N}^d_t), \qquad (7.18)$$

where (as before) T_t are net nominal taxes in period t. The term $\underset{\sim}{N}^d_t$ shows government demand for labor to maintain its stock of fiat money. Following the discussion of bank money, let $\underset{\sim}{N}^d_t$ depend on the number of transactions in which government money is used, τ^*_t, or

$$\underset{\sim}{N}^d_t = \theta^* (\tau^*_t) = \theta^* \left(v^*_t \frac{M^s_t}{\underset{\sim}{P}_t} \right), \qquad \theta^*_{\tau^*} > 0, \qquad (7.19)$$

where v^*_t is the average number of transactions in which a unit of real government money (in terms of period t's prices) is used in period t. Call v^* the transaction velocity of government money, in analogy to the v of the banking sector in chapter 6. Notice that θ^* is assumed homogeneous of degree zero in the nominal variables P and M. This plays a key role in the results below, just as degree-zero homogeneity of θ did in chapter 6's discussion of bank money.

Rearranging (7.18), discounting, summing over all t ($t \geqslant 0$), and dividing by P_0 yields the government sector constraint

$$\sum_{t=0}^{\infty} \frac{T_t}{P_0 \Pi(1+i)} = \sum_{t=0}^{\infty} \frac{\Pi(1+\Delta P/P)}{\Pi(1+i)} G^d_t - \sum_{t=1}^{\infty} \frac{(i_t - r^*_t) M^s_t}{P_0 \Pi(1+i)}$$

$$+ \frac{V_0}{P_0} + \frac{M^s_0}{P_0} + \frac{r^*_0 M^s_0}{P_0} + \sum_{t=0}^{\infty} \frac{w_0}{P_0} \frac{\Pi(1+\Delta w/w)}{\Pi(1+i)} \underset{\sim}{N}^d_t. \qquad (7.20)$$

Substituting (7.20) and the (appropriately modified) expressions for Div_t and div_t into (7.17) yields the household sector constraint that

$$\sum_{t=0}^{\infty} \frac{w_0}{P_0} \frac{\Pi(1+\Delta w/w)}{\Pi(1+i)} N^s_t - \sum_{t=0}^{\infty} \frac{w_0}{P_0} \frac{\Pi(1+\Delta \widetilde{w}/w)}{\Pi(1+i)} (N^d_t + \overline{N}^d_t)$$

$$- \sum_{t=0}^{\infty} \frac{w_0}{P_0} \frac{\Pi(1+\Delta w/w)}{\Pi(1+i)} \underset{\sim}{N}^d_t - \sum_{t=0}^{\infty} \frac{\Pi(1+\Delta P/P)}{\Pi(1+i)} C^d_t$$

$$- \sum_{t=0}^{\infty} \frac{\Pi(1+\Delta \underset{\sim}{P}/P)}{\Pi(1+i)} G_t + \sum_{t=0}^{\infty} \frac{\Pi(1+\Delta \widetilde{P}/P)}{\Pi(1+i)} (Y^s_t - \Delta K^d_t)$$

$$- \sum_{t=1}^{\infty} \frac{\Pi(1+\Delta P/P)}{\Pi(1+i)} \{(i_t - r^*_t) \, \mathrm{mh}_t + (i_t - r_t) \, \overline{\mathrm{mh}}_t\}$$

$$- \sum_{t=1}^{\infty} \frac{\Pi(1+\Delta \widetilde{P}/P)}{\Pi(1+i)} \{(i_t - r^*_t) \, \mathrm{mb}_t + (i_t - r_t) \, \overline{\mathrm{mb}}_t\}$$

$$-\sum_{t=1}^{\infty} \frac{\Pi(1+\Delta\widetilde{P}/P)}{\Pi(1+i)} \{(i_t - r_t^*)\, m_t^F - (i_t - r_t)\, \overline{m}_t\}$$

$$+\sum_{t=1}^{\infty} \frac{(i_t - r_t^*)M_t^s}{P_0\Pi(1+i)} \tag{7.21}$$

must equal or exceed zero (with non-satiation, must equal zero). Expression (7.21) makes use of the fact that

$$\begin{aligned}
& MH_0 + MB_0 + MF_0 - M_0^s + \overline{MH}_0 + \overline{MB}_0 - \overline{M}_0 + V_0^h + \overline{V}_0 \\
& - V_0 + \overline{B}_0 - B_0^h + r_0\overline{MH}_0 + r_0\overline{MB}_0 - r_0\overline{M}_0 + r_0^*MH_0 \\
& + r_0^*MB_0 + r_0^*MF_0 - r_0^*M_0^s = 0
\end{aligned}$$

which follows from this system's accounting identities

$$MH_0 + MB_0 + MF_0 = M_0^s,$$

$$V_0^h + \overline{V}_0 = V_0,$$

$$B_0^h = \overline{B}_0,$$

$$\overline{MH}_0 + \overline{MB}_0 = \overline{M}_0.$$

The Price-Induced Effect on Wealth

Differentiating (7.21) with respect to P_0 yields the price-induced effect on wealth. As before, assume that, when P_0 rises, w_0 changes proportionately, no expected rate of price or wage inflation alters (unit-elastic expectations), and no bond or bank interest rate (i or r) alters. A rise in P_0 may, however, cause the government to alter its r^* in every period, so dr_t^*/dP_0 must be taken into account. The price-induced effect on wealth is

$$-\left[\frac{\partial Y_0^s}{\partial(MB_0/P_0)} \frac{MB_0}{P_0^2} + \frac{\partial Y_0^s}{\partial(\overline{MB}_0/P_0)} \frac{\overline{MB}_0}{P_0^2} \right]$$

$$+\left[\sum_{t=1}^{\infty} \Pi\left(1 + \frac{\Delta\widetilde{P}}{P}\right) \left\{ (i_t - r_t) \frac{d\overline{m}_t}{dP_0} - (i_t - r_t^*) \frac{dm_t^F}{dP_0} \right\} \right.$$

$$\left. -\sum_{t=0}^{\infty} \frac{w_0}{P_0} \frac{\Pi(1+\Delta\widetilde{w}/w)}{\Pi(1+i)} \frac{d\overline{N}_t^d}{dP_0} \right]$$

$$+\left[\sum_{t=1}^{\infty} \frac{\Pi(1+\Delta P/P)}{\Pi(1+i)} (mh_t + mb_t + m_t^F) \frac{dr_t^*}{dP_0} \right.$$

$$- \sum_{t=1}^{\infty} \frac{M_t^s}{P_0 \Pi(1+i)} \frac{dr_t^*}{dP_0} \Bigg]$$

$$+ \left[\sum_{t=1}^{\infty} \frac{(i_t - r_t^*)}{\Pi(1+i)} \frac{d(M_t^s/P_0)}{dP_0} - \sum_{t=0}^{\infty} \frac{w_0}{P_0} \frac{\Pi(1+\Delta w/w)}{\Pi(1+i)} \frac{dN_t^d}{dP_0} \right]$$

$$\tag{7.22}$$

which has four terms to analyze. The first term in square brackets in (7.22) is just the impact on wealth of the initial-condition effect (through the two sorts of money) on the non-financial business sector, and is familiar from chapters 4, 5, and 6. The second term in square brackets is the price-induced effect on wealth through banks and the banks' initial-condition effect when there are no government restrictions on r, the case analyzed extensively in chapter 6. The only difference here is that the opportunity cost per dollar of reserves is no longer i but $i - r^*$. Under the conditions of chapter 6, the second bracketed term in (7.22) reduces to an initial condition effect on the banking sector.

Under conditions discussed below, the third and fourth terms in (7.22) reduced to an initial-condition effect through government money.

The third term in square brackets reflects the fact that r_t^* varies with P_0. To evaluate this term, note that if the system is on a path where markets clear over time, then

$$\Pi(1 + \Delta P/P)(\mathrm{mh}_t + \mathrm{mb}_t + m_t^F) = M_t^s/P_0$$

and hence the third bracketed term equals zero. In words, a rise in P_0 may cause a change in r_t^*. Suppose for illustration that r_t^* rises so that people are wealthier in that they get more interest on the government money they hold, but poorer in that they have higher taxes to finance the extra interest the government pays on the money it has outstanding. If the private sectors are aiming at nominal holdings of government money that equal the stock the government plans to supply in each period, the increase in r^* has no net effect on wealth. If expectations do not coincide, the effect through the third term is clearly ambiguous.[2]

This leaves the fourth term in square brackets in (7.22), which is evaluated at initial levels of $r_t^* = \bar{r}_t^*$. This term is conveniently considered as the sum of

$$\partial \left\{ \sum_{t=1}^{\infty} \frac{(i_t - r_t^*)M_t^s}{P_0 \Pi(1+i)} - \sum_{t=1}^{\infty} \frac{w_0}{P_0} \frac{\Pi(1+\Delta w/w)}{\Pi(1+i)} N_t^d \right\} \Big/ \partial P_0 \tag{7.23}$$

and

$$- \frac{\partial(w_0/P_0) N_0^d}{\partial P_0}, \tag{7.24}$$

where both are evaluated at the initial $r^* = \bar{r}^*$. Similarly to the analysis of the price-induced effect on wealth through bank money in chapter 6, (7.23) shows the effect through government money supplies, while (7.24) is an initial-condition effect.

The Price-Induced Effect on Wealth Through Government Money

First consider (7.23). Following chapter 5's discussion, $(i_t - r_t^*)M_t^s$ is the net revenue government receives in period t from having an outstanding money supply of M_t^s. The suggestion that government pay interest on its money is not necessarily a suggestion that it abandon control over the nominal money stock. To the contrary, in some discussions of this suggestion, the government is envisioned as controlling the sequence M_t^s $(t \geqslant 1)$ with the aim of controlling the temporal course of the price level.[3] Rather, the argument is that once government has chosen the sequence $M_t^s(t \geqslant 1)$, it should pay interest on its money at the rate r_t^*.

r_t^* could be chosen in two plausible ways. The first approach chooses r_t^* to set the marginal value to the public of having one more unit of government money in any period equal to the marginal cost of supporting that unit in that period. Call this the "marginal cost equals marginal benefit" condition. Johnson (1969) argues that the relevant distinction is not between "outside" and "inside" money, but whether the money pays competitively determined interest. In his view, any money paying competitively determined interest, including government money, is not part of the price-induced effect on wealth (though his argument is not very explicit). However, he also argues that if a money issuer has a positive net present value as a result of its money activity, then the money is part of the effect. Thus, a second approach sets r_t^* at a level that eliminates any profit from government money issue. Call this the zero-profit condition. In the case Johnson considers, $\theta^* = 0$ for all m, and hence there is no difference between the two approaches, with each requiring $r^* = i$. Patinkin's discussion of the role of bank money in the price-induced effect on wealth makes the zero-profit condition the key to bank money not entering the price-induced effect on wealth (see the discussion of Patinkin's analysis in section 7.3.) Patinkin's (1969, 1972) general assumption is that the "marginal benefit equals marginal cost" approach implies the zero-profit approach, but in fact the two rules yield different results.[4]

"Marginal Benefit Equals Marginal Cost" Case.

"Marginal Benefit Equals Marginal Cost" Case. This interpretation requires that, once government has chosen the sequence M_t^s, it sets r_t^* so that

$$(i_t - r_t^*) - \underset{\sim}{w}_t \, \theta_{r^*}^* \, v_t^* \, \frac{1}{\tilde{P}_t} = (i_t - r_t^*) - \frac{w_0}{P_0} \, \theta_{r^*}^* \, v_t^* \, \frac{\Pi(1 + \Delta \underset{\sim}{w}/w)}{\Pi(1 + \Delta \underset{\sim}{P}/P)}$$
$$= 0 \quad (t \geqslant 1). \tag{7.25}$$

Thus, government chooses r^* so that $i_t - r_t^*$, the marginal cost to the public of having the use of one more nominal government dollar in period t, just equals the marginal cost of maintaining the dollar in that period – the usual efficiency criterion.

The price-induced effect on wealth through government money, expression (7.23), can be written as

$$\left\{ \sum_{t=1}^{\infty} \frac{-(i_t - r_t^*) M_t^s}{P_0^2 \Pi(1+i)} + \sum_{t=1}^{\infty} \frac{w_0}{P_0} \, \frac{\Pi(1 + \Delta \underset{\sim}{w}/w)}{\Pi(1+i)} \, \theta_{r^*}^* \, v_t^* \, \frac{M_t}{P_0^2 \Pi(1 + \Delta \underset{\sim}{P}/P)} \right\}$$

$$+ \left\{ \sum_{t=1}^{\infty} \frac{(i_t - r_t^*)}{P_0 \Pi(1+i)} \, \frac{dM_t^s}{dP_0} - \sum_{t=1}^{\infty} \frac{w_0}{P_0} \, \frac{\Pi(1 + \Delta \underset{\sim}{w}/w)}{\Pi(1+i)} \, \theta_{r^*}^* \right.$$

$$\left. \times \frac{v_t^* \, dM_t^s/dP_0}{P_0 \Pi(1 + \Delta \underset{\sim}{P}/P)} \right\} \tag{7.26}$$

under the assumptions that w_0 varies proportionately with P_0, the future i_t are constant, and government's wage and price expectations are unit elastic. Clearly, the sign of (7.26) depends on the two expressions in braces. From the marginal condition for efficiency (7.25), both expressions equal zero, no matter what the elasticity of M_t^s with respect to P_0 in any period t ($t \geqslant 1$).

In words, in the case of "marginal benefit equals marginal cost," a rise in P_0 causes a zero price-induced effect on wealth through government money ($t \geqslant 1$). The reason for this is simple. Think of the government as running a profit-maximizing, though price-taking, "money business" where all profits go to reduce taxes. Since the marginal condition holds, a small change in real money balances has no effect on the real present value of the future operations of this business, and hence the real present value of future taxes does not change. This is so whether the change in the real government money stock arises from changes in M or P, because θ^* is homogeneous of degree zero in these nominal magnitudes.[5]

Notice that (7.26) equals zero whatever the value of dM_t/dP_0. This is in distinction to Johnson's (1969) discussion where optimality is assumed to require a fixed stock of real balances (OM_2 in his figure 1, p. 33). It appears that Johnson assumes that M must vary proportionately with P_0.

Thus, future government money is not a part of the price-induced effect on wealth, because government sets the marginal condition (7.25) and because θ^* is homogeneous of degree zero in nominal values. Further, the interest payment that causes this in no way requires weakening control over the money supply.[6]

Zero-Profit Case This case turns on the sign of $\theta^*_{r^*r^*}$. To start, assume increasing marginal cost, or $\theta^*_{r^*r^*} > 0$. The zero-profit condition can only be met by average-cost pricing. In figure 7.2, with real balances M/P_A, the difference $i - r^*$ must be the smaller $i - r^*_C$ rather than the level $i - r^*_A$ under the case of "marginal benefit equals marginal cost." Setting r^*_C leads to inefficiency of government's "money business" and makes taxes higher than otherwise. If P rises to P_B, M/P falls, and at the same $i - r^*_C$ the inefficiency is reduced and so taxes fall. Thus, the price-induced effect on wealth through future government money is positive in this case, not negative. (Recall that the effect of the induced change in r^* is captured in the third term in (7.22) and hence is ignored here.)

The graphical analysis in figure 7.2 corresponds to expression (7.26). Suppose a rise in P reduces M/P. Since $i - r^* < $ MC, this rise in P has a positive effect on wealth. In fact, as long as $\theta^*_{r^*r^*} > 0$ (so MC is rising), and MC $>$ AC, this case of average-cost pricing means that any rise in P_0 that

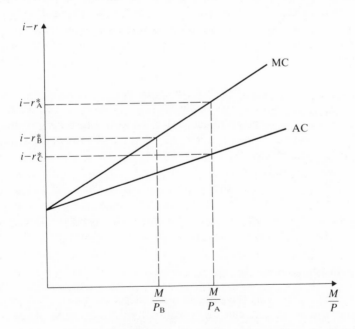

Figure 7.2 Government money and interest payments in the price-induced effect on wealth

reduces the real value of future government money stocks causes a positive effect on wealth. However, if M_t^s is unit elastic relative to P_0, so real balances do not change, or if MC is constant, this price-induced effect on wealth is equal to zero.

Money, Competitive Interest, and the Price-Induced Effect on Wealth   The analysis and results of the price-induced effects on wealth through bank and government money are exactly symmetric. If wealth-maximizing, price-taking and quantity-setting banks pay a competitive rate of interest on their money, and their resource use is homogeneous of degree zero in nominal values, then bank money does not enter the price-induced effect on wealth, as shown in chapter 6. The discussion in section 7.1 showed that if banks are restricted in the rate they are allowed to pay, then bank money can easily enter the effect, and will enter the effect if the real demand for bank money is affected by price level changes. The present chapter also showed that if the government pays a competitively determined rate of interest on its money, then government money does not enter the effect. By competitive interest is meant the government follows a "marginal benefit equals marginal cost" condition, not a zero-profit condition (though these two are the same when government's marginal cost is constant). Neither the bank nor government money business need make zero profits for the two monies to fail to enter the effect. Government money does, however, enter the effect if a competitive rate of interest is not paid (and future money stocks are not unit elastic relative to the current price level), as chapters 4 and 5 discuss.

In chapter 5, with $r^* = 0$, if the M_t^s ($t \geqslant 1$) do not increase proportionately with P_0, the price-induced effect on wealth through government money is negative. In this chapter, the effect is zero under the case of "marginal benefit equals marginal cost." In the zero-profit case, the effect turns on $\theta_{r^*r^*}^*$; the effect is positive if $\theta_{r^*r^*}^* > 0$, that is, there is increasing marginal cost, and if marginal cost is constant, the effect is zero. In chapter 5, if the M_t^s are unit elastic relative to P_0, then the price-induced effect on wealth through government money is zero. Here, this is true also under both approaches to setting r^* and whatever $\theta_{r^*r^*}^*$ is.

The Government's Initial-Condition Effect

The remaining part of the price-induced effect on wealth is (7.24), an initial-condition effect, and, as is habitually the case, it has been overlooked in the literature. As long as $\theta_{r^*}^*$ is positive, (7.24) is

$$\frac{-\partial(w_0/P_0)\,N_0^d}{\partial P_0} = \frac{w_0}{P_0}\,\theta_{r*}^*\,v_0^*\,\frac{M_0^s}{P_0^2} > 0. \tag{7.28}$$

In period 0, a rise in P_0 such as from P_A to P_B in figure 7.2 reduces M_0^s/P_0 and hence reduces government's total real cost of maintaining the money stock, the area under the MC curve (plus a constant). This decline in costs is the government sector initial-condition effect; the household sector is wealthier because its taxes are cut by exactly this fall in costs. If P_0 initially takes on the value that had been expected, then

$$\frac{w_0}{P_0}\,\theta_{r*}^*\,v_0^*\,\frac{M_0^s}{P_0^2} = (i_0 - r_0^*)\,\frac{M_0^s}{P_0^2} > 0, \tag{7.29}$$

where r_0^* is the value that was set at the end of last period to rule currently.

Suppose that government pays competitive rates r^* and thus the price-induced effect on wealth through government money, expression (7.23), is zero. Further, let the banking sector pay competitive rates r so that the price-induced effect on wealth through bank money is zero. There still remain the household, business, banking sector, and now the government sector, initial-condition effects to help render the price level determinate.[7] These initial-condition effects are supplemented by the velocity effect on bank money (discussed in chapter 5), and by the velocity effect on government money (discussed below).

As noted repeatedly, initial-condition effects work in two ways. First, they contribute to the price-induced effect on wealth. Second, they directly affect demand and supply in various current markets. The second channel is now the key, since the net influence on wealth of the initial-condition effect through both types of money can be shown to be zero when government pays a competitive r^*.

An increase in real government money balances yields marginal benefits for the household, banking, and non-financial business sectors; if these sectors are optimizing, the marginal benefits just equal $i_0 - r_0^*$, provided that P_0 is initially at the level that was expected. In this case an increase in P_0 causes initial-condition effects on wealth through government money of $-(i_0 - r_0^*)\mathrm{MH}_0/P_0^2$, $-(i_0 - r_0^*)\mathrm{MF}_0/P_0^2$, and $-(i_0 - r_0^*)\mathrm{MB}_0/P_0^2$. For example, the marginal benefit to the household sector from an increase in MH_0/P_0 equals $i_0 - r_0^*$ at an optimum, and the change in MH_0/P_0 with a rise in P_0 is $-\mathrm{MH}_0/P_0^2$. Adding these three initial-condition effects on wealth to the government sector's initial-condition effect in (7.29) gives $(i_0 - r_0^*)M_0^s/P_0^2 - (i_0 - r_0^*)\mathrm{MH}_0/P_0^2 - (i_0 - r_0^*)\mathrm{MF}_0/P_0^2 - (i_0 - r_0^*)\mathrm{MB}_0/P_0^2 \equiv 0$ since $\mathrm{MH}_0 + \mathrm{MF}_0 + \mathrm{MB}_0 \equiv M_0^s$. In words, the net of the initial-condition effects in the price-induced effect on wealth through government money is zero; what one sector gains in wealth, others lose because each sector was at the margin.

While the initial-condition effects on wealth through government money cancel in the price-induced effect on wealth, there is no presumption that they have zero net effect in various current markets. For example, the current level of output falls; the demand for labor by banks and government falls, as likely happens to that of the non-financial business sector (since real balances and labor are likely complementary factors of production). The initial-condition effects still play a stabilizing role in the economy.

Finally, recall from chapter 6, section 6.3, that the net influence on wealth of the initial-condition effects through bank money was zero even in the case where government interest rate r^* on its fiat money was zero. But now that all the initial-condition effects through government money net to a zero effect on wealth, it is clear that the net of all initial-condition effects in the price-induced effect on wealth is zero. The general non-zero net initial-condition effect on wealth found above in chapters 4–6 was simply because the government was not paying a competitive rate of interest.

The Effect on r_0^* *of an Increase in* P_0 One loose end is the question of what happens to r_0^* when P_0 rises and hence θ_0^* changes. Government might simply stick with the value set in the previous period, or might revise r_0^*. The r_0^* that *ex ante* satisfied the government's condition for money will not do so now unless θ_0^* is constant. Government may have bound itself to the *ex ante* r_0^*, or may now adjust r_0^* to reflect the change in τ_0^* (in fact, may adopt the policy of adjusting r^* *ex post* to reflect any change). Choice between these two rules, however, has no effect on wealth. One way to see this is that $r_0^* \, M_0^s$ does not enter the household sector budget constraint (7.21) or any marginal condition.[8] Intuitively, if government, say, raises r_0^* to reflect an unexpectedly low τ_0^*, it must increase taxation by the value of these extra interest payments; the private sector receives more interest but pays taxes higher by the same amount.

The Government Money Velocity Effect

The discussion of (7.23) and (7.24), the price-induced effect on wealth through government money and the government's initial-condition effect, turned heavily on the transactions velocity of government money, both current and future. As in chapter 6, proper analysis requires separation of price-induced effects and velocity effects. Holding constant P_0, w_0/P_0, all interest rates and expected rates of inflation, the government money velocity effect on wealth is

$$\partial \left\{ \sum_{t=1}^{\infty} \frac{(i_t - r_t^*)M_t^s}{P_0 \Pi(1+i)} - \sum_{t=0}^{\infty} \frac{w_0}{P_0} \frac{\Pi(1 + \Delta \underset{\sim}{w}/w)}{\Pi(1+i)} \underset{\sim}{N}_t^d \right\} \Big/ \partial v_0^*. \quad (7.30)$$

This is conveniently expressed as the sum of

$$\partial \left\{ \sum_{t=1}^{\infty} \frac{(i_t - r_t^*)M_t^s}{P_0 \Pi(1+i)} - \sum_{t=1}^{\infty} \frac{w_0}{P_0} \frac{\Pi(1 + \Delta \underset{\sim}{w}/w)}{\Pi(1+i)} \underset{\sim}{N}_t^d \right\} \Big/ \partial v_0^*, \quad (7.31)$$

and

$$-\frac{\partial(w_0/P_0)\underset{\sim}{N}_0^d}{\partial v_0^*}. \quad (7.32)$$

In considering government monetary policy and its response to changing conditions, it is just as reasonable to assume a relationship between M_t^s and v_0^* as between M_t^s and P_0.

Expression (7.31) can be written as

$$\left\{ \sum_{t=1}^{\infty} \frac{(i_t - r_t^*)}{P_0 \Pi(1+i)} \frac{dM_t^s}{dv_0^*} \right.$$

$$- \sum_{t=1}^{\infty} \frac{w_0}{P_0} \frac{\Pi(1 + \Delta \underset{\sim}{w}/w)}{\Pi(1+i)} \underset{\sim}{\theta}_{\tau^*}^* v_t^* \frac{1}{P_0 \Pi(1 + \Delta \underline{P}/P)} \frac{dM_t^s}{dv_0^*} \right)$$

$$- \sum_{t=1}^{\infty} \left\{ \frac{w_0}{P_0} \frac{\Pi(1 + \Delta \underset{\sim}{w}/w)}{\Pi(1+i)} \underset{\sim}{\theta}_{\tau^*}^* \frac{M_t^s}{P_0 \Pi(1 + \Delta \underline{P}/P)} \frac{dv_t^*}{dv_0^*} \right\}, \quad (7.33)$$

where (7.33) is evaluated at constant $r^* = \bar{r}^*$, similar to the discussion surrounding the price-induced effect on wealth through government money. From (7.25), the marginal condition for government money, the first term in (7.33) equals zero. As long as expected future velocity is positively related to current velocity $(dv_t^*/dv_0^* > 0)$ and increased transactions require more inputs, or $\theta_{\tau^*}^*$ is positive, the second term must be negative. Hence, (7.31) is negative in this case.[9]

Under either condition for setting r^*, "marginal benefit equals marginal cost" or "zero profits", (7.32) equals

$$-\frac{w_0}{P_0} \theta_{\tau^*}^* \frac{M_0^s}{P_0} < 0.$$

Thus, in the case where government sets marginal benefit equal to marginal cost, the sum of (7.31) and (7.32), the government money velocity effect on wealth, is negative.

Now consider the results under the zero-profit condition. When analyzing the price-induced effect on wealth through government money, a key issue was whether $\theta^*_{r^*,r^*}$ was positive or zero; here the value of $\theta^*_{r^*,r^*}$ does not matter. Assuming that both $dM^s_t/dv^*_0 > 0$ and $\theta^*_{r^*,r^*} > 0$, the first term in (7.33) is negative, along lines analyzed in connection with the price-induced effect on wealth through government money. With $dv^*_t/dv^*_0 > 0$, the second term is also negative. Thus, even if $dM^s_t/dv^*_0 = \theta^*_{r^*,r^*} = 0$, (7.33) is negative. Since (7.32) is negative, it follows that under the zero-profit condition the velocity effect on wealth is negative.

Neutrality with Competitive-Interest-Bearing Money

Suppose all holdings of government money and bank money are doubled. If all price expectations are unit elastic and all interest rates are constant, and if θ and θ^* are homogeneous of degree zero in nominal values, then a doubling of P_0 maintains the same real equilibrium. If the economy is on an intertemporal equilibrium path, this experiment does not displace it. For example, since maintaining $\overline{m}_t$ ($t \geq 1$) requires a rise in $\overline{M}_t$, this will occur voluntarily under the banks' homogeneity condition. The simultaneous doubling of all stocks of money along with the doubling of P_0 means there are no initial-condition effects.

However, if initial holdings of a government money are doubled, with unchanged holdings of bank money, a doubling of P_0 causes initial-condition effects. In this experiment, government money is not neutral in the short run. However, over the longer run, bank money will expand endogenously and the same real equilibrium time path can once again be reached. Thus, money is neutral in the longer run.

In other words, modifying the analysis of chapter 6 by allowing competitive interest on government money has no effect on neutrality.

Determinacy of the Price Level

Suppose P_0 is arbitrarily increased from its initial equilibrium value. What forces exist to push it back to equilibrium? To begin with, there are initial-condition effects on the household, banking, non-financial business, and government sectors. Recall that with competitive interest payments by government on its money, the impact on wealth of the initial-condition effects may well net to zero. However, these initial-condition effects will alter current output supply and labor demand, creating disequilibrium.

If no interest rates change, if price and wage expectations are unit elastic, if bank money and government money resource use are homogeneous of degree zero in nominal values, and if the government pays interest based on the condition of "marginal benefit equals marginal cost," then there are no wealth or substitution effects.

While there is no effect on wealth due to the rise in P_0, some real asset stocks will no longer equal the level desired; this is very similar to the "portfolio effect" of Gurley and Shaw (discussed in chapter 2 above). Suppose that all government money stocks are constant at M_0, the case of Yap-Island money. The rise in P_0 causes no effect on wealth through government money because competitive interest is paid. Ignoring the initial-condition effects, m_1^d is unchanged. However, m_1^s has fallen since P_0 and P_1 are up, while $M_1^s = M_0$ is unchanged.

The household sector's wealth is unchanged in the following sense. The rise in P_0 reduces household holdings of real government money and equally the real stock the government must support. A unit fall in this stock reduces net interest income by $i - r^*$. However, it reduces taxation by an equal amount from the government's marginal condition, since the government need now support only a smaller real money stock. Since wealth is unchanged, the household sector wants to keep its use of real government money at its previous level. At the higher price level, however, the actual stock has fallen. Exactly the same forces are at work with bank money, except that banks are willing to expand their nominal money stock to return their real stocks to the same level. Government is viewed, however, as picking a sequence M_t that may be less than unit elastic, in part out of a desire to stabilize the time path of prices.

Thus, there exist initial-condition and portfolio effects to give determinacy of the price level.

7.3 Patinkin's Critique of Pesek and Saving

This section discusses Pesek and Saving's (1967) book, Patinkin's (1969, 1972) critique of Pesek and Saving, and Saving's (1970, 1971) and Patinkin's (1971) further exchange. After this flurry in the late 1960s and early 1970s, there was relatively little theoretical discussion in the literature of the price-induced effect on wealth. This lack was not due to everyone coming to agreement on all issues. Rather, economists seemed to lose interest because it was not clear how to make progress on the issues involved, and the profession's interest was taken up with the rational expectations revolution.

For three decades, Patinkin's (1956; rev. edn 1965) work has been a standard in general equilibrium monetary theory. The first major challenge to it was Gurley and Shaw's (1960) analysis where government could cause real effects by shifting the ratio of government bonds to money while holding the total of the two fixed, a "portfolio effect." Further, in Gurley and Shaw's view the real balance effect need not exist if all money is inside money, and the price level would still be determinate through a portfolio effect, as discussed in chapter 2. Patinkin smoothly incorporated these points into his (1965) revised edition in his discussion of the "net real financial asset effect" (chapter XII, section 4). Pesek and Saving's (1967) book was another major challenge, where they argued that bank money was part of the price-induced effect on wealth. Patinkin's (1969) review of the book, revised and extended in 1972, made a splendidly plausible job of disposing of this challenge.

This essay does not reach Pesek and Saving's conclusions. Patinkin seems to have disposed of their challenge by a series of analytical confusions, however, the most serious of which is a failure to understand the Hicksian analysis of this case. This is indeed serious, for Patinkin (1965) argues that he uses Hicksian wealth effects in his analysis.

Pesek and Saving's Analysis

Pesek and Saving focus much of their analysis of the price-induced effect on wealth on the question of what part of the money stock could or should be viewed as debt. They view debt as simultaneously the asset of one agent and the equal liability of another. Hence, in the aggregate the asset and liability net out and cannot contribute to the price-induced effect on wealth. This is exactly the view that had been taken by Gurley and Shaw (1960) and by Patinkin (1965) in arguing that bank money is not part of the price-induced effect on wealth; while bank money is an asset to its holders, it is an equal liability to its issuers. Pesek and Saving, however, argue that government money and some fraction of bank money is not properly viewed as debt, and hence is part of the price-induced effect on wealth.

This book adopts the view, in chapters 5 and 6, that the debate over whether money is debt is essentially semantic and shows that the debate is, in any case, irrelevant to the analysis of the price-induced effect on wealth. Consequently, Pesek and Saving were on the wrong track. However, it is worthwhile pursuing their argument.

Pesek and Saving argue that government money M is not viewed as imposing any liability on government but is an asset to private sector money-holders. Hence, government money is not a debt, and contributes the amount M/P to society's real wealth.

They then turn to banks and suppose that a bank is allowed to issue a given amount $\overline{M}^*$ of non-interest-bearing bank money which trades on a one-for-one basis with government money. In addition, the bank must stand ready to repurchase its dollars at any time with government dollars. Thus, the bank must hold reserves $M^F = e\overline{M}^*$, $0 < e < 1$, where e is determined by the public's proclivity to trade-in bank dollars.

Pesek and Saving argue that the bank must be restrained in the amount it can issue. After all, if it is essentially costless to print a bank dollar but each dollar buys \$1 worth of real goods, the bank will stop printing dollars only when \$1 worth of goods is virtually valueless and equals the cost of printing another bank dollar. Thus, Pesek and Saving argue that a finite, determinate price level in a world of private banks requires outside limits such as $\overline{M}^*$ on the issuance of bank dollars. The only restriction really required for a finite price level, however, is imposition and enforcement of the instant repurchase provision that government and bank money trade at par. There was a finite stock of bank money and a finite, determinate price level in chapter 6 where banks must keep their money at par with government money and banks in that chapter paid a competitive rate of interest. As section 7.1 showed, restricting the interest rate that banks can pay on their money reduces the stock of bank money below what it would be for a given price level if interest were competitively set.

In Pesek and Saving's view, the non-bank private sector gives up $e\overline{M}^*$ of government dollars and gets $\overline{M}^*$ bank dollars. $\overline{M}^*$ is not a debt of the banking sector according to Pesek and Saving. Thus, the net increase in wealth is $\overline{M}^* - e\overline{M}^*$. Hence, the contribution of government and bank money to real wealth is $(M + \overline{M}^* - e\overline{M}^*)/P$. When P rises, the price-induced effect on wealth is $-(M + \overline{M}^* - e\overline{M}^*)/P^2$, with the component through government money $-M/P^2$ and the bank money component $-(\overline{M}^* - e\overline{M}^*)/P^2 = -(1-e)\overline{M}^*/P^2$.

Chapter 5 showed that the price-induced effect on wealth through government money is $-M/P^2$ only if M is constant (the Yap-Island case); assume this is so. To analyze the effect through bank money, ignore the bank's initial-condition effect. Then, chapter 6 argued that with an unregulated rate of bank interest and wealth-maximizing, price-taking and quantity-setting banks, the price-induced effect on wealth through bank money is very likely zero, since $\theta(\cdot)$ is likely homogeneous of degree zero in nominal values. Pesek and Saving find their negative effect of $-(1-e)\overline{M}^*/P^2$ for two reasons. First, they do not allow banks to optimize and attract deposits in a competitive manner, with r varying to give equilibrium, as in chapter 6 where the price-induced effect on wealth through bank money is zero. Second, even in their framework, the bank is restricted to $\overline{M}^*$ in nominal rather than real terms. If $\overline{M}^*$ and the associated reserves are allowed to vary proportionately with P, the effect found by Pesek and Saving (1967) vanishes, as is shown below.

Pesek and Saving (1967) have one key insight.[10] The balance sheet of a bank will say that its assets equal its liabilities plus net worth (with this sum often simply called "liabilities"); however, the market value of the bank can be positive even though its assets must always equal liabilities through accounting definitions. This positive market value of banks arises in their analysis because government restrictions allow the bank to earn monopoly rents with a real capitalized value of $(1 - e)\overline{M}^*/P$, as Patinkin (1969) points out. Thus, the assumption that assets equal liabilities is not sufficient to ensure that the real net present value of banks is zero, though Patinkin's (1965) edition falls into this error (chapter XII, section 5; see also Patinkin's (1972, chapter 9, p. 184) acknowledgment of this error).

Chapter 6 investigates the price-induced effect on wealth by asking how the real net present value of future bank dividends changes with P_0. The initial real net present value may be zero, if banking is a competitive constant-cost industry with free entry. Alternatively, the industry may show increasing costs and infra-marginal firms may pay positive dividends as differential rents to non-explicit factors put up by bank owners. And, finally, restriction on entry may make this figure positive for the industry even when the interest rate r on bank money is competitively determined. The issue of the price-induced effect on wealth is independent of the initial value of the real net present value of future bank dividends, and instead depends on whether wealth-maximizing banks pay a competitive r, so that all bank marginal conditions hold, and on whether bank resource use is homogeneous of degree zero in nominal values. Thus, Pesek and Saving's insight that the market value of banks can be positive even though bank's assets and liabilities are equal is valid but irrelevant to the price-induced effect on wealth through bank money in the general analysis of chapter 6. The issue is how the real net present value of banks' future dividends changes in response to changes in P_0, not whether this real net present value is initially positive or zero.

Pesek and Saving (1967) try to explain the positive market value of the bank, even though its assets and liabilities are equal, by arguing that the liabilities are not really debt. A saving bank that earns monopoly rents will be in exactly the same situation as the bank, however, even though Pesek and Saving would not include the savings deposits as money. Trying to explain the market value of the bank over its liabilities by arguing that money is not debt misses the point (monopoly rents) and is misleading.

Further, their emphasis on bank money not being debt leads Pesek and Saving into error on the question of interest on bank money. They argue that the fact that one bank dollar that pays no interest is worth $1 means that the capitalized value of the money services from one dollar is worth

$1. If the dollar now pays interest at say one-half of the bond rate i, then the dollar is both money and debt. But since the dollar is still worth only $1, and the present value of the interest is $0.50, evidently the capitalized value of the money-services component of the dollar is now worth only $0.50. If $r = i$, the money-services component of a dollar is valueless in this view. Interest on bank money destroys moneyness, they argue.

Johnson (1969) and Friedman and Schwartz (1969) pointed out the classic confusion here between total value and value at the margin. When $r = 0$, people hold a small enough amount of bank money so that the discounted value of the money services of the marginal dollar is $1. If $r = 0.5i$, people expand their use of bank dollars because this is now cheaper. The total value of bank money services consumed rises, but the marginal value falls until the discounted value of the marginal stream is worth $0.50. If $r = i$, people use even more bank dollars, increasing the total value of money services used, but driving the marginal value to zero. If the marginal cost of supporting one more bank dollar is zero, $i = r$ is an efficiency condition and it is simply an error to say the moneyness of bank money has been destroyed.

With this review as background, the next subsections try to clear up some of the key issues raised by Pesek, Saving and Patinkin.

Patinkin's analysis confuses the question of the size of the contribution of bank money to the price-induced effect on wealth with the question of the source (or cause) and size of the real present value of the dividend stream from the bank sector. That is, Patinkin seems to believe that the present value of the dividend stream from the banking sector must be positive if a non-zero price-induced effect on wealth through banks is to exist, and that, further, a positive dividend stream implies a lack of perfect competition. Contrarily, he believes that perfect competition implies zero bank profits. What follows is intended to sort this all out.

"Monopoly Rights" and Bank Money

A crucial case in the literature is where banks issue a number of dollars that is invariant with price changes; both Pesek and Saving (1967), and Patinkin (1969, 1972) spend much time on this case. Suppose that banks are granted the right by the government to issue only $100 of non-interest-bearing nominal dollars which are almost identical with government money (Patinkin, 1969). This particular $100 is just a type of Yap-Island money, fixed in quantity, and many Yap-Island money results are to be expected (see chapter 4). Suppose, in addition, that banks are required to hold reserves of $20 of government money to satisfy the condition of convertibility on demand of bank money into government money. If the bank is allowed to issue the money in period ℓ, its profits in that period are $80. Conceptually, it sells $20 of bank money for $20 of government money to hold as reserves, and distributes the remaining $80 of bank money as dividends to its owners. And, of course, if the right to issue the $100 in period ℓ is granted in period 0, the present value of this $80 has effects in period 0 on the behavior of the household sector, which is the owner of the banking sector.

This case illustrates several of Patinkin's (1969) points. First, the right to issue $100 (subject to the $20 reserve requirement) creates an effect on wealth ($100 − $20 = $80). Second, this is so even before the money is issued, because, third, the effect on wealth in either case is due to the right to issue money and earn the monopoly rent, not the money *per se*.[11]

To continue analysis of this problem, suppose P_0 rises. For example, a doubling of P_0 causes a price-induced effect on wealth through the banking sector equal to minus the real present value of $40. Regarding this experiment, Patinkin's view seems to be that in this case where some individual has $80 worth of "monopoly rights" (his phrase) to issue $100 subject to the required reserves of $20, there is a price-induced effect on wealth through the banking sector, but this effect is fundamentally based on the monopoly rights, not on the money having been issued. From these results for a very particular case, however, he draws as a *non sequitur* the very general proposition that under reasonable assumptions a price-induced effect on wealth through the banking sector requires a positive net worth of the sector, which he identifies with the positive value of the monopoly rights.

This view is seriously misleading. First, only in special cases does the existence of monopoly rights to issue money imply a non-zero price-induced effect on wealth through the banking sector. Suppose that the government grants to some individual the right to issue $100 in terms of P_0, subject to the requirements of holding $20 of government money in terms of P_0. Then a doubling of P_0 doubles both of these nominal quantities and there is no price-induced effect on wealth through banks. The proper conclusion is that the price-induced effect on wealth follows in Patinkin's example from restrictions on the nominal quantity of bank money.[12] In the case where banks can issue a given amount of money in real terms, there is a zero price-induced effect on wealth through bank money, even though there exist monopoly rents to banks.

Second, in the case discussed in chapter 6, where banks pay a competitively determined interest rate and hold reserves to keep the two monies trading at par, the sign of the effect though future bank money depends on the homogeneity of banks' demand for resources. It has nothing to do with whether restrictions on entry may have caused the existence of monopoly rents or whether non-explicit factors cause the banking industry to show increasing costs with differential rents earned by infra-marginal banks. Even if banks earn zero rents, lack of homogeneity of degree zero in nominal values will lead to a non-zero price-induced effect on wealth through bank money.

Finally, section 7.1 considered the case where r is restricted and a rise in the demand for bank money creates a wealth effect through banks. This effect arises because $i - r >$ MC. Average cost (AC) may, however, have the relationship $i - r >$ AC or $i - r =$ AC. In the latter case, monopoly rents are zero and there is still an effect on wealth through bank money. Thus, in the example Patinkin uses, the price-induced effect on wealth through bank money is indeed related to monopoly rents. In general, however, there is no necessary relationship at all to monopoly rights.

The Price-Induced Effect on Wealth Through Banks – Perfect Competition

Patinkin's discussion of Pesek and Saving's argument that bank money is part of the price-induced effect on wealth concludes that what is really included is the change in the real capitalized value of the monopoly rents. As seen above, this requires that the right to issue bank money be stated in nominal terms; if stated in real terms, the real capitalized value of monopoly rights is constant and is not part of the effect. Patinkin then turns to the case of a competitive banking industry, which he identifies as one where zero profits are made, at least in the long run when entry will eliminate profits. His view is that zero profits together with real operating costs that vary proportionately with real balances imply that the price-induced effect on wealth through (future) bank money is zero (1972, chapter 9, p. 187). Further, he seems to believe this is so even if r is not competitively determined (1972, chapter 9, p. 189).

Patinkin considers the effect on wealth through banks of a decline in the price level when the banking sector is competitive, i.e. it earns zero rents. He writes (Patinkin, 1972, pp. 184–5):

> The crucial question in this analysis is what assumption the banking sector makes about the impact of this price decline on the physical volume of administrative operations (per unit of time) needed to maintain the stock of bank money constant . . . and hence on the banks' costs. If, for example, banks assume that this volume will remain the same, then the lowered price level means that the banks' nominal costs of operations per unit of time are lower, and hence their profits are greater. Hence the nominal net worth of the banking sector – that is, the capitalized value of these profits – increases; and

this, of course, causes a corresponding increase in the net worth of the nonfinancial sector. This increased net worth is matched in the balance sheet of the banking sector by the introduction of an asset "Goodwill . . . ."

It does not, however, seem reasonable that the banking sector would make this assumption. For – in the absence of money illusion – it might well be expected to take account of the fact that if the price level is, say 10 percent lower, then each individual transaction with the bank (namely, each deposit made and each check drawn) will also be roughly 10 percent less in nominal value. Under these circumstances the banks will assume that the physical volume of bank operations connected with maintaining the nominal stock of bank money fixed at its original level will be roughly 11 percent $\{ \approx [(1.00/0.90) - 1.00]100\}$ greater than it was before the price decline. But since the prices of the factors of production engaged in these operations have (by assumption) declined by 10 percent, total nominal operating costs will remain more or less the same. Hence, net profits will remain the same [i.e., equal to zero] and hence so will the nominal net worth of the banking system [i.e., equal to zero]. In this case, . . . the increase in the real net worth of the private sector will equal the increase in the real value of government fiat money – in accordance with the traditional contention. (Material in brackets added.)

The flavor of Patinkin's analysis can be captured in a simplified version of the model used in chapter 6. (The model of chapter 6 and the simplified version used here neglect service charges on transactions using bank money, a standard omission in discussions of bank money's role in the price-induced effect on wealth, as Saving (1977) notes.) Suppose $MF = e\overline{M}$ and $\overline{N}^d = \theta(\tau) = \theta(v\overline{M}/P)$; this makes bank resource use homogeneous of degree zero in nominal values. Notice that in the second paragraph of the above quote, Patinkin evidently assumes v is constant so that an increase in M/P raises τ proportionately. Then bank dividends in any period are the net interest earned on deposits, $(i - r)\overline{M}$, less the interest foregone by holding reserves, iMF, and the cost of labor services the bank uses, $w\overline{N}^d$, that is, dividends are[13]

$$\begin{aligned} \text{div} &= (i - r)\overline{M} - i\text{MF} - w\overline{N}^d \\ &= \{i(1 - e) - r\}\overline{M} - w\overline{N}^d. \end{aligned} \quad (7.34)$$

The first-order condition for a wealth maximum is

$$\frac{d\,\text{div}}{d\,\overline{M}} = \{i(1 - e) - r\} - \frac{w}{P}\,\theta_\tau v = 0. \quad (7.35)$$

The second-order condition requires that $\theta_{rr} > 0$ if the bank is to attain an optimum for a given r; or if θ_r is a constant, r must adjust to make (7.35) hold, with $\overline{M}$ being indeterminate for any individual bank. Conceptually, in (7.35) $i(1-e)-r$ is the value of the marginal product of $\overline{M}$, while $(w/P)\,\theta_r\,v$ is the (nominal) marginal cost $(\mathrm{MC}_{\overline{M}})$ of $\overline{M}$ and $(w/\overline{M})\theta(v\overline{M}/P)$ is nominal average cost $(\mathrm{AC}_{\overline{M}})$.

Patinkin is interested in what happens to real dividends, div/P, or

$$\frac{d\,(\mathrm{div}/P)}{dP} = \frac{(d\,\mathrm{div}/dP)\,P - \mathrm{div}}{P^2}.$$

He assumes $\mathrm{div} = 0$ in perfect competition. Hence $d(\mathrm{div}/P)/dP$ depends on $d\,\mathrm{div}/dP$. In turn, with fixed $\overline{M}$ and MF as Patinkin assumes, nominal revenues $\{i(1-e)-r\}\overline{M}$ are given and the change in div depends only on nominal costs $w\theta(v\overline{M}/P)$. Thus,

$$\frac{d\,\mathrm{div}}{dP} = \frac{d\{-w\theta(v\overline{M}/P)\}}{dP} = \frac{d\{-P(w/P)\theta(v\overline{M}/P)\}}{dP}$$

$$= \frac{\overline{M}}{P}\left\{-\frac{w}{\overline{M}}\,\theta\left(\frac{v\overline{M}}{P}\right) + \frac{w}{P}\,\theta_r\,v\right\}$$

$$= \frac{\overline{M}}{P}\left(-\mathrm{AC}_{\overline{M}} + \mathrm{MC}_{\overline{M}}\right) \geqslant 0 \qquad (7.36)$$

as $\mathrm{MC}_{\overline{M}} \geqslant \mathrm{AC}_{\overline{M}}$.

With U-shaped AC curves, equilibrium may be where $\mathrm{MC}_{\overline{M}} = \mathrm{AC}_{\overline{M}}$, if entry drives down r to eliminate any rents. Suppose that this is so. Then $d\,\mathrm{div}/dP = 0$ from (7.36). But since $\mathrm{MC}_{\overline{M}} = \mathrm{AC}_{\overline{M}}$, it also follows that $\mathrm{div} = 0$ initially. Hence there is no change in div/P and thus no price-induced effect on wealth.

This argument is somewhat misleading, and obscures the fact that what is really going on is use of the marginal condition (7.35). The assumption of $\mathrm{div} = \mathrm{div}/P = 0$ implies that revenue per unit of bank money, $i(1-e)-r$, equals nominal average cost, $\mathrm{AC}_{\overline{M}} = (w/\overline{M})\theta$. The further assumption of U-shaped cost curves and a zero-profit equilibrium means that $\mathrm{MC}_{\overline{M}} = \mathrm{AC}_{\overline{M}}$. Here is where the wealth maximization assumption is introduced, though perhaps without appropriate emphasis. Does $\mathrm{AC}_{\overline{M}} = \mathrm{MC}_{\overline{M}}$ imply that $d\,\mathrm{div}/dP = 0$? No. Instead $\mathrm{AC}_{\overline{M}} = i(1-e)-r$ (from zero profits) and $\mathrm{AC}_{\overline{M}} = \mathrm{MC}_{\overline{M}}$ (from wealth maximization at zero profits) imply together that $i(1-e)-r = \mathrm{MC}_{\overline{M}} = (w/P)\,\theta_r\,v$, the marginal condition (7.35). This marginal condition is in fact all that is needed; the intermediate steps using zero profits are irrelevant, as is now shown.

Suppose that $\mathrm{MC}_{\overline{M}} > \mathrm{AC}_{\overline{M}}$ due to restrictions on entry. Real dividends are

$$\frac{\mathrm{div}}{P} = (i - r) \frac{\overline{M}}{P} - i \frac{\mathrm{MF}}{P} - \frac{w}{P} \overline{N}^{\mathrm{d}}$$

$$= \{i(1 - e) - r\} \frac{\overline{M}}{P} - \frac{w}{P} \theta \left(\frac{v\overline{M}}{P} \right). \tag{7.37}$$

An increase in P, with $\overline{M}$ held constant, causes

$$\frac{\mathrm{d}(\mathrm{div}/P)}{\mathrm{d}P} = - \{i(1 - e) - r\} \frac{\overline{M}}{P^2} + \frac{w}{P} \theta_r v \frac{\overline{M}}{P^2}$$

$$= \frac{M}{P^2} \left[- \{i(1 - e) - r\} + \frac{w}{P} \theta_r v \right]$$

$$= 0 \tag{7.38}$$

from the marginal condition for $\overline{M}$ in (7.35). Note that this is entirely independent of whether $\mathrm{MC}_{\overline{M}} = \mathrm{AC}_{\overline{M}}$. Intuitively, the increase in P changes real balances. But the marginal condition says that a small change in real balances has no effect on the real dividends of a wealth-maximizing, price-taking, quantity-setting bank with costs homogeneous of degree zero.

Thus, both this essay and Patinkin get the same result, $\mathrm{d}(\mathrm{div}/P)/\mathrm{d}P = 0$, but under greatly differing assumptions. Patinkin argues that div $= 0$ and consequently he devotes his attention to showing that d div$/\mathrm{d}P = 0$. This essay instead shows that whatever div ≥ 0 is, $\mathrm{d}(\mathrm{div}/P)/\mathrm{d}P = 0$ for wealth-maximizing, price-taking, quantity-setting banks with costs homogeneous of degree zero.

In other words, Patinkin's zero-profit condition misses the point. The two key conditions are that (a) r adjusts to make all wealth-maximizing banks price-takers and quantity-setters (whether entry is limited or not) so that each bank sets the marginal condition (7.35), and (b) θ is homogeneous of degree zero in nominal values. Section 7.1 showed that, if r does not adjust, there is a role for bank money in the price-induced effect on wealth. Chapter 6 showed that lack of appropriate homogeneity means that bank money enters the price-induced effect on wealth. Once conditions (a) and (b) are assumed, nothing further is gained by Patinkin's assumption div $= 0$.

Proportionality of Costs

Patinkin's assumption that "total *nominal* operating costs . . . are invariant under a change in P (that is, real operating costs per unit of bank money outstanding are inversely proportionate to $P \ldots$)'' (1972, chapter 9, p. 187; see also the above quote from pp. 184–5) obscures the issue and plays no role. It says that $\overline{N}^d = \theta_r \, v\overline{M}/P$ where θ_r is a constant, i.e. $AC_{\overline{M}} = MC_{\overline{M}}$ for all $\overline{M}$. All that is necessary for the result of no price-induced change in div/P is that banks be wealth-maximizing price-takers (r adjusts to let them be price-takers) and that $\overline{N}^d$ be homogeneous of degree zero in nominal values. Further, even for Patinkin's unnecessary result that the price-induced change in div equals zero when div = 0, all that is required is the appropriate homogeneity, not his assumed proportionality. In addition, this proportionality assumption seems inconsistent with his later assumption of a U-shaped average cost curve (see the quote below from pp. 189–90).

Patinkin Versus Saving

Saving (1970) argues that bank money can play a role in the price-induced effect on wealth. Patinkin (1971, p. 273) argues that "constancy of operating cost implies constancy of bank profits at their original competitive level [i.e. zero]" (bracketed words added). This is the same argument as that discussed above. Saving (1971) responds that div = 0 (in present notation) is not sufficient for d div/dP = 0, which is true. He then argues that if the cost function is homogeneous of degree zero in P and $\overline{M}$ and div = 0, then d div/dP = 0. Clearly, this exchange misses the key point that homogeneity plus wealth-maximizing price-taking behavior gives d(div/P)/dP = 0 whatever div or div/P is.

Evaluating the Effect with a Constant Stock of Bank Money

Both Patinkin and Saving assume that $\overline{M}$ is held constant, while chapter 6 allowed $\overline{M}$ (and $\overline{m}$) to vary endogenously, as is appropriate in the Hicksian analytical framework (chapter 3, section 3.2). This makes no difference, however, in evaluation of the price-induced effect on wealth provided that r is set competitively and the homogeneity condition holds. Write

$$\frac{d(\text{div}/P)}{dP} = \frac{\partial(\text{div}/P)}{\partial P} + \frac{\partial(\text{div}/P)}{\partial \overline{M}} \frac{d\overline{M}}{dP},$$

where d(div/P)/dP is the total change in div/P due to a rise in P when the induced change in $\overline{M}$, d$\overline{M}$/dP, is taken into account, and d$\overline{M}$/dP > 0 is found from disturbing the bank's marginal condition (7.35). But this same marginal condition simply says that $\partial(\text{div}/P)/\partial \overline{M} = 0$, and hence

$$\frac{d(\text{div}/P)}{dP} = \frac{\partial(\text{div}/P)}{\partial P}$$

whether $\overline{M}$ is allowed to vary or not. This simply restates the results in chapter 6, section 6.2.

In Patinkin's case with θ_r constant and $\mathrm{AC}_{\overline{M}} = \mathrm{MC}_{\overline{M}}$ equal to a constant, a rise in P causes an indeterminate change in the individual bank's $\overline{M}$, since the size of the bank is indeterminate, while with an increasing $\mathrm{MC}_{\overline{M}}$ in the relevant range $d\overline{M}/dP > 0$ to keep $\overline{m}$ constant.

Rents and the Price-Induced Effect on Wealth

The banking industry as a whole can earn rents if entry to the industry is restricted. Furthermore, if banking is an increasing-cost industry because some banks are more efficient than others, then even without entry restrictions rents will be earned by the infra-marginal efficient banks. Of course these rents can be capitalized and imputed to the factor that generates them. After this imputation, profits will equal zero. Indeed, rents can be imputed to the factor "monopoly" if they are due to restrictions on entry.

These imputed costs are not fixed, however, the way, say, labor costs are. With a given wage rate w and real money stock $\overline{M}/P$, the wage bill is $w\,\theta(v\overline{M}/P)$ whatever revenues are. Rents, however, are a residual that vary *pari passu* with revenues in this example.

These points are relevant to Patinkin's (1972, pp. 189–90) consideration of a banking industry which is not perfectly competitive:

> Thus assume that there is restricted entry into this industry in the form of (say) the necessity to obtain a government license to operate a bank. This case is a combination of the ones described above. Namely, if the government grants such a license as a gift to a group of individuals, then the net worth of the private sector is immediately increased by the value of the license. . . . On this increased net worth (assuming the salability of the license) banks will earn the market rate of return. As in the preceding [discussion of a competitive zero-profit industry], the nature of the real-financial-asset effect in such an economy will then depend on the effects of a price decline on the net worth of the banking sector. (Bracketed material added.)

It is not clear what is meant here. The holder of the monopoly license is richer by having the license given to him/her, but how the real value of the license varies with P is unclear. On the one hand, the imputation of the value sets profits equal to zero and from Patinkin's past discussion one might assume the change in profits with P is thus zero. On the other hand, the flow cost of the monopoly license is not "hard," as are wage costs, but is instead a residual term. In fact, this essay's previous analysis shows that the zero-profit condition is irrelevant to whether bank money is part of the price-induced effect on wealth. Nevertheless, Patinkin's emphasis on the zero-profit condition if there is to be no price-induced effect on wealth through (future) bank money makes it seem he expects a non-zero price-induced effect on wealth in the case of restricted entry.

Patinkin continues:

> Alternatively, we can assume that there is free entry into the banking industry, but that the imperfect competition manifests itself in the form of an agreement among the banks (which may be government-imposed) not to compete with each other either with respect to the price of their product (i.e., not to sell bank money at a discount with respect to government fiat money – a restriction inherent in the banks' commitment always to exchange bank deposits and fiat money at a one-to-one ratio) or with respect to the price they pay to attract reserves (a restriction inherent in, say, the prohibition of interest payments on deposits). Thus the banking sector is effectively a cartel on both the buying and selling sides. Now, if the banks' cost curves are U-shaped, then firms will continue entering the industry until profits are driven down to their normal levels – in which case bank money will not be part of net wealth, in accordance with the argument . . . above. Clearly, such a cartel could also operate without free entry – in which case the considerations of the preceding paragraph [i.e., the previous quote from Patinkin] would continue to be relevant. (Bracketed material added.)

Once again, the zero-profit condition is asserted as the key. It appears, then, that for Patinkin restrictions on r play no necessary role in the price-induced effect on wealth. Rather, a non-zero effect turns on whether entry reduces profits to zero. Section 7.1 shows, however, that restrictions on r make bank money a part of the price-induced effect on wealth whether profits are positive or zero.

Who Earns the Rents?

The analysis above is phrased in terms of banks' dividends. One reason for expecting positive dividends is monopoly rent; another is differential rent earned by specialized, extra-productive factors in an increasing cost industry. If the monopoly rights are owned by bank owners, or they contribute the specialized factors, it is clear that these rents and their capitalized value can be positive in equilibrium. Whether these rents are positive and, if so, are assigned a capital value on the banks' books, so that measured profits are zero, is irrelevant. The zero-profit condition does not determine whether bank money enters the price-induced effect on wealth.

It is quite possible, of course, that specialized factors are not owned by the banks. An example is differential managerial ability on the part of hired, non-owner employees. In this case, eventually the specialized factors earn the rent, not the banks. Banks' measured profits and rents are both zero. The capitalized value of these rents plays the same role, however, as the present value of bank dividends above. When the price level rises, the issue is whether these rents are "squeezed." If wealth-maximizing banks are price-takers with resource use homogeneous of degree zero in nominal values, the real present value of these rents is unaffected. If banks are quantity-takers, these rents are squeezed in exactly the same way as in section 7.1. The issue of bank money's role in the price-induced effect on wealth is not who owns the rights to these rents, but whether they are squeezed. And, once again, whether measured profits or rents are zero is not relevant.

Patinkin's Analysis Versus the Hicksian Apparatus

Patinkin's (1969, 1972) analysis is faulty in terms of the Hicksian apparatus. To illustrate this, return to the issue of the price-induced change in bank dividends, d div/dP. Patinkin writes (1969, pp. 1153–4) regarding d div/dP

> All depends on the assumptions banks make about the effect of such a decline on their future operating costs. But this is really only part of the picture. For in all of the foregoing we have tacitly assumed that the banks take as given their outstanding volumes of credit and bank money, respectively.
>
> There is, however, another – and fundamental – point that I have so far ignored. The foregoing discussion has shown that bank money is part of net wealth for purposes of the real-balance effect only by virtue of the fact that the price decline increases the nominal net worth of the banking system. But by so doing, it also increases the rate of return in the banking industry above the competitive one. Hence new firms will be attracted into the banking industry until the profit rate is driven down once again to the competitive level. Correspondingly, the increase in the net worth of the banking system generated by the price decline is inversely related to the length of time banks assume their above-normal profits will continue. The shorter this period, the better the approximation of the real-balance effect which defines it solely in terms of government fiat money, as distinct from bank money.

Patinkin's first paragraph says that the quantity of bank money may be expected to change, and the clear implication is that this change should also contribute to the price-induced effect on wealth through banks. In two ways, this is misleading regarding the Hicksian analytical technique. First, banks under perfect competition are price-takers and quantity-setters, and supply as many bank dollars as they like – they do not *expect* their deposits to change; *they* actively vary deposits to maximize wealth. Second, this active choice of quantities to maximize wealth is precisely why the induced changes in quantities make no contribution to the price-induced effect on wealth, as explicitly shown above: the contribution to bank profits of a marginal dollar in deposits is zero at an optimum. (As section 7.1 showed, if banks cannot attract all the deposits they like, they are interested in the quantity of bank money demanded, and there is a price-induced effect on wealth through the bank sector. This effect is not what Patinkin is talking about.)

The second paragraph of the above quote is also misleading regarding the price-induced effect on wealth through banks. It plays the familiar theme of denying the possibility of "profits" – or rent – save as a short-run phenomenon indicative of lack of full adjustment. Entry (or exit) of firms is easily handled in the Hicksian framework; see, in particular, Hicks (1946, pp. 101–3, and p. 200). It is useful to see where Patinkin's chain of reasoning goes astray. He asserts that, when P (and w) declines, (a) this induces a positive effect on wealth through banks if and only if the effect on the present value of the bank dividend stream is positive, (b) perfect competition requires a zero present value for the dividend stream, (c) thus, if the change in (a) is positive, firms enter the banking industry to reduce profits to zero, and, hence (d) the final price-induced effect on wealth is zero.

The correct sequence starts with the fact that a decline in P (a') may induce an effect on wealth through banks; but it goes on to (b') the total effect of a parametric change on the dividend stream is the sum of the effect in (a') plus any other induced effects (including any role played by firms entering or leaving). The price-induced effect on wealth through banks is given in (a') and is independent of the value in (b'). That is, the contribution of the price-induced effect does not depend on the sum of all the effects but helps determine the sum. (See the analysis in chapter 3, section 3.1.)

Perhaps an illustration is useful. From the household sector's budget constraint (6.7), the initial impact on wealth of technological progress is

$$\sum_{t=0}^{\infty} \frac{\partial Y_t^s}{\partial \alpha} \frac{1}{\Pi(1+i)}$$

or

$$-\sum_{t=0}^{\infty} \frac{\partial \theta_t}{\partial \alpha} \; \frac{w_0}{P_0} \; \frac{\Pi(1 + \Delta w/w)}{\Pi(1 + i)}$$

if the progress occurs in the non-financial or banking sectors, respectively (see chapter 3, section 3.2 for this result). $\partial Y_t^s / \partial \alpha$ and $\partial \theta_t / \partial \alpha$ are evaluated at initial quantities, before any reaction; assume the former partial derivative is positive and the latter negative, to earn the title "progress." This parametric change causes other changes. The business sector is likely to change demands for factors, depending on how α affects marginal productivity. In addition, the household sector reacts to the change in wealth. Both sectors' reactions cause price changes, and price changes cause wealth, substitution, initial-condition and velocity effects. It may happen that the net result of all this is a zero change in the real present values of both sectors' dividends. But surely this outcome is not taken as saying $\partial Y_j^s / \partial \alpha$ or $\partial \theta_j^d / \partial \alpha$ must therefore be zero, or that the effect on wealth of technological progress is zero. Patinkin's reasoning can be bent to use his zero-profit condition to deny the existence of any change in wealth through either the non-financial or the financial business sector.

In Patinkin's (1969, p. 1152) discussion of technological progress in the banking industry, he writes that

> If there should occur an exogenous technological improvement in the process by which bank money is produced (or, more generally, in the financial sector of the economy), then total wealth will increase and this increase in wealth will accrue to those individuals who for one reason or another possess the rights to these improvements. Correspondingly, a *monetary expansion* which is *generated* by such a technological improvement *will* (just like a costless increase in government fiat paper money) *initially generate a wealth effect*. (My italics.)

Thus, he has wealth increasing through technological progress, without any reference to whether further induced changes reduce profits to zero; this seems inconsistent with quotes above. Also, he has the associated monetary expansion part of the effect on wealth. But just as it was shown above that the change in $\overline{M}$ when P rises, $d\overline{M}/dP$, contributes nothing to the effect, with technological progress the induced change in $\overline{M}$, $d\overline{M}/d\alpha$, makes no contribution.

7.4 Conclusions

Government restrictions on entry can cause monopoly rents for the banking industry. Further, if banking is an increasing-cost industry, there will be differential rents earned by some factors. As long as banks in the industry behave as wealth-maximizing price-takers and quantity-setters, the existence of a price-induced effect on wealth through bank money will turn on the degree of homogeneity of θ. With θ homogeneous of degree zero in nominal values, there will be a zero effect even if there are monopoly rents due to restricted entry or differential rents due to increasing costs. Without the proper homogeneity, there will be a non-zero effect even if monopoly rents are zero (see chapter 6, section 6.7).

NOTES

1 Note that the average cost (AC) curve at $\bar{m}_2$ may be below or equal to $i - r$, giving positive or zero profits. (With negative profits, the bank would exit from the industry.) Thus, the discussion in this section has nothing to do with whether bank profits equal zero.
2 This discussion of the price-induced effect on wealth considers the effect of a price change on r^*, while previous sections did not consider simultaneous variations in r when price changes. Indeed, the discussion in the next section criticizes Patinkin's analysis for including in the price-induced effect on wealth any other effects that might accompany a rise in P_0. This seemingly asymmetrical treatment results from government controlling r^*. Thus, dr^*/dP_0 has the same role as $d\bar{N}_t^d/dP_0$ for banks, which do not set r.
3 See Friedman (1969).
4 Friedman's (1969) concern is efficiency, and thus he proposes the "marginal benefit equals marginal cost" approach. This part of his discussion is not concerned with the price-induced effect on wealth. He does not distinguish the cases (analyzed below) in which the two approaches to setting r^* are not equivalent.
5 The present value of the government's money business is given above as

$$\sum_{t=1}^{\infty} \frac{(i_t - r_t^*)M_t^s}{P_0\Pi(1+i)} - \sum_{t=0}^{\infty} \frac{w_0}{P_0} \frac{\Pi(1+\Delta w/w)}{\Pi(1+i)} \underset{\sim}{N_t^d} - \frac{M_0}{P_0} - r_0^* \frac{M_0}{P_0}$$

$$= \sum_{t=1}^{\infty} \left\{ \frac{(i_t - r_t^*)M_t^s}{P_0\Pi(1+i)} - \frac{w_0}{P_0} \frac{\Pi(1+\Delta w/w)}{\Pi(1+i)} \underset{\sim}{N_t^d} \right\}$$

$$- \left\{ \frac{w_0}{P_0} N_0^d \right\} - \frac{M_0}{P_0} - r_0^* \frac{M_0}{P_0} .$$

The price-induced change in the first set of terms in braces on the right-hand side was just shown to equal zero. The change in the second term in braces is an initial-condition effect discussed below. Clearly each of the final two terms falls with a rise in P_0, or adds to the real present value of the government's money business. However, while M_0/P_0 and r^*M_0/P_0 can be thought of as liabilities of the government's money business, they are assets of the household sector (either owned directly or by the businesses and banks that the household sector owns). Thus, the M_0/P_0, r^*M_0/P_0 terms drop out of the household sector's budget constraint (7.21) and analysis of the government's money business ignores these terms.

6 One loose end is the question of what happens to r_t^* when P_0 rises. Total differentiation of the marginal condition (7.25) with respect to P_0 yields the induced change in r_t^*

$$\frac{dr_t^*}{dP_0} = \left\{ \frac{w_0}{P_0} \; v_t^* \; \frac{\Pi(1 + \Delta w/w)}{\Pi(1 + \Delta \underline{P}/P)} \; \theta^*_{r^* r^*} \; \frac{v_t^* \, M_t^s}{P_0^2 \Pi(1 + \Delta \underline{P}/P)} \right\}$$
$$- \left\{ \frac{w_0}{P_0} \; v_t^* \; \frac{\Pi(1 + \Delta w/w)}{\Pi(1 + \Delta \underline{P}/P)} \cdot \theta^*_{r^* r^*} \; v_t^* \; \frac{dM_t^s/dP_0}{P_0 \Pi(1 + \Delta \underline{P}/P)} \right\},$$
(7.27)

where allowance is made for the possibility that M_t^s varies in response to changes in P_0. Equation (7.27) yields several special cases for this change in r^*.

(i) Initially, M_t ($t \geqslant 1$) equals M_0^s, and $dM_t/dP_0 = 0$ ($t \geqslant 1$) – the Yap-Island case. Then, $dr_t^*/dP_0 \gtreqless 0$ as $\theta^*_{r^* r^*} \gtreqless 0$. With $dM_t^s/dP_0 = 0$, the second term in braces in (7.27) equals zero. The first term says that an increase in P_0 reduces M_t^s/P_t, given P_t/P_0, and hence reduces transactions τ_t^* using real government money, as long as its velocity v_t^* is constant. Thus, the real marginal cost to the government of maintaining its money stock changes since τ^* falls. This marginal cost depends on $\theta_{r^*}^*$. Thus, when τ^* changes, the issue is whether $\theta^*_{r^* r^*} \gtreqless 0$. It seems likely that $\theta^*_{r^* r^*} \geqslant 0$, increasing or constant marginal costs. With $\theta^*_{r^* r^*} > 0$, the fall in τ^* reduces $\theta_{r^*}^*$, and hence must be balanced by a fall in $i - r^*$; the government does this by raising r^*, or $dr^*/dP_0 > 0$. However, if $\theta^*_{r^* r^*} = 0$, the price-induced fall in τ^* does not affect $\theta_{r^*}^*$ and hence r^* is unaltered.

Figure 7.2 illustrates the case when $\theta^*_{r^* r^*} > 0$, so MC is rising. With $M_t^s = M$ for all P_t, m_t varies with P_t and hence P_0, with unit-elastic expectations. Thus, a rise in P from P_A to P_B reduces m and hence MC. To keep $i - r^*$ equal to MC, $i - r^*$ must fall; with i given, r rises from r_A^* to r_B^* as (7.27) says.

(ii) M_t^s is unit elastic with respect to P_0 ($t \geqslant 1$). Then $dr_t^*/dP_0 = 0$ no matter what the value of $\theta^*_{r^* r^*}$. Note that this unit-elastic case is precisely the one many monetary theorists would rule out in order to ensure the determinacy of the price level. (For determinacy, see below.)

Intuitively, in this case the marginal cost of maintaining and servicing the government money stock does not change because m_t is constant, so r^* cannot change. The increase in P_0 would by itself reduce all τ_t^* and hence affect

$\theta_{r^*}^*$. However, since all M_t^s rise proportionately with P_0, the M_t^s/P_t are unaffected, as are the τ_t^*.

(iii) $\theta_{r^*r^*}^* = 0$. In this case, dr_t^*/dP_0 equals zero no matter what the elasticity of M_t^s with respect to P_0. With constant marginal cost, r^* will not change.

(iv) N_t^d/τ_t^* equals a constant for all values of τ_t^*. Then, $\theta_{r^*}^* = N_t^d/\tau_t^*$, and $\theta_{r^*r^*}^* = 0$; thus (iii) applies. In fact, under (iv) the zero-profit condition yields the same results as the "marginal benefit equals marginal cost" condition. (iv) then is the analog for the government of Patinkin's (1969, 1971, 1972) assumption of proportionality for banks (discussed below).

(v) If government money is costless to issue and maintain, or $N_t^d = \theta^*(\tau_t^*) = 0$, then under either condition $r_t^* = i_t$ and (7.27) equals zero.

7 See chapter 5 for a discussion of the sense in which initial-condition effects help render the price level determinate.

8 Before period 0 begins, r_0^* does of course affect household, bank, and non-financial businesses' marginal conditions, for the higher is r_0^* *ceteris paribus* the less expensive it is to use government money in period 0. But once period 0 begins, initial government money holdings are bygones.

9 When velocity rises, the effect on r^* is found by differentiating (7.25) totally,

$$\frac{dr_t^*}{dv_0^*} = \left\{ -\frac{w_0}{P_0} \theta_{r^*}^* \frac{\Pi(1+\Delta w/w)}{\Pi(1+\Delta P/P)} - \frac{w_0}{P_0} \theta_{r^*r^*}^* \frac{\Pi(1+\Delta w/w)}{\Pi(1+\Delta P/P)} v_t^* \right.$$
$$\times \frac{M_t^s}{P_0\Pi(1+\Delta P/P)} - \frac{w_0}{P_0} v_t^* \frac{\Pi(1+\Delta w/w)}{\Pi(1+\Delta P/P)} \theta_{r^*r^*}^* v_t^*$$
$$\left. \times \frac{dM_t^s/dv_0}{P_0\Pi(1+\Delta P/P)} \right\},$$

the sign of which is indeterminate, since $\theta_{r^*r^*}^* \geqslant 0$.

10 See Johnson (1969) for emphasis on this point.

11 The same points would be true for permission to start in the future a competitive banking industry where, however, entry is limited and thus monopoly rents are earned. As long as wealth-maximizing, price-taking and quantity-setting banks pay a competitive r and the homogeneity condition holds, the price-induced effect on wealth through bank money is zero whether the banking industry is yet in existence and whether the value of the industry is positive or not.

12 Fixity of the nominal quantity of bank money in the face of a change in the price level is not sufficient to give a non-zero price-induced effect on wealth through bank money. If banks pay a competitively determined r, if the homogeneity condition holds for any resources that must be used, and if the quantity of bank money was initially optimal, then the price-induced effect on wealth through bank money is zero, as can be seen from the discussion below around (7.35) and in chapter 6, section 6.2, around (6.11).

13 This simplified formulation neglects any capital contributed by bank-owners and the imputed market rate of return on it.

Part IV

THE INTEREST-RATE-INDUCED EFFECT ON WEALTH, AND GOVERNMENT BONDS

8
The Interest-Rate-Induced Effect on Wealth, and Government Bonds as Net Wealth

The price-induced effect on wealth received extensive attention in the post-World War II period. Another effect on wealth of concern to monetary theory is the impact of variations in the rate of interest. This effect has received much less attention than the price-induced effect though it is often raised in the literature and its importance is widely recognized. This chapter discusses the interest-rate-induced effect on wealth, as well as the closely related issue of whether some fraction of government bonds is part of the household sector's net wealth.

Leijonhufvud (1968) and Pesek and Saving (1967) argued that Keynes thought a decrease in the (long-term) rate of interest caused a positive effect on wealth, an increase in consumption, and thus a decrease in saving out of given level of income. These authors cite the same passages from the *General Theory* (1936) in so arguing. Patinkin (1969, p. 1158) rejects these arguments.

Pesek and Saving (1967) try to prove that a decrease in the interest rate, when all short-term rates are and remain equal, has a positive impact on wealth. They acknowledge that for a single individual the effect may go either way. Their argument that the aggregate effect is determinate and positive is nonrigorous, and unconvincing.

Leijonhufvud's (1968) work on Keynes proposes a price-theoretic foundation for the negative interest-rate-induced effect on wealth in which, he argues, Keynes believed. Leijonhufvud approaches the problem with the Hicksian analytical apparatus and correctly focuses on the issues of the mortality of the current generation and its behavior about bequests. Leijonhufvud's conclusion is valid under certain conditions in the approach used here.

This essay analyzes the interest-rate-induced effect on wealth with the Hicksian apparatus used above. The effect is zero if (a) all economic actors hold the same price, wage and interest rate expectations, (b) all future markets are initially "close" to intertemporal market clearing, and (c) either the population is constant and immortal or the current generation leaves utility-maximizing bequests and always uses bequests to offset changes in wealth that are simply distribution effects for the current *vis-à-vis* future generations.

Once analysis introduces the government sector and the possibility of financing its deficits through bond sales, a key issue is whether government plans to redeem its bonds through taxation (or, equivalently, ultimately pay interest on the bonds through taxation) and increases in the money supply, versus simply rolling over the bonds and paying interest on them by issuing new bonds. Under the conditions used in analysis above and in this chapter, if the government plans to redeem its bonds through taxation (or issuing new money), these bonds are not net wealth. (Chapter 9 relaxes some conditions, particularly introducing uncertainty, and reconsiders this issue.) There is good reason to believe that government will plan to redeem any increase in its bonds through increased taxation (conceptually holding constant the government money stock's time path). Holding constant the time path of the stock of government money, it is only when government plans to redeem its bonds through taxation that there can exist a perfect foresight intertemporal equilibrium time path. (Of course such government behavior is not sufficient to guarantee existence of equilibrium.) Otherwise, there may exist a sequence of temporary equilibria where expectations must often necessarily be disappointed. Further, as people catch on to this fundamental disequilibrium problem, the existence of even a sequence of temporary equilibria becomes quite tenuous.

Analysis of these problems is made clearer by distinguishing the case where the world ends in some period N, versus the case of a world without end. In the finite-time-horizon case, each private citizen must end period N with zero debt outstanding. If the government intends to do the same, this is equivalent to its planning ultimately to redeem all of its debt through taxation. The alternative is to plan to sell bonds in period N with the promise to pay interest in period $N+1$; such sales are not possible, since no one will buy the bonds, and there cannot exist a perfect foresight equilibrium time path under these conditions.

In the case of an infinite time horizon, government can always issue new debts to refinance its old debt. There is never a period N in which all debts must be redeemed. Hence, the exact problem with the finite-horizon case does not arise. However, a perfect foresight, intertemporal equilibrium time path cannot exist in this case, because government behavior means that Walras's law does not hold in the sequence of time periods. In particular, if it is assumed that prices and interest rates have adjusted to set excess demands in all non-bond markets equal to zero there are still excess supplies of bonds in some time periods – equilibrium cannot exist.

8.1 The Interest-Rate-Induced Effect on Wealth

The interest-rate-induced effect on wealth is investigated by the now familiar procedure of differentiating the household sector's budget constraint, in this case with respect to the interest rate. This section assumes a constant population of immortal individuals; most of the above analysis can perhaps be most easily interpreted under this assumption. As in chapter 3, finding determinate results for the interest-rate-induced effect on wealth requires two assumptions. First, all people hold intertemporal price, wage and interest rate expectations in common, though these expectations need not turn out to be accurate. Second, intertemporal quantities demanded and supplied are equal; there is planned market clearing over time, though the planned quantities need not turn out to be actual quantities. These are the assumptions Hicks (1939, 1946) uses to find a zero interest-rate-induced effect on wealth, though in a model that does not include government money.

Sections 8.2 and 8.3 relax the assumption of a constant population of immortal individuals. How the current generation handles bequests then becomes the key issue. If the current generation makes bequests on utility-optimizing grounds, there is a zero interest-rate-induced effect on wealth. Otherwise, the effect on current consumption is likely to be negative, as Leijonhufvud (1968) argues. Such an effect is a distribution effect between the current and future generations.

In the moneyless economy of chapter 3 – the sort of economy Hicks describes through much of *Value and Capital* – the price-induced effect on wealth is of course zero, and the interest-rate-induced effect is also zero under the two conditions described above. With the introduction of money, the price-induced effect on wealth is generally believed to be negative (though it is zero in the case where future money supplies are unit elastic with respect to the current price level). It is tempting to suppose that introducing money also changes chapter 3's results of a zero interest-rate-induced effect on wealth. In fact, the results are exactly the same in money and moneyless economies.

As indicated above, a key analytical issue is how the government plans to finance its outstanding bonds. In turn, this can be considered in the finite and infinite-horizon case. This section considers the finite-horizon case, while section 8.4 discusses the infinite-horizon case.

Finite Time Horizon

The government's budget constraint is

$$T_t = \underline{P}_t G_t - \Delta M_t^s - P_{b,t} V_{t+1}^s + V_t^s \qquad t = 0, N \qquad (8.1)$$

where the world ends at the conclusion of period N. Discount (8.1) and sum over all N periods to find

$$\sum_{t=0}^{N} \frac{T_t}{\Pi(1+i)} = \sum_{t=0}^{N} \frac{P_t G_t}{\Pi(1+i)} - \sum_{t=1}^{N} \frac{i_t M_t^s}{\Pi(1+i)} - \frac{M_{N+1}^s}{\Pi(1+i)} + M_0^s$$

$$- \frac{P_{b,N} V_{N+1}^s}{\Pi(1+i)} + V_0^s, \tag{8.2}$$

where (8.2) uses the fact that

$$\frac{P_{b,t} V_{t+1}^s}{\Pi^t(1+i)} = \frac{V_{t+1}^s}{\Pi^{t+1}(1+i)} \tag{8.3}$$

since

$$P_{b,t} = \frac{1}{1+i_{t+1}}.$$

For later discussion, note that the constraint (8.2) could alternatively be expressed as

$$\sum_{t=0}^{N} \frac{T_t}{\Pi(1+i)} = \sum_{t=0}^{N} \frac{P_t G_t}{\Pi(1+i)} - \sum_{t=0}^{N} \frac{\Delta M_t^s}{\Pi(1+i)} - \frac{P_{b,N} V_{N+1}^s}{\Pi(1+i)} + V_0^s.$$

$$\tag{8.2a}$$

Every private individual must end with zero debt outstanding. Temporarily assume that this is so for the government also; section 8.4 discusses how government attempts to evade this constraint are likely to fail. Since the government must end with the zero debt outstanding,

$$V_{N+1}^s = 0 \tag{8.4}$$

and the government budget constraint (8.1) for $t = N$ is

$$T_N = P_N G_N - \Delta M_N^s + V_N^s. \tag{8.5}$$

In other words, an increase in V_N^s causes an equal increase in taxes T_N.

The constraint (8.4) that the government will pay its debt then means that (8.2) is

$$\sum_{t=0}^{N} \frac{T_t}{\Pi(1+i)} = \sum_{t=0}^{N} \frac{P_t G_t}{\Pi(1+i)} - \sum_{t=1}^{N} \frac{i_t M_t^s}{\Pi(1+i)} - \frac{M_{N+1}^s}{\Pi(1+i)} + M_0^s + V_0^s.$$

$$\tag{8.6}$$

Note that there is no promise that the government will ultimately retire its money stock, so M_{N+1}^s may easily be positive.[1] Alternatively, (8.2a) becomes

$$\sum_{t=0}^{N} \frac{T_t}{\Pi(1+i)} = \sum_{t=0}^{N} \frac{\underset{\sim}{P}_t G_t}{\Pi(1+i)} - \sum_{t=0}^{N} \frac{\Delta M_t^s}{\Pi(1+i)} + V_0^s, \tag{8.6a}$$

or

$$\sum_{t=0}^{N} \frac{T_t}{\Pi(1+i)} + \sum_{t=0}^{N} \frac{\Delta M_t^s}{\Pi(1+i)} = \sum_{t=0}^{N} \frac{\underset{\sim}{P}_t G_t}{\Pi(1+i)} + V_0^s. \tag{8.6b}$$

Note that V_0 was determined last period, in period -1, and hence is fixed at a given level, say, $V_0^{s'}$, or

$$V_0^s = V_0^{s'}. \tag{8.7}$$

Constraint (8.6b) says the present value of taxation and new money issuance finances the present value of government purchases of goods and services plus the value of government debt outstanding. Equation (8.6a) says that if G_t, $\underset{\sim}{P}_t$, and ΔM_t^s are held constant, an increase in V_0^s must be accompanied by an equal increase in the present value of taxation. It is precisely this that is meant by saying that outstanding government bonds must be redeemed by taxation. Further, in present value terms, there is no difference between increasing taxes today to redeem a perpetuity and increasing future taxes to pay the interest on such a bond. Hence, using taxation to redeem the bond is equivalent to using taxation to pay its interest.

The Interest-Rate-Induced Effect on Wealth

Chapter 3, section 3.3, showed how the consumer's optimization problem and also the interest-rate-induced effect on wealth can be analyzed by using the intertemporal budget constraint. The household sector's budget constraint, based on (5.3) in chapter 5, says that

$$\sum_{t=0}^{N} \left\{ \frac{w_t N_t^s}{\Pi(1+i)} + \frac{\mathrm{Div}_t}{\Pi(1+i)} - \frac{T_t}{\Pi(1+i)} - \frac{P_t C_t^d}{\Pi(1+i)} \right\}$$

$$- \sum_{t=1}^{N} \frac{i_t \mathrm{MH}_t}{\Pi(1+i)} - \frac{\mathrm{MH}_{N+1}}{\Pi(1+i)} + \mathrm{MH}_0 + V_0 \tag{8.8}$$

must equal or exceed zero, where for convenience no banking sector is assumed. The term $\mathrm{MH}_{N+1}/\Pi(1+i)$ indicates that the household sector realizes that it will face the end of the world stuck with some money balances. The present value of the non-financial sector's dividend stream is

$$\sum_{t=0}^{N} \frac{\mathrm{Div}_t}{\Pi(1+i)} = \sum_{t=0}^{N} \frac{\widetilde{P}_t(Y_t^s - \Delta K_t^d)}{\Pi(1+i)} - \sum_{t=0}^{N} \frac{\widetilde{w}_t N_t^d}{\Pi(1+i)}$$

$$- \sum_{t=1}^{N} \frac{i_t \mathrm{MB}_t}{\Pi(1+i)} - \frac{\mathrm{MB}_{N+1}}{\Pi(1+i)} + \mathrm{MB}_0, \tag{8.9}$$

where it is assumed for convenience (as in past chapters) that the business sector has no debt. The term MB_{N+1} recognizes that the business sector will also be stuck with some money balances at the end of the world.

Substituting (8.6) and (8.9) into the household sector's budget constraint (8.8) gives the new budget constraint that

$$\sum_{t=0}^{N} \left\{ \frac{w_t N_t^s - \widetilde{w}_t N_t^d}{\Pi(1+i)} + \frac{\widetilde{P}_t(Y_t^s - \Delta K_t^d) - P_t C_t^d - \underset{\sim}{P}_t G_t}{\Pi(1+i)} \right\}$$

$$- \sum_{t=1}^{N} \frac{i_t(\mathrm{MH}_t + \mathrm{MB}_t - M_t^s)}{\Pi(1+i)} \tag{8.10}$$

must equal or exceed zero. (8.10) uses the facts that the private sector's initial holdings of debt identically equal the number of bonds the government has outstanding, and that $\mathrm{MH}_0 + \mathrm{MB}_0 \equiv M_0^s$. It also assumes that the household sector recognizes that $M_{N+1}^s \equiv \mathrm{MH}_{N+1} + \mathrm{MB}_{N+1}$ whatever value of M_{N+1}^s the government currently plans on.[2]

Note that in (8.10) the V_0 in the government budget constraint (8.6) and in the household sector budget constraint (8.8) necessarily net to zero. It is in this sense that government bonds cannot be a part of net wealth in the world considered here. However, this topic is returned to below for worlds that never end.

The interest-rate-induced effect on wealth, when all i_t are equal and rise together, is found as the derivative of (8.10) with respect to i,

$$- \sum_{t=1}^{N} t \left\{ \frac{w_t N_t^s - \widetilde{w}_t N_t^d}{(1+i)^{t+1}} + \frac{\widetilde{P}_t(Y_t^s - \Delta K_t^d) - P_t C_t^d - \underset{\sim}{P}_t G_t}{(1+i)^{t+1}} \right\}$$

$$+ \sum_{t=1}^{N} t \frac{i(\mathrm{MH}_t + \mathrm{MB}_t - M_t^s)}{(1+i)^{t+1}} - \sum_{t=1}^{N} \frac{\mathrm{MH}_t + \mathrm{MB}_t - M_t^s}{(1+i)^t} \gtreqless 0. \tag{8.11}$$

The sign of (8.11) is clearly ambiguous. This is just the analog of the well-known fact that the similar experiment at the individual level gives ambiguous results. Note that the time subscript runs from $t = 1$ for output and labor markets; a rise in i does not affect the present value of current excess demands in these markets.

The Sign of the Interest-Rate-Induced Effect on Wealth

Hicks (1939; rev. edn 1946) and Leijonhufvud (1968) explain the ambiguity in the following way. An increase in i will reduce the present value of $1 that is received in the future; but an increase in i will reduce this present value by more the further in the future is this $1. The change is

$$- t \, \frac{1}{(1+i)^{t+1}}$$

for $1 that is t periods in the future. The typical individual plans to have his/her expenditures exceed income in some periods and income exceed expenditures in other periods. Any individual must plan on having the present value of his/her expenditures over income in some periods equal the present value of the excess of his income over expenditures in other periods, or the present value of his "borrowings" from the economy must equal the present value of his "lendings" to the economic system. When i rises, the present value of both his borrowings and lendings falls – but which falls more? This depends on which is "on average" further in the future. If, for example, the individual is currently lending in order to live beyond his earnings in old age, his lendings are on average closer in time than his borrowings, and the increase in i raises his wealth. His current lending now earns more interest, so he can consume even more in the future. Of course other individuals may well be in the opposite situation.

In fact, recognition that there are two sides to the credit market, borrowing and lending, is the key to evaluating (8.11). If two individuals are trading intertemporally, what one borrows, the other must lend if there is equilibrium. Hence, the increase in wealth that one gains from an increase in i, the other loses, and the net effect on wealth of the change in i must be zero. In (8.11), suppose that all individuals, businesses, and government have the same expectations, or

$$\begin{aligned} w_t &= \widetilde{w}_t = \underset{\sim}{w}_t \\ P_t &= \widetilde{P}_t = \underset{\sim}{P}_t \end{aligned} \qquad t = 1, N. \tag{8.12}$$

Further, let individuals' planned quantities be consistent in the labor, output, and money markets, or

$$N_t^d = N_t^s, \tag{8.13a}$$

$$C_t^d + G_t + \Delta K_t^d = Y_t^s \qquad t = 1, N, \tag{8.13b}$$

$$\text{MH}_t + \text{MB}_t = M_t^s. \tag{8.13c}$$

Then, from (8.12) and (8.13),

$$w_t N_t^s - \tilde{w}_t N_t^d = \tilde{P}_t(Y_t^s - \Delta K_t^d) - P_t C_t^d - \underline{P}_t G_t$$
$$= i(\text{MH}_t + \text{MB}_t - M_t^s) = 0 \tag{8.14}$$

and thus (8.11), the interest-rate-induced effect on wealth, equals zero. Hence, (8.12) and (8.13a)–(8.13c) are sufficient for a zero interest-rate-induced effect on wealth in this case.

In words, the interest-rate-induced effect on wealth is zero if all actors hold the same price expectations over time – (8.12) – and their planned quantities are consistent over time – (8.13a), (8.13b) and (8.13c). Note that this does not require that price expectations actually turn out to be correct, or that markets actually end up clearing at the expected quantities. However, if the economy is on a unique perfect foresight, intertemporal equilibrium time path, *ipso facto* the effect is zero.

It would be fatuous to argue in connection with the preceding result that the economy is usually on an equilibrium intertemporal path. Price and quantity expectations are often unfulfilled. However, for the effect on wealth to be consistently of one sign, expectations must be consistently biased in one direction, and it would seem that experience should remove this bias or at least make its effects rather small. If expectations are not consistently biased one way or the other, the average algebraic value of the effect on wealth should be close to zero, even if some deviations from average are quite large.

Two points from the above deserve more discussion. First, suppose that there are recognizable generations, that new people will be born and the current generation will perish. The implications of this for the interest-rate-induced effect on wealth are discussed in sections 8.2 and 8.3, under the assumption that government will redeem its currently outstanding debt with taxation. Second, section 8.4 explores the implications of not assuming the government will pay its debt with taxation. Both sections assume for convenience that the world never ends (N goes to infinity), but that government pays off its bonds with taxation. The issue of the sense in which government must pay off its bonds with taxation is taken up in section 8.4.

A "Keynesian" Disequilibrium

It is sometimes possible to say something interesting about the interest-rate-induced effect on wealth in certain cases where the system is not on a path where planned intertemporal quantities clear markets. A key case in Keynesian analysis is an autonomous decrease in current aggregate demand. Suppose for concreteness that this sudden excess supply of output in period 0 is balanced by positive excess demand for output in later periods. For example, in the household sector budget constraint in (8.10), let a current fall in consumption (or increase in current saving) demand be balanced by a rise in future consumption demand, or $C_t^d + \Delta K_t^d + G_t \geqslant Y_t^s$ ($t \geqslant 1$). This is what occurs when a current increase in planned saving is unaccompanied by an increase in money demand or fall in labor supply.

In this example, the only non-zero terms in the budget constraint (8.10) are $P_0\{Y_0^s - (C_0^d + \Delta K_0^d + G_0)\} > 0$ balanced by an equal but opposite

$$\sum_{t=1}^{N} \frac{P_t\{Y_t^s - (C_t^d + \Delta K_t^d + G_t)\}}{(1+i)^t} < 0.$$

Thus, the interest-rate-induced effect on wealth (8.11) is

$$-\sum_{t=1}^{N} t\, \frac{P_t\{Y_t^s - (C_t^d + \Delta K_t^d + G_t)\}}{(1+i)^{t+1}} > 0.$$

Before the decline in current aggregate demand, the effect (8.11) was zero because the economy as a whole was neither a net borrower nor lender. Now, however, with the fall in current aggregate demand the economy plans to save more and lend more, and has thus become a net lender. With the rise in the interest rate, a net lender is better off, and hence (8.11) is now positive.

It is sometimes argued (for example, Pesek and Saving, 1967; Leijonhufvud, 1968) that Keynes believed that the interest-rate-induced effect on wealth is negative. In this "Keynesian" case, it is in fact positive.[3]

8.2 The Interest-Rate-Induced Effect on Wealth, and Intergenerational Redistribution

The above discussion, from chapter 4 on, can perhaps best be thought of as considering the case of a constant population of immortal individuals (or at least individuals who live until the economy ends in period N). The following sections consider individuals of finite life span in an economy that goes on long after them (for ever, for convenience). Two polar extremes are considered. First, those currently alive care nothing for these who will be born (their offspring), leaving them no bequests. Second, those currently alive care for their offspring and leave them bequests determined by rational optimization. The first case is discussed in this section, the second in section 8.3. In the case of no bequests, the interest-rate-induced effect on wealth that shows up in current markets is highly likely to be negative, and government bonds will appear to the current generation as net wealth.

No Bequests

Suppose that everyone currently alive will live until the end of period ℓ. Suppose that the next generation will be born at time h, $\ell > h \geqslant 1$. Thus, the life spans of the two generations overlap. This is necessary if there is to be an interesting solution to the problem of how the current generation transfers the ongoing machinery of the economy (the business sector and household money balances) to the new generation in this world with no bequests.

To discuss this problem conveniently, suppose a world of Yap-Island money, with no government sector and no bank money; qualifications will then be added. The generation born at time h has no claim to any income save its own labor income. In particular, the rights to all of the non-labor income from h to eternity are held at time h by the generation currently alive in period 0. But this current generation cannot consume the non-labor income to which it has rights between period $\ell + 1$ and the infinite number of periods following – it will be dead. Consequently, it wishes to sell the rights to this non-labor income to the new generation, in return for funds which it will use for extra consumption – that is, for consumption beyond the current generation's labor plus non-labor income. Clearly, this extra consumption must occur somewhere between time h and time ℓ. When the current generation comes to time h, a constraint on its extra expenditure between times h and ℓ is that the present value of its consumption of goods and services, including money services, over its income must equal the present value of non-labor income from time $\ell + 1$ to infinity. This constraint can be expressed as

$$\sum_{t=\ell+1}^{\infty} \left\{ \frac{\Pi(1+\Delta \widetilde{P}/P)}{\Pi(1+i)} (Y_t^s - \Delta K_t^d) - \frac{w_0}{P_0} \frac{\Pi(1+\Delta \widetilde{w}/w)}{\Pi(1+i)} N_t^d \right.$$

$$\left. - \frac{\Delta MB_t}{P_0 \Pi(1+i)} \right\} + \sum_{t=h}^{\ell} \left\{ \left[\frac{\Pi(1+\Delta \widetilde{P}/P)}{\Pi(1+i)} (Y_t^s - \Delta K_t^d) \right. \right.$$

$$-\frac{w_0}{P_0}\,\frac{\Pi(1+\Delta\tilde{w}/w)}{\Pi(1+i)}\,N_t^{\mathrm{d}} - \frac{\Delta MB_t}{P_0\Pi(1+i)}\Bigg]$$

$$-\left[\frac{\Pi(1+\Delta P/P)}{\Pi(1+i)}\,C_t^{\mathrm{d}'} + \frac{\Delta MH_t'}{\Pi(1+i)} - \frac{w_0}{P_0}\,\frac{\Pi(1+\Delta w/w)}{\Pi(1+i)}\,N_t^{\mathrm{s}'}\right]\Bigg\}$$

$$(8.15)$$

must be greater than or equal to zero (must equal zero, assuming non-satiation), where $C_t^{\mathrm{d}'}$ and $N_t^{\mathrm{s}'}$ refer to the current generation's output demand and labor supply and $\Delta MH_t'$ its planned accumulation of money balances. The summation over the first set of braces is the real present value of businesses' dividends from $t = \ell + 1$ to the end of time, the rights to which are owned by the current generation; this generation will be dead, however, by the end of period ℓ. In the second set of braces, the first set of terms in square brackets gives dividends over the time from period h to period ℓ when the two generations coexist; as of time h, the present value of these dividends belongs to the current generation. The second set of terms in square brackets gives the current generation's consumption and accumulation of dollars in excess of its labor income. Assume for convenience that households and businesses expect the same P_t, w_t. Then, expenditure by the current generation is "extra" in period t if expenditures on consumption and money accumulation exceed dividend (non-labor) income plus labor income, or if

$$P_t C_t^{\mathrm{d}'} + \Delta MH_t' > P_t(Y_t^{\mathrm{s}} - \Delta K_t^{\mathrm{d}}) - w_t(N_t^{\mathrm{d}} - N_t^{\mathrm{s}'}) - \Delta MB_t. \quad (8.16)$$

$P_t(Y_t^{\mathrm{s}} - \Delta K_t^{\mathrm{d}}) - w_t N_t^{\mathrm{d}} - \Delta MB_t$ is period t's non-labor income, and $w_t N_t^{\mathrm{s}'}$ is the labor income of the current generation. $N_t^{\mathrm{d}} - N_t^{\mathrm{s}'}$ is the amount of labor that must be supplied by the younger generation. In any period where equilibrium $N_t^{\mathrm{d}} - N_t^{\mathrm{s}'}$ is greater than zero, the new generation is earning income that could be used to buy resources from the current generation. But even when $N_t^{\mathrm{d}} - N_t^{\mathrm{s}'}$ is positive, (8.16) need not hold. Either the new generation may devote all of its labor income to consumption, or it may actually borrow from the current generation in order to consume beyond income.

The Interest-Rate-Induced Effect on Wealth for the Current Generation

An equal rise in all i when they are initially equal can have a wealth effect on current demands and supplies only through affecting the current generation. Suppose that, from periods 0 through h, all price expectations are consistent, as are all planned quantities demanded and supplied. Then, the part of the interest-rate-induced effect on wealth from times 0 to h must be zero according to preceding arguments. Hence, any effect on wealth arises through (8.15), where the derivative is

$$
- \sum_{t=\ell+1}^{\infty} t \left\{ \frac{\Pi(1+\Delta \widetilde{P}/P)}{(1+i)^{t+1}} (Y_t^s - \Delta K_t^d) - \frac{w_0}{P_0} \frac{\Pi(1+\Delta \widetilde{w}/w)}{(1+i)^{t+1}} N_t^d \right.
$$

$$
\left. - \frac{\Delta \mathrm{MB}_t}{P_0(1+i)^{t+1}} \right\} - \sum_{t=h}^{\ell} t \left\{ \left[\frac{\Pi(1+\Delta \widetilde{P}/P)}{(1+i)^{t+1}} (Y_t^s - \Delta K_t^d) \right. \right.
$$

$$
\left. - \frac{w_0}{P_0} \frac{\Pi(1+\Delta \widetilde{w}/w)}{(1+i)^{t+1}} N_t^d - \frac{\Delta \mathrm{MB}_t}{P_0(1+i)^{t+1}} \right]
$$

$$
- \left[\frac{\Pi(1+\Delta P/P)}{(1+i)^{t+1}} C_t^{d'} + \frac{\Delta \mathrm{MH}_t'}{P_0(1+i)^{t+1}} \right.
$$

$$
\left. \left. - \frac{w_0}{p_0} \frac{\Pi(1+\Delta w/w)}{(1+i)^{t+1}} N_t^{s'} \right] \right\}. \tag{8.17}
$$

The assumption that the quantities in all markets (current and future) are consistent is of no avail in determining the sign of (8.17), for after ℓ the current generation has zero demand for output and zero supply of labor – it is dead. And between h and ℓ, equilibrium in general requires $C_j^d < Y_j^s - \Delta K_j^d$ and $N_j^d > N_j^{s'}$, because the new generation consumes part of output and supplies part of labor. Thus, the convenient canceling employed above, when planned quantities are consistent intertemporally, is unavailable.

To evaluate (8.17), it is useful to look at (8.15) as a present value magnitude that varies with i, where the $C_t^{d'}$, $N_t^{s'}$, N_t^d, $Y_t^s - \Delta K_t^d$, w_0/P_0, $\Delta w/w$, $\Delta P/P$, $\Delta \widetilde{w}/w$, $\Delta \widetilde{P}/P$, $\Delta \mathrm{MB}_t$, $\Delta \mathrm{MH}_t'$ for all $t \geq h$ are all evaluated at their initial values. This present value can be plotted against the interest rate. Non-satiation requires that (8.15) equal zero at the initial interest rate, that is, the present value of "extra" consumption must equal the present value of *post mortem* non-labor income. The sign of (8.17) is just the slope of the function relating present value to the interest rate, evaluated where (8.15) equals zero.

In figure 8.1, suppose that the curve relating present value to i intersects the i axis at i', so that (8.15) equals zero at i'. There are many possible shapes of such a curve. If the curve intersects the i axis only once, it may have a negative slope as does curve A, or a positive slope as does B. If the curve intersects several times, its slope through i' may be negative (curve D) or positive (curve C). Clearly, this problem is very similar to the question of how many interest rates can set the net present value of a capital

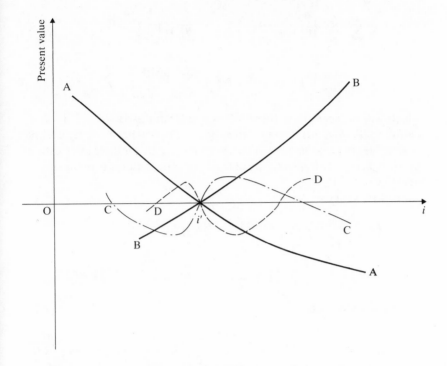

Figure 8.1   Interest rates and the wealth of the current generation

project equal to zero (the multiple roots problem).

Under plausible conditions, however, curve A is the only one that can exist. The argument depends on two steps: first, as i approaches zero, (8.15) approaches plus infinity; second, Descartes's law of signs is used to show that (8.15) has one positive real root.

Expression (8.15) necessarily becomes positive as i approaches zero if dividends are positive in every period, with a lower bound $a > 0$. The sum of the present value of dividends from $\ell + 1$ to infinity is the first set of expressions in braces in (8.15), and the present value of dividends is greater than or equal to $\sum_{t=\ell+1}^{\infty} \dfrac{a}{(1+i)^t}$, which approaches infinity as i approaches zero. As i goes to zero, terms in the second set of braces in (8.15) approach some finite number

$$ -\left\{ \sum_{t=h}^{\ell} \Pi\left(1 + \frac{\Delta P}{P}\right) C_t^{d'} + \sum_{t=h}^{\ell} \frac{\Delta MH_t'}{P_0} \right. $$

$$- \sum_{t=h}^{\ell} \frac{w_0}{P_0} \Pi \left(1 + \frac{\Delta w}{w} \right) N_t^{s'} - \sum_{t=h}^{\ell} \Pi \left(1 + \frac{\Delta \widetilde{P}}{P} \right) (Y_t^s - \Delta K_t^d)$$

$$+ \sum_{t=h}^{\ell} \frac{w_0}{P_0} \Pi \left(1 + \frac{\Delta \widetilde{w}}{w} \right) N_t^d + \sum_{t=h}^{\ell} \frac{\Delta \mathrm{MB}_t}{P_0} \Bigg\} ,$$

which will be negative if there is positive "extra expenditure" in every period so (8.16) holds. Overall, then, (8.15) approaches a strictly positive number as i approaches zero. Thus, even if there are multiple intersections in figure 8.1, there is necessarily at least one intersection where the slope is negative.

Further, suppose that

$$\Pi \left(1 + \frac{\Delta P}{P} \right) C_t^{d'} + \frac{\Delta \mathrm{MH}_t'}{P_0} - \frac{w_0}{P_0} \Pi \left(1 + \frac{\Delta w}{w} \right) N_t^{s'}$$

$$- \Pi \left(1 + \frac{\Delta \widetilde{P}}{P} \right) (Y_t^s - \Delta K_t^d) + \frac{w_0}{P_0} \Pi \left(1 + \frac{\Delta \widetilde{w}}{w} \right) N_t^d$$

$$+ \Delta \mathrm{MB}_t > 0 \tag{8.18}$$

for all $\ell \geqslant t \geqslant h$. This says that in every period from h to ℓ the current generation spends beyond its income. This implies that all terms in the second set of braces in (8.15) are negative. Continue to assume all terms in the first are positive. Then, (8.15) can be looked on as a polynomial in $\{1/(1+i)\}^t$. According to Descartes's law of signs, the number of positive real roots of such a polynomial is equal to the number of times the coefficients go from one sign to the other, less some even number $k \geqslant 0$. Now, all the coefficients of $\{1/(1+i)\}^t$ are negative from $t = h$ to $t = \ell$, and, from $t = \ell + 1$ on, the coefficients are positive. Thus, the polynomial has at most one positive real root. But, of course, one of its positive real roots is i'. Hence, i' is the only positive real root. Thus, the curve relating present value to i must be curve A, where the slope is negative. Thus, in this case, the effect on wealth of an increase in i is negative.

The intuition for this result is straightforward. The rise in i reduces the present value of what the current generation is selling, future non-labor income, and since these flows are far in the future, the rise in i reduces the present value substantially. Of course the present value of "extra expenditures" falls also, but not as substantially since the "extra expenditures" are relatively close in time.

Another way to think of this is to add the assumptions that price expectations are consistent and quantities are market clearing. Then any current effect is just a distribution effect since section 8.1 showed that, with immortal individuals, these assumptions give a zero interest-rate-induced effect on wealth. Thus, whatever the effect on wealth for the current generation, the future generation has an equal but opposite effect. The issue then is why a rise in i helps the future generation. The typical member of this generation plans each period between h and ℓ to save and purchase the capital K_h and real balances $(M/P)_h$ which the old generation cannot take with it, or there is a given amount to buy over time, $K_h + (M/P)_h$. If the interest rate were zero, this would have to be done purely out of labor income. With $i > 0$, the capital acquired in period h will earn a return that helps buy further capital, and the larger i is the less is the burden of acquiring $K_h + (M/P)_h$ by the end of ℓ. In other words, the future generation will spend its earlier years being a net lender, and a rise in the interest rate thus makes it better off, with the current generation being worse off since it is the corresponding net borrower.

The Argument with Government Fiat Money and Taxes

Replacing Yap-Island money with government fiat money and introducing government expenditures cause no great differences from the previous subsection's analysis. However, the introduction of government borrowing does raise a new issue; now government can subsidize one generation at the expense of another.

From the point of view of the current period, the real present value of the government's total net taxes in period t is

$$\frac{T_t}{P_0\Pi(1+i)} = \frac{\underset{\sim}{P_t}G_t}{P_0\Pi(1+i)} - \frac{\Delta M_t^s}{P_0\Pi(1+i)} - \frac{P_{b,t}V_{t+1}}{P_0\Pi(1+i)}$$

$$+ \frac{V_t}{P_0\Pi(1+i)}. \tag{8.19}$$

The fraction of total taxes in period t paid by the current generation is a_t, where

$$a_t = 1 \qquad h \geqslant t > 0$$

$$a_t \gtreqless 1 \qquad \ell \geqslant t > h \tag{8.20}$$

$$a_t = 0 \qquad t \geqslant \ell + 1.$$

Government can use tax policy to subsidize one generation at the expense of the other in two ways. Take as an example the case where the current generation is subsidized. First, out of a given present value of net taxation government can shift taxation to future periods when the current generation is not alive and hence does not pay taxes.[4] Second, for any given time path of taxes, government can reduce the fraction of taxes the current generation pays during the period when the two generations coexist. Neither action will necessarily change the result that the interest-rate-induced effect on wealth is negative when there are no bequests.

The real present value of the current generation's taxes (indicated by a prime) is

$$
\sum_{t=0}^{\infty} \frac{T_t'}{P_0 \Pi (1+i)} = \sum_{t=0}^{\infty} \frac{a_t T_t}{P_0 \Pi (1+i)}
$$

$$
= \sum_{t=0}^{\infty} \frac{a_t (\underset{\sim}{P}_t G_t - \Delta M_t^s - P_{b,t} V_{t+1} + V_t)}{P_0 \Pi (1+i)}
$$

$$
= \sum_{t=0}^{h} \frac{(\underset{\sim}{P}_t G_t - \Delta M_t^s - P_{b,t} V_{t+1} + V_t)}{P_0 \Pi (1+i)}
$$

$$
+ \sum_{t=h+1}^{\ell} \frac{a_t (\underset{\sim}{P}_t G_t - \Delta M_t^s - P_{b,t} V_{t+1} + V_t)}{P_0 \Pi (1+i)}. \qquad (8.21)
$$

The introduction of taxes modifies (8.15) to

$$
\sum_{t=\ell+1}^{\infty} \left\{ \frac{\Pi(1+\Delta \widetilde{P}/P)}{\Pi(1+i)} (Y_t^s - \Delta K_t^d) - \frac{w_0}{P_0} \frac{\Pi(1+\Delta \widetilde{w}/w)}{\Pi(1+i)} N_t^d \right.
$$

$$
- \frac{\Delta MB_t}{P_0 \Pi(1+i)} \right\} + \sum_{t=h}^{\ell} \left\{ \frac{\Pi(1+\Delta \widetilde{P}/P)}{\Pi(1+i)} (Y_t^s - \Delta K_t^d) \right.
$$

$$
- \frac{w_0}{P_0} \frac{\Pi(1+\Delta \widetilde{w}/w)}{\Pi(1+i)} N_t^d - \frac{\Delta MB_t}{P_0 \Pi(1+i)} - a_t \frac{T_t}{P_0 \Pi(1+i)}
$$

$$
- \left[\frac{\Pi(1+\Delta P/P)}{\Pi(1+i)} C_t^{d'} + \frac{\Delta MH_t'}{P_0 \Pi(1+i)} - \frac{w_0}{P_0} \frac{\Pi(1+\Delta w/w)}{\Pi(1+i)} N_t^{s'} \right] \right\}
$$

$$
(8.22)
$$

by subtracting $a_t T_t / P_0 \Pi (1+i)$ from the income that finances extra consumption and money accumulation. However, as long as "extra expenditures" are positive in every period, even after taking account of the current generation's taxation, or

$$
\Pi \left(1 + \frac{\Delta P}{P} \right) C_t^{d'} + \frac{\Delta MH_t'}{P_0} > \frac{w_0}{P_0} \Pi \left(1 + \frac{\Delta w}{w} \right) N_t^{s'}
$$

$$
+ \Pi \left(1 + \frac{\Delta \widetilde{P}}{P} \right) (Y_t^s - \Delta K_t^d) - \frac{w_0}{P_0} \Pi \left(1 + \frac{\Delta \widetilde{w}}{w} \right) N_t^d
$$

$$- \frac{\Delta MB_t}{P_0} - \frac{a_t T_t}{P_0}, \qquad\qquad (8.23)$$

the argument showing that curve A in figure 8.1 applies will still hold, and the interest-rate-induced effect on wealth is negative.

Similar modifications for the case where bank money exists are straightforward. In general, the interest-rate-induced effect on wealth is very likely negative for current generations in the absence of bequests.

Government Bonds Are Net Wealth

Suppose that the government gives V_0 of its bonds to the current generation and plans to retire them in some period $t \geq \ell$ by levying taxes whose present value is $P_{b,0} V_0$. Since the current generation pays none of these extra taxes but does receive V_0, clearly it is wealthier by $P_{b,0} V_0$. This results in an increase in current aggregate demand; government bonds are net wealth.[5] More generally, to the extent that the present value of the taxes necessary to service the bonds is placed on future generations, the bonds are net wealth to the current generation. Thus, with any expansion in V_0 one must know the associated tax plan to determine what fraction of the additional bonds constitutes net wealth from the current generation's viewpoint.

Note, however, that this is a type of distribution effect. While the current generation is wealthier by $P_{b,0} V_0$ the future generation is poorer by $P_{b,0} V_0$. The latter cannot of course reduce its current consumption, which is necessarily zero, and hence the sum of the current and future generations' current demand for output rises.

8.3 Bequests and the Interest-Rate-Induced Effect on Wealth

The preceding section assumed that the current generation left no bequests and, indeed, had no concern for future generations. Under this assumption, the interest-rate-induced effect on wealth is quite likely to be negative. This is in contrast to the earlier discussion of this chapter where it is zero, under the assumption of consistent price and wage expectations and planned market-clearing quantities. The reconciliation of these two results involves noticing that, when the interest rate rises, the induced wealth loss of the current generation in section 8.2 is the future generation's gain – the total effect on wealth is zero under the price and quantity assumptions. But what matters to current demand (indeed all demands in period t for $h > t \geq 0$) is the effect on the current generation's wealth.

Thus, in essence, the effect on wealth found in the preceding section is a redistribution effect necessitated by the technical condition that a generation cannot demand or supply goods in a period in which it is not alive. The increase in the interest rate raises the wealth of the future generation, but this increase cannot raise current demand to offset the reduction in demand occasioned by the current generation's wealth loss.

However, this technical imposition of a redistribution effect will be overcome, thus rendering the interest-rate-induced effect on current demands zero, if the current generation leaves bequests and decides on them by an optimizing process in which it compares the future generation's utility with its own.[6]

Suppose that the bequests are made because the utility of the future generation enters the utility function of the current generation. In this case, it can be shown that when the rise in i reduces the current generation's wealth, this generation reacts by reducing bequests by the same amount as the wealth loss. Thus, on balance there is no change in the current generation's wealth and hence no wealth effect on current-period demands.

In a simplified analysis, let the utility U^c of the current generation depend on its wealth $W^c(i)$, which is a function of i, less the present value of its bequests B, and on the utility U^F of the future generations, and let U^F depend on the future generation's wealth plus the present value of the bequests B it receives,[7] or

$$U^c = U^c\{W^c(i) - B, U^F\}, \tag{8.24}$$

$$U^F = U^F\{W^F(i) + B\}. \tag{8.25}$$

For any i, the current generation maximizes its utility by choosing B to set

$$\frac{dU^c}{dB} = -\frac{\partial U^c}{\partial W^c} + \frac{\partial U^c}{\partial U^F}\frac{dU^F}{dW^F} = 0. \tag{8.26}$$

From the above analysis in sections 8.1 and 8.2, an increase in i causes

$$\frac{dW^c}{di} < 0, \quad \frac{dW^c}{di} + \frac{dW^F}{di} = 0, \text{ and hence } \frac{dW^F}{di} > 0. \tag{8.27}$$

If the current generation reacts by reducing B by the fall in W^c it keeps both generations at the same level of utility. For if $dB/di = dW^c/di$, then $dB/di = -dW^F/di$ and $d(w^F+B)/di = 0$, so

$$\frac{dU^F}{di} = \frac{dU^F}{dW^F}\frac{d(W^F+B)}{di} = 0, \tag{8.28}$$

and thus

$$\frac{dU^c}{di} = \frac{\partial U^c}{\partial W^c} \frac{d(W^c - B)}{di} + \frac{\partial U^c}{\partial U^F} \frac{dU^F}{dW^F} \frac{d(W^F + B)}{di} = 0. \quad (8.29)$$

Further, optimality requires that $dB/di = dW^c/di$. Differentiating the current generation's marginal condition (8.26) with respect to i gives

$$\frac{d(dU^c/dB)}{di} = -\frac{\partial^2 U^c}{\partial W^{c2}} \left(\frac{dW^c}{di} - \frac{dB}{di} \right)$$

$$-\frac{\partial^2 U^c}{\partial W^c \partial U^F} \frac{dU^F}{dW^F} \left(\frac{dB}{di} - \frac{dW^c}{di} \right)$$

$$+\frac{\partial^2 U^c}{\partial U^{F2}} \frac{dU^F}{dW^F} \frac{dU^F}{dW^F} \left(\frac{dB}{di} - \frac{dW^c}{di} \right)$$

$$+\frac{\partial U^c}{\partial U^F} \frac{d^2 U^F}{dW^{F2}} \left(\frac{dB}{di} - \frac{dW^c}{di} \right) = 0 \qquad (8.30)$$

which implies in general

$$\frac{dB}{di} = \frac{dW^c}{di}.$$

In words, the rise in i hurts the current generation and equally helps the future one. The current generation reduces B by the amount of the fall in its wealth induced by the rise in i, and thereby keeps both generations as well off as before. Further, this offsetting reduction in B is not only feasible, the current generation finds it optimal; with the total wealth of the two generations combined held constant when i rises, the available set of U^c, U^F is unchanged and so the current generation chooses the same point as before.

It would be fatuous to argue that every parent cares very much or well for his offspring – and there are, of course, orphans. Nevertheless, to the extent that parents care for children beyond the minimum prescriptions of law – through providing education, diversions, goods in kind, as well as bequests (for bequests can be consumed before the donor's death) – there is some process of distributing wealth between generations, and some cushions of wealth to be taken back (or increased) when interest rate variations redistribute wealth. When the interest rate rises, the current generation may recompense itself by forcing offspring to pay for their own education[8] – leaving each generation's wealth exactly as before the change in i. This mechanism cannot work in the case of orphans or children dependent on law (rather than parental benevolence) for their welfare. In addition, some members of the current generation are childless. Thus, a rough conjecture is that the interest-rate-induced effect on wealth is negative, but not nearly as great as it would be were parental concern rare.

Government Bonds Are Not Net Wealth

Suppose as in section 8.2 that the government gives the current generation $P_{b,0} V_0$ bonds, to be redeemed by extra taxes levied in period $t \geqslant \ell$. Clearly, W^c rises and W^F falls by the same amount. Based on this section's analysis, the current generation will not change any of its demands but will simply keep the $P_{b,0} V_0$, accumulate its interest over time, and pass on the total to the younger generation as an extra bequest (cf. Barro, 1974).

8.4 The Government Does Not Redeem Its Debt Through Taxation

If the government does not plan to redeem its debt by taxation but simply plans to pay interest on the debt by issuing more debt, then a perfect foresight, intertemporal equilibrium path cannot exist. This does not mean that a sequence of temporary equilibria cannot exist. Rather, in such a sequence, expectations are systematically falsified. Further, when people catch on to the fundamental problem, even this sequence of temporary equilibria cannot exist.

The argument below considers separately the two cases of a finite and an infinite time horizon. With a finite time horizon, equilibrium cannot exist in period N. If people understand this, equilibrium cannot exist in $N-1$, and so forth back to period 0. An alternative demonstration shows that simultaneous assumption of intertemporal equilibrium plus the government not redeeming its debt through taxation implies a logical contradiction, since non-zero excess demand for bonds would exists in equilibrium. The same logical contradiction holds in the infinite-time-horizon case.

Finite Time Horizon

Non-existence of a perfect foresight, intertemporal equilibrium is first shown by starting in period N and working backwards.

Non-Existence: Argument by Recursion　If government does not intend to use taxation to redeem its bonds, its intertemporal budget constraint is very different from the usual case considered above, for example in chapter 5 or in (8.2) in section 8.1. To see this, take a concrete example. Suppose that in period 0 the government decides to issue no more dollars ($\Delta M_t^s = 0, t = 0, N$), to finance all purchases of goods with current taxes ($T_t = \underline{P}_t G_t$), and to finance the interest and principal on current bonds outstanding by simply issuing and selling more bonds. (The assumption of a constant money supply is solely for convenience.) Thus, with the current number of one-period bonds outstanding V_0, the government must pay interest and principal equal to V_0 and hence sell new bonds with the value $P_{b,0} V_1 = V_0$. Further, in every period the government will issue new bonds so that

$$P_{b,t} V_{t+1} = V_t \qquad (t = 0, N). \tag{8.31}$$

In this simple case, then, the government budget constraint in each period is, using (8.31),

$$T_t = \underline{P}_t G_t^d - P_{b,t} V_{t+1} + V_t - \Delta M_t^s = \underline{P}_t G_t^d. \tag{8.32}$$

Hence, discounting and summing,

$$\sum_{t=0}^{N} \frac{T_t}{\Pi(1+i)} = \sum_{t=0}^{N} \frac{\underline{P}_t G_t}{\Pi(1+i)} - \sum_{t=0}^{N} \frac{\Delta M_t^s}{\Pi(1+i)}$$

$$= \sum_{t=0}^{N} \frac{\underline{P}_t G_t}{\Pi(1+i)} - \frac{M_{N+1}^s}{\Pi^N(1+i)} - \sum_{t=1}^{N} \frac{i_t M_t^s}{\Pi(1+i)} + M_0^s$$

$$= \sum_{t=0}^{N} \frac{\underline{P}_t G_t}{\Pi(1+i)}, \tag{8.33}$$

since $M_t^s = M_0^s$ ($t \geq 0$) by assumption. This intertemporal government budget constraint can be compared with the case where government does plan to redeem its bonds with taxation,

$$\sum_{t=0}^{N} \frac{T_t}{\Pi(1+i)} = \sum_{t=0}^{N} \frac{\underline{P}_t G_t}{\Pi(1+i)} - \sum_{t=0}^{N} \frac{M_{N+1}^s}{\Pi(1+i)}$$

$$- \sum_{t=1}^{N} \frac{i_t M_t^s}{\Pi(1+i)} + M_0^s + V_0$$

$$= \sum_{t=0}^{N} \frac{\underline{P}_t G_t}{\Pi(1+i)} + V_0, \tag{8.34}$$

since once again $M_t^s = M_0^s (t \geq 0)$ by assumption. But if the government tries to choose (8.33) rather than (8.34), it will have problems carrying out its plan.

Government must set $V_{N+1} = 0$ in order to be honest and end with all its debts extinguished; this gives (8.34), the usual constraint used above. Suppose, however, that this is not government's aim, and it plans on (8.33) by never redeeming its bonds. In period N, the private sector's net demand for bonds to buy now and carry into the next period, B_{N+1}^d, is of course zero, under non-satiation and the provision that no private individual can die with positive personal debt outstanding. Thus, if government sets $V_{N+1} > 0$, to pay interest and principal in N, then the excess demand for bonds in period N, ExDB_N, is

$$\text{ExDB}_N \equiv B_{N+1}^d - V_{N+1}^s$$
$$= -V_{N+1}^s < 0, \tag{8.35}$$

and there is a positive excess supply of bonds. (The notation $\text{ExD}J_t$ refers to the excess demand for good J in period t.) Since there is no price vector that will make $B_{N+1}^d > 0$ and thus cause the bond market to clear, there can be no equilibrium in either the bond market or other markets (as a whole) in period N.

If people in period $N-1$ understand that will happen in N, markets will also not clear in $N-1$. From (8.32) and (8.33), people who buy government bonds in period $N-1$ know that any interest they get in N will be derived from sales of bonds in N, V_{N+1}. However, if they understand that no one will buy these bonds, they know they will not be paid the promised return in N and hence will not buy bonds in $N-1$. Thus, in $N-1$, $\text{ExDB}_{N-1} < 0$ and there is disequilibrium in the sense of the bond market not clearing and hence other markets not clearing in $N-1$. But if people understand this argument for periods N and $N-1$, in the same way no one will want to buy government bonds in $N-2, N-3, \ldots$, back to period 0. In other words, if people understand that ultimately the government will reach a period when it plans on not paying its debts, then people will not now want to hold government debt. In this case, then, where government plans to roll over its debt and finance the interest by issuing new debt, a perfect foresight, intertemporal equilibrium path cannot exist.

Heuristically, current-period wealth-holders are reluctant to buy bonds now because they fear that, before they can be repaid, the public will catch on that government bond holders cannot ultimately be paid. Government must keep peoples' faith in its honesty regarding debt or it ultimately cannot use debt financing and it is likely that government will find it progressively more difficult to sell its debt.

On an intuitive level, it would seem that in a world of uncertainty about government's honesty over debt, people will demand a higher return on the debt, or will require a higher i and thus pay a lower P_b. For example, if people are uncertain about whether government will ultimately try to set

$V_{N+1} > 0$, they will demand a larger i in earlier periods, because they never know when the public's faith will collapse. Alternatively, government could obviate the need for $V_{N+1} > 0$ by resorting to money creation. This money creation would not only pay for some interest and redeem some debt, but the accompanying increase in prices would reduce the real value of any debt, V_t/P_t. Hence, fear that the government might have to face setting $V_{N+1} > 0$ entails fear of the alternative inflationary monetary policy that erodes the real return on debt. This fear also argues for a higher rate of interest.

During much of the Reagan administration, there were very large deficits and these were financed in large part by bond sales. There is nothing in the analysis above that raises doubts about deficits *per se*, even large deficits. Deficits that are financed by bonds need cause no fear about repayment or inflationary finance, if the government is committed to redeeming the debt through taxation (or equivalently, paying interest through taxation). Worry arises from the possibility that government will never redeem the debt and will begin to pay interest on it simply by issuing new debt. Indeed, this fear had to be present during the Reagan administration, since consensus forecasts were for quite substantial future deficits even if the economy returned to full employment. Given the administration's taxing and spending policies, to some people the two alternatives seemed to be a rapidly growing national debt that would never be redeemed, where debt would be rolled over and interest would be paid by issuing more debt, or resort to a inflationary monetary policy. These fears may have been part of the explanation of the high real rates of interest found during the administration.

Non-Existence: Argument by Contradiction   Another way to approach the issue is to use the household sector budget constraint that

$$\sum_{t=0}^{N} \left\{ \frac{w_t N_t^s}{\Pi(1+i)} + \frac{\text{Div}_t}{\Pi(1+i)} - \frac{T_t}{\Pi(1+i)} - \frac{P_t C_t^d}{\Pi(1+i)} \right\}$$

$$- \sum_{t=1}^{N} \frac{i_t \text{MH}_t}{\Pi(1+i)} - \frac{\text{MH}_{N+1}}{\Pi(1+i)} + \text{MH}_0 + V_0 \qquad (8.36)$$

must be greater than or equal to zero. Substitute into (8.36) the expression for business dividends,

$$\sum_{t=0}^{N} \frac{\text{Div}_t}{\Pi(1+i)} = \sum_{t=0}^{N} \left\{ \frac{\widetilde{P}_t(Y_t^s - \Delta K_t^d)}{\Pi(1+i)} - \frac{\widetilde{w}_t N_t^d}{\Pi(1+i)} \right\}$$

$$-\sum_{t=1}^{N} \frac{i_t \mathrm{MB}_t}{\Pi(1+i)} - \frac{\mathrm{MB}_{N+1}}{\Pi(1+i)} + \mathrm{MB}_0, \tag{8.37}$$

and the government budget constraint when taxation is not used to redeem debt,

$$\sum_{t=0}^{N} \frac{T_t}{\Pi(1+i)} = \sum_{t=0}^{N} \frac{\underline{P}_t G_t}{\Pi(1+i)} - \frac{M_{N+1}^s}{\Pi^N(1+i)} - \sum_{t=1}^{N} \frac{i_t M_t^s}{\Pi(1+i)} + M_0^s$$

$$= \sum_{t=0}^{N} \frac{\underline{P}_t G_t}{\Pi(1+i)}, \tag{8.38}$$

where again $M_t^s = M_0^s$ $(t \geqslant 0)$ is assumed. This gives the constraint that

$$\sum_{t=0}^{N} \left\{ \frac{w_t N_t^s - \widetilde{w}_t N_t^d}{\Pi(1+i)} + \frac{\widetilde{P}_t(Y_t^s - \Delta K_t^d) - P_t C_t^d - \underline{P}_t G_t}{\Pi(1+i)} \right\}$$

$$- \frac{\mathrm{MH}_{N+1} + \mathrm{MB}_{N+1} - M_{N+1}^s}{\Pi^N(1+i)} - \sum_{t=1}^{N} \frac{i_t(\mathrm{MH}_t + \mathrm{MB}_t - M_t^s)}{\Pi(1+i)} + V_0 \tag{8.39}$$

must equal zero, assuming non-satiation. Notice that (8.39) differs from other versions of the budget constraint in that V_0 remains after substitution. This is because government does not intend ever to pay off V_0, and the V_0 in (8.36) is not canceled by a V_0 in (8.38) when substituting. Thus, if government does not plan to redeem its debt through taxation, then government debt is part of net wealth. However, the story does not end there.

Suppose that $w_t = \widetilde{w}_t$, $P_t = \widetilde{P}_t = \underline{P}_t$ for all t. Suppose further that the private sector plans to end period N with money holdings $\mathrm{MH}_{N+1} + \mathrm{MB}_{N+1}$ that just equal the amount of government money outstanding, $M_{N+1}^s = M_0^s$ in this case. Then, the constraint (8.39) is

$$\sum_{t=0}^{N} \left\{ -\frac{w_t \mathrm{ExD} N_t}{\Pi(1+i)} - \frac{P_t \mathrm{ExD} Q_t}{\Pi(1+i)} - \frac{i_t \mathrm{ExD} M_t}{\Pi(1+i)} \right\} + V_0 = 0, \tag{8.40}$$

where, in period t, $\mathrm{ExD} N_t$ is the excess demand for labor services, $\mathrm{ExD} Q_t$ the excess demand for output, $\mathrm{ExD} M_t$ the excess demand for money and $\mathrm{ExD} B_t$ the excess demand for bonds. From (8.40), an intertemporal equilibrium does not exist. To see this, note that when there is equilibrium in any period t and hence

$$\mathrm{ExD} Q_t = 0$$

$$\text{ExD}M_t = 0 \tag{8.41}$$

$$\text{ExD}N_t = 0,$$

then, from Walras's law, $\text{ExD}B_t = 0$. Suppose that it is asserted that an intertemporal perfect foresight equilibrium price vector exists, in the sense that when people see and expect this price vector (8.41) holds for all t. The equilibrium conditions (8.41), combined with the intertemporal budget constraint (8.40), give the implication

$$V_0^s = 0. \tag{8.42}$$

In other words, the existence of equilibrium implies a logical contradiction if $V_0^s \neq 0$.

The contradiction arises because government is demanding more resources from society than it can pay for through printing money or taxing society. When people buy a bond, they give up resources and ultimately expect to be provided with resources of the same present value in the future, while government has no intention of providing these resources through taxation or printing money. This contradiction will hold for any price vector. Hence, there is no way for the pricing system to coordinate demands and supplies to set demands equal to society's resources.[9]

Infinite Time Horizon

Suppose N is allowed to grow to infinity. This changes nothing in the above analysis, since nothing depends on N's size.

If the time horizon does not merely approach infinity, however, but actually is infinite, matters are different. This occurs because, with a large but finite N, the passage of a year brings society one year closer to its end, but with an infinite horizon one never gets closer to an end that never occurs.

With an infinite horizon, there will never be an $N+1$ period and hence never an N in which government bonds cannot be sold. Hence, the "argument by recursion" from above cannot be used in this case to show why the government will be forced to adopt a policy of redeeming its bonds through taxation. So far, government can just go on rolling over its debt, paying interest by issuing more debt.

Consider the example, however, where there is no new money issued, there is no redemption of government bonds, and all government purchases are financed by taxation on a pay-as-you-go basis, so

$$T_t = \underset{\sim}{P_t} G_t.$$

Then, by altering the upper summation limits to infinity, the household sector budget constraint (8.39) applies, with $\mathrm{MH}_{N+1} + \mathrm{MB}_{N+1} - M^s_{N+1}$ removed. In the same way, (8.40) also holds, with the upper summation limits now infinity. The same problem arises as before, that there exists no intertemporal equilibrium time path, because government is taking more resources than its taxation and money issuance allow.

Temporary Equilibria

While a perfect foresight, intertemporal equilibrium path cannot exist if government does not plan to pay off its debt, a sequence of temporary equilibria can. In particular, given expected prices, wages and interest rates, it is possible there are values of P_0, w_0 and i_0 for which

$$\mathrm{ExD}Q_0 = \mathrm{ExD}N_0 = \mathrm{ExD}M_0 = 0. \tag{8.43}$$

Walras's law ensures that, if (8.43) holds, then

$$\mathrm{ExD}B_0 = 0.$$

The above discussion shows that eventually, however, some of the expected P_t, w_t, i_t will turn out not to hold for there is no intertemporal equilibrium path. This will eventually lead to people catching on that their expectations are unrealistic, since there can be no intertemporal equilibrium path. When they discover that no expectations can come true, presumably the economic system collapses.

Before that, however, one can offer some non-rigorous conjectures about the system. Under the case assumed above of zero money supply growth and current taxation equal to current government purchases, government bonds in the hands of the public will rise every period by a factor of unity plus the one-period rate of interest, or the sequence is V_0, $V_1 = (1+i_1)V_0$, $V_2 = (1+i_2)V_1 = (1+i_2)(1+i_1)V_0, \ldots$, etc. Thus the household sector will feel ever wealthier over time. Furthermore, since government finances its debt by rolling it over and issuing new debt to pay the interest, $P_{b,t}V^s_{t+1} = V^s_t$, government bond sales will rise in the same sequence. Intuitively, both the increases in wealth and government bond sales put continuing upward pressure on the interest rate over time, so that the interest rate becomes ever higher; as wealth rises, aggregate demand rises, requiring a higher interest rate to clear the output market, and in the bond market the increase in government sales causes the excess supply of bonds to rise, drawing down the price of bonds and driving up the interest rate. However, even when people have adapted to rising rates, this sequence cannot be a perfect foresight path. A conjecture is that, however fast people expect i to rise, actual i generally rises even faster. Presumably, this puts upward pressure on prices as the demand for money drops in response to rises in i. It is likely that increases in i outstrip inflation, so real rates of interest rise over time.

Government Bonds Are Net Wealth

As in the previous two sections, suppose that the current generation is given $P_{b,0} V_0$ bonds but is now told that taxes will never be raised to redeem them. This clearly raises the wealth of the current generation whether or not that generation cares nothing for the future generation, and hence affects current demands. Even with bequests, the future generation faces no extra taxes due to $P_{b,0} V_0$, so the current generation feels wealthier and raises its current demands for superior goods.

Summary

A four-way classification is useful. (This classification neglects the possibility of government paying some of its interest with money supply growth, but the necessary complications are easily added.) The government can plan on paying all interest with taxes (at some point, even if it sometimes temporarily allows debt to grow), or it can plan on paying at least some interest by issuing ever more debt. In the private sector, the current generation may have no concern for the future generation and leave no bequests, or the current generation may have concern and leave bequests. Table 8.1 shows the four cases, A–D, and their implications for

Table 8.1   Interactions of how government finances its debt and whether the household sector leaves bequests

| | | Government Sector: Interest paid by | |
		(I) Taxation	*(II) Issuing More Bonds*
Private Sector	*Bequests*	**A.** (1) Interest-rate-induced effect on wealth equals zero (2) Government bonds are not net wealth (3) Intertemporal equilibrium may exist	**C.** (1) Interest-rate-induced effect on wealth is indeterminate, but is likely positive (2) Government bonds are net wealth (3) Intertemporal equilibrium cannot exist
	No Bequests	**B.** (1) Interest-rate-induced effect on wealth is very likely negative (2) Government bonds are net wealth (to the current generation) (3) Intertemporal equilibrium may exist	**D.** (1) Interest-rate-induced effect on wealth is indeterminate, but is likely positive (2) Government bonds are net wealth (to the current generation) (3) Intertemporal equilibrium cannot exist

the interest-rate-induced effect on wealth, the issue of whether government bonds are net wealth and finally the issue of whether an intertemporal equilibrium path can exist.

In case (II), where interest on at least some fraction of the currently outstanding national debt will be paid by perpetually issuing new bonds, intertemporal equilibrium simply cannot exist, whether the economy's horizon is finite or infinite. Since the current national debt does not necessitate offsetting taxation of equal real present value, then some portion of the national debt is viewed by the current generation as part of wealth, and this is so whether or not the current generation leaves bequests. As for the sign of the interest-rate-induced effect on wealth, it is not possible to determine this by using the assumption of intertemporal equilibrium, since such a time path cannot exist in this case; the effect is indeterminate. However, in a loose way, the effect may well be positive. The private sector as a whole views itself (mistakenly) as a rentier earning interest income on V_0. With a rise in i, it can now afford to consume more in all periods. This view is "loose" in the sense that no intertemporal set of private sector plans can ever be completely fulfilled due to the government's policies necessarily resulting in disequilibrium over time.

In case (I), where bonds are ultimately redeemed through taxation, the interest-rate-induced effect on wealth in current markets is zero if there are utility-maximizing bequests, and negative if no bequests, under the conditions discussed above. With bequests, government bonds are not considered net wealth by the current generation, since any increase in these bonds benefits the current generation at the expense of future generations through government-imposed redistribution. The current generation then increases its bequests by exactly the amount of the redistribution and is hence no wealthier due to the increase in the number of government bonds outstanding. In the case of no bequests, an increase in government bonds makes the current generation wealthier at the expense of future generations; the current generation does nothing to offset this redistribution, and hence government bonds act as net wealth. Finally, with and without bequests, there is no guarantee that an equilibrium will exist, but as opposed to case (II), there is no necessity for an intertemporal equilibrium not to exist.

8.5 Does the Ratio of National Debt to GNP Matter?

It is common in monetary and macroeconomics to write behavioral functions, say the consumption function, with government debt as an argument, often as a ratio to income.[10]

Calling real income Y and nominal income PY, then the ratio of government debt to GNP is real debt per unit of output, or $P_b V/PY = (P_b V/P)/Y$. Does the ratio $P_b V/PY$ influence C? Often this is viewed in the context of constant per capita income, where Y and population (POP) grow at a constant rate g. Based on the analysis of the above sections, it can be shown the $P_b V/PY$ will influence consumption only if (a) the bequest motive does not operate fully, or (b) the government does not plan on ever redeeming its bonds (plans on paying interest by issuing more debt).

Suppose the government up to period 0 has used no debt. Now it suddenly gives each person in the economy V' bonds. Then, $P_b V_0 = POP P_b V'$. From the above discussion, the effect of $P_b V_0$, or $P_b V_0/P_0$, depends on what is done about taxes. Suppose that the bonds V_0 are perpetuities paying \$1 per year in interest[11] (so $P_b = \$1/i$), and the government tells each person that his/her taxes will be higher each year by \$$V'$. Suppose further that each of the people in POP_0 is immortal. Clearly, then, V_0 has no effect on their decisions.

In the next period, $POP_1 = (1+g) POP_0$, and $Y_1 = (1+g) Y_0$. For convenience, assume that the price level is constant through time. Consider the case where the government distributes V' bonds to each of the new people, so $P_b V/PY$ is constant. If the government informs the recipients that their taxes will be higher by \$1 per year for each bond, the new people are in unchanged circumstances due to the bonds, so their behavior is unaffected. Thus, $P_b V_1/P_1 Y_1 = P_b V_0/P_0 Y_0$ and consumption behavior in both periods 0 and 1 is no different from the case where $V_t = 0$ for all t.

What if all the extra taxes are imposed on POP_0? If the bequest motive operates, the older generation simply reduces its transfers to the younger; there is no effect on consumption in either period. If the bequest motive is absent, there is a net distribution to the younger generation and thus consumption demand falls in period 0 and rises in period 1. Hence, $P_b V/PY$ is constant between periods in both examples, but consumption demand is higher in 1 than in 0 if the bequest motive does not operate.

Alternatively, suppose that no bonds are distributed to the new people and their taxes are not raised. Then their consumption behavior is unaffected. While $P_b V_0/P_0 Y_0 > P_b V_1/P_1 Y_1$ since $V_1 = V_0, P_1 = P_0$ and $Y_1 > Y_0$, there is no change in per capita consumption demand between periods 0 and 1, since people from period 0 are unaffected.

Further, in all these cases, it can make no difference whether a particular generation pays extra taxes that equal the current interest from their V', or simply have an increase in tax liabilities with a present value of $P_b V'$.

So far, $P_b V/PY$ can affect aggregate demand only if the bequest motive fails to work fully. Even there, variations in $P_b V/PY$ must represent inter-generational transfers. Further, debt policy that redistributes wealth and affects per capita demand need not result in a positive correlation between per capita aggregate demand and $P_b V/PY$, as shown by the example where each generation's bond holdings rise but the current generation pays all of the extra taxes for both generations and thus cuts current demand.

It is sometimes argued that it makes a difference when the growth rate of the debt $(P_b V)$ exceeds that of nominal GNP $(=PY)$. To see this is not necessarily so, suppose that $V_1' = 2V_0'$, so each member of the new generation receives twice as many bonds as in the old, and suppose the new people simply pay taxes twice as high as before. Continue to assume a constant P so $\Delta(PY)/PY = g$. Then, $P_b V_0/P_0 Y_0 < P_b V_1/P_1 Y_1$, $(P_b V_1/P_1 Y_1)/(P_b V_0/P_0 Y_0) - 1 > 0$, and $(P_b V_1)/(P_b V_0) - 1 > g$. But since this larger V_1 does not affect the new people, the growth of the ratio $P_b V/PY$ has no effect.

Financing Interest Payments with New Debt

Suppose that the economy ends in period N. It is obvious that if the government is going to set $V_{N+1} = 0$ the strategy of deferring some taxes early on by issuing more bonds must give a present value of extra taxes equal to $P_b V_0$. Thus, $P_b V/PY$ rises for a time with C unaffected, and then falls as taxes rise to pay off the debt, again with C unaffected.

The government can make $V_{N+1} > 0$ and the present value of extra taxes less than $P_b V_0$; this, however, prevents the existence of an inter-temporal equilibrium path. As discussed above, there might be some temporary equilibrium where consumption demand is larger due to the rise in $P_b V_0$. Section 8.4 argued, since an intertemporal equilibrium cannot exist when government plans $V_{N+1} > 0$, there can be only a loose, intuitive argument about this policy's effect on wealth. It does seem likely, however, that per capita consumption will grow over time, as will $P_b V/PY$, though the relationship need not be constant. Ultimately, government must abandon its planned $V_{N+1} > 0$ as people catch on to the implications of the plan, as section 8.4 argued.

If the economy goes on for ever, there is never a period N where the government tries to sell $V_{N+1} > 0$. However, as section 8.4 showed, there still will not exist an intertemporal equilibrium path if the government finances its debt by issuing new debt.

One strand of literature argues that the question of whether or not government bonds are net wealth depends on whether $i \lessgtr g$ (see Feldstein, 1976; Barro, 1976). However, this argument is really about whether an intertemporal equilibrium path exists. The issue of the relationship of i to g is just a crude way of restricting growth of the national debt. The remainder of this section discusses this issue.

The argument is that the government tries to avoid levying new taxes by simply selling new bonds each period. Suppose, however, that as in Barro (1976), and Feldstein (1976), $P_b V$ cannot grow faster than the real economy (again assuming zero inflation). Barro (1976, p. 343, n. 2) justifies this restriction "by assuming that the value of the outstanding stock of debt at any point in time is bounded by the government's collateral, which I assume can be measured by the present value of future taxing capacity . . . the government's collateral grows at rate g. . . . If government debt grew at a rate faster than g, then the outstanding stock would eventually exceed the government's collateral."

Assuming for convenience that P_b and P are constant, then the assumption is $\Delta V/V \leqslant g$. Suppose that V is allowed to grow at g. For concreteness, assume that the bonds discussed are initially issued as transfers to POP_0 and any extra taxes entailed by these bonds are paid by that generation. The issue then is the relation of the present value of the extra taxes to $P_b V_0$. The extra taxes T_t^* in any period t equal the interest payments $iP_b V_t = V_t$ on bonds outstanding less the sale of new bonds $P_b \Delta V_t = P_b(V_{t+1} - V_t) = P_b g V_t$. The present value of T_t^* is most conveniently calculated in continuous time. The extra taxes T_t^* at time t are

$$T_t^* = i P_b V_t - P_b \dot{V} = V_t - P_b g V_t = (i-g)P_b V_t = (i-g)P_b V_0 e^{gt},$$

since V grows at rate g. The present value of the stream T_t^* is

$$\int_0^\infty e^{-it} T_t^* \, dt = (i-g) P_b V_0 \int_0^\infty e^{-(i-g)t} \, dt. \tag{8.44}$$

Consider first the case where $i > g$. Then, from (8.44), the present value of T_t^* is

$$P_b V_0 (i-g) \frac{1}{i-g} = P_b V_0.$$

Thus, under the restriction $\Delta V/V \leqslant g$, the present value of the extra taxes necessary to support the "gift" of $P_b V_0$ is in fact $P_b V_0$, so there is no effect on wealth.

Note that the point of this discussion is not that $P_b V/PY$ stays constant as time goes on with $i > g$. Rather, in the early stages, use of bond sales will reduce extra taxation, but only at the cost of raising V_t. Eventually, V_t

is so large that the extra taxes are greater than they would have been without the bond sales. The present value of the early decrease in extra taxation due to bond sales is exactly balanced by the later increase in extra taxation. The generation in period 0 thus saves the excess of interest over extra taxation in the earlier periods to pay for the reverse in later periods. In this case, then, there is no effect on wealth, and this is independent of the intertemporal course of $P_b V/Y$.

Now consider the case where $g > i$. From (8.44), if $g > i$, then the present value of extra taxes goes to minus infinity. In words, the government is able to increase its bonds outstanding so fast that the recipients of the initial transfer end up never having to repay it and also receive additional transfers whose values go to infinity. Clearly, the government could expand V at a lower rate and make the net present value of T^* equal zero so that government bonds $P_0 V_0$ are a part of net wealth. This does not mean that government bonds are net wealth. It simply means that the restriction $\Delta V/V \leqslant g$ is not sufficient when $i < g$ to remove the possibility of government trying to pay for interest on its bonds by issuing new bonds. (The case where $i < g$ implies inefficient over-accumulation of capital, as in the discussion of "golden rules"; see Phelps, 1966.)

When there is a finite N, it is clear that the issue of the possible existence of intertemporal equilibrium turns on whether $V_{N+1} > 0$. If government sets $V_{N+1} = 0$, it does not matter how large $\Delta V/V$ is for $t < N$. Eventually, taxes pay for the initial bond transfer (assuming a given sequence of M_t^s).

However, when N is infinite, there is no question of $V_{N+1} = 0$. Here the issue is whether taxes must pay for $P_b V_0$. If $\Delta V/V$ must not exceed g, and if $i > g$, the answer is that the government eventually pays for the bonds with taxes. But if $i \leqslant g$, the government is able, if it wants, to expand V so fast that the initial bond transfer is never paid for with taxes. This does not mean the bonds are net wealth. Rather it means that no intertemporal equilibrium path exists.

NOTES

1   In the next-to-last period, each individual will want to hold some real balances at the start of period N to facilitate transactions. It is true, though, that as period N goes on, each individual will be eager to dispose of money balances and reluctant to accept money, since there will be no period $N+1$ and hence there is no advantage to ending N with positive balances. Hence, the assumption that the price level P_N is constant through period N is likely to be false. Similarly, prices in earlier periods will be higher in reflection of this coming rise than if the economy never ended. (See Brock (1975), Fischer (1979a).)

However, if N is quite far in the future, these reflections in current prices of the chaos of the end will be very slight and can safely be ignored.

Assuming an infinite-lived economy avoids the above problem, though surely is not more realistic. However, infinite time horizons lead to other analytical difficulties discussed below.

2 There is an alternative way of ensuring that $M^s_{N+1} = MH_{N+1} + MB_{N+1}$. If market-clearing quantities are assumed for all periods, as below, including for N, then zero excess demands for output and labor services imply a zero excess demand for money, since the excess demand for bonds has to be zero in N, as section 8.4 discusses in detail.

3 As chapter 3 discussed, almost all of this book's effects on wealth are evaluated for price-takers and quantity-setters. Chapter 10, section 10.3, however, briefly discusses the case where the price-taking decision-makers are quantity constrained (Clower, 1965). A common assumption in macroeconomics is unemployment in the labor market but, subject to this quantity constraint on supplies of labor services, market clearing elsewhere. This is the assumption in IS–LM unemployment models. In such a case, a rise in the quantity of labor services demanded increases the wealth of quantity-constrained households. In contrast, quantity-setting households are unconcerned with the quantity demanded for they believe they choose exactly how many hours to work.

Suppose that there is initially an unemployment equilibrium and i rises. This reduces the demand for future capital, and, assuming that capital and labor are complements, reduces future demands for labor, as chapter 10, section 10.3 discusses. Hence, the household sector is poorer. In other words, there is a negative interest-rate-induced effect on wealth in this case, where there would not be if supplies of labor services were not quantity constrained. Taking quantity-constrained behavior as a sign of disequilibrium, it is true that in disequilibrium this effect can be negative. This is in contrast with the text where the disequilibrium was not associated with quantity constraints. Evidentlv, then, one must specify with care the meaning of the term disequilibrium.

4 This is strictly speaking true in the world assumed so far with lump-sum taxes. If taxes are raised with marginal tax rates, however, increases in future taxes that are associated with higher tax rates on capital will reduce the value of capital in the eyes of future generations and hence reduce the value of extra consumption that the current generation can finance by selling its assets to future generations. Chapter 9 discusses some issues of non-lump-sum taxes and effects on wealth.

5 Cf. Tobin (1980, chapter 2).

6 The basic idea here is similar to Barro (1974). The parent thinks of allocating the total wealth of all generations. An interest-rate-induced reallocation of wealth across generations that leaves total wealth unchanged is simply offset by familial action.

7 Of course, U^c is likely to enter U^F, but this symmetry is not needed here for the key points made. However, see note 8 for the problem of corner solutions.

8 It may be that the older generation is at a corner solution of $B = 0$ when it prefers $B < 0$. Legal and social institutions may make it difficult for the older

generation to set $B < 0$, though the example of forcing the child to pay for (a larger proportion of) his/her education shows there is not a flat prohibition. More generally, if the current generation's utility enters the future's utility function, $U^F = U^F(W^F + B, U^c)$, then the two generations can agree on $B < 0$. The problem of a corner solution arises when intergenerational concern is asymmetrical, or, out of the feasible set of U^c, U^F, the two generations do not agree on the optimum. If this is so, then $B > 0$ means that the current generation's choice prevails, while with $B < 0$ the future generation's does.

9 See also Lucas's (1984) very cryptic, but somewhat similar, argument that government must plan on paying off its bonds.

Note that no member of the private sector plans on facing the end of the world with positive holdings of government bonds, and instead plans on converting them to resources. This is the source of the non-existence of equilibrium when government plans on paying interest on its bonds by selling new bonds. However, as in note 1, the private sector can plan on facing the end of the world with positive cash balances since these may be useful in transactions right to the end.

10 For example, Tobin (1980), Smith (1982).

11 This is a change from this book's usual assumption above of single-period bonds, but is done solely for convenience and makes no fundamental difference to any argument.

9

Government Bonds as Net Wealth:
An Uncertainty Analysis

Chapter 8 discussed the issue of whether government bonds are part of the household sector's net wealth. The answer is "No" if the world consists of a constant population of immortal individuals, or if bequests are determined by utility maximization in a world of finite-lived individuals. However, the result that government bonds are not part of net wealth was found in a world of total certainty, where all taxes were lump sum and every individual could borrow or lend as much as desired subject only to an intertemporal budget constraint. This chapter investigates how relaxing these assumptions changes the effect of government bonds.

9.1 Introduction

For over two decades, the question of whether some fraction of government bonds is net wealth has received a good deal of discussion, both at the theoretical level[1] and the empirical.[2] Much of the theoretical debate has centered on Barro's ingenious demonstration that, under certain circumstances, the bequest motive leads currently living decision-makers to act as if they were infinitely lived, as chapter 8 discussed. This in turn gives the so-called Ricardian doctrine that government bonds and the associated lump-sum tax changes have no net effects on current aggregate demand. Of course, many defend the traditional Keynesian position that an increase in bonds outstanding will raise current aggregate demand. Many of the criticisms of the modern versions of the Ricardian doctrine have focused on the Barro argument regarding bequests; at some points the Barro argument is in fact quite weak, as discussed below.

The main focus of this chapter, however, is on three other prominent arguments against the Ricardian doctrine. First, the wealth in government bonds is certain while the implied taxes are uncertain. Some economists argue that the discount rate on the certain bonds is lower than on the uncertain taxes and hence net wealth rises. Section 9.2 shows, however, that the uncertainty reduces welfare and, with decreasing absolute risk aversion, current aggregate demand falls.

Second, section 9.3 analyzes the argument that government bonds add to current liquidity and thus increase current aggregate demand in a world where people are subject to a liquidity constraint as well as an intertemporal wealth constraint. Government bonds then allow liquidity-constrained people to avoid the private market; instead "the government lends to them at its borrowing rate of interest, an option not otherwise available in the credit market" (Tobin, 1980). Or, as in Niehans (1978), liquidity-constrained individuals can be thought of as borrowing in the private market but with government repayment guarantees. However, individuals feel liquidity constrained because of the risks they offer lenders. Government loan guarantees do not reduce the risk the system must bear, but instead shift part of it from lenders to taxpayers. Taxpayers now pay extra taxes in default situations where previously lenders would have lost; the risk is simply shifted. If this shifting affects lenders, it does so as a free-rider problem where each lender believes that some of the extra taxes, in the event the guarantee is used, will be paid by others. Further, existence of an effect also requires that guaranteed loans are not inframarginal, and this seems likely only if all loans are guaranteed or lenders are faced with a new, unforeseen guarantee program after they have made all the loans they planned on.

A third line of argument supposes that non-zero marginal tax rates are used to pay off bonds, rather than lump-sum taxes. Such arguments are often confused, as section 9.4 discusses. First, it is clear that changes in relative intertemporal tax rates have real effects. However, there is no necessary relationship between bond financing and changes in marginal tax rates. Either can change without the other; for example, bonds could be redeemed with cuts in tax credits and personal exemptions that raise average but not marginal tax rates. Second, it is often assumed that marginal tax rates are held constant when people find their income low, by chance or design. However, the necessity of meeting interest payments may mean the tax rate rises when income falls. More generally, this sort of confusion of partial versus general equilibrium analysis can lead to opposite conclusions. For example, in the case where everyone practises tax avoidance, this forces up marginal tax rates to generate the revenue necessary to pay off bonds. Welfare and current consumption actually fall. Finally, if individuals' incomes are less than perfectly correlated, a tax system with positive marginal tax rates may offer a form of diversification that the market might not provide for (say) labor income. However, this is wholly independent of whether debt financing is ever used. Further, while diversification through the tax system may be beneficial, there are costs through distortions. With these conflicting forces of diversification and distortion, there is no *a priori* reason to believe that an increase in non-zero marginal tax rates (to match bond financing) would be better than a reduction.

Section 9.5 summarizes the discussion and offers some conclusions. There are serious weaknesses in Barro's intergenerational argument that make it reasonable that some fraction of government bonds is net wealth. However, arguments based on the uncertainty of taxes, the liquidity constraint and non-lump-sum taxes are not very persuasive.

9.2 Taxes are Uncertain

Many argue that bond financing increases current aggregate demand because the bonds are certain wealth but the implied taxation is uncertain. Tobin (1980, pp. 60–1) writes

> Keynesians have always argued that the discount rate for future taxes is the one appropriate for the streams on which the taxes are levied; given the uncertainties in those streams, that rate is higher than the discount rate for government obligations. The differential means that government bond issue does indeed raise net wealth even if taxpayers correctly expect that taxes will be increased to service the added debt.

In the absence of distribution effects, an increase in government bonds that is financed by taxes with no uncertainty attached has no effect on wealth or current aggregate demand (chapter 8). This section shows, however, that when the future taxes needed to pay off the bonds are uncertain (even though lump sum), government bonds reduce aggregate demand, under the conventional assumption that absolute risk aversion is decreasing. While any one person may escape taxes, the system as a whole cannot; the addition of risk on top of expected taxes reduces demand.

Assume that every individual has the same endowment $\bar{c}$ in each period, and a time-separable welfare function equal to the sum of instantaneous utilities discounted at the constant rate $\delta > 0$, where δ and the instantaneous utility function over consumption (c) are the same for each person. This suffices to eliminate distribution effects here.

Certainty Case – Individual Optimization

Suppose that individual A has the same instantaneous utility function u_A in each period; in the two-period case, the welfare function U_A is

$$U_A = u_A(c_1) + \frac{1}{1+\delta} u_A(c_2).$$ (9.1)

Before bond and tax actions by the government, the budget constraint[3] is

$$c_1 + \frac{1}{1+r} c_2 = \bar{c}_1 + \frac{1}{1+r} \bar{c}_2, \quad c_2 = \bar{c}_2 + (1+r)(\bar{c}_1 - c_1),$$ (9.2)

where r is the (real) rate of interest on no-default bonds. Thus,

$$U = u(c_1) + \frac{1}{1+\delta} u\{\bar{c}_2 + (1+r)(\bar{c}_1 - c_1)\}.$$ (9.3)

With $\bar{c}_1, \bar{c}_2$ non-stochastic, $E(U) = U$ and

$$\frac{dU}{dc_1} = \frac{dE(U)}{dc_1} = u'(c_1) - \frac{1}{1+\delta} u'\{\bar{c}_2 + (1+r)(\bar{c}_1 - c_1)\} (1+r).$$ (9.4)

Setting $dU/dc_1 = 0$ gives

$$u'(c_1) = \{(1+r)/(1+\delta)\} u'(c_2).$$ (9.5)

With $\bar{c}_1 = \bar{c}_2$ and everyone identical, equilibrium requires that $c_1 = \bar{c}_1$, $c_2 = \bar{c}_2$, and hence $u'(\bar{c}_1) = u'\{\bar{c}_2 + (1+r)(\bar{c}_1 - c_1)\} = u'(\bar{c}_2)$. Thus, $(1+r)/(1+\delta) = 1$ and $r = \delta$ in equilibrium.

The IC' curve in figure 9.1 shows combinations of c_1, c_2 that keep

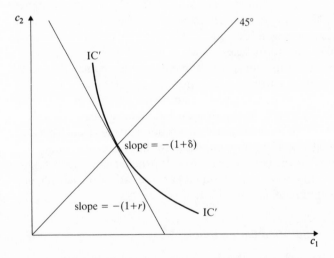

Figure 9.1 Consumption choice in a two-period world, time-separable utility

U_A constant at a given level. The marginal rate of substitution (MRS) is $-u'(c_1)\{u'(c_2)/(1+\delta)\} = -(1+\delta)u'(c_1)/u'(c_2)$. Along the 45° line, $c_1 = c_2$ and $u'(c_1) = u'(c_2)$, so MRS $= -(1+\delta)$ at all points. Since $\bar{c}_1 = \bar{c}_2$, A must end up consuming $\bar{c}_1 = c_1 = c_2 = \bar{c}_2$ and hence the MRS $= -(1+\delta)$. The budget constraint (9.2) has the slope $-(1+r)$ and since equilibrium requires $-(1+r) = $ MRS, it follows that $-(1+r) = -(1+\delta)$ and hence $r = \delta$.

The Individual Is Given a Government Bond

Suppose that A is given a non-stochastic quantity b of government bonds in period 1. The first-order condition becomes

$$\frac{\partial U}{\partial c_1} = u'(c_1) - \frac{1}{1+\delta}\, u'\{\bar{c}_2 + (1+r)(\bar{c}_1 - c_1) + (1+r)b\}(1+r) = 0.$$

(9.6)

If b is increased,

$$\frac{\partial^2 U}{\partial(c_1)^2}\frac{dc_1}{db} + \frac{\partial^2 U}{\partial c_1 \partial b} = 0$$

(9.7)

and thus (evaluating at $r = \delta$, $c_1 = c_2 = \bar{c}_1 = \bar{c}_2$, $b = 0$)

$$\frac{dc_1}{db} = -\frac{\partial^2 U}{\partial c_1 \partial b}\bigg/\frac{\partial^2 U}{\partial(c_1)^2} = (1+r)/(2+r).$$

(9.8)

Hence, $1 > dc_1/db > 0$. Further, $dc_2/db = (1+r) - (1+r)(dc_1/db) = (1+r)/(2+r) = dc_1/db$. In fact, for $r = \delta$, c_1 will equal c_2 whatever b is; from the first-order condition in this case with $r = \delta$, $u'(c_1) = u'(c_2)$, and this equality holds with identical instantaneous $u(\cdot)$ just in case $c_1 = c_2$.

In figure 9.1, suppose that b rises by unity, shifting the budget constraint to the right by unity. With $r = \delta$, the new equilibrium quantities c_1, c_2 must be on the 45° line, with $c_1 = c_2$ once again.

If A must pay the taxes to finance b, or pays $T = b(1+r)$, then clearly any change in b has no effect on c_1 since the budget constraint is unchanged.

Effect on Aggregate Demand

Consider the effect on aggregate demand of an increase in b when the other n individuals pay the associated taxes. To explore this, tentatively let r stay at δ. Then, every unit increase in b causes A's c_1 and c_2 to rise by $(1+r)/(2+r)$ each.

Let individual j pay taxes T_j. Let all individuals have the same instantaneous utility function as A and the same non-b endowments. Suppose each T_j has $E(T_j) = b(1+r)/n$, and the variance of T_j is the finite σ_j^2, which can vary across j. Since $T_n = (1+r)b - \Sigma_{j=1}^{n-1} T_j$, σ_n^2 depends on the $(n-1)$ covariance matrix.

Suppose $\sigma_j \to 0$, or the model is the certainty case. For each j,

$$\frac{dc_{1,j}}{db} = - \frac{dc_{1,A}}{db}\bigg/ n. \tag{9.9}$$

For every unit increase in b, $c_{1,j}$ decreases by $(1+r)/(2+r)n$; indeed, in equilibrium along the 45° line in figure 9.1,

$$c_{1,j} = \bar{c}_1 - \frac{1+r}{2+r}\frac{b}{n}. \tag{9.10}$$

Thus, $\Sigma_{j=1}^n dc_{1,j}/db = - dc_{1,A}/db$, and hence the change in aggregate demand is zero. Further, the necessary change in the equilibrium r is also zero.

Taxes are Stochastic

Uncertainty about taxes makes people feel worse off. The contrary view, as in the quote at the start of this section, likely arises from thinking that each person will at most have to pay his/her pro rata share of the taxes due to bonds plus interest, with the possibility of paying less. Thus, as a best guess you will have to pay $b(1+r)/n$, but if you die you pay less. However, this view neglects the fact that if someone else dies you may have to make up part of his/her share and hence can end by paying more than $b(1+r)/n$.

Note that with complete, frictionless markets, all taxpayers could insure among themselves and agree that each will pay $(1+r)b/n$ no matter what the *ex post* distribution of tax bills. Thus, Tobin's problem assumes some frictions, and hence so do we.

The introduction of uncertainty in taxes makes current aggregate demand fall, which can be seen by supposing such uncertainty does not alter behavior. With given taxes, (9.10) holds. If (9.10) continues to hold, then $u'_j(c_1) = u'_j[\bar{c}_1 - \{(1+r)/(2+r)\}(b/n)]$ and $E(c_{2,j}) = \bar{c}_2 - \{1/(2+r)\}E(T_j) = \bar{c}_2 - \{(1+r)/(2+r)\}(b/n) = \bar{c}_1 - [(1+r)/(2+r)](b/n)$, so $E(c_{2,j}) = c_{1,j}$. But with $u''' > 0$, as with constant relative risk aversion or with absolute risk aversion that is either constant or decreasing,

$$E[u'_j\{\bar{c}_2 - T_j(1+r)/(2+r)\}] > u'_j\{E(c_2)\} = u'_j(c_1). \tag{9.11}$$

Thus, from (9.11),

$$dE(U_j)/dc_1 = u'_j - E(u'_j) < 0 \qquad (9.12)$$

when evaluated with c_1 from (9.10). But since the first-order condition with $r = \delta$ is

$$dE(U_j)/dc_1 = u'_j - E(u'_j) = 0, \qquad (9.13)$$

(9.12) implies that, when uncertainty is introduced, j will want to reduce $c_{1,j}$ in order to raise $c_{2,j}$.[4]

Figure 9.2 shows the initial equilibrium at c'_1, c'_2 with no uncertainty. At this pair, the marginal condition is satisfied. With uncertainty, c'_1 implies $E(c_2) = c'_2$. If the $u'(c_2)$ curve is linear, $E\{u'(c_2)\} = u'E(c_2)$ and individual j has no incentive to alter plans. (To see this, think of c_2 as uniformly distributed around c'_2.) If the $u'(c_2)$ curve is non-linear as with $v'(c_2)$, however, then clearly $E\{v'(c_2)\} > u'(c'_2)$. (Again, think of a uniform distribution around c'_2; the probability-weighted value of $v'(c_2)$ is greater than $u'(c'_2)$.) This induces j to cut back on c_1 to raise $u'(c_1)$ and reduce $E\{v'(c_2)\}$ and thus make the marginal condition hold once again. A curvilinear relationship such as $v'(c_2)$ arises if $u''' > 0$.

Intuitively, period 2's utility may be severely adversely affected by a realization of $T_j > b(1+r)/n$. To ensure against this eventuality, j reduces period 1 consumption to provide a cushion for period 2. Thus, at $r = \delta$, the introduction of b causes $c_{1,A}$ to rise by $\{(1+r)/(2+r)\}b$, but the

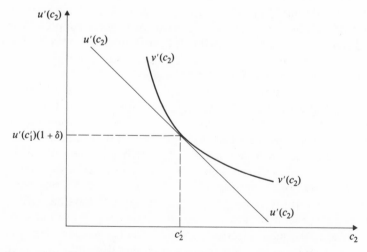

Figure 9.2 The effect of tax uncertainty on consumption choice

consumption demand of the rest of the economy falls by more than $\{(1+r)/(2+r)\}b$. In the aggregate, current demand falls; hence r must fall to restore equilibrium. The increase in b is contractionary, not expansionary.

The Appropriate Discount Rate for Taxes

As long as each person is risk averse ($u'' < 0$), the introduction of risk in taxes reduces E(U). However, the effect on c_1 depends on the change in E$\{u'(c_2)\}$. With $u''' = 0$, there is no change, since T_j enters u' linearly. With $u''' > 0$, an increase in σ_j raises E$\{u'(c_2)\}$ and hence causes c_1 to fall. The introduction of risk can be thought of as holding constant E(T) = $(1+r)b$ but changing the discount rate R used on E(T).[5] The change in R with the introduction of risk changes the net effect of bonds plus taxes, $(1+r)b/(1+r) - E(T)/(1+R) = (1+r)b/(1+r) - (1+r)b/(1+R)$, from zero to negative. Hence, with risk, $(1+r)/(1+R) > 1$ and therefore $R < r$, just the opposite of the Keynesian argument quoted above.

9.3 Liquidity Constraints

". . . the government lends to them at its borrowing rate of interest, an option not otherwise available in the credit market" Tobin (1980).

Many argue that current aggregate demand is less than otherwise because borrowers suffer liquidity constraints and cannot borrow to the extent they would like. Liquidity constraints in this book arise from the fact that lenders view collecting on the loans as costly or even impossible in some states of the world. All such difficulties are referred to as "default."

Certainly in the Great Depression or in severe recessions a substantial number of people have little or no remaining non-human capital on which they can borrow, or more generally people can face very unattractive terms for further borrowing. The suggestion is often made that government could borrow at its relatively low rate and relend to such people, or more generally act as an intermediary. However, this argument fails to take into account that private borrowers face difficulties because of the possibility of default on their loans. If government acts as an intermediary, but does not change the rules on borrowers' defaulting, then it can be shown that (a) for government intermediation to have an effect it must take over the loan market, or somehow make government loans the marginal loans, (b) such an effect arises through a sort of free-rider behavior, and (c) such an effect reduces aggregate demand rather than raising it, as modeled here.

While not considered here, government can always change rules on the states in which private default is permitted, but this is entirely separable from whether it also acts as an intermediary. Changes in default rules may or may not increase aggregate demand. For example, changes designed to spur aggregate demand may reduce allocative efficiency and wealth and thus reduce demand. Abstracting from efficiency questions, changes that "favor" borrowers over lenders will have a net effect similar to a distribution effect, perhaps small and uncertain in sign. One type of change in default rules is a permanent shift in the economic rules of the game. This must be distinguished from changes that remove the "dead hand of the past" without changing future rules. For example, it might have been beneficial for legislation in 1933 to reduce the nominal value of all contractual debt to adjust for the price declines since 1929. If one of the problems of the Depression was that the economy was caught in a "debt-deflation" process as described by Irving Fisher, such legislation would have had the effect of increasing endowments and aggregate demand. This issue is ignored in what follows.

Equilibrium with the Possibility of Default

Two individuals, A and B, trade with each other. $\bar{c}_{1,A}$ and $\bar{c}_{1,B}$ are not stochastic but $\bar{c}_{2,A}$ and $\bar{c}_{2,B}$ are. Suppose that, in equilibrium, A borrows from B in period 1 to finance $c_{1,A} > \bar{c}_{1,A}$. Expected utility is

$$E(U_A) = E\{u_A(\bar{c}_{1,A} + b^*)\}$$
$$+ \{1/(1+\delta_A)\} E[u_A\{\bar{c}_{2,A} - (1+r^*)b^* + D\}]$$

$$E(U_B) = E\{u_B(\bar{c}_{1,B} - b^*)\}$$
$$+ \{1/(1+\delta_B)\} E[u_B\{\bar{c}_{2,B} + (1+r^*)b^* - D\}], \qquad (9.14)$$

where r^* is the contractual real rate of interest on default-possible bonds b^* and D is the amount by which A defaults on his/her payments to B. The rules governing D are taken as exogenous. Choice of b^* determines $c_{1,A}$ since $c_{1,A} = \bar{c}_{1,A} + b^*$. Since $\bar{c}_{1,A}$, $\bar{c}_{1,B}$ are certain, first-order conditions are

$$dE(U_A)/db^* = u'_A(\bar{c}_{1,A} + b^*) - \{1/(1+\delta_A)\}$$
$$\times E[u'_A\{\bar{c}_{2,A} - (1+r^*)b^* + D\}(1+r^* - dD/db^*)]$$
$$= 0 \qquad (9.15)$$

$$dE(U_B)/db^* = -u'_B(\bar{c}_{1,B} - b^*) + \{1/(1+\delta_B)\}$$
$$\times E[u'_B\{\bar{c}_{2,B} + (1+r^*)b^* - D\}(1+r^* - dD/db^*)]$$
$$= 0 \qquad (9.16)$$

Let the equilibrium $b^* = b^{*\prime}$ and the equilibrium contractual real rate be $r^{*\prime}$, found from solving (9.15) and (9.16) simultaneously.

The default provisions raise current aggregate demand over what it would be without such provisions at the same $r^{*\prime}$ and hence increase the equilibrium $r^{*\prime}$. (This is true with $u'' < 0$ and $u''' > 0$.)[6]

In general, both sides of the loan market *ex ante* favor well-tailored default rules as opposed to a rule under which non-payment can never occur. Under very many systems, $dD/db^* > 0$ and both sides of the market must take this into account as in the marginal conditions (9.15) and (9.16).

Government-Guaranteed Loans

Government can guarantee that it will not default. Rather than explore government intermediation through the case where government borrows at a lower than private rate and relends to some private people, this chapter follows Niehans (1978) and explores liquidity constraints by supposing that the government guarantees private borrowing in certain ways. Suppose that, for any b^*, A can default exactly the same as before in any state of nature, or $D(b^*)$ and dD/db^* are unaffected by guarantees. However, in some states the guarantees affect the defaulted payments received by B, or affect $D_B(b^*)$ and make $D_B < D$.

The key to the analysis is that any difference $D - D_B$ is made up by the government, and $D - D_B$ must be financed by extra taxes. Suppose that these extra taxes fall on B. Then $T_B = D - D_B$, and the sum of default and taxes is $D_B + T_B = D$. Thus, A's first-order condition remains (9.15) but B's becomes

$$dE(U_B)/db^* = -u_B'(\bar{c}_{1,B} - b^*) + 1/(1+\delta_B)$$

$$E[u_B'\{\bar{c}_{2,B} + (1+r^*)b^* - D_B - T_B\}(1+r^* - dD_B/db^* - dT_B/db^*)]$$

$$= 0. \tag{9.17}$$

A number of cases are of interest. First, suppose that B fully takes account of the relationship between T_B and b^*. Then, since $D_B + T_B = D$, $dD_B/db^* + dT_B/db^* = dD/db^*$, (9.16) and (9.17) are identical, and the government guarantee program leaves the equilibrium $b^{*\prime}$ and $r^{*\prime}$ unchanged. B is no more willing to lend than before because he/she sees through the veil of government guarantees and realizes that any gains made because of less default are exactly offset by higher taxes, giving a zero net gain.

When there are multiple lenders, an effect can arise through a free-rider problem. B knows that lending one more dollar to A, in any state where A defaults, will increase A's default by dD/db, raise the defaulted amount to B by $dD_B/db < dD/db$ and raise taxes in default by dT/db. However, some of these extra taxes may well be levied on other lenders. If dT/db is split evenly over n lenders, then B views $dT_B/db = (dT/db)/n$ and $d(D_B + T_B)/db = dD_B/db - (dT/db)/n$ which approaches dD_B/db as $n \to \infty$. Hence, with many lenders, each ignores dT/db and focuses only on $dD_B/db < dD/db$.

This free-rider problem may not arise. (a) Lenders have an incentive to form a "lenders' cartel" to internalize the problem, and conceivably could induce government to regulate the cartel. (b) Alternatively, the loan guarantees may be viewed as infra-marginal, as discussed below. In any case, note that government-induced free riding will be beneficial here just in case the default rules are poorly drawn and in a way that can be offset by free riding.

Second, suppose that B does not recognize the relationship T_B and b^*, but the guarantees are infra-marginal, in the sense that the last dollar borrowed has no government guarantee. Thus, B views $dT_B/db^* = 0$ and this is true at the margin, so again (9.16) and (9.17) yield the same solution, since $dD_B/db^* = dD/db^*$.

This case is not at all implausible. In this simple model, the temporal sequence of government and private loans makes no difference, so effectively any private unguaranteed loan made is the marginal loan. The guarantees affect behavior only in two ways. (a) The government could guarantee all loans; the government in effect becomes the only borrower facing private lenders. (b) The government can guarantee only X percent of the loans and try to make this X percent marginal to what would have been lent anyway. This is not easy to do; it is akin to using tax incentives to increase investment while trying to give tax breaks only on marginal investments. This case might occur if, for example, the economy is in an unexpectedly severe recession and guarantees are unexpectedly offered. However, if these guarantees are foreseen, the unguaranteed loans remain the marginal ones, even if made temporally before the guaranteed loans, and the guarantees have no effect.

One complication in this second case is that the lenders may not demand r^* on the guaranteed infra-marginal loans, but accept a smaller r (even though these loans are just as risky in the aggregate once T_B is taken into account). This would be in effect a transfer from B to A of $r^* - r$ per infra-marginal dollar lent, raising $c_{1,A}$ and reducing $c_{1,B}$. Assume that these distribution effects net to zero.

Third, if B ignores the relationship between T and b^*, with the guarantees not infra-marginal, then the guarantees actually reduce current aggregate demand. At $r^{*'}$, the guarantees do not affect A's supply of bonds but raise B's demand for them, corresponding to a fall in $c_{1,B}$ and thus in aggregate demand. The fall in current aggregate demand occurs because government guarantees work by stimulating lending at $r^{*\prime}$ and hence reducing the lenders' demand for current consumption, rather than by shifting borrowers' demand for loans.

9.4 Non-Lump-Sum Taxes

Sections 9.2 and 9.3 assumed lump-sum taxes. However, it is often argued that consideration of non-lump-sum taxes improves the case for viewing government bonds as net wealth. Three such arguments are discussed below.

Tobin (1980, p. 59) supposes a case where ". . . current lump-sum transfer payments or per capita tax credits are financed by debt issues to be serviced, at least in part, by future wealth taxes. Few of us would doubt that the combination induces some substitution against saving . . ." and thus an increase in current aggregate demand.

It is well known that variations in marginal tax rates affect inter-temporal decisions, and of course use of such taxes may be made in connection with bond financing. However, this connection is not necessary; variations in marginal tax rates can be used for stabilization policy even if bond financing is never used, and bond financing does not imply use of non-lump-sum taxes. The connection is a distraction, as discussed below.

A second argument is the fact that marginal tax rates will "generally induce tax-reducing behavior" (Tobin, 1980, p. 58); in other words, you may be able to avoid paying the taxes implicit in the bond transfer made to you. For the economy as a whole, however, this argument is fallacious. In the aggregate, a given amount of taxes must be paid to redeem the bonds issued, and tax-reducing behavior is necessarily met by an increase in tax rates. In addition, tax-reducing behavior leads to deadweight loss that reduces welfare and current aggregate demand.

A third argument is related but depends on uncertainty. If the marginal tax rate on income is raised, after-tax income's "variance is reduced by the increase in tax rate" (Tobin, 1980, p. 60), and the individual raises his current demand. This implicitly assumes that when income is low, taxes will be low since the tax rate is constant. On the aggregate level, total taxes are constant in order to pay off the bonds, and hence when income is lower than average the tax rate is higher. However, variance for the individual might be reduced if disturbances are not perfectly correlated across individuals. This leads to a discussion of "diversification through the tax system." There is no presumption, however, that an increase in existing marginal tax rates would improve welfare.

Effect of an Increase in Future Tax Rates

A simple example illustrates how an increase in the future marginal tax rate stimulates current aggregate demand, a well-known result. However, it also makes clear that this result in no way depends on bond financing.

Suppose that there is only one individual (or many identical individuals). Let the government give the individual b $1 bonds this period and redeem them through a sales tax on next period's consumption that raises $b(1+r)$ dollars. Then, the individual's tax is $T = tc_2 = (1+r)b$ and the tax rate is $t = b(1+r)/c_2$. Note that while the individual may take t as parametric, from the government's point of view t is an endogenous variable that in particular rises as he/she reduces c_2 in order to try to save on taxes; the amount of taxes is independent of the individual's tax-reducing behavior and equals $(1+r)b$. This t will raise the intertemporal relative price of c_2 in terms of c_1. At the initial equilibrium r', current aggregate demand rises. Thus, r must rise to return the system to equilibrium. Hence, in this case the effect of tax-shifting behavior is indeed to raise current aggregate demand, just as Tobin argues.

This is not at all surprising. It is precisely the well-known rationale for, say, varying investment tax credits intertemporally for stabilization purposes.

It is important to note that the bond transfer is in principle quite independent of the tax-rate rise and its effects on current aggregate demand. For example, suppose no bond transfers are made, but let period 2 taxes equal $t_0 + tc_2$. If tax credits say were used to set t_0 equal to the $-b(1+r)$ from the previous example with t as before, then the same results as above hold. In the first case, b bonds were issued in the current period and t for the next period was set so that the effect on wealth was zero but there was a substitution effect against c_2 and in favor of c_1. In the second case, no bonds are involved but t_0 and t are chosen to cause a zero effect on wealth and the same substitution effect as before in favor of c_1.

It might be argued, however, that when b bonds have already been issued, necessarily t rises. This is not so; the government could change the intercept of next period's tax schedule by, for example, reducing everyone's standard deduction or failing to raise it to offset the effects of inflation.

Tax-Reducing Behavior

Tax-reducing behavior seems to mitigate some of the harm of taxes for the individual. However, at the aggregate level the taxes have to be paid and tax-reducing behavior increases welfare loss. This can be illustrated in connection with the Barro argument about intergenerational linkages. Tobin (1980, p. 59) writes that marginal tax rates

> may also induce substitution in favor of leisure and other uses of time that escape the scrutiny of the tax collector. Anticipating such substitution by his heirs, a Barro model parent will know that to maintain her heirs' utilities, it is unnecessary to maintain their endowments against expected increases in wage taxes. Substitutions will do part of the job, so the parent may in good conscience consume herself some of the fruits of her tax reductions.

The heir's budget constraint is $\alpha b(1 + r) + \pi + (w/P)(1 - t)N - c \leqslant 0$, where α is the fraction of the parent's transfer b that is passed along with interest to the heir, π is the non-labor income ("profits") from the business sector, w/P is the real wage rate, N is the amount of labor the heir supplies, and t is now the marginal tax rate on wage income. Equilibrium requires the government to choose t to set $tNw/P = b(1 + r)$. Hence, if the heir is to be able to consume the same consumption/leisure bundle with and without the government's bond-transfer/tax strategy, the parent

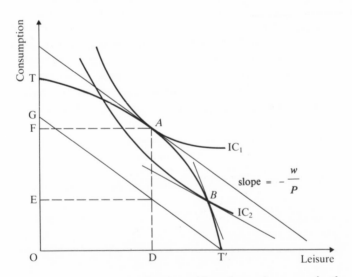

Figure 9.3   The reduction in welfare due to increases in the
marginal tax rate

must set $\alpha = 1$. Further, if the heir tries to reduce his tax bill by reducing N, t will simply rise to keep tNw/P constant.

In figure 9.3, in the absence of taxation the heir trades off leisure for consumption along the leisure–consumption transformation function TT' at point A, his/her optimum. (TT' arises from a standard production function with diminishing marginal physical product, combined with a total amount of time per period T'; reading to the left from T' along the horizontal axis gives the labor input to the production process.) Supplying DT' labor earns OE, and with $\pi = $ EF, he/she consumes OF. In the absence of taxes, T'G and the tangent line through A are parallel and differ by $\pi = $ EF. When bonds are issued and taxation imposed, a parental transfer of $b(1+r)$ allows the heir still to pick any point on TT'. However, with the tax rate t, the marginal rate of transformation is $-w/P$ while the marginal rate of substitution is $-(1-t)w/P$, and rather than A an inferior point such as B is picked. Indeed, the more that tax-reducing behavior reduces Nw/P, the larger is t and the greater the wedge between the MRT and MRS.[7]

In consequence, the parent would have to transfer more than $b(1+r)$ in order to make up for both the amount of future taxes the heir must pay and the welfare cost of the distortion. Current aggregate demand falls.

Taxes and Stochastic Future Income

Tobin argues that positive marginal tax rates reduce uncertainty and hence increase current aggregate demand: "Taxation of income, wealth or consumption lowers . . . variance." "His future consumption is more secure. He will therefore consume more now . . . variance is . . . reduced by the increase in the tax rate." (Tobin, 1980, p. 60). However, it is a partial equilibrium view that the marginal tax rate is constant so that, when income falls, taxes fall. In a general equilibrium view, when income falls the tax rate rises to keep taxes constant.

As before, continue to suppose a one-person economy, but now let $\bar{c}_2$ be stochastic. The individual wants to maximize

$$E(U) = u(c_1) + \{1/(1+\delta)\}\, E[u\{(1-t)\bar{c}_2 + (1+r)(\bar{c}_1 + b - c_1)\}].$$

The first-order condition is

$$dE(U)/dc_1 = u'(c_1) - \{(1+r)/(1+\delta)\}\, E[u'\{(1-t)\bar{c}_2 + (1+r)(\bar{c}_1 + b - c_1)\}] = 0.$$

If t is set at a level that is expected to yield $T = (1+r)b$, or set so that $t = (1+r)b/E(\bar{c}_2)$, then the individual is indeed better off with $b > 0$ and hence $t > 0$ and he/she will increase c_1 as long as $u''' > 0$. This is because any shortfall of $\bar{c}_2$ below $E(\bar{c}_2)$ gives a net reduction of $(1-t)\{\bar{c}_2 - E(\bar{c}_2)\}$ instead of the full shortfall $\{\bar{c}_2 - E(\bar{c}_2)\}$.

But this does not take account of the fact that taxes must be $T = t\bar{c}_2 = (1+r)b$, whatever $\bar{c}_2$ turns out to be. Hence, when $\bar{c}_2$ falls, t rises. In fact, $(1-t)\bar{c}_2 + b(1+r) = \bar{c}_2$ and the bond/tax strategy has no effect whatsoever provided the individual knows how the tax rate varies.[8]

Diversification of Income Risk

The above example assumes that all (period 2) income variations are perfectly correlated, or arise solely from aggregate disturbances. However, when income disturbances arise from a variety of circumstances that are imperfectly correlated, non-zero marginal tax rates offer the potential for increasing current aggregate demand.

In the more general case, for every individual $c_2 = \bar{c}_2 + b(1+r) - T$, and let $E\{(\bar{c}_2) + b(1+r) - T\} = E(\bar{c}_2)$. The variance of c_2 is $\sigma^2 = \sigma_{\bar{c}}^2 + \sigma_T^2 - 2\,\text{cov}(\bar{c}_2, T)$. When every individual's tax bill is constant, as above, $\sigma^2 = \sigma_{\bar{c}}^2$, or the variances of before- and after-tax income are equal. This was because t rises with declines in $\bar{c}_2$. But consider a case where it turns out that t is (almost) constant. Suppose that there are n individuals, and suppose to start that $\bar{c}_{2,i}$ is orthogonal to $\bar{c}_{2,j}$ for all $j \neq i$, with $E(\bar{c}_{2,j}) = E(\bar{c}_2)$ for all j. Then, $t = nb(1+r)/\Sigma\bar{c}_{2,j}$, and $1/t = \Sigma\bar{c}_{2,j}/nb(1+r)$; hence, $E(1/t) = \Sigma E(\bar{c}_{2,j})/nb(1+r)$, while $\text{var}(1/t) = \sigma_{\bar{c}}^2/nb^2(1+r)^2$; as $n \to \infty$, $\text{var}(1/t) \to 0$ and $t \to$ a constant. In this case, fluctuations in $\bar{c}_{2,j}$ are not accompanied by changes in t, so the variance of after-tax income is reduced by having $t > 0$. Thus, every individual is *ex ante* better off, and if $u''' > 0$, current aggregate demand rises. t can remain constant when $\bar{c}_{2,j}$ is low because everyone else's $\bar{c}_2$ is approximately average so there is no need to raise (noticeably) t.

This system-wide gain arises because every j has his/her future income dependent on one security $\bar{c}_{2,j}$ in a world where there are n securities whose returns are uncorrelated. In effect, the tax system allows the individual some diversification over the n securities, as discussed in modern portfolio theory to which Tobin contributed so greatly.

If these securities can be traded costlessly in private markets, everyone would diversify, and with $n \to \infty$, $\sigma^2 \to 0$ or the variance of period 2 consumption goes to zero. In other words, private action would eliminate the income variance. (Indeed, in the absence of private action, government should set $t = 1$ to reduce σ^2 to zero in this model.)

A number of points should be made. First, any net benefits derived by diversification through the tax system are of course independent of use of

b, that is, can be derived if $b = 0$ at all times. Second, marginal tax rates are a costly way of achieving diversification because they distort choices (as seen in the example around figure 9.3).

Third, such a government plan, if beneficial, supposes that private transactions costs are so high that private arrangements could not do the job equally well (or better, by avoiding use of marginal tax rates). If all $\bar{c}_2$ is from securities, there is surely no need for "diversification through tax rates" in the United States and other countries with highly developed capital markets. However, it is quite difficult to diversify away the specific risk of labor income, especially when human wealth is a large fraction of an individual's portfolio. In such a world, a system of marginal tax rates (and perhaps progressive rates combined with an unemployment insurance scheme) may well be an improvement over lump-sum taxes.

Fourth, it is not clear that an increase in tax rates (accompanied by either an increase in b or a decrease in t_0) increases current aggregate demand. Presumably there is an optimum t that balances the gains of diversification against the costs of distortions. No reason has been put forward to suppose at any particular time that t is too low.

9.5 Conclusions

Critiques of the modern Ricardian doctrine often attack the bequest motive, discussed below. Three other criticisms focus first, on the fact that wealth in bonds is certain while the associated taxes are uncertain; second, on the possibility that government bonds might mitigate a liquidity constraint and thus expand current aggregate demand; and, third, on the fact that lump-sum taxes might not be used to finance implied interest and principal payments.

Critique of these Arguments

Section 9.2 shows that uncertain taxes reduce current aggregate demand if $u''' > 0$ as with decreasing absolute risk aversion. Since the total amount of taxes to be collected is given, for every individual who is lucky enough to pay less than his/her share, others must pay more, and this risk is a "bad."

Section 9.3 views liquidity constraints as arising as a rational response to the fact that repayment of loans to private individuals is uncertain, or there may be "default." If government action takes the form of guarantees on these loans, but the rules under which borrowers can default are unchanged, the government will end by raising taxes in some states to cover what would otherwise be defaulted payments. For the system as a whole, there really is no difference, then, between default and guarantees that are met by added taxation. Lenders may not recognize the guarantees' effect on taxes; or each individual lender may try to free-ride on the fact that others will pay a share of the taxes that might be needed to make good the guarantees on loans he/she makes. Even so, guarantees affect the volume of loans only if the marginal loan is guaranteed, perhaps by guaranteeing all loans. Effective government guarantees cause a fall rather than a rise in aggregate demand; borrowers do not want to consume more than before at the initial interest rate while lenders lend more and hence consume less.

Section 9.4 discusses the well-known point that changes in the intertemporal profile of marginal tax rates have real effects. However, there is no necessary connection between bond financing and such changes; either can be used without the other. Marginal tax rates lead to tax-reducing behavior and hence distortions in consumption and production. Given the total resources to be extracted, tax-reducing activities make people worse off ultimately rather than better, contrary to what is often argued.

Marginal tax rates reduce the variance of after-tax income if the rates are constant as income fluctuates. In a case where tax revenues must be constant, the variance of income for the system as a whole is not reduced by bond financing redeemed by marginal tax rates. In a world where variations in individuals' incomes are not perfectly correlated, it is possible that marginal tax rates provide a kind of "diversification through the tax system" that is beneficial. This would occur if diversification through private markets is more costly. Since marginal tax rates also induce distortions, it is not clear that given a particular marginal tax rate an increase in it would be beneficial.

On balance, these arguments are not very persuasive that some positive fraction of government bonds is net wealth.

Critique of Barro's Argument

The modern Ricardian doctrine depends greatly on Barro's (1974) demonstration that under certain conditions the bequest motive will make people act as if they are immortal. Thus, when current lump-sum taxes fall by b but future taxes rise by the present value of b, the infinitely lived individual or the one with the Barro bequest motive does not alter his/her consumption time path because wealth is unchanged.

One weak point in this argument is that many people have no children and for them the Barro bequest motive cannot be operative – the chain is broken. Individuals with children receive a tax cut which they save to pass on to the children who will pay the taxes; those without children increase their consumption, so total current consumption rises (Tobin, 1980, pp. 55–6).

This argument depends on a (perfectly plausible) distribution effect. The current generation is wealthier at the expense of the future generation, and thus raises its consumption demand. The future generation is poorer, and reduces its consumption in all periods. If the future generation is not yet alive, it cannot reduce its current consumption to balance the rise in the present generation's.

Notice that much of the "future" generation may already be alive and at work. A tax cut now that is balanced by a rise in taxes in ten years will involve no future taxes for the childless who die within ten years. These avoided taxes will be paid both by workers who are now young and by those who enter the work force over the ten years. It is only those youngsters who are not presently consuming who will not cut back present consumption in light of this transfer.[9] While the redistribution must increase current consumption demand, the effect will be quite small if future taxes are raised only one year from now, and has its full effect only if none of the people who will pay the future taxes are currently active workers and consumers.

A weakness in the Barro argument with much greater potential significance is that the current generation may have little or no regard for the future generation's well-being. In this case, the government's redistribution is gleefully accepted by the older generation and current aggregate demand rises. The extent of the rise in current aggregate demand depends as above on the degree to which the future generation that suffers is already currently consuming.

The current extent of regulation of parents' behavior towards children, and the number of violations that come to light, suggests that society believes that, while there are many tragic exceptions, the bequest motive in the aggregate works roughly well. This view may be quite wrong, however. If it is, most markets may be yielding suboptimal outcomes. The appropriate solution is deep intervention in the family, not piecemeal intervention in individual markets. In other words, if the bequest motive works rather badly, the issue is much graver than tax-bond policy, and on second-best grounds the appropriate tax-bond policy is not at all obvious.

NOTES

1 See Barro (1974, 1976), Buchanan (1976), Feldstein (1976), Tobin (1980). Chan (1983) has an analysis of the uncertainty effects of taxation that is similar to that

of section 9.2; he also discusses the "insurance" aspects of taxation (as Barro briefly does) along lines similar to section 9.4, but explicitly does not allow for changes in leisure–labor decisions as is done below. Barsky *et al.* (1986) consider the effects of current transfers financed by increased future marginal tax rates; they do not take into account, however, the points in section 9.4 regarding changes in the leisure–labor choice or the independence of "insurance" aspects of marginal tax rates from the level of government debt (a point Chan notes).

2 See Taylor (1971), David and Scadding (1974), Kochin (1974), Yawitz and Meyer (1976), Barro (1978), Buiter and Tobin (1979), Tanner (1979a,b), Feldstein (1982), Seater (1982), Kormendi (1983), Reid (1985).

3 Subscripts referring to individuals are dropped where their omission will not lead to confusion.

4 Clearly, the effect on c_2 depends on how σ_j affects $E\{u'(c_2)\}$. $u'' < 0$ means that u' is a downward-sloping function of c_2. If derivatives higher than u'' are zero (quadratic utility), then T_j enters u' linearly and σ_j does not enter $E(u')$. With $u''' \neq 0$, σ_j enters $E(u')$, and enters positively if $u''' > 0$. If all derivatives above the third are zero, higher moments of T_j do not enter $E(u')$. If the latter derivatives are non-zero, then the net effect of an increase in σ_j depends on these derivatives and how higher moments of T_j vary with σ_j.

Suppose that, for every j, $u(c_2)$ is the quadratic $u(c_2) = ac_2 - ec_2^2 (a, e > 0)$. Then, $du(c_2)/dc_1 = a(dc_2/dc_1) - 2ec_2(dc_2/dc_1) = -a(1+r) + 2ec_2(1+r)$ since $dc_2/dc_1 = -(1+r)$. c_2 depends on T and hence $E\{du(c_2)/dc_1\}$ depends on $E(T)$. However, since c_2 depends linearly on T, σ_T^2 does not enter $E\{du(c_2)/dc_1\}$. With the cubic $u(c_2) = ac_2 - ec_2^2 + fc_2^3 (a, e, f > 0)$, $u''' > 0$ and $du(c_2)/dc_1 = -a(1+r) + 2ec_2(1+r) - 3fc_2^2(1+r)$. The term c_2^2 means $du(c_2)/dc_1$ depends both on T and T^2, and hence σ_T^2 enters $E\{du(c_2)/dc_1\}$. Further, $dE\{du(c_2)/dc_1\}/d\sigma_T^2 < 0$ since $f > 0$ and a rise in σ_T^2 reduces c_1.

5 This seems to be the approach Tobin has in mind, but this is less appropriate than the dynamic stochastic programming approach of, for example, Samuelson (1969) and Merton (1969).

6 An increase in D, with dD/db^* held constant, reduces $E[u_A'\{\bar{c}_{2,A} - (1+r^*)b^* + D\}]$. Thus, A wants to borrow and consume more in the first period to reduce u_A' similarly in (9.15). The rise in D conversely raises $E[u_B'\{\bar{c}_{2,B} + (1+r^*)b^* - D\}]$ and thus B wants to consume less and lend more in period 1. With $u''' > 0$ and δ_A not too dissimilar to δ_B, the net effect can be shown to be a rise in current aggregate demand.

A rise in dD/db^*, with D held constant, leads to a fall in $E[u_A'\{\bar{c}_{2,A} - (1+r^*)b^* + D\}(1+r^* - dD/db^*)]$, and hence an increase in A's borrowing and consumption in period 1. The rise in dD/db^* leads B to want to consume more and lend less in period 1. Thus, a rise in dD/db^* unambiguously leads to an increase in current aggregate demand and the equilibrium $r^{*'}$.

Combining the two experiments, it is clear that a rise in both the level and height of the function relating D to b^* causes an increase in aggregate demand and a rise in the equilibrium $r^{*'}$.

7 As is well known from public finance, whatever is the tax rate t, the heir would

be better off with right-angle indifference curves, since this would result in no alteration of quantities chosen compared with the case of $t = 0$.

8 If $\bar{c}_2$ is not an endowment but is produced, the existence of (stochastic) marginal tax rates will induce distortions and hence reduce welfare. This will reduce current aggregate demand.

9 The future generation will spread its cut in wealth over more years, since it lives longer (on average) than the current generation. Hence, redistribution among the generations, even if all future members are currently at work, will raise current aggregate demand.

Part V

MEASURING CHANGES IN REAL WEALTH

10

Problems in Measuring Changes in Real Wealth

The work in chapters 3–9 allows comparison of theoretically appropriate measures of changes in wealth with types of wealth measures in general use both in empirical and theoretical work in monetary economics and macro-economics. This chapter shows that measures commonly used have sub-stantial qualitative and quantitative defects.

In deciding on a measure of wealth to use in empirical work, one approach is to try to reach general agreement on what wealth is, and then use a constructed series that corresponds as well as possible to the agreed definition. Another approach is to develop a model and find the effect on wealth of various changes, as was done above at length for variations in the general level of prices and interest rates. In this second approach, an appropriate wealth measure faithfully mirrors the effects on wealth implied by theory. Some measures of wealth may be robust over a wide range of theories; whichever theory is true, the measure will move in the appropriate way even though the way it moves may vary across theories. Other measures will be valid only in very particular worlds. For example, representing the contribution of the non-financial firm sector to real wealth by its physical capital stock is not generally adequate, though this is sometimes done in simple models and some textbook descriptions. Again, the interest-rate-induced effect on wealth was zero under some assump-tions in chapter 8, negative under others. A given measure might move correctly with a change in interest rates if one set of assumptions is valid but not if another is true.

The general point is that the theory will imply the properties of a correct measure of wealth to use on the assumption that the theory is valid. Any suggested proxy for wealth movements must be investigated under the assumptions of the theory to see if the proxy behaves well.

Chapter 3 developed the Hicksian equivalent variation approach for measuring changes in wealth when all decision-makers are price-takers and quantity-setters, in the sense that they believe that they can buy or sell as much as they like at current and expected prices, wages and interest rates. Chapters 4–7 then used this apparatus to investigate the price-induced effect on wealth, and chapters 8 and 9 used it to discuss the interest-rate-induced effect on wealth. Changes in the real wage rate, expected inflation and other economic variables also cause changes in wealth that can be investigated in the same way, as they are below.

Wealth variables play an important and seemingly growing role in macroeconometric models, particularly the larger, Keynesian models. Very often the measure of wealth used is real non-human wealth, frequently defined as a sum of various measures of financial wealth in real terms. Variations in measured real non-human wealth will very often be quite different from the true effects on wealth found in previous chapters, as section 10.1 discusses.

This difference has three causes. First, empirical wealth measures often neglect changes in the real present value of future tax liabilities. Thus, as chapter 5 showed, the price-induced effect on wealth will be zero if future government money stocks are unit elastic with respect to changes in the current price level; this effect of changes in future money supplies on wealth works through changes in future taxes. By contrast, many of the usual empirical measures will give the conventional real balance effect $-M_0^s/P_0^2$ even when this is quite inappropriate. Further, to the extent that government bonds are not part of net wealth, inclusion of these bonds in financial wealth but omission of future tax liabilities that offset these bonds leads to a misstatement of the price-induced effect on wealth, as is well known. Both of these problems are discussed below.

Second, some changes in non-human wealth are accompanied by simultaneous, offsetting or partially offsetting changes in human wealth. In an example discussed below, an increase in the current real wage rate w/P reduces the real value of banks and non-financial firms, and measured non-human wealth declines. The same rise in w/P, however, increases the human wealth of those supplying labor services to business, evaluated at initial labor supplies. If the demand and supply of labor services are equal, the two effects cancel – they are a distribution effect[1] and as such are typically ignored in monetary economics. Unless appropriate measures of both human and non-human wealth are included, there can be systematic and substantial misstatements of changes in wealth. It is not easy, however, to construct a series on changes in real human wealth because these must be evaluated at initial labor supplies, as in chapter 3. Instead, constructed measures are likely also to include induced changes in amounts of labor services supplied and thus mismeasure real human wealth.

Third, commonly used measures of non-human wealth look at changes in the real present value of household income flows but not at changes in the real present value of household expenditures. As an example, an increase in the general level of interest rates will give a change in wealth of zero under two sets of conditions discussed in chapter 8. The real value of businesses will decline, however, or real non-human wealth will fall. When focusing on the change in real non-human wealth in this case, what is neglected is that the real present value of household planned consumption and use of money services, less the real present value of planned sales of labor services, will also fall, and by such an amount that the net interest-rate-induced effect on wealth is zero. Thus, looking only at the fall in non-human wealth will systematically and substantially overstate the fall in real wealth in this and similar cases. Even if real human wealth (appropriately measured) is included along with real non-human wealth, the interest-rate-induced effect on wealth will still be mismeasured because the change in the real present value of household planned consumption and use of money services will be overlooked. In fact, inclusion of real non-human wealth aggravates the measured fall rather than reducing it, as section 10.1 discusses.

These are not irremediable problems. For example, if real non-human wealth is used as an explanatory variable, one can attempt to purge it of false movements induced say by changes in interest rates. Rather, the point is that empirical wealth variables should not be used uncritically. It might well be good practice to adjust measured changes in wealth to try to make them conform to theoretically appropriate changes.

This does not mean that past work using wealth variables is incorrect or useless. It does mean that changes in wealth in such work cannot in general be interpreted as Hicksian changes in wealth, the type of wealth changes familiar from microeconomics, and it is theoretically unclear what these measured changes in wealth mean. Further, this suggests that there might be some gain from doing empirical work with measures of wealth constructed such that their changes are supposed to correspond to Hicksian changes in wealth. Section 10.2 briefly explores some of the costs of using mismeasured changes in wealth as currently done.

Theoretical discussions of changes in wealth often encounter the same difficulties discussed for empirical measures. Many theoretical discussions do not find an explicit Hicksian equivalent variation as in chapters 3–8 but instead work with a definition of real non-human wealth and ask how this varies in response to a particular change (Patinkin, 1965, 1969, 1972; Saving, 1970, 1971). For some experiments this approach gives the correct results. An example is the price-induced effect on wealth when government money is constant over time. For other experiments, the approach gives quite erroneous results. An example is a change in the general level of interest rates. Another example of erroneous results is the price-induced effect on wealth in the case where future money supplies are unit elastic relative to the current price level but the definition used for real non-human wealth does not include the present value of real future taxes. In this case, the measured change in real non-human wealth is the conventional real balance effect $-M_0^s/P_0^2$, while the true change is zero, as chapter 5 discusses. Thus, much theoretical work falls into the same difficulties as empirical work. Further, the theoretical work leads empirical researchers down the wrong garden path.

Work in previous chapters provides a theoretically appropriate measure of changes in real non-human wealth for the worlds discussed in those chapters, as section 10.1 argues. Even this measure, however, gives mistaken information about total changes in wealth in many instances. As discussed above, this is because using only real non-human wealth neglects both real human wealth and also planned household expenditures on consumption and money services. Different definitions of non-human wealth will give poorer performance, but even the best will be quite inadequate unless the empirical worker systematically makes adjustments to current measured observable wealth series.

Mismeasurement of changes in wealth has two serious effects for the economic observer, as section 10.2 discusses. First, the observer will frequently see measured movements in wealth that do not correspond to true changes in wealth. Given estimated slope coefficients on the effect of wealth changes on say consumption, the observer will sometimes predict consumption changes that are not there, because measured wealth varies when there is not a true change in wealth. And sometimes the observer will miss changes in consumption because true changes in wealth are overlooked. Second, the error in the measurement of true changes in wealth is correlated with other explanatory variables such as changes in interest rates and real wage rates. The estimated slope coefficients will generally be biased and inconsistent.

This book explores effects on wealth on the assumption that all decision-makers are price-takers and quantity-setters, viewing themselves as able to buy and sell as much as they want at current and expected prices, wage rates, and interest rates. Very many macro models make this assumption. Other very influential views, however, see decision-makers as facing not only the price vector, their endowments and their utility or profit functions, but also quantity constraints (Clower, 1965; Leijonhufvud, 1968). Section 10.3 discusses some implications of this approach for measuring changes in wealth. Most familiarly, perhaps, many IS–LM macro models view workers as constrained to sell fewer hours of labor services than they would like, with price-taking, quantity-setting behavior in all other markets, subject to this labor-market constraint. As might be expected, true wealth effects in a model with quantity-constrained behavior are different from those developed in previous chapters. The apparatus used here can be straightforwardly adapted to handle the implications of quantity constraints for changes in wealth. Quantity constraints do not remove the problems associated with usual empirical measures of wealth and indeed introduce difficulties of their own.

10.1 True Versus Measured Changes in Wealth

This section discusses some of the differences between true changes in wealth, such as those discussed in previous chapters, and measured changes in wealth, focusing on measures of non-human wealth. Often these differences are very large. The strategy in this section is to look first at appropriately measured changes in real non-human wealth and to show how even these differ substantially from the true, total Hicksian changes in wealth. While real non-human wealth is appropriately measured in these experiments, focusing only on this variable neglects other important influences on wealth and thus leads to mismeasurement of changes in wealth. The section's next step is to show how mismeasurement of real non-human wealth can further affect the discrepancy between changes in real non-human wealth and true Hicksian changes in wealth.

From chapters 5 and 6, the household sector's budget constraint can be written, assuming non-satiation, as

$$
\sum_{t=0}^{\infty} \frac{\Pi(1+\Delta P/P)}{\Pi(1+i)} \, C_t^d + \sum_{t=1}^{\infty} \frac{\Pi(1+\Delta P/P)}{\Pi(1+i)} \, i_t \mathrm{mh}_t
$$

$$
+ \sum_{t=1}^{\infty} \frac{\Pi(1+\Delta P/P)}{\Pi(1+i)} \, (i_t - r_t) \, \overline{\mathrm{mh}}_t - \sum_{t=0}^{\infty} \frac{w_0 \Pi(1+\Delta w/w)}{P_0 \Pi(1+i)} \, N_t^s
$$

$$
= \sum_{t=0}^{\infty} \frac{\mathrm{Div}_t}{P_0 \Pi(1+i)} + \sum_{t=0}^{\infty} \frac{\mathrm{div}_t}{P_0 \Pi(1+i)}
$$

$$
- \sum_{t=0}^{\infty} \frac{T_t}{P_0 \Pi(1+i)} + \frac{\mathrm{MH}_0}{P_0} + \frac{\overline{\mathrm{MH}}_0}{P_0} + \frac{V_0}{P_0} - \frac{\overline{B}_0}{P_0} + \frac{r_0 \overline{\mathrm{MH}}_0}{P_0}
$$

$$
= \frac{E_0}{P_0} + \frac{\mathrm{EB}_0}{P_0} - \frac{\mathrm{PVT}_0}{P_0} + \frac{\mathrm{MH}_0}{P_0} + \frac{\overline{\mathrm{MH}}_0}{P_0} + \frac{V_0}{P_0} - \frac{\overline{B}_0}{P_0} + \frac{r_0 \overline{\mathrm{MH}}_0}{P_0},
$$

$$(10.1)$$

where E_0 is the value at time 0 of equity in non-financial firms, EB_0 the equity in banks, and PVT_0 the present value of taxation,

$$E_0 \equiv \sum_{t=0}^{\infty} \frac{\mathrm{Div}}{\Pi(1+i)}, \ \mathrm{EB}_0 \equiv \sum_{t=0}^{\infty} \frac{\mathrm{div}}{\Pi(1+i)}, \ \mathrm{PVT}_0 \equiv \sum_{t=0}^{\infty} \frac{T}{\Pi(1+i)}.$$

Using the right-hand side of (10.1), define real non-human wealth at time 0 as

$$\frac{W_{\mathrm{NH},0}}{P_0} \equiv \frac{E_0}{P_0} + \frac{\mathrm{EB}_0}{P_0} - \frac{\mathrm{PVT}_0}{P_0} + \frac{\mathrm{MH}_0}{P_0} + \frac{\overline{\mathrm{MH}_0}}{P_0} + \frac{V_0}{P_0} - \frac{\overline{B}_0}{P_0}$$

$$+ \frac{r_0 \overline{\mathrm{MH}_0}}{P_0}. \tag{10.2}$$

Analogously, from the left-hand side of (10.1), real human wealth $W_{\mathrm{H},0}/P_0$ can be defined as

$$\frac{W_{\mathrm{H},0}}{P_0} \equiv \sum_{t=0}^{\infty} \frac{w_0}{P_0} \frac{\Pi(1+\Delta w/w)}{\Pi(1+i)} N_t^s.$$

Finally, define real wealth devoted to expenditures on consumption and on money services as

$$\frac{W_{\mathrm{EX},0}}{P_0} \equiv \sum_{t=0}^{\infty} \frac{\Pi(1+\Delta P/P)}{\Pi(1+i)} C_t^d + \sum_{t=1}^{\infty} \frac{\Pi(1+\Delta P/P)}{\Pi(1+i)} i_t \mathrm{mh}_t$$

$$+ \sum_{t=1}^{\infty} \frac{\Pi(1+\Delta P/P)}{\Pi(1+i)} (i_t - r_t) \overline{\mathrm{mh}}_t.$$

Another way of thinking of the household sector's budget constraint is that

$$\frac{W_{\mathrm{NH}}}{P} + \frac{W_{\mathrm{H}}}{P} - \frac{W_{\mathrm{EX}}}{P}$$

must equal zero, assuming non-satiation. The effect on wealth of any change is then found by differentiating this expression with consumption, labor supply and households' planned use of money services held constant in real terms, as chapter 3 discussed in detail.

The large majority of work using wealth variables focuses on real non-human wealth, W_{NH}/P. Some work also uses real human wealth W_{H}/P, particularly work using permanent income, which is sometimes thought of as an attempt to measure W_{NH}/P and W_{H}/P as a sum. Apparently all empirical work and most theoretical work[2] neglects W_{EX}/P.

Real Non-Human Wealth

Begin with a consideration of real non-human wealth W_{NH}/P, as defined in (10.2). $E_0/P_0 + EB_0/P_0$ is the real value of equities in the economy and $MH_0/P_0 + V_0/P_0$ the real value of government debt held by the household sector, adopting the convention of referring to money as debt (see chapter 5's discussion). The usual definitions of real wealth used in empirical work are somewhat similar to $W_{NH,0}/P_0$. They typically neglect the tax term PVT_0/P_0, however, and also neglect $r_0 MH_0/P_0$, and sometimes use total government money M_0^s in place of MH_0.

Empirical work typically uses a time series on W_{NH} or W_{NH}/P. W_{NH}/P can change over time for a number of reasons; in some cases the true, total change in wealth and the change in W_{NH}/P are equal, but in other cases they are not. Think of W_{NH}/P as changing for five reasons. First, observable endogenous variables such as P, w/P, and i can change and thus alter say E/P, the real value of equity in non-financial firms. Second, unobservable variables such as $\Delta P/P$, $\Delta \tilde{P}/P$, $\Delta w/w$, $\Delta \tilde{w}/w$ can alter; whether these variables are endogenous depends on the strategy of the modeler. Third, exogenous variables such as the state of technology, the productivity of factors, and so forth can change, or expectations about future values of these can change; denote all of these by α. Fourth, policy variables such as M^s and V can alter, as can the sequence $\{T_t\}$. Fifth, the passage of time can alter W_{NH}/P. For example, suppose P, i, etc. do not change but Div is growing over time. Then period after period E/P is rising. This is an increase in wealth that then plays a role in explaining increased demand for consumption and for money services, etc. Thinking of the length of the period as small, so that variations in W_{NH}/P can be approximated as in continuous time,

$$
\begin{aligned}
d(W_{NH}/P) ={}& \frac{\partial (W_{NH}/P)}{\partial P} \, dP + \frac{\partial (W_{NH}/P)}{\partial (w/P)} \, d(w/P) \\[2mm]
&+ \frac{\partial (W_{NH}/P)}{\partial i} \, di + \frac{\partial (W_{NH}/P)}{\partial (\Delta P/P)} \, d(\Delta P/P) + \dots \\[2mm]
&+ \frac{\partial (W_{NH}/P)}{\partial \alpha} \, d\alpha + \frac{\partial (W_{NH}/P)}{\partial MH} \, dMH \\[2mm]
&+ \frac{\partial (W_{NH}/P)}{\partial V} \, dV + \frac{\partial (W_{NH}/P)}{\partial T_0} \, dT_0 \\[2mm]
&+ \frac{\partial (W_{NH}/P)}{\partial T_1} \, dT_1 + \dots + \frac{\partial (W_{NH}/P)}{\partial t} \, dt. \quad (10.3)
\end{aligned}
$$

Some but not all of these movements in W_{NH}/P are genuine Hicksian changes in real wealth, $d(W/P)$. In other words, relying on changes in W_{NH}/P to measure appropriately defined changes in real wealth $d(W/P)$ leads to error in many (though not all) cases.

The Effect on Wealth of a Rise in the Real Wage Rate

To see this, look again at the household sector budget constraint in terms of the current-period price level P_0, which says that

$$\sum_{t=0}^{\infty} \frac{w_0}{P_0} \frac{\Pi(1+\Delta w/w)}{\Pi(1+i)} N_t^s - \sum_{t=0}^{\infty} \frac{w_0}{P_0} \frac{\Pi(1+\Delta \widetilde{w}/w)}{\Pi(1+i)} (N_t^d + \overline{N}_t^d)$$

$$+ \sum_{t=0}^{\infty} \frac{\Pi(1+\Delta \widetilde{P}/P)}{\Pi(1+i)} (Y_t^s - \Delta K_t^d) - \sum_{t=0}^{\infty} \frac{\Pi(1+\Delta P/P)}{\Pi(1+i)} C_t^d$$

$$- \sum_{t=0}^{\infty} \frac{\Pi(1+\Delta \widetilde{P}/P)}{\Pi(1+i)} G_t$$

$$- \sum_{t=1}^{\infty} \frac{\Pi(1+\Delta P/P)}{\Pi(1+i)} (i_t \, \mathrm{mh}_t + (i_t - r_t)\overline{\mathrm{mh}}_t)$$

$$- \sum_{t=1}^{\infty} \frac{\Pi(1+\Delta \widetilde{P}/P)}{\Pi(1+i)} (i_t \, \mathrm{mb}_t + (i_t - r_t)\overline{\mathrm{mb}}_t)$$

$$+ \sum_{t=1}^{\infty} \frac{\Pi(1+\Delta \widetilde{P}/P)}{\Pi(1+i)} \{(i_t - r_t)\overline{m}_t - i_t m_t^F\} + \sum_{t=1}^{\infty} \frac{i_t M_t^s}{P_0 \Pi(1+i)}$$

$$(10.4)$$

must equal zero, assuming non-satiation. This is just (10.1) with appropriate substitution for E_0/P_0, PVT_0/P_0 and other variables.

As an example of the differences between a measured change in real non-human wealth and the appropriate Hicksian measure, let the real wage rate w/P rise. From (10.4), the Hicksian (w/P)-induced change in wealth is

$$\sum_{t=0}^{\infty} \frac{\Pi(1+\Delta w/w)}{\Pi(1+i)} N_t^s - \sum_{t=0}^{\infty} \frac{\Pi(1+\Delta \widetilde{w}/w)}{\Pi(1+i)} (N_t^d + \overline{N}_t^d). \qquad (10.5)$$

The sign of expression (10.5) is ambiguous without further assumptions. Suppose, then, that expectations are consistent, so that $\Delta w/w = \Delta \widetilde{w}/w$ for all t, and that planned quantities are market clearing, or

$N_t^d + \overline{N}_t^d = N_t^s$ for all t. Then (10.5) equals zero and there is a zero (w/P)-induced change in wealth. The rise in w/P has simply redistributed wealth among members of the household sector, from those who are firm-owners to those who are labor suppliers. Firm-owners must pay more for labor services and are thus less wealthy, while suppliers of labor services are more wealthy, with the changes in wealth canceling. There are, of course, substitution effects both on the demand and supply sides of the market, but there is no aggregate effect on wealth.

Now look at how the rise in w/P affects real non-human wealth W_{NH}/P. This is the approach taken in almost all theoretical discussions of wealth changes in monetary economics and macroeconomics, though the most common disturbance considered is a rise in the price level, not the real wage rate. The effect of a rise in w/P on W_{NH}/P works through changing E/P and EB/P, where

$$\frac{E}{P} = \sum \frac{\text{Div}}{P_0 \Pi(1+i)} = \sum_{t=0}^{\infty} \frac{\widetilde{P}_t(Y_t^s - \Delta K_t^d)}{P_0 \Pi(1+i)}$$

$$- \sum_{t=0}^{\infty} \frac{w_0}{P_0} \frac{\Pi(1+\Delta\widetilde{w}/w)}{\Pi(1+i)} N_t + \sum_{t=0}^{\infty} \frac{\Delta MB_t}{P_0 \Pi(1+i)}$$

$$- \sum_{t=0}^{\infty} \frac{\Delta\overline{MB}_t}{P_0 \Pi(1+i)} + \sum_{t=0}^{\infty} \frac{r_t \overline{MB}_t}{P_0 \Pi(1+i)}$$

and

$$\frac{EB}{P} = \sum \frac{\text{div}}{P_0 \Pi(1+i)} = \sum_{t=1}^{\infty} \frac{(i_t - r_t)\overline{M}_t}{P_0 \Pi(1+i)} - \sum_{t=1}^{\infty} \frac{iMF_t}{P_0 \Pi(1+i)}$$

$$- \sum_{t=0}^{\infty} \frac{w_0}{P_0} \frac{\Pi(1+\Delta\widetilde{w}/w)}{\Pi(1+i)} \overline{N}_t^d + \frac{MF_0}{P_0} + \frac{\overline{B}_0}{P_0} + \frac{\overline{V}_0}{P_0}$$

$$- \frac{\overline{M}_0}{P_0} - r_0 \frac{\overline{M}_0}{P_0}.$$

Then,

$$\frac{\partial(E/P)}{\partial(w/P)} = - \sum \frac{\Pi(1+\Delta\widetilde{w}/w)}{\Pi(1+i)} N_t^d$$

and

$$\frac{\partial(EB/P)}{\partial(w/P)} = - \sum \frac{\Pi(1+\Delta\widetilde{w}/w)}{\Pi(1+i)} \overline{N}_t^d,$$

and thus

$$\frac{\partial(W_{\mathrm{NH}}/P)}{\partial(w/P)} = - \sum_{t=0}^{\infty} \frac{\Pi(1+\Delta\tilde{w}/w)}{\Pi(1+i)} (N_t^d + \overline{N}_t^d) < 0. \tag{10.6}$$

While the true (w/P)-induced change in real wealth is $\partial(W/P)/\partial(w/P) = 0$ in the case examined above, it is clearly negative here as measured by $\partial(W_{\mathrm{NH}}/P)/\partial(w/P)$. What the change in W_{NH}/P neglects is the increase in the wealth of those who supply labor.

The true (w/P)-induced change in wealth $\partial(W/P)/\partial(w/P)$ is zero under the assumptions $\Delta\tilde{w}/w = \Delta w/w$ and $N^d + \overline{N}^d = N^s$ for all t, but the measurement error in using $\partial(W_{\mathrm{NH}}/P)/\partial(w/P)$ is independent of these assumptions. Subtract (10.6) from (10.5) to get the difference between the true and the measured change in wealth, or the measurement error, as

$$\frac{\partial(W/P)}{\partial(w/P)} - \frac{\partial(W_{\mathrm{NH}}/P)}{\partial(w/P)} = \sum \frac{\Pi(1+\Delta w/w)}{\Pi(1+i)} N_t^s$$

$$- \sum \frac{\Pi(1+\Delta\tilde{w}/w)}{\Pi(1+i)} (N_t^d + \overline{N}_t^d)$$

$$+ \sum \frac{\Pi(1+\Delta\tilde{w}/w)}{\Pi(1+i)} (N_t^d + \overline{N}_t^d)$$

$$= \sum \frac{\Pi(1+\Delta w/w)}{\Pi(1+i)} N_t^s.$$

Thus, the change in wealth is understated by

$$\sum \frac{\Pi(1+\Delta w/w)}{\Pi(1+i)} N_t^s,$$

whether or not $\Delta w/w = \Delta\tilde{w}/w$ and $N^s = N^d + \overline{N}^d$ for all t. The mismeasurement does not depend here on the value of $d(W/P)$. The impact of a rise in w/P on W_{NH}/P mismeasures the true effect on wealth by approximately 100 percent, using dW_{NH}/P as the base.

Similarly, a rise in expected wage inflation, with $\Delta w/w = \Delta\tilde{w}/w$, leads to a zero Hicksian effect on wealth if $N^s = N^d + \overline{N}^d$ for all t. Whether or not labor markets are clearing, the change in W_{NH}/P overstates the true changes by

$$\sum \frac{w_0}{P_0} \frac{\partial\Pi(1+\Delta w/w)/\partial(\Delta w/w)}{\Pi(1+i)} N_t^s.$$

*The Effect on Real Human Wealth of a Rise in the Real Wage
Rate*

Expanding the concept of real wealth to include real human wealth improves the theoretical performance, but has some serious practical problems.

Recalling the definition of real human wealth as

$$\frac{W_{H,0}}{P_0} \equiv \sum \frac{w_0}{P_0} \frac{\Pi(1 + \Delta w/w)}{\Pi(1 + i)} N_t^s,$$

the (w/P)-induced change in $W_{H,0}/P_0$ is

$$\frac{\partial(W_{H,0}/P_0)}{\partial(w/P)} = \sum \frac{\Pi(1 + \Delta w/w)}{\Pi(1 + i)} N_t^s,$$

when N_t^s is held constant for all t in finding a Hicksian equivalent variation. Clearly, $\partial(W/P)/\partial(w/P) = \partial(W_{NH}/P)/\partial(w/P) + \partial(W_H/P)/\partial(w/P)$, since W_{EX}/P is unchanged as a result of being evaluated for given time paths of consumption and money services. If both human and nonhuman wealth are included, the change in their sum gives the true change in wealth when w/P changes. As can be seen, this is also true when $\Delta w/w$ and $\Delta \tilde{w}/w$ vary together.

Empirical work that uses W_{NH}/P and omits W_H/P reduces the overall explanatory power of equations. Omissions of W_H/P will not affect the bias or consistency of estimated slope coefficients, if W_H/P is orthogonal to include explanatory variables. In this instance, changes in W_{NH}/P and W_H/P are clearly not uncorrelated, and omission of W_H/P can then lead to biased and inconsistent estimates of the coefficient on W_{NH}/P. Similarly, if w/P is used as an explanatory variable, it is not orthogonal to changes in W_H/P. If the theory says that variations in w/P contribute relatively little to changes in W_{NH}/P, the problem of bias and inconsistency is relatively unimportant. But then one test of the theory is precisely whether this restriction on co-movements of w/P and W_{NH}/P holds empirically.

The above example of a change in w/P suggests using the sum of $W_{NH}/P + W_H/P$ as the wealth variable. There is a grave difficulty, however, in using a time series on W_H/P. The change $\partial(W_H/P)/\partial(w/P)$ was found by holding constant N_t^s for all t. In fact, N_t^s will generally vary with w/P and these changes in N_t^s are induced effects rather than part of a change in wealth (see chapter 3, section 3.1). Hence any series on W_H/P would have to have such (w/P)-induced changes in N_t^s removed. The same sort of adjustment would have to be made for variations in $\Delta w/w$, $\Delta \tilde{w}/w$.

Even supposing that an appropriately adjusted series on W_H/P is constructed, inclusion of both forms of wealth does not solve the measurement problem when other variables beyond w/P change, for example, the general level of interest rates.

An Increase in the General Level of Interest Rates

From chapter 8, if either all individuals are immortal and currently alive, or all currently alive individuals leave utility-maximizing bequests,[3] then the aggregate interest-rate-induced effect on wealth is zero under the assumptions that all price and wage expectations are consistent and market-clearing quantities are planned for every period. The induced change in real non-human wealth W_{NH}/P is negative, however. Take, for example, the effect on the real equity of non-financial firms, E/P, of a rise in the interest rate where all i are equal,

$$\frac{\partial(E/P)}{\partial i} = \frac{\partial \Sigma(\text{Div}_t/P_0(1+i)^t)}{\partial i}$$

$$= \sum_{t=0}^{\infty} (-t) \frac{\text{Div}_t}{P_0(1+i)^{t+1}},$$

which is negative if $\text{Div}_t > 0$ for all t (and in general negative for the economy[4] even if $\text{Div}_t < 0$ for some t).

The zero interest-rate-induced effect on wealth arises through negative and equal changes on both sides of the household sector budget constraint (10.1). The right-hand side falls because the real value of equities (net of the real present value of taxation) declines. The left-hand side declines because the real present value of household planned consumption and use of monetary services goes down by more than the real present value of planned labor services supplied (W_H/P).

On the left-hand side of (10.1) W_H/P falls, but since W_H/P enters negatively the left-hand side rises through this channel. In other words, the decline in the real present value of households' planned consumption and use of money services must be even greater than if W_H/P had not changed. This means that $\partial(W_{NH}/P)/\partial i + \partial(W_H/P)/\partial i < \partial(W_{NH}/P)/\partial i < 0$. While $\partial(W_{NH}/P)/\partial i$ overstates the fall in wealth, adding in $\partial(W_H/P)/\partial i$ increases the overstatement.

Thus, using the sum of (appropriately measured) real human and non-human wealth solves the mismeasurement problem for changes in some variables such as w/P, but increases the problem for changes in others such as i.

In the case of a rise in the general level of interest rates, the fall in real non-human wealth overstates the true change in wealth by 100 percent when the true change is zero and the measured change is used as the base.

Not only is the error large in relative size, it can also be shown to be large in absolute value.[5]

Even when there are no bequests, the measured fall in W_{NH}/P due to a rise in i overstates the Hicksian effect on the wealth of those currently alive. This is so because focusing on the fall in W_{NH}/P takes no account of the reduction in the present value of the excess of the economy's consumption expenditures and use of money services less wage income, the left-hand side of (10.1).

Suppose that changes in the series $W_{NH}/P + W_H/P - W_{EX}/P$ are used to measure changes in real wealth, with changes in W_H/P and W_{EX}/P measured at initial values of N_t^s, C_t^d, etc. The measured interest-rate-induced effect is then zero, since the variable is identical with that in the household sector budget constraint (10.4). For this experiment, then, the measured changes in $W_{NH}/P + W_H/P - W_{EX}/P$ give the correct answer.

The problem, however, is that movements in W_{EX}/P must be purged of any changes due to induced variations in consumption demand or use of money services. This is similar to how changes in W_H/P have to be purged of induced movements in labor supply. In fact if the budget constraint holds every time it is observed, $W_{NH}/P + W_H/P - W_{EX}/P = 0$ at all times, and changes in the three real wealth components (W_{NH}/P, W_H/P, W_{EX}/P) due to changes in any variable are exactly offset by induced changes in quantities demanded and supplied. The unpurged measure W_{EX}/P cannot possibly say anything about changes in wealth.

Measuring Price-Induced Changes in Wealth

A major question in monetary economics has been the role of price-induced changes in wealth, and measuring such changes is taken up separately here. Virtually always, the approach in past work has been to focus on induced changes in W_{NH}/P. Though this is incorrect as a general procedure for evaluating changes in wealth, it gives the correct answer for the price-induced effect on wealth if the correct definition of W_{NH}/P is used. This is because the change in P does not affect the left-hand side of (10.1), that is, does not affect W_H/P or W_{EX}/P.

Consider the effects on real wealth and on real non-human wealth of a rise in P_0, or $\partial(W/P)/\partial P$ and $\partial(W_{NH}/P)/\partial P$. To begin, assume that M^s is constant over time at its initial value M_0^s, as in chapter 4, and assume that banks pay a competitive rate of interest on their deposits. Then, as chapters 4–7 showed, the price-induced effect on wealth, neglecting initial-condition effects,[6] is simply the conventional real balance effect, $-M_0^s/P_0^2$. In this case,

$$\frac{\partial(W_{\mathrm{NH}}/P)}{\partial P} = \frac{\partial\{(E_0+\mathrm{EB}_0-\mathrm{PVT}_0+\mathrm{MH}_0+\overline{\mathrm{MH}}_0+V_0-\overline{B}_0+r_0\overline{\mathrm{MH}}_0)/P_0\}}{\partial P_0}$$

$$= -\frac{M_0^s}{P_0^2}. \tag{10.7}$$

One way to check on this is to notice that the left-hand side of (10.1) does not change with P_0, so any Hicksian price-induced effect on wealth comes from the change in the right-hand side W_{NH}/P, or is the middle partial derivative in (10.7). However, from chapter 4 the effect is $-M_0^s/P_0^2$. Thus, the two measures of the change in wealth are the same. This equality is somewhat fortuitous, however, in the sense that slight changes in the definition of W_{NH}/P, or omission from it of unobserved variables, will remove the equivalence, as shown in two examples.

First, suppose real non-human wealth is redefined as

$$\frac{W'_{\mathrm{NH}}}{P_0} \equiv \frac{E_0}{P_0} + \frac{\mathrm{EB}_0}{P_0} + \frac{M_0^s}{P_0} + \frac{V_0}{P_0}.$$

If one simply starts out to define real non-human wealth, W'_{NH}/P looks quite reasonable. By comparison to W_{NH} in (10.2), W'_{NH} neglects PVT_0, $\overline{B}_0$, and (less importantly) $r_0\overline{\mathrm{MH}}_0$, and uses M_0^s instead of MH_0. Then, neglecting the impact on wealth of initial-condition effects,

$$\frac{\partial(W'_{\mathrm{NH}}/P_0)}{\partial P_0} = \frac{\partial(E_0/P_0)}{\partial P_0} + \frac{\partial(\mathrm{EB}_0/P_0)}{\partial P_0} - \frac{M_0^s}{P_0^2} - \frac{V_0}{P_0^2}$$

$$= -\frac{\mathrm{MB}_0}{P_0^2} - \frac{\overline{\mathrm{MB}}_0}{P_0^2} - r_0\frac{\overline{\mathrm{MB}}_0}{P_0^2}$$

$$- \frac{\mathrm{MF}_0 + \overline{B}_0 + \overline{V}_0 - \overline{M}_0 - r_0\overline{M}_0}{P_0^2} - \frac{M_0^s}{P_0^2}$$

$$- \frac{V_0}{P_0^2} < -\frac{M_0^s}{P_0^2},$$

assuming that $\overline{M}_0 + r_0\overline{M}_0 \doteq \mathrm{MF}_0 + \overline{B}_0 + \overline{V}_0$. $\partial(W'_{\mathrm{NH}}/P)/\partial P$ mismeasures the change in real wealth (a) by neglecting future taxes and the fact that V_0 adds equally to their present value, (b) by neglecting the household sector's debts $\overline{B}_0$ to banks while including fully the value of bank equity EB_0 that includes these debts, and (c) by including M_0^s without realizing that MB_0 and MF_0 (which together with MH_0 equal M_0^s) are already entered through E_0 and EB_0.

Second, consider omitting PVT/P from W_{NH}/P. It is difficult to estimate time series on PVT. But suppose that aside from PVT, W'_{NH}/P is fixed to correspond to W_{NH}/P. Suppose that real non-human wealth is redefined as

$$\frac{W''_{\text{NH}}}{P_0} \equiv \frac{E_0}{P_0} + \frac{\text{EB}_0}{P_0} + \frac{\text{MH}_0}{P_0} + \frac{\overline{\text{MH}_0}}{P_0} + \frac{V_0}{P_0} - \frac{\overline{B}_0}{P_0} + \frac{r_0\overline{\text{MH}_0}}{P_0}$$

and the government money stock is still constant at M_0^s. Then,

$$\frac{\partial(W''_{\text{NH}}/P_0)}{\partial P_0} = -\frac{M_0^s}{P_0^2} - \frac{V_0 + \overline{V}_0}{P_0^2} = -\frac{M_0^s}{P_0^2} - \frac{V_0^s}{P_0^2} < -\frac{M_0^s}{P_0^2}.$$

This result follows from the fact that W''_{NH}/P_0 differs from W_{NH}/P_0 in omitting $-\text{PVT}/P$ and that, in this case, a rise in P gives

$$\frac{\partial(-\text{PVT}/P)}{\partial P} = +\frac{V_0^s}{P_0^2};$$

in words, a rise in the price level that reduces the real value of the private sector's holdings of government bonds equally reduces the real present value of its tax liabilities.

Suppose, then, that W''_{NH} is fixed up by subtracting V_0^s/P_0, to give

$$\frac{W'''_{\text{NH}}}{P_0} = \frac{E_0}{P_0} + \frac{\text{EB}_0}{P_0} + \frac{\text{MH}_0}{P_0} + \frac{\overline{\text{MH}_0}}{P_0} + \frac{V_0}{P_0} - \frac{\overline{B}_0}{P_0} + \frac{r_0\overline{\text{MH}_0}}{P_0} - \frac{V_0^s}{P_0}.$$

Then,

$$\frac{\partial(W'''_{\text{NH}}/P_0)}{\partial P_0} = -\frac{M_0^s}{P_0^2}.$$

It appears that the W'''_{NH}/P definition at least gives the correct price-induced effect on wealth, even if it must necessarily be incorrect for changes in i, w/P, etc. as discussed above. Suppose, however, that instead of future government money stocks all equaling M_0^s, these are unit elastic relative to P_0. From chapters 5 and 6, neglecting initial-condition effects, the true effect on wealth of a rise in P_0 is zero. But from the definition of real non-human wealth in W'''_{NH}/P, the change is $-M_0^s/P_0^2$, and is clearly in error. It goes wrong by neglecting the fact that government is going to raise its future issuance of money in response to the rise in P_0 and that therefore future taxes will not be as large as if future money issuance did not respond to the rise in prices.

The Effects of Technical Progress and Economic Growth

Consider two final experiments. Suppose a rise in α is taken as technical progress, so that for given N_t^d, K_t^d, output rises or $\partial Y_t^s/\partial\alpha > 0$. The Hicksian effect on wealth is

$$\sum \frac{\Pi(1+\Delta\widetilde{P}/P)}{\Pi(1+i)} \; \frac{\partial Y_t^s}{\partial\alpha} > 0$$

(see chapter 3). The change in W_{NH}/P is the same. (For both measures of wealth changes, the α-induced changes in N^d and K^d result in a marginal physical product, the value of which just equals marginal factor cost. Hence, these induced changes in factor use contribute nothing to the true change in wealth or the change in W_{NH}/P.) As a second experiment, let time move ahead one period and suppose that all prices and quantities are as expected, though they are not necessarily the same as in period 0. Then for example, from the definition of E/P in (10.1), unless dividends are constant over time, one sees $E_1/P_1 \neq E_0/P_0$. Indeed, if wealth accumulation is going on over time so dividends are growing, $E_1/P_1 > E_0/P_0$ on average (or in expected value terms), and this increases W/P by an equal amount. This change is a Hicksian effect on wealth that helps to explain the change from C_0^d to C_1^d, from mh$_0$ to mh$_1$, etc., similarly to the discussion in chapter 3, section 3.1.

Thus, in these last two experiments, the true changes in real wealth equal the changes in real non-human wealth.

What to Do

The following section argues that mismeasurement of changes in wealth leads to substantial problems. Here the question is what to do about this mismeasurement. There seems no way around having to purge movements in measured wealth of changes that do not correspond to true changes in wealth.

One approach is to continue to use real non-human wealth, though with care to see that it is measured as closely as possible to the right-hand side of (10.1). The key difficulty here is to find a good proxy for the present value of tax liabilities.

Some movements in W_{NH}/P will correspond one-to-one with true changes in wealth. Other changes in W_{NH}/P, however, will occur when the true changes in wealth are zero. Examples are changes in i and w/P (under some assumptions spelled out above). One could use econometric techniques to estimate those movements in W_{NH}/P that are due to changes in i and w/P, etc., and purge the W_{NH}/P series of such changes. Notice that theory has to be invoked to say which parts of movements in W_{NH}/P should be purged. For example, in ridding changes in W_{NH}/P of effects due to changes in i, the extent of purging depends on whether utility-maximizing bequests are assumed, and whether consistent price and wage expectations and market-clearing quantities are assumed.

An alternative is to develop a measure of human wealth and work with the sum $W_H/P + W_{NH}/P$. Some changes in W_H/P and W_{NH}/P that correspond to a true change in wealth of zero net out in the sum $W_H/P + W_{NH}/P$. An example is a change in the real wage rate. As discussed above, however, this presumes that W_H/P is adjusted to remove from it the induced changes in labor supplies in each period due to changes in w/P, i, etc., since Hicksian wealth effects are measured at unchanged labor supplies.

In other cases, such as an increase in i, the changes in W_{NH}/P and W_H/P both mismeasure the true change in wealth and the mismeasurements reinforce each other. Thus, use of $W_H/P + W_{NH}/P$ does not remove the problem of having to purge the measured real wealth series of variations that do not correspond to true variations in real wealth.

10.2 Mismeasurement, Forecasting, and Estimation

The consequences of mismeasuring changes in wealth are not trivial. Even if the true coefficients are (somehow) known, mismeasurement leads to erroneous forecasts and to misinterpretations of observed events. Mismeasurement also leads to biased and inconsistent estimates of slope coefficients, generally both for the wealth variable and for other explanatory variables.

Technical Progress

To see these points, consider a simple example. Suppose that there is technical progress or α rises. As seen above, this causes a true increase in real wealth and a measured increase in real non-human wealth that are equal – $d(W_{NH}/P) = d(W/P)$ in this case. For simplicity, assume that in response the only endogenous price variable that changes to reequilibrate the system is the real wage rate, w/P, due to a change in w. (More realistically, P, i, and many other variables are likely to have to change, but these are neglected to make the discussion here more straightforward.) The problem is to analyze the magnitude of the α-induced change in w/P.

Look first at the business sector and neglect for simplicity the response of the banking sector's labor demand. The change in the quantity of labor demanded is

$$\frac{dN^d}{d\alpha} = \frac{\partial N^d}{\partial \alpha} + \frac{\partial N^d}{\partial (w/P)} \frac{d(w/P)}{d\alpha}.$$

$\partial N^d/\partial \alpha > 0$ shows the assumption that technical progress by itself raises the quantity of labor demanded by shifting the demand curve for labor to the right; $\partial N^d / \partial (w/P) < 0$ shows that a rise in w/P by itself reduces N^d through an upward movement along the labor demand curve; and $d(w/P)/d\alpha$ is the α-induced change in the equilibrium w/P. $d(w/P)/d\alpha$ is the endogenous change in w/P that must be solved for.

Finding $d(w/P)/d\alpha$ requires the labor supply function. The change in N^s is

$$\frac{dN^s}{d\alpha} = \frac{\partial N^s}{\partial (W/P)} \frac{\partial (W/P)}{\partial \alpha} + \frac{\partial N^s}{\partial (w/P)} \frac{d(w/P)}{d\alpha}. \tag{10.8}$$

$\partial N^s / \partial (W/P)$ is the effect on N^s of an increase in wealth and $\partial (W/P)/\partial \alpha$ is the α-induced change in real wealth discussed above in section 10.1. Their product gives the shift in the labor supply curve. $\partial N^s / \partial (w/P) > 0$ is the substitution effect on N^s due to a rise in the real wage rate w/P and describes upward movement along the labor supply curve.[7] Combining the changes in N^d and N^s, the change in the real wage rate is

$$\frac{d(w/P)}{d\alpha} = \frac{(\partial N^s / \partial (W/P)) (\partial (W/P)/\partial \alpha) - \partial N^d / \partial \alpha}{\partial N^d / \partial (w/P) - \partial N^s / \partial (w/P)} > 0$$

if leisure is a superior good, so $\partial N^s / \partial (W/P) < 0$. In words, technical progress raises the demand for labor while the rise in real wealth from technical progress reduces labor supply if leisure is a superior good, and hence the real wage rate must unambiguously rise. (The effect on equilibrium employment depends on whether the labor-demand or labor-supply shift dominates.)

Now examine how the change in N^s is analyzed if W_{NH}/P is used. That is, assume $\partial Y_t^s / \partial \alpha$ and $d(w/P)/d\alpha$ are known and ask how N^s will change. To begin, assume that the true slope coefficients, $\partial N^s / \partial (w/P)$ and $\partial N^s / \partial (W/P)$, are known. The problem is that the change in wealth is mismeasured because $\partial (W_{NH}/P)/\partial (w/P) < 0$, while the true change in wealth due to a rise in the real wage rate is $\partial (W/P)/\partial (w/P) = 0$ from section 10.1 above (under assumptions discussed there). Hence, the true change in wealth is simply that due to technical progress, $\partial (W/P)/\partial \alpha$; however, the measured change adds the effect due to w/P rising, $\{\partial (W_{NH}/P)/\partial (w/P)\} \{d(w/P)/d\alpha\}$, and sums to $\partial (W/P)/\partial \alpha + \{\partial (W_{NH}/P)/\partial (w/P)\} \{d(w/P)/d\alpha\}$.

Thus the predicted change in N^s (evaluated using W_{NH}/P) is

$$\left. \frac{dN^s}{d\alpha} \right|_{W_{NH}/P} = \frac{\partial N^s}{\partial (W/P)} \left\{ \frac{\partial (W/P)}{\partial \alpha} + \frac{\partial (W_{NH}/P)}{\partial (w/P)} \frac{d(w/P)}{d\alpha} \right\}$$

$$+ \frac{\partial N^s}{\partial (w/P)} \frac{d(w/P)}{d\alpha}.$$

Subtracting this from the true change in N^s gives

$$- \frac{\partial N^s}{\partial (W/P)} \frac{\partial (W_{NH}/P)}{\partial (w/P)} \frac{d(w/P)}{d\alpha} < 0.$$

In other words, using W_{NH}/P leads to an understatement of the increase in wealth and thus the prediction of a smaller leftward shift (or fall) in labor supply than actually occurs.[8] The reason for this understatement is that the (w/P)-induced increase in the wealth of labor suppliers is overlooked. While firm-owners are poorer through the rise in w/P, and this is captured in the change in W_{NH}/P, the increase in human wealth is overlooked. Neglecting distribution effects between those who own shares in firms and those who do not, the change in w/P induces no change in wealth and hence by itself no shift in the labor supply curve to the right that conflicts with the leftward shift in labor supply caused by the α-induced increase in wealth.

Using the mismeasured change in real wealth would lead the forecaster who expects a rise in α to predict a smaller reduction in labor supply than actually occurs (or perhaps even to forecast a rise). Looking back, the observer committed to the wealth measure W_{NH}/P would then have to rationalize this forecast error. He/she might do so by postulating either another influence that was overlooked and is now in the error term, or by including an additional explanatory variable that happened to be correlated with the error, or he/she might adjust the initial slope coefficients that are, by assumption, the true values. All of these attempts are misguided and all have their more or less obvious costs.

An Increase in Consumption Demand

The problems caused by mismeasurement can be seen in yet another way by supposing, just for illustration, that N^s is insensitive through substitution effects to the interest rate, or $\partial N^s/\partial i = 0$. Further, suppose the economy is one of the worlds analyzed in chapter 8 where the interest-rate-induced effect on wealth is zero. Then, let current consumption demand C^d autonomously rise with no associated autonomous change in N^s. Let the implied increase in aggregate demand be choked off by a rise in i, $di/dC^d > 0$, with no change in any other endogenous variable, in particular, no change in w/P. What is the effect of this experiment on the quantity of labor supplied? The change in N^s is zero, or

$$\frac{dN^s}{dC^d} = \frac{\partial N^s}{\partial i} \frac{di}{dC^d} + \frac{\partial N^s}{\partial (W/P)} \frac{\partial (W/P)}{\partial i} \frac{di}{dC^d} = 0,$$

since by assumption the substitution effect $\partial N^s/\partial i = 0$, and, following chapter 8, the true interest-rate-induced effect on wealth $(\partial(W/P)/\partial i)$ is also assumed zero (as before, $\partial N^s/\partial(W/P)$ is the slope coefficient showing the change in N^s due to the rise in real wealth).

However, the measured change in non-human wealth is $\partial(W_{NH}/P)/\partial i < 0$. The prediction here is a rise in N^s, or

$$\frac{dN^s}{dC^d} = \frac{\partial N^s}{\partial(W/P)} \frac{\partial(W_{NH}/P)}{\partial i} \frac{di}{dC^d} > 0,$$

since $\partial N^s/\partial(W/P) < 0$ under the assumption that leisure is a superior good.

Biased and Inconsistent Estimates of Slope Coefficients

It is highly unlikely that the observer will in fact find the true slope coefficients when mismeasured changes in wealth are used. This is not the place for an econometric discussion, but the nature of some of the problems can be sketched in an intuitive way. By using dW_{NH}/P instead of dW/P, the observer is using a proxy that is not perfectly correlated with the true variable. Alternatively, the problem can be thought of as measuring the true variable with error, and what would seem to be substantial error in light of the above examples of changes in the real wage rate or the general level of interest rates. If a measurement error, uncorrelated with any other variable, were the only problem, the estimated slope coefficient on the changes in real wealth would simply be biased toward zero.

There is a further problem, however, because the error in wealth measurement is correlated both with the true change in wealth and with some other explanatory variables. In the example of the effect of technical progress on the quantity of labor supplied, the change in the real wage rate was correlated with the measurement error in the change in wealth. In the example of an autonomous increase in consumption demand, the measurement error in the change in wealth was correlated with the interest rate movement. This is a very general phenomenon and can be expected to cause problems for changes in i, P, w/P, $\Delta P/P$, $\Delta w/w$, etc., when these and real non-human wealth are included as explanatory variables. Because of this correlation, the estimated slope coefficients on these variables generally will be biased and inconsistent.

As an example, consider

$$Y = a + bX + cdW + u, \tag{10.9}$$

where the equation is a behavioral function, Y the change in a choice variable, X a vector of endogenous and exogenous explanatory variables, dW the time rate of change in wealth and u a random term. b is a vector conformable to X, with the b-element for say w/P showing substitution effects. u is likely to be correlated with elements of X (and even dW). For example, a realization $u > 0$ may affect the equilibrium w/P. Thus, some appropriate econometric techniques such as instrumental variables may have to be used to get around this problem. The problem would be to choose instruments that are highly correlated with X but uncorrelated with u. The difficulty of main concern in this subsection, however, is that the proxy dW' is used for dW,

$$\mathrm{d}W' = \mathrm{d}W + e,$$

where e is measurement error. Substituting into (10.9) gives

$$\begin{aligned}
Y &= a + bX + c(\mathrm{d}W' - e) + u \\
&= a + bX + c\mathrm{d}W' + (u - ce) \\
&= a + bX + c\mathrm{d}W' + u',
\end{aligned} \tag{10.10}$$

where $u' = u - ce$.

As shown above, e is generally correlated with both dW' and X. Hence, estimates of b and c are generally biased and inconsistent, with even the directions of bias generally unknown. Furthermore, instrumental variables or other techniques designed to get around the correlation of X and u cannot be expected in general to solve as a by-product the problem of the correlation of e with X and dW'. The measurement error in dW must be explicitly addressed.

10.3 Measuring Wealth Effects When There Are Quantity Constraints

Throughout this book, the assumption has been that decision-makers are price-takers and quantity-setters (save in the case of government regulation of interest rates on bank deposits in chapter 7). As a quantity-setter, each believes he/she can buy or sell as much as desired at going prices; wealth effects have been measured under the assumption that each acts on this belief. At every point, the discussion has pointed out the implications for the measurement of the induced effects on wealth of whether price and wage expectations are consistent and planned demands and supplies would lead to market clearing. Even when current markets are not in equilibrium, however, the various effects on wealth have been measured under the assumption that people act as though they could carry out their planned transactions. Much of macro and monetary economics uses the assumption of decision-makers as price-takers and quantity-setters, and discussions in this genre can be comfortable with this book's analysis.

Examples are Patinkin (1956, 1965, 1969, 1972), Gurley and Shaw (1960), Pesek and Saving (1967), Bailey (1971) in his discussions that assume full employment, and authors using market-clearing rational expectations models.

Other influential macro discussions use a distinctly different assumption. They assume that decision-makers face not only price vectors, endowments and their utility or profit functions, but also quantity constraints on amounts they may buy and sell (Clower, 1965; Leijonhufvud, 1968). In essence, "false trading" (in Hicks's phrase) goes on at prices where at least some markets do not clear, and this may happen some or most of the time in various economists' views. The Hicksian practice of evaluating wealth effects for people who act as price-takers with no additional quantity constraints, even if the set of prices does not give market clearing, basically assumes that false trading never actually occurs or that false trading is a relatively trivial problem most of the time. False trading can be unimportant either because it occurs infrequently, or only to a small extent, or because there is some cheap and fast recontracting mechanism to remove the effect of even large amounts of false trading.

Some economists view quantity constraints as forming a key part of what is distinct about macroeconomics and use the assumption of quantity constraints in much of their reasoning. The quantity-constraint assumption is perhaps most commonly made about the labor market. Here it is assumed that $N^s > N^d$, so that the amount of labor services that workers can actually supply is $N = N^d$, and there is thus aggregate unemployment. Frequently, it is also assumed that all other markets clear subject to this labor market constraint. Two examples are familiar IS–LM analyses. In the first, the nominal wage rate is institutionally fixed above the market-clearing level, with the price level adjusting to put the economy on the labor demand curve at all times at N^d less than the full-employment level. Plugging this level of employment into the economy's production function gives real output and income, with the IS–LM intersection at this level of income implying that all non-labor markets are clearing (subject to the labor constraint). In the second IS–LM example, there is an institutionally fixed real wage rate above the full-employment level, with both nominal wages and prices adjusting to put the economy on the labor demand curve at this real wage rate and at the implied level of employment. The rest of the model works similarly to the fixed nominal wage case, with all markets clearing save that for labor.

Wealth Effects with a Labor-Market Constraint

In such a case, where all non-labor markets clear subject to the labor-market quantity constraint, suppose there is technical progress that not only increases wealth by $\partial(W/P)/\partial\alpha$, but also shifts up the labor demand curve by increasing the marginal physical product of labor. For simplicity, assume the real wage rate does not change, as in the second IS–LM case mentioned above. The initial effect on firms' output in any period is $\partial Y_t^s/\partial\alpha$, which is part of the discounted sum that is the change in real wealth $\partial(W/P)/\partial\alpha$. Since the real wage rate is fixed, the total change in N^d, $dN^d/d\alpha$, is simply the rightward shift of the labor demand curve, $\partial N^d/\partial\alpha$. This change in labor use thus gives a further change in Y^s each period of

$$\frac{\partial Y^s}{\partial N^d}\,\frac{dN^d}{d\alpha}.$$

In every period, the changes in N^d and the consequent change in Y^s raises profits by $P(\partial Y^s/\partial N^d)\,dN^d/d\alpha \ - \ w\,dN^d/d\alpha \ = \ \{P(\partial Y^s/\partial N^d) - w\}$ $dN^d/d\alpha$. If the firms' marginal condition $\partial Y^s/\partial N^d \ - \ w/P \ = \ 0$ holds as assumed, then the further induced change in wealth through firms, beyond $\partial Y^s/\partial\alpha$, is zero. This is the sort of reasoning used repeatedly above, and its application here should be no surprise since firms here are price-takers who rightly assume they can hire and sell as they like at the P, w they take as given.

On the other side of the market, previous chapters evaluated the effect on wealth by holding constant N^s. This was done under the assumption that workers believe they are quantity-setters and can sell as much of their services as they like. Now there is a quantity constraint and they know they can sell only less than they would like. The rise in α partially relaxes this constraint by raising aggregate N^d at the given w/P, or $\partial N^d/\partial\alpha > 0$ and the labor demand curve shifts to the right. When it does so, N rises with $dN = dN^d$. Hence, at least some workers are free to sell more labor than before and they do so. The rise in wealth through this channel is

$$\sum_{t=1}^{\infty} \frac{w_0}{P_0}\,\frac{\Pi(1+\Delta w/w)}{\Pi(1+i)}\,\frac{dN_t^d}{d\alpha} > 0.$$

The difference is that in previous analysis the labor suppliers were price-takers and could set the quantity of labor services they sold. A shift in N^d did not affect their plans unless it induced a price change, for example, in w/P. Here they are quantity constrained and a shift in N^d affects plans directly.[9]

The basic point of this example is very general. Any change that affects a binding-quantity constraint induces a change in wealth. This change in wealth is equal to the effect on wealth of a shift in the constraint multiplied by the induced shift in the constraint.

As another example in the labor market, a rise in i has a zero effect on wealth under certain conditions discussed in chapter 8. The rise in i, however, causes substitution effects away from capital use by firms and thus reduces the demand for labor in future periods, assuming that labor and capital are complements. By making the quantity constraint on employment more stringent, the firms' substitution effects due to a rise in i lead to a negative effect on wealth. Thus, changes in endogenous variables like i as well as in exogenous variables like α can shift quantity constraints and induce changes in wealth.

Implications of Quantity Constraints

A number of points can be made about effects on wealth when there are quantity constraints. First, neither the Hicksian wealth effects that this book focuses on nor the quantity-constrained effects are "right" and others "wrong." The appropriate analysis of effects on wealth depends on the model used and the situation analyzed.

Second, the Hicksian apparatus is quite robust and analysis using it can be generalized to include quantity constraints, as illustrated above, and to include other modifications. The particular results developed in previous chapters are characteristically Hicksian in the sense of being close to those in *Value and Capital*. These results depend on each decision-maker thinking as a price-taker and quantity-setter free to choose quantities, but the basic analytical approach is easily modified to reflect actual institutional arrangements.

Third, usual measures of real non-human wealth will fail to detect the effects on wealth that depend on labor-quantity constraints. This is because these latter effects arise through changes in real human wealth. Suppose, however, that a separate measure of variations in real human wealth accurately tracked changes in wealth arising from variations in labor-quantity constraints. This would still leave many of the problems discussed above regarding mismeasurement of effects on wealth that arise from looking at variations in real non-human wealth, and those that arise from neglecting the expenditures side of the budget constraint. In other words, appropriate analysis of $W_H/P + W_{NH}/P$ would solve the quantity-constraint problems analyzed in this section but would leave many of the problems discussed in the previous sections of this chapter.

For example, suppose w/P rises. An appropriate measure of real human wealth would rise by

$$\sum_{t=0}^{\infty} \frac{\Pi(1+\Delta w/w)}{\Pi(1+i)} N_t + \sum_{t=0}^{\infty} \frac{w_0}{P_0} \frac{\Pi(1+\Delta w/w)}{\Pi(1+i)} \frac{\partial N_t}{\partial(w_0/P_0)},$$

so that the combined real wealth measures $W_{\text{NH}}/P + W_{\text{H}}/P$ would give a change of

$$\left\{ \sum_{t=0}^{\infty} \frac{\Pi(1+\Delta w/w)}{\Pi(1+i)} \, N_t - \sum_{t=0}^{\infty} \frac{\Pi(1+\Delta \widetilde{w}/w)}{\Pi(1+i)} \, (N_t^{\text{d}} + \overline{N}_t^{\text{d}}) \right\}$$

$$+ \left\{ \sum_{t=0}^{\infty} \frac{w_0}{P_0} \, \frac{\Pi(1+\Delta w/w)}{\Pi(1+i)} \, \frac{\partial N_t}{\partial (w_0/P_0)} \right\}.$$

The first set of braces contains the appropriate measure of the Hicksian effect on wealth in the absence of constraints (so $N = N^{\text{s}}$) or when the constraints do not change (and thus $N = N^{\text{d}} + \overline{N}^{\text{d}}$). The second set of braces gives the effect on wealth due to a (w/P)-induced change in the labor constraint. The sum of the two terms in braces is then the correct measure of the true (w/P)-induced effect on wealth. Use of an appropriate real human wealth variable along with some real non-human wealth measures will not, however, capture the effect of changes in i on the present value of planned consumption and use of money services; along the lines of section 10.1, such combined measures will give an inaccurate change in wealth by neglecting W_{EX}/P. Similarly, the use of real human wealth will not suffice in most cases to make correct the measurement of the price-induced effect on wealth if real non-human wealth is mismeasured along lines discussed in section 10.1. Thus, attempting to remedy the defects in conventional measures of real non-human wealth by including even good measures of real human wealth (including effects of quantity constraints) will still leave several difficulties along lines discussed in section 10.1 above.

Fourth, it is not entirely straightforward to obtain measures of human wealth that accurately reflect changes in constrained quantities such as labor services. In the case of technical progress discussed above, it might seem that all of the increase in employment is part of the change in wealth. In most cases of quantity constraints, however, some actors will be constrained and some will not. If there is involuntary unemployment of say 2 percent beyond the natural rate, this does not mean that every worker supplies 2 percent fewer hours than desired. Instead, most work close to as many hours as desired while a relative few work far less than they desire. When employment rises, some of the increase may come from those for whom the quantity constraint was not binding. For example, suppose that the technical progress induces a rise in the real wage rate, as happens in an IS–LM analysis with a fixed nominal wage rate and a fall in the price level induced by a rise in output. Then some of those already employed or voluntarily unemployed, may react to the rise in the real wage rate and account for part of the increased number of hours of employment. To the extent that this is true, part of the increase in employment does not represent a loosening of the constraint and hence should not be counted as part of the increase in wealth.

Similarly, suppose the world is such that the economy is sometimes at the natural rate of unemployment and labor suppliers can be viewed as quantity-setters. Changes in employment in this case do not enter the change in wealth. But suppose that sometimes there is higher, involuntary unemployment. Changes in employment in this case do enter the true change in wealth. Once again, the appropriate measure of the change in wealth depends on the theory used.

NOTES

1 Note that this is not a distribution effect between the firm and household sectors. Rather, it is a distribution effect across households that are equity owners and those that are labor suppliers. Clearly, some households that both supply labor services and own some equity may find their wealth positions unaffected by the rise in w/P, while those who own less equity relative to their supply of labor services are better off and households in the opposite position are worse off.

2 Not all theoretical work neglects W_{EX}/P. See chapter 8's discussion of work by Hicks, Leijonhufvud, Cassell and Matthews, for example.

3 This assumes either that there are no corner solutions, so that all parents plan positive bequests, or that negative bequests are possible.

4 While a sequence of Div in which some are negative allows for multiple internal rates of return, a neo-classical firm, with non-lumpy capital and positive but diminishing marginal productivity, will generally choose investments where an increase in i reduces net present value.

5 As an example, suppose the economy grows forever at the real rate g, there is no inflation, and current dividends Div_0 have already been paid (or rather, the stock has gone ex dividend). Then, if Div_1 is next period's dividends, the current real value of non-financial firms is

$$E_0/P_0 = \text{Div}_1/P_0(i-g).$$

Assuming that i is initially 10 percent and rises to 11 percent while g is constant at 5 percent, E_0/P_0 falls by 16.67 percent. (If instead $g = 0.0$ percent, the fall is 9.1 percent.)

Note that since business is assumed to issue no bonds in the text, empirically E_0 should be taken as the value of business equity plus debt, so the base for the change is larger than if it were only equity.

6 As pointed out in previous chapters, the initial-condition effects on the different sectors, and their implications for wealth, have simply been overlooked in past

literature. It serves little purpose to include these effects here and reiterate how they have been overlooked. Indeed, the point here is that, even in the absence of such effects, there are difficulties in obtaining good empirical measures of the price-induced effect on wealth.

7 This assumes that the (w/P)-induced wealth effects net to zero because labor markets are initially close to equilibrium and distribution effects can be neglected.

8 Alternatively, the example could assume that $d(w/P)/d\alpha$ is unknown and has to be predicted along with the equilibrium change in N^s (equal to that in N^d). Except in trivial cases, all endogenous variables will necessarily be misforecasted when mismeasured changes in wealth are used.

9 This is exactly parallel to the case in chapter 7 where regulation sets the interest rate paid on bank deposits below the market-clearing level. Here the real wage rate is somehow set above the market-clearing level.

References

American Economic Association 1952: *Readings in Price Theory*. Homewood, Ill: R. D. Irwin Inc.

Bailey, Martin J. 1971: *National Income and the Price Level: A Study in Macrotheory* (2nd edition). New York: McGraw-Hill.

Barro, Robert November/December 1974: Are government bonds net wealth? *Journal of Political Economy*, 82, 1095–117.

—— April 1976: Reply to "Perceived Wealth in Bonds and Social Security" and "Barro on The Ricardian Equivalence Theorem." *Journal of Political Economy*, 84, 343–9.

—— August 1978: Comment from an unreconstructed Ricardian. *Journal of Monetary Economics*, 4, 569–81.

Barsky, Robert B., Mankiw, N. Gregory and Zeldes, Stephen P. September 1986: Ricardian consumers with Keynesian propensities. *American Economic Review*, 76, 676–91.

Bear, D. V. T. 1961: The relationship of saving to the rate of interest, real income, and expected future prices. *Review of Economics and Statistics*, 43, 27–35.

Brock, William A. April 1975: A simple perfect foresight monetary model. *Journal of Monetary Economics*, 1, 133–50.

Buiter, Willem H. and Tobin, James 1979: Debt neutrality: a brief review of doctrine and evidence. In George M. von Furstenberg (ed.), *Social Security vs. Private Saving*, Cambridge, Mass.: Harper & Row, Ballinger, 39–63.

Buchanan, James April 1976: Barro on the Ricardian equivalence theorem. *Journal of Political Economy*, 84, 337–42.

Cassel, Gustav 1903: *The Nature and Necessity of Interest*. New York: Macmillan.

Chan, Louis Kuo Chi May 1983: Uncertainty and the neutrality of government financing policy. *Journal of Monetary Economics*, 11, 351–72.

Christ, Carl F. August 1957: Patinkin on money, interest and prices. *Journal of Political Economy*, 65, 347–54.

Clower, Robert W. 1965: The Keynesian counter-revolution: a theoretical appraisal. In Frank H. Hahn and Frank P. R. Brechling (eds), *The Theory of Interest Rates*, London: Macmillan.

David, Paul A. and Scadding, John L. March/April 1974: Private savings: ultrarationality, aggregation and 'Denison's law'. *Journal of Political Economy*, Part I, 82, 225–49.

Einzig, Paul, 1949: *Primitive Money in Its Ethnological, Historical and Economic Aspects*. London: Eyre & Spottiswoode.

Enthoven, Alain C. 1960: Appendix. In John G. Gurley and Edward S. Shaw, *Money in a Theory of Finance*, Washington: The Brookings Institute.

Feldstein, Martin S. April 1976: Perceived wealth in bonds and social security: a comment. *Journal of Political Economy*, 84, 331–6.

—— July 1982: Inflation, tax rules and investment: some econometric evidence. *Econometrica*, 50, 825–62.

Fischer, Stanley April 1979a: Anticipations and the nonneutrality of money. *Journal of Political Economy*, 87, 225–52.

—— November 1979b: Capital accumulation on the transition path in a monetary optimizing model. *Econometrica*, 47, 1433–9.

Fisher, Irving 1911; rev. edn 1913; *The Purchasing Power of Money*. New York: Macmillan.

Friedman, Milton and Schwartz, Anna J. February 1963: Money and business cycles. *Review of Economics and Statistics*, 45, 32–64.

—— February 1969: The definition of money: net wealth and neutrality as criteria. *Journal of Money, Credit and Banking*, 1, 1–14.

—— June 1985: Has government any role in money? Unpublished working paper.

Gurley, John G. and Shaw, Edward S. March 1956: Financial intermediaries and the saving–investment process. *Journal of Finance*, 11, 257–76.

—— 1960: *Money in a Theory of Finance*. Washington: The Brookings Institute.

Haavelmo, Trygve 1960: *A Study in The Theory of Investment*. Chicago: University of Chicago Press.

Haines, Walter W. 1966: *Money, Prices, and Policy* (2nd edn). New York: McGraw-Hill.

Hansen, Bent 1970: *A Survey of General Equilibrium Systems*. New York: McGraw-Hill.

Herskovitz, Melville J. 1965: *Economic Anthropology: The Economic Life of Primitive Peoples*. New York: W. W. Norton.

Hicks, John R. 1939; rev. edn 1946: *Value and Capital*. London: Oxford University Press.

—— 1956: *Revision of Demand Theory*. Oxford: Clarendon Press.

—— June 1957: A rehabilitation of "classical" economics? *Economic Journal*, 67, 278–89.

Hicks, John R. and Allen, R. G. D. February/May 1934: A reconsideration of the theory of value. *Economica*, New Series 1, 52–76, 196–219.

Johnson, Harry G. May 1961: The general theory after twenty-five years. *American Economic Review*, Supplement 51, 1–17.

—— 1962: *Money, Trade and Economic Growth: Survey Lectures in Economic Theory*. Cambridge, Mass.: Harvard University Press.

—— February 1969: Inside money, outside money, income, wealth and welfare in monetary theory. *Journal of Money, Credit and Banking*, 1, 30–45.

Kalecki, Michael April 1944: Professor Pigou on "The stationary state" – a comment. *Economic Journal*, 54, 131–2.

Keynes, John M. 1936: *The General Theory of Employment, Interest and Money*. New York: Harcourt, Brace and World, Inc.

King, Robert G. and Plosser, Charles June 1984: Money, credit, and prices in a real business cycle. *American Economic Review*, 74, 363–81.

Klein, Benjamin November 1974: The competitive supply of money. *Journal of Money, Credit and Banking*, 6, 423–54

Kochin, Levis A. August 1974: Are future taxes anticipated by consumers? Comment. *Journal of Money, Credit and Banking*, 6, 385–94.

Kormendi, Roger C. December 1983: Government debt, government spending, and private sector behavior. *American Economic Review*, 73, 994–1010.

Kuenne, Robert E. 1963: *The Theory of General Economic Equilibrium*. Princeton: Princeton University Press.

Leijonhufvud, Axel 1968: *On Keynesian Economics and the Economics of Keynes*. New York: Oxford University Press.

Long, John and Plosser, Charles February 1983: Real business cycles. *Journal of Political Economy*, 91, 39–69.

Lucas, Robert E., Jr April 1972: Expectations and the neutrality of money. *Journal of Economic Theory*, 4, 103–24.

—— June 1973: Some international evidence on output–inflation trade-offs. *American Economic Review*, 63, 326–34.

—— December 1975: An equilibrium model of the business cycle. *Journal of Political Economy*, 83, 1113–44.

—— Autumn 1984: Money in a theory of finance. *Carnegie-Rochester Conference Series in Public Policy*, 21, 9–45.

Lucas, Robert E., Jr. and Sargent, Thomas J. Spring 1979: After Keynesian macroeconomics. *Federal Reserve Bank of Minneapolis Quarterly Review*, 3, 1–16.

Machlup, Fritz March 1957: Professor Hicks' revision of demand theory. *American Economic Review*, 47, 119–35.

Matthews, Robert C. O. June 1963: Expenditure plans and the uncertainty motive for holding money. *Journal of Political Economy*, 71, 201–218.

Mayer, Thomas May 1959: The empirical significance of the real balance effect. *Quarterly Journal of Economics*, 73, 275–91.

Merris, Randall C. November 1985: Explicit interest and demand deposit service charges. *Journal of Money, Credit and Banking*, 17, 528–33.

Merton, Robert C. August 1969: Lifetime portfolio selection under uncertainty: the continuous time case. *Review of Economics and Statistics*, 51, 247–57.

Metzler, Lloyd A. October 1945: Stability of multiple markets: the Hicks condition. *Econometrica*, 13, 277–92.

—— April 1951: Wealth, saving, and the rate of interest. *Journal of Political Economy*, 59, 93–116.

Miller, M. H. and Modigliani, F. October 1961: Dividend policy, growth and the valuation of shares. *Journal of Business*, 34, 411–33.

Mitchell, Douglas W. May 1979: Explicit and implicit demand deposit interest. *Journal of Money, Credit and Banking*, 11, 182–91.

Modigliani, Franco January 1944: Liquidity preference and the theory of interest and money. *Econometrica*, 12, 45–88.

—— March 1977: The monetarist controversy or, should we forsake stabilization policies? *American Economic Review*, 67, 1–19.

Mosak, Jacob L. 1944: *General Equilibrium Theory in International Trade.* Bloomington, Ind.: The Principia Press.

Mundell, Robert June 1963: Inflation and real interest. *Journal of Political Economy*, 71, 280-3.

Muth, John F. July 1961: Rational expectations and the theory of price movements. *Econometrica*, 29, 315-35.

Niehans, Jurg March 1978: Meltzer, wealth, and macroeconomics: a review. *Journal of Economic Literature*, 16, 84-95.

Obstfeld, Maurice and Rogoff, Kenneth August 1983: Speculative hyperinflations in maximizing models: can we rule them out? *Journal of Political Economy*, 91, 675-87.

Patinkin, Don 1956; 2nd edn 1965: *Money, Interest and Prices*. New York: Harper & Row.

—— December 1969: Money and wealth: a review article. *Journal of Economic Literature*, 7, 1140-60.

—— May 1971: Inside money, monopoly bank profits, and the real-balance effect. *Journal of Money, Credit and Banking*, 3, 271-5.

—— 1972: *Studies in Monetary Economics*. New York: Harper & Row.

Pesek, Boris P. and Saving, Thomas R. 1967: *Money, Wealth and Economic Theory*. New York: Macmillan.

Phelps, Edmund April 1966: Models of technical progress and the golden rule of research. *Review of Economic Studies*, 33, 133-45.

Pigou, Arthur C. December 1943: The classical stationary state. *Economic Journal*, 53, 343-51.

Power, John H. April 1959: Price expectations, money illusion, and the real balance effect. *Journal of Political Economy*, 67, 131-43.

Reid, Bradford G. July 1985: Aggregate consumption and deficit financing: an attempt to separate permanent from transitory effects. *Economic Inquiry*, 23, 475-86.

Samuelson, Paul A. 1947: *Foundations of Economic Analysis*. Cambridge, Mass.: Harvard University Press.

—— 1965: *Foundations of Economic Analysis*. New York: Atheneum.

—— August 1969: Lifetime portfolio selection by dynamic stochastic programming. *Review of Economics and Statistics*, 51, 239-46.

Santomero, Anthony M. November 1984: Modeling the banking firm: a survey. *Journal of Money, Credit and Banking*, 16, 576-602.

Sargent, Thomas J. 1973: Rational expectations, the real rate of interest and the natural rate of employment. *Brookings Papers on Economic Activity*, 2, 429-72.

—— April 1976: A classical macroeconomic model for the United States. *Journal of Political Economy*, 84, 207-37.

Sargent, Thomas J. and Wallace, Neil April 1975: "Rational" expectations, the optimal monetary instrument, and the optimal money supply rule. *Journal of Political Economy*, 83, 241-54.

Saving, Thomas R. February 1970: Outside money, inside money, and the real balance effect. *Journal of Money, Credit and Banking*, 2, 83-100.

—— May 1971: Inside money, short-run rents, and the real balance effect. *Journal of Money, Credit and Banking*, 3, 276–80.

—— January/February 1973: On the neutrality of money. *Journal of Political Economy*, 81, 98–119.

—— February 1979: Money supply theory with competitively determined deposit rates and activity charges. *Journal of Money, Credit and Banking*, 11, 22–31.

Seater, J. J. August 1982: Are future taxes discounted. *Journal of Money, Credit and Banking*, 14, 376–89.

Sidrauski, Miguel May 1967: Rational choice and patterns of growth in a monetary economy. *American Economic Review*, 57, 534–44.

Smith, Gary May 1982: Monetarism, bondism and inflation. *Journal of Money, Credit and Banking*, 14, 278–86.

Stein, Jerome L. October 1966: Money and capacity growth. *Journal of Political Economy*, 74, 451–65.

Sweeney, Richard J. 1974: *A Macro Theory with Micro Foundations*. Cincinnati: South-Western Publishing Co.

Tanner, J. Ernest May 1979a: An empirical investigation of tax discounting: a comment. *Journal of Money, Credit and Banking*, 11, 214–18.

—— May 1979b: Fiscal policy and consumer behavior. *Review of Economics and Statistics*, 61, 317–21.

Taylor, Lester D. 1971: Saving out of different types of income. *Brookings Papers on Economic Activity*, 2, 383–407.

Tobin, James April 1955: A dynamic aggregative model. *Journal of Political Economy*, 63, 103–15.

—— 1963: Commercial banks as creators of money. In Deane Carson (ed.), *Banking and Monetary Studies*. Homewood, Ill.: Richard D. Irwin, 408–19.

—— October 1965a: Money and economic growth. *Econometrica*, 33, 671–84.

—— 1965b: The theory of portfolio selection. In Frank H. Hahn and Frank P. R. Brechling (eds), *The Theory of Interest Rates*. London: Macmillan.

—— 1973: Comment on Sargent. *Brookings Papers on Economic Activity*, 2, 473–80.

—— 1980: *Asset Accumulation and Economic Activity*. Chicago: University of Chicago Press.

Villanueva, Delano November 1971: A neoclassical monetary growth model with independent savings and investment functions. *Journal of Money, Credit and Banking*, 3, 750–9.

Yawitz, Jess B. and Meyer, Laurence H. May 1976: An empirical investigation of the extent of tax discounting: comment. *Journal of Money, Credit and Banking*, 8, 247–54.

Index

aggregation 66, 68, 74, 152, 158

Bailey, Martin J. 314
bank money 11, 15–16, 33–4, 35–7, 149, 150, 151–2, 153, 155, 158, 160–2, 163, 167, 168, 170–1, 173, 174, 176–8, 179, 180, 181, 182–3, 187, 188, 189, 190–200, 208, 209, 210, 214, 215, 216–17, 220–2, 226–7, 231
bank reserves 34, 151, 152, 155, 161, 162, 177, 180, 191–4
banking sector 151–2, 176–80, 215–16
   creation of money 176–8, 215
   demand for labor 154–5, 184
   dividend stream 152–4, 155–6, 161, 217
   monopoly rents 224–6
   optimum conditions 155–6, 198
   welfare effect 174–6, 185
Barro, Robert 254, 267, 282, 288
   critique of bequest motive 286–7
   government bonds as net wealth 13, 44, 264, 265, 269, 271, 286
   interest-rate-induced effect on wealth 43
Barskey, Robert B., et al. 288
BB curve 108–11, 116
bequest motive 269, 285, 286–9
bequests 13, 17, 18, 42, 43, 44, 235, 236, 237, 244, 251–4, 261, 262, 263, 269, 285, 286, 287, 318
bonds 70–1, 108–11, 151, 152, 157, 177, 178, 179, 184
Brock, William A. 266
Buchanan, James 287
budget constraint 50, 52, 66, 67, 69, 70, 71–4, 77, 78, 79, 91, 92–3, 95, 102, 118, 119–21, 123, 124, 127, 129, 130, 131, 132, 156–7, 158–9, 166, 194, 200,

budget constraint—*contd*
   201, 202, 227–8, 229–30, 237, 237–40, 250, 254–5, 256, 257, 258, 269, 272, 282–3, 297–8, 300
Buiter, W. and J. Tobin 288
burden of the debt 136

capital stock 75, 93, 151, 183, 231, 249, 267, 318
Cassel, Gustav: interest-rate-induced-effect on wealth 42, 43
Chan, Louis K. C. 287–8
Civil War 190
Clower, Robert W. 267, 296, 314
coin shortage 185
collateral 265
comparative statics 62–3, 84
compensating variation 50, 55, 57
composite good 74, 115
currency drain 177

David, Paul A. and John L. Scadding 288
default 270, 276, 277, 278, 279, 285–6, 288
deficits 257
demand for money 188, 191, 192, 199
Descartes' law of signs 247, 248
destabilizing 111
determinacy of the price level 12, 19, 20, 26, 27, 28, 29–30, 31, 32, 33, 90, 101, 112–13, 114, 117, 118, 124–9, 135, 139–41, 143, 144, 150, 167–9, 181, 212–13, 214, 215
   portfolio effect 26, 30, 38, 167–8, 213, 214
distribution effects 10, 13, 14, 28, 42–3, 49, 50, 60–2, 63, 67, 74, 89, 90, 105–6, 118, 134–6, 180, 236, 237, 248–9, 252, 264, 271, 287, 289, 294, 301, 311, 318